The Collapse of Ancient
States and Civilizations

THE COLLAPSE

OF ANCIENT

STATES AND

CIVILIZATIONS

Edited by

Norman Yoffee and

George L. Cowgill

The University of Arizona Press · Tucson

Second printing 1991

THE UNIVERSITY OF ARIZONA PRESS

Copyright © 1988
The Arizona Board of Regents
All Rights Reserved

This book was set in 10/12 Linotype Sabon.
Manufactured in the U.S.A.
∞ This book is printed on acid-free, archival-quality paper.

Library of Congress Cataloging-in-Publication Data

The collapse of ancient states and civilizations.

    Bibliography: p.
    Includes index.
    1. Civilization, Ancient.   2. Civilization—
Philosophy.   I. Yoffee, Norman.   II. Cowgill, George L.
CB311.C736   1988   930   88-1347
Cloth ISBN 0-8165-1049-0
Paper ISBN 0-8165-1249-3

British Library Cataloguing in Publication data are available.

CONTENTS

PREFACE

This volume is the result of a seminar held at the School of American Research in Santa Fe, March 22 to 26, 1982. In planning the seminar, we hoped that it would contribute to the explanation of sociocultural change and stability. We wanted to explore and, if possible, improve theory about why and how sociocultural characteristics sometimes are reproduced and persist with little change, while in other cases one state of affairs is followed by something that is quite different in important ways. However, we wanted to avoid trying to talk about all sorts of change or all sorts of societies. We have concentrated on instances of political fragmentation (and, to some extent, the decline or transformation of great traditions) in nonindustrialized societies that were complex enough to be, by anybody's definition, states.

There were several reasons for this focus. One was that it is often a good strategy to divide a large, amorphous problem into smaller and better-defined segments, and to address these segments rather than dealing with everything at once. Also, we believed we could identify instances that have enough in common so that it would be instructive to compare them. We planned to look at a moderate number of cases in depth, because, at least until we understand much more than we do now, this strategy is likely to be far more productive than superficial comparison of many instances. The conceptualization of sociocultural change is still in a primitive stage, hampered by received preconceptions and imprecise language. Study of a few cases in depth is more apt to lead one to notice evidence that demands serious rethinking of one's prior opinions. When one looks in a limited way at many examples, there is greater danger of failing to recognize that one's preconceptions and initial categories are simply inappropriate.

A second reason for choosing collapse as our topic was that it seemed especially useful for improving theory because it directly challenges views about sociocultural change that explicitly or implicitly assume that human sociocultural systems, for any of various reasons, inherently tend to persist or expand. The study of collapse is also apt to be enlightening because societies in trouble may often reveal more about what is really vital for their operation than societies in reasonably good shape. One of the reasons it is useful to study troubles that afflict societies is that, probably, most societies most of the time are actually not in very harmonious adjustment. More importantly, if one takes it as axiomatic that stability and/or growth are normal—regarding troubles as secondary deviations or irregularities in dominant processes whose primary feature is development—one is constricted in what one can imagine about instances in which persistence or expansion actually occur. Recent studies of ancient states, with a few notable exceptions, continue to pay disproportionate attention to explaining only certain types of sociocultural change, namely expansion and increasing organizational complexity, while ignoring instances of opposite kinds of change or attributing them to extraneous disturbances.

We should add that we are just as unenthusiastic about viewpoints that take inexorable decline for granted. Obviously, anything that does not last forever has a beginning and an end, and it is axiomatic that early states (somehow) came into being and (somehow) went out of being. This is a simple point that should not be forgotten, but it is too abstract to be of much help in itself. Our view, then, is that neither the beginning of a state, nor its expansion and elaboration, persistence with little change, decline, or end can be taken for granted. One has to ask how and why certain things happened at certain times, and one should also ask why something else did not happen instead. In looking specifically at times of decline or collapse, we hoped to gain not only better understanding of those kinds of phenomena themselves, but also clearer ideas about the things that states must deal with, adequately if not well, in order to persist. An additional goal was to heighten attention as to why sociopolitical elaboration and expansion ever happens at all, and why it happens at some times and places but not at other times or in other places.

A further reason for choosing collapse as a focus was that both of us had previously worked on instances of political fragmentation and/or sociocultural collapse (Yoffee 1977, 1979; Cowgill 1964, 1979a, 1979b). That we had done so is not accidental, and it is at least partly for some of the reasons mentioned above.

In selecting participants for the seminar, we included historians, a political scientist, and a sociologist. We did so because one of the problems besetting work on early states is the tendency for specialists to communicate too little with those in other fields. Mesoamericanists usually know what other Mesoamericanists say and write, those working in Mesopotamia tend to be in touch mainly with one another, and so on. There are exceptions, such as Robert Adams's (1966) close comparison of Mesopotamia and Mesoamerica, but there are too few such studies. A sizable number of archaeologists and anthropologists are interested in theory about early states as a general category. However, these people also often read too little from beyond their own circle. We believed it would be informative and invigorating to get both data and viewpoints from people somewhat outside this network. For one thing, we wanted the participation of a person expert in systems analyses of modern western institutions, rather than of ancient states. Herbert Kaufman (Chapter 9) filled this role admirably for us. Also, there is still no substitute for the insights provided by cases in which rich bodies of contemporary documents coexist with archaeological evidence. In particular, the "fall of Rome"—more properly, the transition from Late Antiquity to the early Middle Ages—is a prime and much-studied instance of the sort of thing we wanted to discuss. Glen Bowersock (Chapter 6) was very enlightening about recent developments on this topic. Similarly, the "dynastic cycle" of traditional China is a well-known phenomenon with a rich and specialized historical literature. Given our interests and our wish to take advantage of relatively well documented cases, it seemed best to concentrate on Chinese material from the Han and later dynasties, rather than on the Shang and Chou evidence to which western archaeologists have tended to pay most attention. We were fortunate in obtaining the participation of an eminent historian, Cho-yun Hsu (Chapter 7). Finally, Shmuel Eisenstadt (Chapter 10) gave us the advantage of his long interest in ancient empires from a sociological viewpoint.

At a time when many have given thought to the limits to growth and the possible decline or end of our own civilization, a volume on the theme of "collapse" inevitably raises thoughts of its immediate relevance. It would be unproductive, however, to take such considerations as a major focus of our inquiry. A preoccupation with recommendations for policy or action addressed to twentieth-century problems would serve mainly to impede the real contributions we believe can be expected and which are overwhelmingly in the domain of pure rather than applied research.

Nevertheless, the matter of contemporary relevance should not be wholly ignored. This issue arises in two quite distinct ways. First, each generation tends to reinterpret the past in terms of its own preoccupations. We must be aware of this tendency to use what we think we know of the present in order to fill gaps in our knowledge of the past. If we merely project our images of the present onto the past, the process becomes circular and the past cannot really teach us anything. Second, one of the principal genuine accomplishments of the social and historical sciences in the past century has been to challenge a wide range of generally accepted "common knowledge" beliefs. Persons who make and carry out policy often pay some attention to supposed "lessons from history." Many of these suppositions are extremely questionable. Beyond its value to scholars, this book will be useful if it helps to expose the dubiousness of some popular assumptions.

We are indeed grateful to the School of American Research and, especially, to Douglas W. Schwartz, president of the School, for having made this seminar possible. Doug's advice and encouragement in planning the seminar are particularly appreciated. The School's superb facilities afforded us not only the opportunity to meet formally but also a stimulating environment in which views could be candidly and informally discussed.

George L. Cowgill and Norman Yoffee

The Collapse of Ancient
States and Civilizations

Orienting Collapse

Norman Yoffee

Archaeologists have traditionally devoted much attention to the rise of civilizations, producing scores of studies that attempt to account for the origin, development, and growth of particular states. In addition to these areally specific inquiries, numerous efforts have been made to construct general principles, laws, and universalistic explanations for the evolution of complex societies. Little by way of justification has been required for both particularist and general concerns. Civilizations have been generally regarded as rare and precious occurrences in the evolution of human culture, the "great divide" (Service 1975:3) that separates relatively egalitarian, kin-based, and traditionally organized societies from urban, politically and economically riven, and centralized ones. Or, in some recent studies (e.g., Bender 1978; Friedman and Rowlands 1977; Price and Brown 1985), it seems that almost any degree of inequality in social organizations represents a set of structural contradictions that must inevitably lead to (and thus can be typed as a stage in) an evolutionary trajectory toward statehood.

Although investigations into the phenomena of "rise" have by no means established a consensus of scholarly opinion on the nature of the transition to civilized society, it is equally clear that discussion of the collapse of ancient states and civilizations, with the notable exception of the Maya and Roman cases, has been most conspicuous by its absence from the literature on social evolution. The concern with rise, to the near exclusion of collapse, in evolutionary studies, has had important theoretical implications: social change has been perceived as a process of mutually supportive interactions that produce an irreversible succession of "emergent" levels of holistic sociocultural integration (Adams, this volume). Collapse, on the other hand, requires that "levels" be broken down into institutional groupings of partly overlapping and partly opposing fields of action that lend the possibility of instability, as well as stability, to overarching societal institutions. Flux and the possibility of reversibility of the forces of social integration can seldom be captured in the rhetoric of evolutionary studies that are generated from examples of the rise of civilizations. Collapse studies thus are important not only because they deal with a set of significant, but often poorly understood, sociocultural phenomena, but because they also provide excellent points of entry into the social configuration of the societies that were doing the collapsing. Collapse studies may therefore also yield fresh perspectives with which to evaluate conditions of rise.

In this volume we propose to consider some aspects of social evolutionary theory through a limited set of case studies of the collapse of ancient states and civilizations. Since it is apparent that the political systems of ancient civilizations did collapse and that these collapses did not follow a common trajectory or proceed to the same level of breakdown, we need not only to explain these instances of social change, but also to develop a methodology for their comparative examination. In this introductory chapter, I present a digest of studies that have considered the problem of collapse. Many of these investigations have either not used modern findings on the nature of ancient states and civilizations or have done so only as incidental to their main evolutionary concern with rise. From this review of prevailing assumptions about the process of collapse, I shall attempt to provide some basic orientating principles through which the empirical investigations of collapse can proceed. Examples from the chapters in this volume will illustrate the major concerns that such evolutionary studies must consider.

THE INEVITABILITY OF COLLAPSE

Ideas about the collapse of civilizations are not restricted, of course, to the twentieth century and to archaeological theory-building. The notion of the ancient Greeks that civilizations are organisms and go through cycles of birth, growth, and death is probably the best known of all ideas of how civilizations decline and fall. This organismic view is by no means moribund. From the early part of this century Oswald Spengler's *Decline of the West* (1918–1922) and Arnold Toynbee's *A Study of History*

(1933–1954, first ten volumes), which were certainly influenced by the Greek view, have found an interested and enthusiastic public.

Both Toynbee and Spengler were world historians in the sense that the entire history of humanity came into their purview. Indeed, for them history was without a central point of reference. In principle, this perspective is not unlike that of the anthropological evolutionists, who hold that any culture, no matter whether known from ethnographic or archaeological evidence and without regard to time or space, can be typed and so identified as representative of a stage of human social development (e.g., Sahlins 1960).

Spengler's "comparative morphology of cultures" identified spiritual principles in which all avenues of human expression, from art and literature to governmental organization, were organically connected. As in the Greek model (Spengler wrote a doctoral dissertation on Heraclitus), each of Spengler's nine or ten cultures produced its own "civilization." By civilization Spengler meant the late, declining phase of a culture, the rigidified form of life that followed the expanding, ripe, mature phase. The cycle of growth was seasonal: heroic Spring emerged, in which powerful, mystical religions were connected to a vigorous rural life; then followed lusty and individualist Summer, in which creative leadership sprang from the thorns; fully ripened Autumn then proceeded, in which centralized monarchies and dynamic urban commerce were supported by rationalist philosophers instead of natural religions; and finally came skeptical Winter, in which a rootless proletariat in megalopoloi were inured to the soulless, civilized way of life (Biddiss 1980).

Spengler's poetry and immense canvas have been criticized for their lack of objective content. Indeed, the whole speculative superstructure rests on the flimsiest of empirical foundations. Likewise, Spengler provides neither reasons for the origin of his cultures nor any explanation for culture change. The biological imagery in Spengler is meant to obviate such questions. Cultures exist with the aimlessness of flowers in the field; Aztec culture perished through Spanish assault "like a sunflower whose head is struck off by one passing" (Biddiss 1980). Spengler was less interested in providing a "falsifiable" model for the rise and fall of civilizations than he was in noting that "Faustian" (i.e., Western European) civilization exhibited in the early twentieth century the same symptoms as other historic, declining cultures. Although decline was the inevitable destiny of cultures, it could last indefinitely as the petrification of vital principles (as was the case for China and India)—"the amorphous scrap-material of history" (Biddiss 1980).

Toynbee, as has often been said, combined a dose of British empiricism with Spengler's mystical cultural organisms. In particular, Toynbee was concerned with formulating explicit and causal statements to account for the origin and collapse of civilizations. Best known of these formulations is his challenge-and-response hypothesis of the growth and development of civilizations. Among diverse cultures, growth is selected for when certain environmental obstacles are presented that humans have to over-come. The stony land of Athens, for example, is contrasted with the fat land of Thebes as an explanation for the development of the "Hellenic model" of historical process. Challenges must not be too daunting, how-ever, for civilizations can never arise in the bleak tundra or the exuberant tropical rainforest. Given the proper obstacles to overcome, an ineffable manifestation of the spirit is gradually set in motion: initial political disunity is transformed into a "universal" state that is the expression of underlying cultural unity. The collapse of civilizations is symmetrically accounted for by a breakdown of creative spirit and the estrangement of the intellectual elite from the masses. This breakdown is not regular, as in Spengler's biological rhythms, but collapse is just as surely the destiny of civilizations. Its course depends on how the civilization responds to its challenges, and it is internal processes (not simply barbarians or other invaders) that deal the final blow to civilizations. In further contrast to Spengler, for Toynbee breakdown may be reversible. This reversal, only discussed in Toynbee's last writings, may apparently occur with the es-tablishment of a "universal church," a distinctive species of institution that transcends the logic of history.

Although his style is less oracular than Spengler's, it has been noted that Toynbee's vast historical erudition is neither objectively employed nor inductive, as Toynbee had claimed (Geyl 1958). Although Toynbee seems to have thought that the breakdown of civilizations is not irrevers-ible, *ancient* civilizations were caught in a historical web of inevitable collapse. For Toynbee, this collapse is an idealist collapse; just as it was environmental obstacles that raised the spirit to consciousness, so in collapse it is the spirit that fails. Since Toynbee's and Spengler's theses are so clearly idealist in tone, it is ironic that a major modern reflection of their prophecies of civilizational doom is a very materialist line of analysis.

Given the modern world's quite realistic concern with overpopulation and a diminishing resource base, the undesirability of economic growth has been turned by the Club of Rome into a prediction of civilizational collapse that seems very Toynbeean (Meadows et al. 1972). Of course, the Club of Rome's *Limits to Growth* report has been much criticized: all bads (pollution, demand on food, and population growth) were as-sumed to be increasing exponentially forever, and all goods (technology) were considered to have finite limits of increase. Feeding these doom-laden assumptions into computers unsurprisingly resulted in predictions of doom (Beckerman 1979). As a result of these criticisms, especially by

Third World economists who saw that slow-growth formulas meant continued economic reliance on industrialized nations, new Club of Rome reports appeared (Mesarović and Pestel 1974). These studies have considered regional problems and have tended not to be so focused on a distant future collapse that they direct society from more urgent problems of inflation, high unemployment, and poverty.

In anthropology this anti-growth mood has been well captured in Roy Rappaport's essay on "maladaptation" (1977). In Rappaport's view, adaptation denotes a systemic homeostasis in which a range of variability is activated in response to various perturbations, especially environmental ones. If adaptation is functional, it is also evolutionary, since once a homeostatic boundary is exceeded, a new adaptive range forms.

For Rappaport social evolution appears consequently as a series of stages (or "punctuated equilibriums"). These stages are measured, in part, according to the increase in special-purpose systems that are coordinated by progressively centralized organizations. In the more complex, differentiated societies certain principles of hierarchical organization inhere. Lower-order subsystems must have degrees of autonomy built in since too much detailed information can overload the capacities of higher-order regulators (which are more concerned with setting system-wide goals and values than with the daily operations of lower-order subsystems).

Rappaport believes that such complex systems are profoundly maladaptive since, instead of maintaining flexible responses to stress, the interconnections in these hierarchical systems mean that change in one component is likely to cause change in all the others. Additionally, the distance between higher- and lower-order regulators (that is, the decision-making institutions within social organizations) results in delays in the transmission of information or a loss of information altogether. Such complex hierarchical systems are maladaptive because diversity and flexibility progressively diminish in them, and the network of overspecialized, interconnected systems is ill equipped to deal with stress on lines of communication and production. When resources become exhausted or cannot be efficiently distributed, collapse or revolution ensues. For Rappaport, therefore, civilization is only an "unsuccessful experiment," and in a blacker mood even human intelligence seems maladaptive (1977:67).

The theme of environmental degradation in the collapse of civilizations that was only touched upon by Rappaport has been explored further in Rice Odell's essays in the Conservation Foundation's *Letter* (1977, 1979, 1980). In developing the theme that "history offers some warnings on environment," Odell writes that the "critical obstacles to environmental protection are not technological, but economic, social, or political" (1977:4). The decline in these institutions that accompanies environmental degradation may be caused by "confiscatory taxation, disruptions of trade, inflation, financial corruption, military weakness or warfare, excessive size of institutions and management failure, weak leadership and loss of nerve, social entropy such as the breakdown of families, political apathy based on religions of personal salvation, or moral decay through excessive permissiveness" (1979:6). Although all or some combination of these may converge and collapse may be the "synergistic result," Odell considers environmental degradation to be among the most important and best attested of the proximate causes of collapse.

It is indeed seen in some cases that environmental degradation played a great role in the collapse of ancient civilizations (see Culbert, this volume), although it is not always clear whether as cause or effect. It is argued by Odell that, as complex societies evolved from simpler social collectivities, harsh demands were placed on local environments. Newly organized states needed to maintain or develop networks of communication and to provide goods, especially food, and services for expanding and/or widespread populations. In many instances the balance effected between the local capacity to produce food and the political goals of the leaders for the distribution of these products was especially fragile. As early growth cycles slowed and new political systems were consolidated, there was more stress on lands, productive technologies, and the networks of communication between bureaucratic, centralized regimes and productive peripheries. Production demands could be set so high as to cause the ruination of arable lands: political collapse and environmental degradation were the predictable twin results.

The implications for research into collapse using this perspective lie not in reconstructing predetermined, natural cycles of behavior as offered by Spengler and Toynbee. It requires, rather, that archaeologists and historians explore the principles of political stability and pathology in early states and civilizations. The investigation of institutional variability and the constraints on the maintenance of centralized political institutions clearly predicates a concern with how political systems managed their productive resources. Such concern with the environmental basis of political stability, however, lies far from any grim teleological forecast of the inevitability of civilizational collapse.

COLLAPSE AS AN EVOLUTIONARY PRODUCT

Although the specific data on collapse that are pertinent to the formulation of a theory of social evolution have not been rigorously collected and comparatively analyzed, nevertheless two important strains in the evolutionist literature have attempted to cope with collapse phenomena. In the first, biological analogy and then sociobiological theory have been offered as explanatory inspiration; in the second, collapse is viewed within the framework of general systems theory.

Biology and Social Collapse

In Elman Service's use of biological analogy, initial social development leads to a "radiating expanding movement" but then settles into the "eventual stasis of success" (1975:313). The "law of evolutionary potential" therefore states that the more specialized and adapted a form in a given evolutionary stage, the smaller the potential for passing to the next stage (Service 1960:97). For Service, although development is attributable to the "solution of problems posed by the outside environment by means created inside itself—i.e., inside its bureaucracy" (Service 1975:321), collapse seems due to the backlash of diffusion. In this perspective, social organizations are clearly modeled as plant or animal species that are initially successful because they adapt well to their niches. Eventually, however, they become statically specialized and overadapted, less viable than more generally adapted competitors who vanquish them.

Social evolutionists like Service seem to have adopted such biological analogies in order to lend the study of social change a more scientific veneer (see discussions in Yoffee 1979 and McGuire 1983). In their evolutionist paradigm, thus, societies are perceived to pass—speciationally—through a series of sequential stages or levels. The assumption is that cultures (wherever they may be found) cluster in discrete stages (e.g., tribes, chiefdoms, states), each stage representing a package of interlinked cultural institutions of government, economy, and social organization. Change must proceed "holistically" since all institutions move in the same direction and at the same pace from stage to stage. This model has been perceived as inadequate to explain the rise of complex societies, for which purpose it was formulated, and its deficiencies are laid open clearly when it is applied to situations of collapse. Most apparent in such studies is that whereas some institutions fail, others do not. Indeed, in none of the examples offered in this volume does collapse represent a total institutional breakdown. Collapse thus cannot be understood through an organic analogy as the endpoint of evolutionary decay. In fact, although collapse must be investigated as a drastic restructuring of social institutions in the absence of a political center, what happens after collapse is as important as the process of collapse itself.

Robert Dunnell (1980) and others have proposed that social evolution goes beyond mere biological analogies and should be considered part of a coevolutionary process that includes both social organizations and biological material. Under the principle of "type reductionism," the mechanisms of social systems ought to be reducible to those of organic systems, since the latter are more fundamental and more general than the former and thus are of more explanatory power. For Dunnell, social evolutionary theory has gone astray because its roots have been in the line of Spencer rather than of Darwin. Spencer's error was that he did not realize that variation is the proper focus of biological evolution and that natural selection and adaptation were simply a posteriori facts that marked statistically reproductive success (Mayr 1974; Lewontin 1983). In Dunnell's argument, archaeologists should concentrate upon how cultural variation is selected through the heritability of traits (as measured by frequencies of artifact classes [Dunnell 1980:62–63, 84–85, 89]). Little interest need be accorded the production of variation, especially any conscious attempts to produce variation, since such variables are randomly generated: "directed, problem-solving, conscious, purposeful, goal-seeking, guided, in a word 'intentional' aspects of human culture are useless [elements] for problem-solving" (Rindos 1985:84).

Human inventions, however, are obviously not the products of random mutations but appear in logical sequences in order to achieve certain goals and to facilitate certain tasks. The empirical study of the mechanisms with which tasks are carried out, how goals are established, and why social change occurs lies within the provinces of social rather than biological theory. This kind of distinction in theory-building is, in fact, especially familiar to biologists. Sir Peter Medawar (1961) has noted explicitly that biology deals with notions that are contextually peculiar to itself—with heredity, sexuality, and disease, for example—things that are not part of chemistry and physics although genes and chromosomes are built of atoms and molecules. Similarly, the evolution of the solar system and the evolution of biological life on earth are obviously related but also must be considered separable for purposes of scientific investigation. In judging "goodness of fit" between appropriate theory and problems needing to be solved, therefore, it is clear that biological and social evolutionary processes differ in their fundamental domains and in the paces and kinds of changes that occur within them. No single theory of evolution can account for both biological and social change.

Collapse Within General Systems Theory

A number of attempts to deal with collapse using the perspective and lexicon of general systems and information theory have also appeared in the evolutionist literature. Kent Flannery, in an important paper (1972) that may be used as the salient example, argued that complexity could be measured according to the amounts of "segregation" (i.e., social differentiation) and "centralization" (i.e., social integration) in a society.

Change, in this scheme, proceeds according to the evolutionary mechanisms of "promotion" (in which a special-purpose system takes on general system characteristics; see Netting 1972 for an example of how a religious system expands its horizons) and "linearization" (in which centralized authority bypasses local authorities to create new possibilities for mobility within the society). These mechanisms for growth, however, can easily become "pathologies" by which central authorities "meddle" in stable lower-order controls and by which a special-purpose system "usurps" the role of the general-purpose system. The resulting "hypercoherence" from these pathologies threatens systemic viability by imperiling the flexibility of institutions to deal with stress selectively. Failure in one part of the system affects all the other parts in a domino theory of disaster.

Although Flannery's evolutionary model usefully identifies some institutional properties in complex societies and the fragility of interdependent linkages of social groupings, it has been criticized for its inability to isolate any specific dimensions of causality in culture change (Athens 1977; Salmon 1982). Part of the problem seems to be that Flannery, writing in the early 1970s, still saw the various evolutionary mechanisms and pathologies as existing in bundles of homeostatic adaptations, in discrete stages and levels. Collapse, thus, was explained by "hypercoherence": when social institutions become so integrally connected that failure in one important subsystem affects all others, the whole hierarchy comes crashing down like a house of cards (Flannery's image was that of a string of Christmas-tree lights that short-circuits when one bulb sparks). Collapses in the real world, however, are seldom wholly catastrophic, but rather must be broken down institution by institution.

Another theoretically parsimonious approach to collapse is "catastrophe theory," a specialized branch of mathematical topology that has been adapted to the analysis of social systems, especially by Colin Renfrew (1978). *Catastrophe* refers to an abrupt and drastic change in the behavior of a system, and catastrophe theory attempts to model such changes as results of internal systemic trajectories rather than of any external factors.

For catastrophe theory it is important that "civilization . . . be expressed in terms of a single variable or several variables" and that "a single variable will suffice to give all the local picture" (Renfrew 1978:212). The Classic Maya collapse can be explained, for example, with recourse to two major variables, I (Investment in Charismatic Authority: "the energy assigned to . . . promote adherence to central authority") and M (Net Rural Marginality: "the economic balance for the rural population" in which marginality increases and productivity per capita decreases) (Renfrew 1978:213). These two variables can then be graphed—for example, in the geometry of the "cusp catastrophe"—and other institutional factors (such as city-state competition, the breakdown of long-distance trading systems, the failure of intensified agricultural regimes) can be discarded or lumped "if there are a priori reasons for using the cusp catastrophe" (Renfrew 1978:212). Mapped on the cusp catastrophe projection, smooth increases in both I and M proceed until they attain the same graphic position. At this point, there is a dramatic reduction in the values of both variables, and a new equilibrium (acephalous society) is established.

Catastrophe theory has effectively alerted us (Culbert, this volume) to the possibility that relatively sudden downward changes in social systems (the Maya collapse, however, persisted well over a century) can be modeled as products of continuous social growth. By aggregating large numbers of institutions into packages that proceed at a uniform pace and in a common trajectory, catastrophe theory seems not very different from traditional stage-level models of social evolutionism, except that it deals with downward as well as upward directions of centralization. Catastrophe theory thus similarly deflects evolutionary studies from the goal of breaking down patterns of complexity formed by many shifting points of interaction that are the result of changing strategies designed to meet long- and short-term risks and opportunities.

Karl Butzer (1980), specifically distancing himself from the stage-level course of evolutionary change and thus rejecting the mechanisms of successive homeostatic equilibriums, contrasts "systems" with "organisms" as appropriate models for understanding collapse. "Metastable equilibriums" provide the needed analytical tool for understanding social change. Collapse results, for example, when a nonproductive superstructure places excessive demands on the productive substrate and thus destroys it (Butzer 1980:518). In civilizations the instability threshold is high because layers of technology, organization, and exchange can mask internal or external stress. It is then a "coincidence of poor leadership, social pathologies, external stress, and environmental perturbation" (Butzer 1980:522) that leads to collapse. Whereas organismic models view collapse as an unalterable natural cycle that ends in social stagnation and death, collapse is merely "stochastic" (which seems to mean that civilizations will not last forever) in Butzer's systems framework. Although Butzer's argument usefully stresses the risks of adopting short-range goals at the expense of long-term stability, this approach to "statistical" collapse appears every bit as teleological as that portrayed in the organismic models (of Spengler and Toynbee). One might just as well argue "that it is the purpose of every individual to die because this is the end of every individual, or that it is the goal of every evolutionary line to become extinct because this is what happened to 99.9 percent of all evolutionary lines that have ever existed" (Mayr 1974:97).

In a wide-ranging general systems approach to collapse, Herbert Simon

(1965) has proposed the notion of "near-decomposability" to explain the breakdown of complex social organizations (among other types of complex systems). For Simon, all complex systems are hierarchically composed of many stable lower-level and intermediate units that are strongly interconnected horizontally but less strongly coupled vertically. Furthermore, those vertical linkages diminish in strength according to their height in the hierarchical scale. Since lower-level controls manage short-term and local affairs, higher-lever controls exist precisely to provide system-wide decision-making capability. In this analysis the process of collapse (but not its cause) is roughly predictable because the products of systemic failure are not randomly formed associations (or social groups) but precisely those intermediate and lower-level units that existed before the formation of higher-level ones. Furthermore, the reversibility of collapse is a clear possibility since the products of decomposition may become the building blocks for subsequent hierarchical arrangement.

One general problem with each of these system analyses is that they tend to encourage us to assume that sociocultural entities are normally highly integrated—highly systemic—with well-developed mechanisms for self-regulation (after Cowgill, this volume). Terms such as *promotion, linearization,* and *near-decomposability* are probably not "wrong"—and may well serve as starters for organizing hard thinking about ideas and data. Nevertheless, the vague language and terminology of systems theory, as used by archaeologists and other social scientists, tends to invite increasingly elaborate abstractions that often impede our ability to break down complex data and may prevent the examination of social institutions that are normally not well integrated (Cowgill, this volume).

Collapse as the Drastic Restructuring of Social Institutions

For the founding fathers of sociology—Marx, Durkheim, and Weber— the collapse of ancient states and civilizations was of little direct concern. Their general goals were rather to understand the nature of modern complex societies and to contrast them with primitive—relatively undifferentiated—ones. Such analyses were intended to account for the appearance and distinctive character of post-medieval European civilization and so to explain why such social systems had not appeared elsewhere. The collapse of ancient states and civilizations was considered essentially a prelude to higher developments. Marx, of course, argued that contradictions within a social order—most especially between the forces and relations of production—can cause a society's breakdown and create the conditions for new levels of sociocultural integration. In Weber's multidimensional model of inequality and political struggle, the persistent nature of some social corporations was underscored even in the face of rapid transformation of other social components. These last observations have been thoroughly explored in a wide variety of historic states by S. N. Eisenstadt. The main points of his investigation (1963, reprinted with an important new introduction in 1969) are recapitulated here.

Eisenstadt argues that historic states are centrally organized with differentiated roles and activities existing within executive, military, and religious hierarchies. Political goals emanate from this center, but in establishing them the center also provides arenas of political struggle within itself. Tension between the center and periphery also exists, since the center is concerned with detaching the means for political action from the periphery, and groups on the periphery are reluctant to surrender their political autonomies. Eisenstadt's periphery consists of traditional aristocracies, kin-based units, peasants, and specialized economic groups, such as craftspeople and merchants. Recruitment to the center rests on either political or economic motives, both of which are detached from the ascriptive qualities of individuals. Indeed, the fundamental organizing principle of early states is precisely that which counteracts the traditionally ascribed ties that characterize much of the periphery. In order to support itself, the center must be able to garner "free-floating resources." That is, it must "disembed" from the periphery those goods and services not irrevocably bound within the subsistence and socially prescribed activities of those groups. In order to channel these resources to itself, the center must address concerns of the periphery through the establishment of judicial activities, by defending the society or expanding the society's boundaries, and by upholding the dominant cultural symbols of the entire collectivity. Thus the center attempts to legitimate the process whereby it withdraws goods and services (e.g., taxes and corvée labor) from the periphery.

Stability in historic states and civilizations is maintained when the periphery considers that the resources it provides the center also return benefits to itself. These benefits may be material—the circulation of goods and services and orderly settlement of disputes—but also lie in manipulation of values and symbols that supply both this- and other-worldly well-being. The locally organized institutional structures of the periphery, however, were never monopolized by the state, neither in the bases of organization or in the internal management of productive resources. Although the political center, for its own goals, may seek to control the extraction, production, and/or distribution of certain key materials, the goods and services required by the state for its continued stability must be acquired from the traditionally organized groups that provide them only in return for some perceived benefits.

By its very nature the set of balances that determines the flow of resources, the establishment of political goals, and the allocation of power between the center and periphery and within the center itself is very fragile. Critical is the management of those free-floating resources. "Meddling" can occur when the center attempts to channel these resources for its own ends and so demands products that the periphery cannot easily supply or is reluctant to provide. Other sources of conflict may emerge when the center refuses to incorporate the needs and orientations of local leadership in the formulation of political goals, in some cases attempting to replace beliefs and values of peripheral groups with the beliefs and values of the central ruling elite. Significant stress can also occur within the center when one interest group is able to reduce or eliminate access to the arena of political struggle by other groups.

Collapse, in general, ensues when the center is no longer able to secure resources from the periphery, usually having lost the "legitimacy" through which it could "disembed" goods and services of traditionally organized groups. The process of collapse entails the dissolution of those centralized institutions that had facilitated the transmission of resources and information, the settlement of intergroup disputes, and the legitimate expression of differentiated organizational components. The maintenance of those institutions demands a flexibility, a "resilience" of responses to stresses that are continually produced, often contradictorally, by the various competing local groups on the periphery and those within the center itself, as well as by external threats or expansionist policies. A "maximizing" strategy, in which the political center tends to channel resources and services for its own, rather than for societal, ends and in which support and legitimation from the periphery are therefore eroded, can lead to collapse (see also Robert Adams 1978). Economic disaster, political overthrow, and social disintegration are the likely products of collapse.

It may be further observed that successful methods of gaining political ascendancy do not necessarily ensure success in maintaining the political system. Political maintenance is achieved by broadening the means of support for the state by meeting needs and demands of old-line elites and by creating institutions that effectively and legitimately restructure the production and distribution of resources. Especially critical for the stability of the state is the transformation of a loyal and personally ascribed cadre of supporters into a bureaucratic hierarchy in which organizational self-perpetuation is subservient to the establishment of political goals.

In his essay in this volume, Eisenstadt is particularly concerned to show that many of the historic states (represented particularly in this volume by Hsu's study) belong to what Jaspers denominated the "Axial Age."

Such civilizations are characterized by the development of new kinds of
ideologies, those

> which strive to present a comprehensive view of the world, not merely of any
> particular group, and argue that the main task is to remake present reality,
> corrupt and imperfect as it is, in accordance with the dictates of higher moral
> order. Socially, Axial civilizations come to be pervaded by new kinds of groups,
> labelled by Eisenstadt "autonomous elites," because their existence, recruit-
> ment, and legitimacy do not depend finally on the political establishment, nor
> on traditional kinship ties, but on individual qualifications, especially intel-
> lectual ability. It is the *raison d'être* of these groups, in turn, to create, prom-
> ulgate, and refine the new ideologies. (Machinist 1986:183)

The concept of the Axial Age (in which various such ideologies were
created) falls squarely in the sociological tradition of distinguishing between different "traditional civilizations" and so indicating wherein lie
the roots of modern societies. In his chapter in this volume, Eisenstadt
thus considers how collapse in some ancient states and civilizations must
not be separated from the larger problem of continuity of those societies.

THE VARIOUS MEANINGS OF COLLAPSE IN ANCIENT STATES AND CIVILIZATIONS

In reviewing the literature on the collapse of ancient states and civilizations, we see that the term *collapse* connotes for many, in a "common
knowledge" way, something quite different and simpler—namely, an end
of things—than the complex set of problems we are trying to explore.
Thus, in the study of collapse we have already referred to the phenomena
of political decomposition, institutional restructuring, and social transformation. It is clear that it cannot be assumed that everyone understands
the same thing by *collapse*.

The distinction between terms such as *decline, decay,* and *decadence*
on the one hand and, on the other hand, terms such as *fall, collapse,*
fragmentation, and *death* is too easily glossed over. Those in the former
group imply changes that are somehow for the worse, especially morally
or aesthetically inferior, but are not necessarily the end of anything. Those
in the latter group, however, imply that some meaningful entity ceased
to exist. In this volume, since we wished to avoid protracted and inevitable
discussions about the criteria that might be used to decide moral or
aesthetic decline (or improvement), we have focused on changes in the
quantity or quality of material phenomena—the economic, technological,
demographic, and, especially, the political aspects of social life.

We have proposed, further, that in turning to phrases that refer to the
termination of something, rather than to its deterioration, it is useful to

distinguish between two semantic categories: those that denote the collapse or end of a civilization and those that refer to the collapse of a state. Cowgill (this volume) has suggested that the term *civilization* refer to those human cultures that are not only socially differentiated and politically centralized but also have the component of what Robert Redfield called a "great tradition" (1956). To speak of the end of a civilization, therefore, would be to refer, among other things, to the termination of that "great tradition." Such cases are indeed rare and are represented only by the Mesopotamian example (Chapters 2 and 3) in this volume. In contrast, the collapse of a state is a phrase with obvious political reference—the falling apart of a large, centralized political system into a number of smaller, politically autonomous units in which permanent specialization of governmental roles is no longer in evidence.

It should be noted, however, that there was more to our desire to concentrate on instances of political fragmentation than an arbitrary wish to narrow our topic. Indeed, in most of the cases examined in this volume, it appears that states may break apart politically without incurring the particularly severe social troubles that preclude their active restructuring. What is also important in this analytical goal of rigorously distinguishing, as far as possible, the boundaries among interconnected social institutions and social groups is that it may also be possible to have acute social organizational problems without political fragmentation. Thus, although political fragmentation is often concomitant with troubles in social, economic, ideological, and/or environmental spheres, it is desirable not to assume that all institutional structures in a society are inextricably and inevitably codetermining. Breaking down complexity in this way, furthermore, increases our ability to distinguish between cause and effect in large-scale institutional collapses. In general, the vicissitudes of civilizations and states, as we have defined them, are distinct topics, and failure to distinguish between them is confusing and a hindrance to research. Thus, we specifically asked the participants of this seminar to focus on episodes in which large-scale, nonindustrialized states were succeeded by substantial periods of political fragmentation.

EXAMPLES OF "COLLAPSE"

The nature of the sources that both allow and limit investigations into collapse is variously represented in the chapters to follow. In the two Mesopotamian examples, Robert Adams and Norman Yoffee are concerned with problems of correlating material culture (e.g., settlement patterns) with a rich, if biased, textual tradition preserved on clay tablets that are themselves part of the archaeological record. It is important, furthermore, in studies of historic Mesopotamian states that the prehistoric roots of Mesopotamian civilization be considered. The patterns of historic Mesopotamian regional interactions took shape millennia before the first cuneiform script was invented.

The Mesopotamian case must consider the problem of several political collapses, each one following a rare and brief period of centralization beyond the boundaries of particular city-states. The reality of these recurrent collapses must be measured against the one-Mesopotamia ideology that provided a continuing justification for the attempts to forge a regional Mesopotamian unity. In Mesopotamia, finally, we have a rare example of both the collapse of a political system and the end of a civilization: Mesopotamian belief systems, cultural traditions—including political ideologies—and even Mesopotamian languages completely disappeared (although certain influences on other cultures can, of course, be traced).

The chapters by Cho-yun Hsu and G. W. Bowersock on Han China and Rome, respectively, are based predominantly on historical material. Hsu's work shows that the collapse of a political system, the Han state, by no means presupposes a similar breakdown of Chinese civilizational values or the elimination of the "carriers" of those ideologies. Indeed, the character of the Chinese bureaucratic system, which took its shape in the Han period, not only contributed to the fall of the dynasty, but facilitated the reformulation of later Chinese states. In the Roman case, Bowersock similarly separates the decline of Rome as a city from the collapse of the Roman empire. The "fall of Rome" is further investigated as a series of social transformations and not as an attempt to affix a date to the collapse, a task that would impossibly simplify the process of how characteristic Roman institutions lived on and were restructured in Late Antiquity.

Patrick Culbert pursues the case of the Maya collapse, perhaps the one that is best known by archaeologists. The impact of the 1970 School of American Research seminar on the Maya collapse (Culbert, ed., 1973) was profound: close examination of exactly what ended and what did not sharpened Mayanists' attention to everything from subsistence bases to political alliances among the ruling elite. Culbert's study depicts the process of internal competition among independent regional states in a culturally bounded Maya sphere of interaction. Competition among these regional states eventually exacerbated the existing tensions in Maya center-periphery relations: the productive rural population became progressively drawn into the orbits of political and cult centers. These centers, foci of population growth and craft and esoteric specializations, however, only exacerbated the problems of securing adequate resources through locally intensified agricultural practices. Finally, continued agricultural intensification degraded arable lands throughout the Maya core area to such an extent that neither exchange nor seizure of scarce food could solve the crisis in subsistence. According to Culbert, only a region-wide failure of the subsistence system could have resulted in such widespread abandonment of cities in the Maya core area as that which characterizes the Classic Maya collapse. Nevertheless, Maya civilization persisted and was restructured, especially in the northern Maya lowlands of Yucatán.

In the collapse of the great metropolis of Teotihuacan, which had dominated its Mesoamerican neighbors for several centuries, René Millon reviews a large range of data to show that the various important problems, both with Teotihuacan's "outer periphery" and with nearer agricultural lands, cannot in themselves explain the pace or character of Teotihuacan's collapse. Rather, Millon wonders, did the apparent desire to maintain an ideological continuity from its earliest days, in spite of the imperial transformations to the political system of Teotihuacan, lead to enormous tension within the Teotihuacan center? It was this internal dislocation of ideological values, and perhaps the loss of status, power, and wealth of certain elites and their followers, that may have brought about the massive, fiery, but selectively "Carthaginian" destruction of Teotihuacan's ceremonial and political precincts. This chapter also contends that the highly formalistic models of economic behavior that have been presented to explain the collapse of Teotihuacan have not considered the full range of data Millon presents here and have neglected important aspects of cultural institutions that affected the internal stability of the state. The destruction of Teotihuacan was vast but not all-encompassing, and social life continued at the site after the end of its imperial political system.

Bennet Bronson's chapter, while focusing on South and Southeast Asia, considers the presence of "barbarians" in general—those people in contact with states but not themselves subject to states—as a factor leading to collapse. Vulnerability to barbarians in northern India, for example, tended to threaten the viability of states, whereas the absence of barbarians in Southeast Asia facilitated the development and maintenance of states there. Barbarians in this perspective can be investigated not merely as outsiders, but as part of a center-periphery phenomenon. They can cause vast military expenditures for states while keeping their own costs of predation low. Few states have been immune from such enthusiastic economists on their borders.

Chapters by Shmuel Eisenstadt and Herbert Kaufman discuss the phenomena of collapse of ancient states and civilizations from the perspectives of sociology and political science, respectively. Eisenstadt's essay focuses on the conditions under which the collapse of ancient states was likely to be followed by the reformulation of those political systems. Applying the logic of formal organizations in the modern world, Kaufman assembles a long list of disequilibrating factors that would make unlikely the long-term survival of any ancient state. For Kaufman chance aggregations of misfortunes could easily bring down such organizations. Kaufman's emphasis on the "delicate balance" of state organizations highlights an important thread that runs through most of this volume: that ancient states never existed at a systemically harmonious level of adjustment. In Santa Fe, Adams suggested that were we to adopt a motto for the seminar, it should be Adam Smith's aphorism: "there's a lot of ruin in a nation."

CONCLUSION

In this volume *collapse* does not, in principle, refer to the death of the great traditions (civilizations) that must be analytically dissociated from the failure of ancient states. Indeed, no state or civilization collapses equally in all its parts and much attention in this volume is paid to what happens after collapse. The term *collapse* is not used in order to project a new analytical cell in which data can be fitted or discarded. It simply serves as a shorthand for a set of research objectives designed to conjoin individual cases so that they may be investigated beyond their familiar ethnospecific environments. In this chapter I certainly have not sought to produce a single powerful explanatory and predictive theory of sociopolitical failure, but rather I have tried to establish a framework in which the data on the collapse of ancient states and civilizations can be intensively examined.

In studying collapse, we have not supposed that ancient states and civilizations are normally well-functioning entities that are upset by external forces that overwhelm them. Indeed, in the cases that are presented, it seems that ancient civilizations do not really function without a good deal of bungling and without generating considerable conflict; they were at best half-understood by the various people who made them, maintained them, coped with them, and struggled against them (see Kaufman and Cowgill, this volume).

Finally, it is appropriate to stress here (see also the preface) that the essays on collapse in this volume are not addressed to any presumed issue of the collapse of any modern civilization (see also Adams, this volume). Indeed, the lessons learned from Spengler's and Toynbee's concern with the fates of their civilizations and how this was translated into their research are clear. One of our prime goals, rather, is to point out that much of what anthropologists and other social scientists have written about the collapse of ancient states, and almost everything that is conveyed outside the groves of academe about such collapses, has been extremely dubious.

In this chapter, I have attempted to delineate the topic of the volume by offering some general themes and tentative theoretical propositions that are discussed, tested, elaborated, criticized, modified, and otherwise responded to in the following essays. We trust that we can at least perform a very useful function in the modern world by exploring how much is patently false in what "everyone knows" about the collapse of ancient civilizations, how much is questionable, and how much, if anything, is firmly rooted in good evidence.

NOTE

Many of the ideas in this chapter and a good deal of its exposition owe much to the clear and helpful observations of George Cowgill. This chapter began as a combination of our two position papers that were distributed well before the seminar and retains some of the form of that combination. The section on the various meanings of collapse and the last section of this chapter, in particular, are abridgments and/or restatements of thoughts more fully developed in George's concluding chapter in this volume.

Contexts of Civilizational Collapse

A Mesopotamian View

Robert McC. Adams

It is probably no accident, in view of the many manifestations of social deterioration or crisis punctuating our lives in the late twentieth century, that the theme of decline or collapse of ancient societies also is undergoing a kind of renaissance. Yet the arguments are unpersuasive that a volume concerned with the decline and formal disappearance of states and civilizations of the fairly remote past has any "presentist" relevance. Our most pervasive present danger, the worldwide threat of nuclear destruction, is unique in being a direct outgrowth not merely of deep-seated instabilities or rivalries like those familiar throughout history but also of material and scientific progress.

This epoch of profound and sustained change is unprecedented both in its long duration and in its all-encompassing spread. Accompanying it has been an awesome technological destruction of distance. The result is that existing civilizations, unlike those whose historical development is represented in this volume, can less and less readily be distinguished from one another or given substance as bounded units. As scholars, most of the contributors to this volume continue to be concerned with regionally autonomous, internally organized processes of cultural growth. But we must acknowledge the contradiction that no small part of the full range of our activities—and perhaps especially those we carry on as scholars—are directed toward a world civilization that is increasingly unitary.

Setting aside the present, we find that there was a degree of local autarky and geographic buffering throughout the millennia of our technically less-advanced past. Interdependencies were correspondingly less dominant, finely tuned, and disastrous in their consequences when allowed to slip out of balance. In the absence of credible sources of disinterested, long-distance aid in times of local crisis, social groupings of any size or character had to give greater attention to preserving resilience and to keeping options open than to maximizing their advantages or well-being at a given moment (Robert Adams 1978). On purely a priori grounds, therefore, it is probably an exaggeration to speak of "lost" civilizations. One way or another, many of their human protagonists managed to leave an imprint on surviving gene pools. And nothing in the archaeological record suggests that their material and cognitive contributions did not mostly prove to be cumulative and ineradicable.

The Classic lowland Maya may seem to offer an example to the contrary. But this was surely an exceptional case, perhaps the only one in which not only a politicoreligious superstructure but a large part of the supporting population disappeared from at least their original setting within the span of a few generations. And even in this case, it is an overstatement to claim that the civilization disappeared with neither direct nor indirect descendants.

Equally to be avoided is the implication that the collapse of ancient states and civilizations was somehow inevitably prefigured in the processes by which they were formed. To assume an interconnection between the ideas of "rise" and "fall" is deceptively easy, calling to mind an oscillatory process or the life cycle of a living organism. But there is, simply, no justification for teleological or vitalistic constructs in the study of social evolution. Societies are not organisms but collectivities that can fragment and recombine on new principles. Extinction in biological evolution admittedly seems to offer an analogue to civilizational collapse. But extinction is dependent on species-limited modes of genetic transmission, whereas for cultures there are no such limitations. Smaller, more primitive human societies may have been swept away without trace from time to time, but it seems fair to assert that no civilization—yet—has ever been wholly extinguished.

Thus it would be a mistake to concentrate on either the absoluteness or the inevitability of collapse. Yet certainly repeated, often protracted, episodes of decline occurred, and at least their comparative aspects constitute a badly neglected theme of study. Apart from the inherent interest in any neglected theme characterizing a substantial part of the historic record, a concern with decline significantly alters the vantage point from which we view the evolutionary process.

The long-accepted opposition between "general" and "specific" evolution, although now increasingly viewed as an arbitrary if not wholly spurious bifurcation of a continuum of possibilities, reflects a traditional anthropological preoccupation with the supposed main line of evolutionary "progress." By focusing on retrogression or collapse, we forcefully reassert the possibility that there can be outcomes other than, for example, negative feedback leading to homeostasis, or excessive extrasystemic stress producing positive feedback and a sudden upward movement on the evolutionary ladder. The theme of decline stimulates recognition that human societies or their constituent elements follow reversible, and in important ways unpredictable, rather than predetermined courses (Boudon 1982). It induces us to ask whether efforts to smooth the frequently abrupt irregularities of change into unilinear processual abstractions may not involve a fundamental distortion of the nature and causation of sociocultural change itself.

That question is naturally not limited to the study of early states and civilizations. One thoughtful answer to it has been offered in the entirely different field of early modern intellectual history:

> It has been assumed that the process of modernization is comprehended by its causes, that once the formation of a new class or the accumulation of capital or the articulation of a new ethic is detected, the means by which this new historical force imposes itself upon actual events is unimportant. The modern transformation of European society has been viewed as a process rather than a series of developments capable of leading to conclusions other than the one actually realized. The means to change are thus subordinated to the initial cause or causes. Means become important, however, if one assumes that there is not an overarching determinant in human affairs but rather a constant flow of events where the consequences of each historical moment become an influence upon the next, each sequence carrying with it possibilities that may not be realized, but that are nonetheless realizable. (Appleby 1978:10)

A comparable viewpoint is also to be found in archaeological and culture historical studies, even though it is at odds with the more doctrinaire positivism of some archaeological theorists. V. Gordon Childe's best-known work, *Man Makes Himself* (1941), encapsulates in at least its title the essential understanding that change is a contingent, interactive outcome rather than a determinate sequence subordinated to first causes. Similarly, Eric R. Wolf (1955:93) has written that

> It is a gross oversimplification to assume that culture changes evenly, and in one direction only; and that phenomena which contradict such linear developments may be disregarded as temporary setbacks. The character of change determines the setbacks it will suffer, and the setbacks themselves are major determinants of future changes and their characteristics.

Or further,

> There exists within evolutionary anthropology a strongly entrenched tradition

which seeks to universalize its explanations. Such theories tend to be extremely reductive, and often condense a multiplicity of processes into unilinear variables. These theories range from a concentration on the extraction of social surplus via increasing divisions of labor and more productive technology . . . ; to status-limitation, perhaps linked to population pressure . . . ; to the effects of population pressure and warfare within circumscribed environments. . . . In the search for universal prime-movers, the concern of these theorists has been extremely retrospective. They tend to see the state as an inevitable and efficient solution to a particular set of problems. But when the evolution of the state is viewed as a unilineal success story, we lose the specificity of history. (Rapp 1977:309–10)

In short, the subject of the decline or collapse of ancient states and civilizations is more than a problem that has somehow failed to receive the attention it deserves. It is also associated with, and lends encouragement to, a new and different set of questions that promises to alter significantly our understanding of processes of growth as well as deterioration. The purpose of what follows is merely to outline these new orientations that a focus on decline makes necessary, and briefly to illustrate them with reference to ancient Mesopotamia. Because of considerations of space, no attempt will be made here fully to describe or document the substantially different account of long-term evolutionary sequences that together they seem to call for.

SCALE, HIERARCHY, AND CONCENTRATION OF STATE AUTHORITY

Anthropological interest in ancient civilizations has for the most part eschewed the study of textual records. This bias partly reflects conflicting demands for disciplinary training that make very difficult the acquisition of the necessary philological competences. But since anthropological practitioners involved with the subject tend to be recruited into it by way of a prior interest in archaeology, it is likely that a preference for behavioral evidence, uncontaminated by the ambiguities about the signification of actions that are inherent in texts, also plays a part (Robert Adams 1984). Given a primarily archaeological data base, the principal areas of concern have involved holistic assessments of social scale and complexity and of patterns of hierarchical authority.

Scale, the most directly measurable topic, may have reference to the extent of territorial integration; to population trends, including especially the degree of nucleation within an ascending hierarchy of settlements culminating in those of "urban" dimensions; to monumentality of public architecture; and to aggregations of wealth, natural resources, agricultural surpluses, or the like. Promoting all such aggregative tendencies were sociopolitical elites, whose growing separation from the communities of which they were part presumably led them to be increasingly authoritarian and self-indulgent. A growing centralization of decision making is implied, hierarchically specialized and employing new means to collect, store, evaluate, and communicate information. All this was frequently accompanied by the introduction of new processes of production and distribution, and by the imposing of new, more centralized controls over old ones. These developments essentially define the rise of the state.

According to most reconstructions of processes culminating in the formation of the early state, the elaboration of social hierarchies was of more decisive importance than an expansion in scale. A plausible, but still essentially speculative, transformation of status hierarchies into more sharply defined class differences has been a special subject of attention. This process is usually assumed to have begun with the ranking of kinship groups, expressed in asymmetrical patterns of spouse selection and perhaps bridewealth payment. Individual lineages gradually took the form of "conical clans," in which the perquisites of wealth, status, and authority became concentrated in the hands of a central core of the group (Fried 1967; Friedman and Rowlands 1977; Haas 1982). Also perhaps accruing to that core or apex was the management of a system of redistribution, although this interpretation, while plausible, is at best very weakly supported by the available archaeological evidence. It has been suggested that the existence of a redistribution system corresponds to a two-tier settlement hierarchy of scattered, relatively autonomous, ceremonial centers each serving as the integrative focus for its own surrounding cluster of smaller, subsistence-oriented communities.

The term *chiefdom* is widely, if loosely and rather uncritically, applied to this kind of system. Centrally involved in the construct is a hereditary succession of individuals whose leadership functions were not yet wholly separable from those of their kindred. There is an underlying assumption that the path to statehood was broadly similar everywhere, taking a succession of integrative forms in which chiefdoms—defined almost entirely on the basis of relatively recent ethnographic analogies—were a crucial intervening phase or stage. Also assumed is the weakening of an earlier, common pattern of extended kin affiliations, so that these ceased to be the primary basis for either superior social status or sociopolitical leadership. All this could well be an accurate description, but once again the archaeological—and somewhat too late to be directly relevant, the textual—evidence is less than conclusive. It clearly supports the emergence of growing socioeconomic differences and of individuals occupying well-defined political roles, but the case for the earlier generality and importance of extended kin groupings is much more tenuous.

From this point forward I will confine my remarks to the Mesopotamian sequence, with which I am most familiar. There is some evidence that political power suggestive of the existence of a state was at first theocratically defined and exercised, with the commonly held belief system acting to blur incipient class divisions. This was followed by a bifurcation between relatively more sacred and more secular institutions (archaeologically differentiated as "temples" and "palaces"). From (admittedly somewhat later) textual evidence it can be shown that secular elites came to dominate the politicomilitary sector while personnel associated with temples were able to retain (or even newly acquire) important economic and managerial roles. Increasing flows of prestige goods, whose production was stimulated by both these sets of institutions, meanwhile helped to validate status systems that were growing more complex and widely ramifying. And at the lowest, most vulnerable levels of the hierarchy, significant numbers of agricultural producers were more or less forcibly divested of their autonomous rights of access to land, water, and other resources.

For some theorists, the introduction of the state signifies no more than the attachment of marginally greater coercive powers to a political apparatus deriving its legitimacy from services performed on behalf of the society at large (Service 1975). This neofunctionalist or "integration" model may be contrasted with a more convincing "conflict" model, supported by Jonathan Haas (1982). The key criterion for the state in the latter model is a qualitative shift in broad patterns of social relations, consistent with a deepening of class divisions and a tendency for asymmetric relations reflecting such alignments to replace others that had been almost wholly embedded in those of kinship. Still another approach centers on neither the elite's integrative functions nor the degree of self-interest involved in its exercise of power, but instead on the degree of concentration that occurred in decision making. Stressing the advantages of a replicable and quantitative assessment, it identifies three- or four-tiered settlement hierarchies with the presence of a state (Wright 1977).

Although they share a concern for hierarchy as expressed in state organization and/or class stratification, the three viewpoints just referred to are derived from discrepant bodies of theory. The first two are divergently related to some aspects of Marxist thought, which underwent alterations in the course of Marx's own writings and continues to be represented by a variety of still-evolving positions. On the other hand, the third borrows heavily from modern work on decision and information theory, and in so doing also relies on some of the assumptions of classical economics.

Two principal strands of Marxist thought are particularly relevant to processes of early state growth. In one, the state is seen as an instrumentality developed in response to growing social differences, not merely in status or wealth but in access to land, labor, and other productive resources. New, formal powers of governance were elaborated in order to defend and extend these differences, rather than to subordinate them, as had been the case earlier, to local or kin loyalties. Such a view places the weight of causation on more or less consciously recognized class antagonisms, a theme on which the available evidence—thus far all of it textual rather than archaeological—is, however, at best exceedingly limited and quite inconclusive. To the contrary, it assigns to the state administration, in spite of its richly documented salience, only a following, "superstructural" role.

The second relevant strand derives from Marx's early speculations about a so-called Asiatic mode of production. As reformulated on the basis of more recent ethnographic and ethnohistorical research, this view involves the exercise of power over a multitude of small, undifferentiated, and autarkic communities by a minority invoking the existence of or need for a higher level of unity:

> This power at first takes root in functions of common interest (religious, political, economic) and, without ceasing to be a functional power, gradually transforms itself into an exploitative one. The special advantages accruing to this minority, nominally as a result of services rendered to the communities, become obligations with no counterpart, i.e., exploitation. The land of these communities is often expropriated to become the ultimate property of the king, who personifies the higher community. We therefore have exploitation of man by man, and the appearance of an exploiting class without the existence of private ownership of land. (Godelier 1978:240)

Here, too, are many difficulties. There are some, to be sure, who reject any empirical interjection in what they prefer to pursue as a strictly theoretical debate (e.g., Hindness and Hirst 1975). For most of us, however, it is a matter of some weight whether the evidence for early civilizations favors the existence of exploitative state superstructures in the absence of private ownership of land. In the case of Mesopotamia, this occurred, if at all, only for a relatively brief period at the very birth of the state. From that point forward, private tenure fluctuated in condition and amount but regularly—and for the most part vigorously—coexisted with variable forms of state domain.

Equally important, it is more than doubtful that an unchanging, cellular structure of village communes was ever separated by a wide gulf from a superimposed, essentially alien state. Most evident in all the early states of which we know is their unstable, contingent character, which is inconsistent not only with older stereotypes of "despotism" but also with the idea that the state could have been consistently and effectively inhibitory to further development. In fact, the very construct of an Asiatic mode of production limits the possibility of decline or collapse to central state functions that increasingly were of marginal benefit to the agricultural population. Yet certainly the entire history of the Mesopotamian case argues for the opposite conclusion. In prosperity as well as in disaster, state power and agrarian well-being were strongly and positively correlated with one another.

The major reference point for this chapter is Mesopotamian civilization. Yet on more general grounds, too, it is difficult to avoid the conclusion that the case for an Asiatic mode of production was inconsistently argued, overgeneralized, and flawed in its interpretation of the very limited data then available, beginning with the versions put forward originally by Marx. Perry Anderson, in a major dissection of the concept, makes a convincing case that Godelier's and other attempts to reinvest it with usefulness and substance can fare no better:

> Modern attempts to build a developed theory of the "Asiatic mode of production" from the scattered legacies left by Marx and Engels—whether in the "communal-tribal" or "hydraulic-despotic" avenues of direction—are thus essentially misguided. They underestimate both the weight of the prior problematic which Marx and Engels accepted, and the vulnerability of the limited modifications which they brought to it. The "Asiatic mode of production," even shorn of its village myths, still suffered the inherent weakness of functioning as a generic residual category for non-European development, and so blending features found in distinct social formations into a single, blurred archetype. The most obvious and pronounced distortion resulting from such a procedure was the persistent attribution of a "stationary" character to Asian societies. (1979:494)

As already noted, those concerned with hierarchies of regulatory functions have tended to follow more narrowly "economic" postulates and to concentrate on administrative aggregates and routines rather than on contingencies and clashes of interest. Most current modeling of early state and/or urban hierarchies within this framework implicitly rests on the assumption of rationally selfish and individualistic location decisions, with these in turn requiring information comparable to that provided by market pricing in order to permit minimization of transport costs. Central-place theory, the most formal and comprehensive expression of this viewpoint, envisions a world artificially devoid of spatial, cultural, or informational constraints, in which producers and retailers cluster so as to reach a maximal pool of consumers at minimal cost. Opportunities to cluster vary by industry, tending toward equilibrium points that are dependent on levels of production and transport technology, population density, and so on. Hence central-place theory predicts the formation of tiered hierarchies of towns and cities, reflecting nodes of progressively higher concentrations of goods and services that are made available to adjacent, smaller communities.

Many of the simplifying assumptions of central-place theory cannot be fully operative in any specific geographical, historical, or cultural milieu, and especially that of preindustrial cities. Boundary discontinuities, resource irregularities, and institutional or cultural obstacles to market pricing—or any other efficient, information-diffusing mechanism with regard to production and distribution costs—all must be taken into account. They may distort beyond recognition the postulated grids of nested, graduated hexagons of territory surrounding each central place, as well as the distinctions between size categories of settlements. However, there are several aspects of the formal modeling of central-place hierarchies that have been shown to be as productive of new insights into early civilizations as they are for contemporary national planning. The rank-size rule, expressing a consistent double-logarithmic distribution of central-place sizes, has been found to apply to some traditional as well as some modern societies. One common deviation from this, a tendency toward enhanced size at the apex of the urban hierarchy known as urban primacy, also has ancient as well as modern examples. Perhaps the modern explanation of it—it is thought to reflect exceptionally strong forces of integration in the society in question—then can be helpful with ancient societies as well. A flattening of the rank-size relationship at its upper end seems to carry the opposite significance. Additionally, central-place theory has sensitized us to the importance of breaks in the distribution of settlement sizes (Johnson 1975; Smith 1985a, b).

To some extent, the widely recognized limitations to the practical application of central-place theory apply to the entire theme of hierarchies. Available models tend to be essentially static. As such, they lead to a rather contrived view of change as an abrupt succession of equilibrium states. The source of change, furthermore, is artificially deflected outside the system under investigation. If population "pressure" or technologically based increases in productivity are proposed as prime movers behind the complex web of changes leading to hierarchies, they must be separated on a priori grounds from such putative effects as spatial clustering of population, hostile or authoritarian patterns of intercommunity interaction, and the like.

Another large area of ambiguity concerns the significance of observed hierarchies. Particularly where textual documentation is lacking, they have had to be reconstructed on the slender basis of arbitrary units of measurement applied to archaeological residues of behavior (e.g., site size or grave "wealth"). The desire to increase the statistical significance of such categories tends to lead to a neglect of the probably greater social significance of the variance within them and the more or less arbitrary boundaries between them. And left unclear, in spite of many innovative and persevering efforts, is what relationship there was between archaeologically derived categories of this kind and the beliefs, associations, and even actions of the ancient peoples whose physical and cultural remains we study.

Conflict, Variance, and Reversibility

Anthropological concern with early states and civilizations is naturally concentrated among archaeologists. As already noted, it has been correspondingly directed toward issues that encourage comparative assessments and can readily be submitted to measurement, such as those of scale, complexity, and hierarchy. It has also been directed away from issues requiring dependence on texts, for reasons rooted not only in archaeologists' prevailing lack of philological skills but in their other methodological challenges and transdisciplinary priorities. Yet it must be remembered that with improvements in early cuneiform writing systems the importance of textual data multiplied manyfold. This came about through broadened use, greater information-carrying capacity, and, not least, enhanced intelligibility of the later texts to modern students. For an understanding of Mesopotamian civilization as a whole, the written record altogether dominates the archaeological one—I do not mean that one can ever replace the other—from at least the mid-third millennium B.C. onward.

It thus happens that most social scientific, as distinguished from humanistic, concern with early civilizations like that of Mesopotamia terminates rather abruptly with the achievement of a state or civilizational level of complexity. The study of social evolution, perhaps continuing an otherwise discarded nineteenth-century attitude, has therefore become largely identified with episodes of "progress." If we are to deal adequately with later historic epochs in Mesopotamia that frequently are dominated by themes of decline or collapse, we will be better served by another problematic.

There is another limitation or bias that is common to the approaches discussed in the preceding section. Perhaps corresponding to the kinds of changes that are easiest to observe in an exclusively prehistoric sequence, they are concerned with identifying regularities of sociocultural change that can be understood as orderly, determinate, relatively long-persistent processes. Little recognition is given to the important part played by recurrent, short-term instability within and between social units. Yet wherever there is adequate textual documentation to supplement the archaeological record, we encounter power arrangements that are characteristically in flux. Virtually continuous, in addition, are environmental variations and ecological imbalances. These, too, are typically destabilizing in their effects and act to promote intra- and intergroup variability and rivalry. Thus there is a need for another approach that concentrates on indeterminacy and reversibility of outcome, an approach that takes variant responses to opportunity and uncertainty and the conflicts that these engender, rather than institutional scale and continuity, as its central subject matter.

Early cities and states are not primarily viewed as the centers of closed, well-ordered systems if one pursues a conflict-and-variance approach. Instead it is a view of them as volatile, often aggressively expansionistic components of open, poorly articulated systems that tends to dominate the interpretive strategy. Quite possibly the Mesopotamian prototypes were initially founded in a climate of increasingly competitive coexistence, in conscious recognition of the advantages of larger numbers of people and concentrations of resources. For it is indeed a truism that

> In the multitude of people is the king's honor: but in the want of people is the destruction of the prince.
>
> (Proverbs 14:28)

But whether initially defensive or predatory in their orientation, neither cities nor larger, territorially organized states could permanently overcome the vulnerability that their physical and social environments imposed on them. This suggests that the paths leading to urban or state development almost certainly were multiple and irregular rather than predictable and determinate.

The amassing of ritual and control functions within a particular center, for example, might or might not have been a derivative of earlier economic or demographic concentrations there. Symbolic considerations, organizational innovativeness or flexibility, degree of internal unity, or merely the readiness to employ coercive force all might contribute to why some centers succeeded and others failed if a milieu of diffuse and protracted conflicts was the dominant challenge to all of them. Nor was success irreversible; concentrations of power in early civilizations were typically fragile and short-lived.

A conflict-and-variance approach should be regarded as an addition to, not a replacement for, the approaches dealt with earlier. Generalizations about hierarchy and scale retain their importance. To overstress situational variability and indeterminacy might almost constitute a denial of the goal of a comparatively based science. But to entertain these alternative emphases does sensitize us to respects in which neighboring power configurations diverged from one another. Contemporaneous Mesopotamian palace and temple organizations illustrate this broad diversity or even redundancy. So do the different paths toward sociopolitical primacy taken by some centers that were dominated by cults and others headed by seemingly more secular elites. But just as similar organizational ends could be achieved by different means, it would not be surprising if relationships between rival institutional pathways remained fluid and were unformalized. Temporary success and dominance of one organizational mode might well have led to rigidities that later held it back, a preindustrial analogue of Veblen's "penalty of taking the lead."

The approach just outlined, like most of those touched on earlier, is not a coherent theory. It embraces, in fact, a number of only loosely associated assumptions and hypotheses. As a whole, however, it gives greater emphasis to higher-order (administrative, ritual, intellectual) functions in which differentiation is likely to be most marked than to standardized, routinized activities. Receiving primary attention are such topics as fluctuations in the scale of social integration; distinctions between primary and secondary paths of urban and state development; class or status disparities reflected in funerary inclusions, house sizes, and, more importantly, in land tenure and other rights of access to productive resources; entrepreneurial activity, whether institutionally embedded or more individualistic and market-oriented; and efforts by elites to secure and rationalize their status and authority.

A further aspect of variance deserves separate mention. It derives from the contemporary World-Systems school's emphasis on asymmetrical or counterposed development of imperial cores and peripheries in the age of European expansion. In transferring such a schema to the archaic Near Eastern empires that first emerged in the second half of the third millennium B.C., the hypothesis is that even these quite short-lived and loosely articulated systems probably followed some policies of selective expropriation and control that intensified cultural, religious, and economic heterogeneity. If so, rather than developmental trends proceeding in parallel in all of their concentric zones, the growth and prosperity of the urban cores of these empires may have come precisely at the expense of the subordinated peripheries. The empirical case for all this is admittedly still in dispute (Larsen, ed., 1978), but at the least it addresses our attention to the possibility that even the earliest territorially extensive systems of dominance were anything but homogeneous.

Imperial cores and peripheries have a further relationship to one another. As noted in Chapter 1, S. N. Eisenstadt (1969) has called attention to the importance of "free-floating resources" in the consolidation of power, and in the Near East (as elsewhere) it was usually the case that the only attractive sources for windfalls of that kind lay across a kingdom's frontiers. Risky as they were, successful foreign campaigns could generate loot, ransom, continuing assessments of tribute, and masses of relatively skilled captives. All could be important in checking the devolution of central dynastic authority into the hands of particularistic city-states or of a landed aristocracy. Hostilities along frontiers thus have to be seen as elements in a strategy of system integration, even if an adverse outcome also could lead to collapse of the central power. What is clear, in any case, is that core-periphery relationships are a necessary aspect of a non-teleological, nonorganismic, truly dynamic view of ancient civilizations.

INTEGRATION OR AUTONOMY OF OTHER CULTURAL SECTORS

The two broad classes of approach that have been discussed earlier share the limitation of concentrating fairly exclusively on the forms and effectiveness of political or economic integration. Although it is easy to justify making this a primary focus, we should not overlook what is thereby left out of account. It can reasonably be expected that technology, for example, followed a quite different path, generally characterized by accumulative growth and normally little deterred by political fragmentation or even economic setbacks.

Subsistence, production, or transport technologies are rooted in basic discoveries or complexes of techniques whose transmissibility across time and space is seldom strongly affected by disturbances to the social order. Yet while the technological corpus may be on the whole subject to unidirectional growth and not shrinkage, the rate of growth has been historically irregular. Periodic pulses of rapid advance have typically been interspersed among longer, more static phases. How closely do such periodicities correspond to phases of advance and decline identified by political or economic criteria? The answer is not at all obvious and warrants further investigation. It is rather surprising to note, for example, that the tide of basic technological discovery is argued by some to have flowed more strongly in Europe during the early Middle Ages, and perhaps even during the so-called Dark Ages following the collapse of the Roman empire in the west, than during either preceding classical times or any following period up until the Industrial Revolution (Lilley 1973:191).

On the other hand, only an excessively narrow view of technology would equate it solely with technics. Any effective employment of technology is infused with matters of scale and organization. A subsistence system, for example, is not merely a repertoire of domesticated plants and animals, a set of tools, and an agricultural calendar governing their management. Instead it also comprises proverbs containing distillations of experience about weather and other hazards, the corvées and design considerations involved in the construction and management of irrigation networks, arrangements for crop shipment and storage, and the organizational arrangements by which seed, tools, and credit are provided. Similarly, a larger view of craft production must begin with the acquisition of raw materials and the marshaling of sources of energy, and go on to include such matters as stability of employment, guild training and recruitment, outlets for distribution, and the like. As our conception of technology broadens in these organizational directions, its independence from political and economic trends surely decreases.

Religion is another sphere of cultural development that maintains at best a problematical relationship to political and economic integration or fragmentation. Christianity became the Roman state religion yet exhibited no serious break in continuity paralleling the "fall" of the western empire. The impressive advances that have been made in understanding Late Classic Maya religion have depended very largely upon the assumption that there was continuity comparable to this in at least cosmology and iconography, surviving the near-abandonment of the Petén, and persisting in neighboring Yucatán until the arrival of the Spaniards many centuries later. To be sure, there may again be institutional and organizational aspects of religion, as with technology, that are more directly dependent on political and economic cycles. It is difficult, for example, to imagine the maintenance of Sumero-Babylonian priesthoods as corporate bodies except within cities economically able to sustain the local establishments of their patron deities. But at least for those aspects of religion constituting a cultural system of some coherence and autonomy, episodes of decline or collapse seem to have been at best very loosely tied to, and hence explainable by, any of the approaches to ancient civilization that we have considered.

CITIES

Cities have repeatedly played a part in the approaches dealt with heretofore—as indices of scale of integration, as nodes of decision in hierarchical systems of state authority, and as contending polities in their own right. But are cities merely locales of change, or of the exercise and decomposition of power, whose main importance for us is that they happen to be particularly well documented archaeologically and textually? Or did they sometimes play an autonomous role of their own, either hastening or resisting trends toward social disintegration? Probably there is no single answer to these questions, but a discussion of some aspects of urbanism may clarify the bonds that either held, or failed to hold, civilizations together.

Urbanism can be construed in purely locational terms as no more than spatial clustering (Sharpless and Warner 1977). Cities from this viewpoint are relatively nucleated, partially ordered collectivities, distinguished from smaller settlements by exceeding certain thresholds of size and density. At the same time, the thresholds themselves cannot be entirely arbitrary. They must bear some relationship, for example, to subsistence productivity and to the prevailing production and transport technology. Moreover, other indices of size may be more sensitive than mere numbers of people: for example, numbers of more or less permanent institutions and of their full-time functionaries; numbers of nonsubsistence producers and of their specialized occupational categories; numbers of levels in social or administrative hierarchies; the breadth of disparities in wealth or status; and rates of flow of goods, services, media of exchange, and information.

Size and density have the virtue of being almost automatically quantifiable. But if they provide potentially clearcut measures of the extent of urbanization, they may also be taken to imply that urbanization is a derivative, dependent phenomenon. Any strictly materialist approach to causality would probably place the attainment of urban size and density not among the fundamental processes of social evolution but instead among the secondary reflections of underlying forces such as productive, technological, or demographic growth.

Still, there is another side to the argument. Early cities and the newly created institutions in them greatly enlarged, and simultaneously set new limits on, the powers and horizons of those who were persuaded or compelled to come together and live in them. As a social invention, the most perceptible and immediate impact of the founding of cities probably was connected with the enhanced security they offered for agricultural reserves, for costly ritual paraphernalia, and for accumulations of personal wealth. Apparently rather abruptly, large, formerly rural populations congregated within cities and built walls to defend them. Deities identified with cities formed a commonly venerated pantheon, and private persons who moved from city to city often continued to be at least administratively identified with their city of origin. Intensifying struggles over political hegemony were conceptualized in dynastic chronicles as indefinitely continuing reversals of fortune, with the individual cities personified as antagonists. Cities, in short, played a central part in the cognitive worlds of their inhabitants. Surely it is reasonable to assume, therefore, that urbanism itself constituted an at least partly independent realm of meaning and motivation for action.

To judge from the fuller information available only in much more recent times, Near Eastern cities have played a part in maintaining, and probably even in shaping, the systems of towns and villages that surrounded them. Traditionally they are sources of the agricultural credit that is vital for bridging bad years in a region of fluctuating, semiarid climate. Their markets and resident entrepreneurs stimulate functional differentiation in village crafts as well as in crop and livestock production. Local differentiation, it may be noted, often reflects artificially induced needs and complementarities rather than being dependent on local environmental differences. Finally, cities house garrisons, schools, records, administrators, agricultural surpluses, and amusements—all attracting and sometimes assisting the rural population, at the cost of continuing exactions of goods and services.

There are complex and interesting links between settlement size and the exercise of state power. Once again they appear most clearly in later records, in this case early Ottoman archives, where the effectiveness of state security has been identified as the key variable (Bates 1980). Strong, centralized administrations encouraged the spread of small settlements, capital investments in such forms of agricultural intensification as waterworks, and thus rural prosperity as well as population growth. Conversely, a decline in government control saw a retreat in agricultural frontiers and populations. Peasants then had to congregate in larger villages and towns that could be defended against nomadic raids with less state assistance.

To be sure, there are dangers in using the relatively more systematic and ample documentation of recent centuries as a basis for reconstructing the ancient past. Cumulative developments in technology (e.g., in communications and firearms) have altered relations between central places and their subsidiaries—and, a fortiori, those between states and their tribalized or nomadic adjuncts and adversaries. Still awaiting study are what must have been substantial changes in the physical and symbolic ways in which power is proclaimed and exercised. The emergence of a commercialized, interdependent world economy has led to a partial dissolution of formerly more localized patterns of economic interchange within the region. But with all these changes, even the relatively remote time of origin of Near Eastern cities cannot be walled off from the more adequately documented processual insights of later historic periods and contemporary ecological realities. Many aspects of the relationship between city and countryside are clearly long-enduring, rooted in uneven patterns of resource distribution and in subsistence complementarities and uncertainties that are dictated by zonal climatic patterns and possibilities for irrigation. Moreover, archaeological surveys provide at least suggestions of similar processes extending well back into the third millennium B.C. These take the form of shifts in the number and distribution of smaller settlements, coinciding with textually attested oscillations between insecurity and strong state authority (Robert Adams 1981).

Except possibly in their earliest origins, therefore, Near Eastern cities cannot be understood as isolated, localized outgrowths of the potential to produce agricultural surpluses. In all textually documentable periods they can be shown to have interacted intensively with one another, sometimes over very long distances. They form systems that sometimes intersect in support of state power and sometimes conspire to achieve its fragmentation. When brought within a single administrative framework, they have tended to stimulate the intensification and diversification of agriculture, whereas at other times urban rivalries have seriously undermined agricultural productivity and rural well-being. To put the matter somewhat pejoratively, urban elites have consistently sought to manipulate the agricultural regime and its practitioners to their own advantage. But the opposite side of the coin is that their objectives were in large part those without which there never would have been an achievement of "high civilization" in the Near East to attract our study.

Even with regard to origins, this suggests that it may be misleading to think of larger centers beginning to develop naturally and from the bottom up, as it were, out of an idealized landscape of undifferentiated small villages. What seems much more likely are patterns of differentiation in productivity, security, population density, resource potential, and many other variables that long preceded urbanism (Kohl and Wright 1977). Fully developed forms of urbanism would have greatly extended the range and complexity of these patterns and no doubt introduced new ones.

Thus we see that processes of urban decline as well as growth characteristically involved whole networks of differentiated centers and hinterlands. Particularly when we are concerned with the breakup of formerly more integrated systems, this demands a contextual approach rather than one limiting itself to isolated centers viewed as ideal-typical units. Within a broad regional perspective, cities following many trajectories of growth and decline take their places as elements in a kaleidoscopic mosaic. Except in a grossly oversimplified way, therefore, urban evolution cannot be reduced to a set of processual regularities, to a consistent, unidirectional series of trends or sequence of stages. Phases of general growth and decline do occur, but equally fundamental are fluctuating patterns of symbiotic specialization, competitive advantage, and stochastic variation.

By this point it should be apparent that, at any rate in Mesopotamia, cities are the primary units in terms of which it is possible to identify civilizational growth or decline. Though dependent upon an agricultural substratum, civilization, at least in all its more complex, "superstructural" dimensions, was essentially urban. That is not to say civilization was identified with a particular set of cities. Most of the great centers of the Sumerian heartland in the third millennium were eclipsed in the second during a much more widely dispersed phase of urban growth, without a corresponding break in formal structure or tradition. But insofar as we can apprehend Mesopotamian civilization, it is inseparable from groups and institutions that flourished only as cities flourished. The decline of Mesopotamian civilization, accordingly, also must have a vital urban dimension.

Conscious Awareness of Altered Social States

Recurring at many points in this discussion has been a dissatisfaction with deterministic and functionalist modes of explanation. The former, concentrating on the role of remote and general prime movers, rests on the presupposition that the often necessarily prolonged courses of change that ensued as a result of the mere existence of those prime movers were unproblematic and inevitable. For the latter, only the ultimate effectiveness of a solution or outcome is presumed worthy of attention, rather than the means by which it was recognized and imposed over a multiplicity of other alternatives. Both thus tend to leave out of account the historical processes of active contention within societies, by which decisions having sharply divergent impacts upon different individuals or groups are resolved upon under conditions of uncertainty. Both also involve an implicit denial of the consequentiality of goal-motivated human action.

The issue of civilizational decline may afford us an opportunity to probe more deeply into the role of motivation than we can under ordinary circumstances. This is not because "real" motives and perceptions are somehow stripped of a mystifying cognitive overlay when major components of a society are withering away or facing destruction, although perhaps that, too, occurs under certain circumstances. But the scholar's rationalization that the outcome was, after all, adaptively superior *is* stripped away. The means by which unwise or dysfunctional solutions were somehow found and imposed instead of superior ones is a problem that cannot be so readily dismissed. And particularly in the circumstance of a widely ramifying social collapse, we may hope to discover something of the extent to which participants in a long-vanished and cognitively remote civilization were able to recognize and generalize about societal conditions and their alteration.

A slight excursus may be necessary in order to establish that there was an unambiguous deterioration during the late second and early first millennia B.C. in Mesopotamia. Chapter 3 makes a primarily political case for this view, which can be supplemented with some demographic and settlement parameters. The pertinent data are derived from archaeological surveys that heretofore have covered a large part of the then-used portions of the central Euphrates floodplain, although it has rightly been pointed out that substantial regions where there must have been relatively young but vigorous Chaldean and Aramean settlement still remain almost entirely unstudied (Brinkman 1984). The available data, at any rate, suggest a steep decline in the occupied area of settlements, continuing through most of the second millennium and possibly beyond it.

Specifically, sites that are thought to have been occupied toward the end of that long span of time cover less than a fourth of the area occupied at its beginning. Paralleling this trend but originating several centuries earlier was a consistent decline in the proportion of all settlement that was urban, here defined in purely quantitative terms as covering forty or more hectares of built-up debris, from almost four-fifths of the total at the end of the Early Dynastic period in the mid-third millennium to around one-sixth in Middle Babylonian times. The result was that the total recorded area of urban settlement had been reduced by the end of the second millennium to perhaps as little as a sixteenth of what it had been earlier (Robert Adams 1981:142). Even given the deficiencies and possible regional biases in the data mentioned above and the clear exceptions to the apparent trend offered by a few urban centers (including outstandingly Babylon itself), it seems undeniable that a major demographic and agricultural as well as urban decline had occurred.

Breaks in the textual record document a parallel deterioration, while also suggesting the abruptness of at least one of its major episodes. We learn of what was certainly a severe social and economic upheaval involving all of the southern Babylonian cities at around 1740 B.C. Text production in most of them came suddenly and simultaneously to an end, with the remaining centers of Nippur and Isin suffering the same fate twenty years later (Stone 1977). Several centuries apparently were to elapse before Nippur was reoccupied, and in many other cases the abandonment was permanent. No matter what their degree of conscious awareness was of the past, in short, it seems clear that during Kassite and Middle Babylonian times people must have lived in a landscape strewn with the physical vestiges of an earlier, historically more expansive and prosperous as well as populous era. If the proportion of desolation was less extreme than that resulting from the Late Classic Maya abandonment, the difference was more one of degree than of kind.

What attestation is there reflecting an awareness that such a massive retrenchment had taken place? John A. Brinkman, who has specialized in Assyriological sources of the later second and early first millennium B.C., maintains that there is essentially none (personal communication, 1983). One can argue, to be sure, that reflective statements about the past would have no place in laconic administrative records. As for literary and ritual texts, written in archaizing Standard Babylonian, it can hardly be surprising that they are confined to asserting continuity rather than to directly taking account of the depressed condition of their times. But does this mean that any larger, genuinely "historical" vision of processes of social decay either did not ever exist or has been irretrievably lost? Not necessarily, for there is some evidence of a shift in perceived relationships to the supernatural that could suggest a new sense of diminishment and vulnerability.

The shift can be illuminated by comparing two literary works that were well known and widely copied, the *Lamentation Over the Destruction of Ur* (Kramer 1940), composed early in the second millennium, and the *Poem of Erra* (Cagni 1977), variously dated in the late second or early first millennium. Both deal with calamities inflicted upon mankind as a result of divine disfavor, and conclude with a reestablishment of harmony as a result of divine discretion. In both, a growing awareness of human suffering plays a considerable part in the reversal of divine attitudes, without any suggestion of the capacity of humans directly to affect the fate decreed for them.

In other respects, however, the two works differ considerably. In the Ur Lament the agencies of destruction are impersonal, and greater emphasis is placed on the abandonment of urban sanctuaries by their divine patrons than on their active wrath. Generalized misfortune and suffering are depicted in poetic terms and affect the whole population without distinction. In *Erra*, by contrast, destruction is portrayed as the outcome of a particular god's active malevolence. He had to secure a degree of consensus within the pantheon before launching his campaign, it is true, but guile and misrepresentation played a part in this. What then ensued was a purposeful overturning of established institutions and relationships. The plague god Erra proclaims his intention thus:

> *I shall cut off [the life] of the righteous man who acts as an intercessor.*
> *The evil man, who cuts throats, him I shall put in the highest places.*
> *I shall so change men's hearts that father will not listen to son*
> *(And) daughter will talk to mother with hatred.*
> *I shall cause them to speak ill and they will forget their god*
> *(And) shall speak gross blasphemy to their goddess.*
> *I shall rouse the th[ief] and bar the way.*
> *People will plunder each other's goods in the city. (9.7–14)*

Apart from castigating a divine course of action as wicked against an implied higher standard of conduct, what is new here is a perceived sense of injustice. An evil deity singles out the wicked for special favor, rather than merely inflicting a calamity on the righteous and unrighteous together.

There are serious risks, of course, in attempting to project general attitudes from individual literary works. Even without considering the more circumscribed appeal of literary traditions as compared to oral ones (of which we know very little), a different choice of examples might alter at least nuances of what is taken as representative of a given time. For example, is the whole genre of laments cast into a somewhat different light by the curious *Lament for Kirga,* which Jacobsen (in Gordon 1959:473–75) suspects may be a kind of bohemian mockery? Or may we need to qualify and soften the apparent contrast in treatment between the early and late second millennium on the basis of the relatively early *Curse of Agade* (Kramer in Pritchard 1969:646–51)? Concepts of justice and righteousness do not appear directly in that text, but there is a possibly anticipatory sense of irony at heedless destructiveness in which "the blood of the treacherous flowed over the blood of the faithful" (1.191). The quandary of the righteous sufferer, the human who if sinning and thereby incurring divine wrath is ignorant of his sin, is also at least implicit in other works dating to the earlier part of the millennium (Lambert 1967:11).

Although a full review of the deeper meaning and diversity of relevant literary materials is beyond my competence, it may be worthwhile briefly to paraphrase W. G. Lambert's extensive treatment of the subject. At around the outset of the second millennium, he notes, no distinction is evident between a moral sin and a ritual omission. By late in the millennium, on the other hand, the notion of a moral sin had clearly emerged. And though morality cannot be said to have extended unequivocally into the world of the gods, Lambert characterizes the latter as having become less amoral and capricious, more respectable and even dull. A tendency toward acting more in unison becomes evident within the pantheon, and there are hints of a "striving for monotheism" (1967:19) in the occasional depiction of lesser deities as aspects of a greater one. Babylonian theologians, having turned away from analogies with natural forces, now "imagined their gods in their own image, and tried to fit the universe into moral laws springing from human conscience" (1967:7). Yet a crucial gulf between the gods and mankind was made more explicit if not widened, in that man was seen as without intuitive sense of sin. Perhaps, it was in one case even speculated, "the gods made men prone to lies and oppression." As this suggests, there is a palpable decline in confidence and self assertion, and

> a sobering of the Old Babylonian *joie de vivre.* Political conditions may also have contributed. A country under foreign rulers and in a somewhat backward state does not promote hedonism. Thus . . . the emphasis now lay on accepting the wretched state imposed by the gods, and continuing the various religious and social duties. (1967:17)

In short, there was a development of doctrines of acquiescence and submissiveness, coupled with a sense of personal guilt and at the same time of helplessness before widely prevailing forces of evil. These are all, to say the least, consistent with a perceived if unacknowledged social decline. What is symbolically portrayed, a world of doubt and shrunken possibilities, corresponds closely to the contrast between everyday experience and the real and remembered vestiges of a greater past.

No trace is found of a counsel that man can aspire to take his fate into his own hands without courting disaster. Individuals are not portrayed as acting as protagonists for human groups, communities, or institutions, nor is any suggestion made that they might enhance their effectiveness by acting in concert. Yet it is also true that both of these stances are newly projected into the world of the gods—gods who, as already noted, were increasingly imagined in human image. A faint but suggestive sense of tension or contradiction appears here, explored (but hardly resolved) with increasing philosophical profundity. Considering the limitations of theologically oriented literary works as the only relevant medium of expression that has come down to us, it can be argued that the evidence for a degree of consciousness about the profound societal reverses that had occurred is as consistent and unambiguous as we have any right to expect.

Openings

It should be clear that this chapter is intended primarily as a programmatic statement rather than as a substantive analysis. Of course, the attractiveness of, or need for, the proposed program is at least somewhat dependent on the illustrative suggestions that have been offered in support of it. The theme of civilizational decline or *collapse*—the completeness of breakdown implied by the latter term should receive further scrutiny— is intrinsically important and understudied. This is particularly the case within an anthropological tradition. But beyond the outward movement of our collective span of attention to fill a comparative void, I have suggested that this redirection of effort should have some more general effects upon prevailing frameworks of thought with regard to ancient states and civilizations and their significance for the social sciences.

These desirable consequences involve not the replacement of existing paradigms of study but their supplementation or broadening. The principal new or enlarged dimensions of inquiry that have been dealt with are the following:

1. Fundamentally, our involvement should be with the whole record of an ancient civilization such as that of Mesopotamia, without disciplinary or methodological biases or barriers. Except for the earliest phase of that civilization, which when it is considered alone represents an arbitrarily truncated and thus distorted part of it, texts often provide the

primary part of the record. Through altered patterns of graduate education and through provisions for more effective interdisciplinary discussions and research, we need to find ways to be less circumscribed by viewpoints deriving from our own archaeological training and findings. It is likely to be only through our own efforts that the vast body of cuneiform documents, for example, receives the attention that its *anthropological* significance warrants.

2. The pursuit of a number of new themes will become possible and natural through a more substantial inclusion of textual data within the field of study. Respects in which archaeological and textual findings can be made complementary, such as in the reconstruction of organizational, exchange, and institutional patterns, are fairly obvious. But beyond these, reference has been made to the need to include microdynamics of various kinds—short-term reversibility, variance around prevailing norms, irregular sequences of change that are misrepresented when they are smoothed into long-term trends, competition, coercion, withdrawal, and conflict—more prominently within the field of study. Only with greater reliance on textual resources can we move very far in most of these directions. And in any case why should we not move, through greater reliance on texts, just as far as we can? Yet it is also the case that these represent *anthropological* problems, for whose pursuit archaeologists (if perhaps for the most part in interdisciplinary teams) will have to assume primary responsibility. Humanists have their own, and different, priorities.

3. We have a demonstrated preference for relatively closed units of analysis—the archaeological site report or the ethnographic community study. Archaeological surveys and regional studies by social anthropologists have broadened the outlook somewhat, but there is still an overreliance on arbitrary boundaries (e.g., those dependent on modern administrative definitions, or defined in terms of some currently convenient and unambiguous environmental classification). Perhaps drawing sharp boundaries has something to do with a predisposition for methodological or quantitative rigor. But the world we seek to understand is not, and was not, made that way! Certainly for the study of anything as large-scale, long-lived, and complex as an ancient civilization, we need to recognize that its context was a vaguely defined and essentially open system of competing, complementary, and highly interactive units. In any long-term analysis it has to be taken for granted that their relations to one another, their relative positions of domination or subordination, were shifting and impermanent.

4. Archaeological thinking about causation also reflects disciplinary limitations or biases. There is entirely too much attention given to so-called prime movers, at least in part because our data do not normally allow us to deal analytically with microsequences of change in which

there is always a complex interplay of long-term and short-term causal factors. With greater attention to the textual record we can move at least some distance toward correcting this shortcoming.

5. Similarly, archaeological thinking is quite naturally concentrated on behavioral residues of various kinds. But as *anthropologists*, properly regarding as within our field of study whatever can be learned from any source that is relevant to an understanding of an ancient civilization, we cannot justify self-imposed limitations. Implicitly to ignore "superstructures" that lie beyond at least the present reach of archaeology and to confine attention to "infrastructures" consisting of subsistence routines, modes of production, and the like, is an entirely worthwhile line of approach for some investigators to pursue. But it is disingenuous to cloak this single strand of what needs to be a multistranded fabric with its own philosophical rationale—some ur-Marxist shading of materialism or any other. The texts open up areas of meaning, consciousness, and motivation whose intersection with, and sometimes determinate influence over, our favored behavioral residues has to be assumed and therefore looked for.

I have argued, in short, that the study of the decline or collapse of a state or civilization invites, and in the end is likely to require, a series of broadenings and innovations that are worthwhile in their own right. They include some attention to new directions in anthropological theory; greater sensitivity to the biases and limitations of prevailing approaches we have tended to take for granted; reexamination and enlargement of temporal and spatial frameworks about which we have grown too comfortable and unreflective; and a variety of difficult measures to take more adequate account of textual data that is directly relevant to our interests. Above all, any real advance in studies of processes of decline or collapse will depend upon a growing tolerance for diversity in choice of problem and approach. If the example is successful, we may hope that the quality of openness will find encouragement in other fields as well.

The Collapse of Ancient Mesopotamian States and Civilization

Norman Yoffee

Although Mesopotamianists have argued about the exact date of birth of the state in Mesopotamia (e.g., Wright 1977), few have ventured to specify a date for the origin of Mesopotamian civilization (Yoffee n.d.). The distinction between the terms *state* and *civilization* is not just semantic, nor does it lie in the appearance of certain "indicators" (Service 1975:178) or of a certain "style" (Chang 1980:365). By Mesopotamian civilization I mean that fragile, but reproducible, set of cultural boundaries that encompass a variety of peoples, political and social systems, and geographies marked as Mesopotamian and that, importantly, include the ideal of a political center. This cultural concept is admittedly abstract, especially in comparison to the very hard political definition of the state, although I shall be concerned later with indicating that this cultural definition is also quite tangible. Certainly, the difference between Mesopotamian civilization and the Mesopotamian state is real and easily apparent. Indeed, in the political sense of the state, historians and archaeologists are well aware that the term *Mesopotamia* is by no means easy to define and even has the disconcerting ability to dematerialize entirely, since "Mesopotamia" existed predominantly as a cellular pattern of city-states that rarely acted in political concert. Nevertheless, there can be demonstrated, throughout millennia before the existence of the state and hundreds of years after it, a very specific and shared cultural sense of Mesopotamia that is independent, within limits that will be specified in this chapter, of the presence of a Mesopotamian state.

In contrast to questions of origin, both the collapse of the Mesopotamian state and the collapse of Mesopotamian civilization have been discussed and their dates ascertained. Thus, no one could argue, after the conquest of Babylonia by Cyrus the Great of Persia in 539 B.C., that a Mesopotamian political system was ever again autonomous and dominant in the land, that the rulers of Mesopotamia thought of themselves as Mesopotamian, or that Mesopotamia existed in any way apart from a larger and non-Mesopotamian institutional order in which it was firmly embedded.

On the other hand, no one would imply by this determination of the end of the Mesopotamian state that Mesopotamian civilization—literature, customs, languages—came to an abrupt and final conclusion. It is clear, however, that Mesopotamian civilization did end—the only example in this volume in which not only a characteristic political system collapses, but also the cultural tradition in which the state is embedded. We may assign this terminus to A.D. 75, since this is the year in which the last known cuneiform document was dated (Sachs 1976). This assignment is, to be sure, arbitrary, yet it is based on what seems to be a particularly appropriate Mesopotamian way of deciding the presence or absence of Mesopotamian culture. Also, after A.D. 75, no vestige of a Mesopotamian economic or belief system or any Mesopotamian language can be determined to have persisted, although, of course, legacies of these cultural institutions can be traced in other civilizations. In this essay, therefore, I propose to trace the causes of these two different, but equally palpable collapses and to investigate the relationships between them.

Before the final political collapse of the Mesopotamian state there were many other extraordinary failures of centralized Mesopotamian political systems. In none of these collapses, however, was there precluded the possibility that new, characteristic Mesopotamian polities would emerge from the decomposition of their predecessors. These collapses have been ascribed to a variety of causes in both contemporary and modern analytical writings: nonindigenous peoples, bureaucratic mismanagement, disruption of trade routes, environmental degradation, divine behavior especially in reaction to human sin, and others. Such reasons for collapse have often been selected according to the biases of the writer, ancient as well as modern, and according to the nature of the data—from temple or palace archives or from trade colonies—which represent those oddments from the past that were recorded, have managed to survive the ages, and have been fortuitously recovered (and published) in the present. Several of these Mesopotamian political collapses will be surveyed here. By filtering, as it were, the biases inherent in particular areal and temporal sources, this wide-ranging discussion will aim to discern what patterns of political behavior, if any, are basic within Mesopotamian civilization, as well as to consider what may be specific to any phase of its political history.

Having considered political collapses, I shall then investigate the collapse of Mesopotamian civilization. Although cultural institutions are certainly not mechanically linked, in packages, with political ones, as some systemic, evolutionary accounts have implied (see Chapter 1), it would be fatuous to maintain that cultural and political domains are conveniently separable. In this case I shall argue that it was not only the physical elimination of the last "Mesopotamian" political system but, more importantly, the disappearance of the peculiar ideal of a Mesopotamian state that led to the end of Mesopotamian civilization.

PORTRAITS OF THE COLLAPSES OF MESOPOTAMIAN STATES

The Old Akkadian Period (ca. 2350–2150 B.C.)

From the mosaic of competing city-states that characterized the Early Dynastic periods of the early third millennium B.C., Sargon forged the first pan-Mesopotamian state. In his struggle to unite the various Mesopotamian city-states, Sargon clearly took advantage of the deeds of predecessors. Specifically, by conquering the confederation put together by Lugalzagesi of Umma, he was able at a stroke to unite the southern part of Mesopotamia with his own central district. Sargon, however, departed from the practice of all his predecessors by attempting to legitimize his deeds as king of all Mesopotamia, not just as king of a dominant city-state. Having begun his ascent to power from the venerable city of Kish, he built a new capital at Agade (or Akkad; Weiss 1975). This new capital symbolized a change in the political tradition in Mesopotamia, ending, at least for a time, the internecine rivalries and transcending the local political traditions in the city-states to a higher conception of a single Mesopotamian political system.

The birth legend of Sargon, known only from first-millennium texts (Lewis 1980; and possibly designed to reflect the actions of the Assyrian king Sargon II), attempts to suffuse the new king with an extraordinary past, perhaps even insinuating that he was the love-child produced from the mating of a god with a mortal at the New Year's "sacred marriage rite" (Kramer 1969). Although arising to power as a usurper in the line of succession at Kish, Sargon was apparently not an outsider in the royal bureaucracy there; his deeds are sometimes thought to highlight his Semitic background (Bottéro 1967:103–4). Indeed, with the conquest of Sargon the administrative language of the realm became predominantly Akkadian, as opposed to Sumerian, which was the language of almost all the Mesopotamian documents of the Early Dynastic periods. After

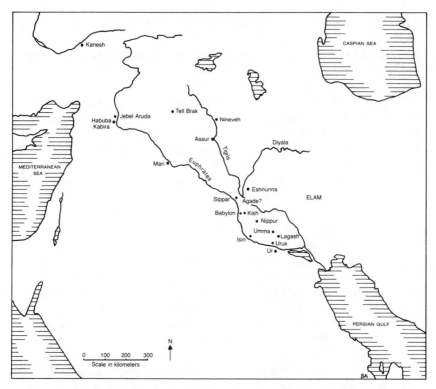

Figure 3.1 Mesopotamian sites mentioned in this chapter.

the collapse of Akkad, Sumerian was again the administrative language of the land under the next unified Mesopotamian state, the Third Dynasty of Ur. In fact, during the Akkadian period, Sumerian continued to be written in southern Mesopotamia while, even before the ascendancy of Sargon, Akkadian scribes copied classics of Sumerian literature (Biggs 1967). Though Semitic speakers seem to have predominated in central Mesopotamian cities (Gelb 1977, 1981), Sumerians and Akkadians must be seen as part and parcel of the amalgam of Mesopotamian society in the third millennium (Jacobsen 1939b, 1978–79). The use of the Akkadian language in Akkadian administration thus was not an ethnic demonstration of Semitic pride, but was, in some measure, a political tactic to disenfranchise the old bureaucracy localized in city-states and to create one responsible to the new order in the capital of Agade (I owe this idea to Piotr Michałowski). The conclusion is not that Akkadians were invaders in the land or that Akkadian was a new language on the Mesopotamian scene. Rather, when an administrative bureaucracy adopts a new official language, those who know that language are presented with new means of political and social mobility. The "Sumerian" city-states of the south—in which, however, not everyone was a strictly monolingual Sumerian speaker (Wilcke 1975; Kraus 1970)—were obviously not favored by this policy. Nevertheless, resistance to Sargon's dynasty can be seen as motivated by political and social, not ethnic and linguistic, antagonisms.

According to Glassner (1979), not only was the political system of Mesopotamia revolutionized by Sargon, but so too were important aspects of Mesopotamian economic and social affairs. Through his campaigns, Sargon's reorganized Mesopotamian army secured trade routes north to Anatolia, west to the Mediterranean, and east to Iran (see summaries in Hallo 1971a and Bottéro 1967). A new kind of social mobility became possible for Mesopotamians who joined these expeditionary troops and were recruited to the newly centralized bureaucracy (Foster 1982; Powell 1973; Diakonoff 1969); this mobility, to be sure, is prefigured by the recruitment of troops by Eanatum of Lagash, who had temporarily established a dominion over rival city-states.

The fall of the house of Sargon was anticipated by the rebellions of the city-states that regularly followed the death of one king and the accession of a new Akkadian ruler. The most spectacular and best attested of these revolts occurred during the early years of Naram-Sin, the grandson of Sargon (Grayson and Sollberger 1976; Jacobsen 1978–79; Michałowski 1980). After defeating a coalition of seventeen kings, Naram-Sin proceeded to resecure Sargon's distant conquests and to maintain these far-flung territories, as is indicated by his fortifications of Tell Brak in Syria and by his monuments erected in Anatolia and the Zagros (e.g., Farber 1983). As Speiser pointed out long ago (1952), the fall of the Akkadian dynasty must in part be ascribed to the activities of "tribal" peoples ("barbarians" in Bronson's terms, this volume) who were perforce brought into contact with the Akkadian empire, but who were never effectively controlled by the distant, centralized Mesopotamian bureaucracy.

Collapse can also be ascribed to the failure of Sargon and his descendants to integrate the traditional leadership of the city-states into the new venture of imperial expansion. Perhaps this experiment into Mesopotamian political unity would have been successful had the Akkadian kings not been so preoccupied with military expeditions outside Mesopotamia. The resulting lack of attention to internal problems of centralization, combined with the increased demands to fund these foreign expeditions, eventually increased the traditional centripetal tendencies among the city-states and also made the empire vulnerable on its flanks. Victim to these economic and political dislocations and unable to marshal support from the city-states that were determined to reestablish their local autonomies, the Akkadian dynasty collapsed and Agade itself became a small, rural site (Brinkman 1968:145 n. 874), remembered only vaguely in later legend and still without archaeological identification. The historical irony, of course, is that the prime causes for the collapse of the dynasty of Sargon are just those deeds—extensive military conquests and the foundation of a new Mesopotamian capital—that have captured the minds of both Mesopotamian and modern observers of this period. The ideal of political unification in Mesopotamia may have lain in the logic of evolutionary development that long preceded Sargon, but it was that great king who transformed this logic into a palpable historical paradigm. It can be no accident that the "Sumerian King List" (see below), which relates that only one city-state at any given time was normatively preeminent over all others, was composed well after the reign of Sargon.

The Third Dynasty of Ur (ca. 2100–2000 B.C.)

After the fall of Akkad, a period of decentralization ensued in southern Mesopotamia when many city-states, such as Lagash, were quite autonomous (Falkenstein 1957, 1966), whereas others, such as Sippar (Glassner 1979:292–96), may have owed allegiance to the non-Mesopotamian Gutians, "the scorpion of the mountains" (Kramer 1964). The hero Utuhegal of Uruk then attacked the Gutians, ending whatever fleeting hegemony they may have achieved (Hallo 1971b). After Utuhegal's death, Ur-Nammu, his brother (Wilcke 1971; cf. Sollberger 1954–56), who had been appointed governor in Ur, "directed his steps from below to above" and became king. He proceeded to seize control of neighboring southern city-states and even attempted expeditions to the north in the pattern of Akkadian kings. He also claimed the royal titles of those kings. The territory of Ur seems not to have been greatly expanded by Ur-Nammu's son Shulgi, although he campaigned vigorously to the east of the Tigris. The administration of the state, however, and its economic base were completely reorganized by Shulgi (Wilcke 1971; Jones 1976). Establishing a vast bureaucratic pyramid in the land to collect taxes and tribute (Hallo 1960), to make legal decisions, and to restrict (but not completely prevent) private alienation of land (Steinkeller 1976), the kings of the Third Dynasty of Ur systematically controlled local economies and maintained administrative networks that were responsible to the supercentralized bureaucracy in Ur (Gelb 1969; Diakonoff 1969). At the apex of this edifice stood the king, deified (like Naram-Sin before him) and actually worshipped in temples in the provinces (e.g., in Eshnunna, where a temple to Shu-Sin has been excavated; Frankfort, Lloyd, and Jacobsen 1940).

The dynasty fell precipitously. The two immediate successors of Shulgi ruled nine years each and were occupied principally with defending outer provinces (Michałowski 1976; Wilcke 1970) and taxing the local economies to fund these ventures. During the twenty-four-year reign of the last king, Ibbi-Sin, the fabric of the administration rapidly unraveled (Jacobsen 1953). Local city-states began to assert their independence from Ur and a governor of Mari on the Euphrates, Ishbi-Erra, moved to consolidate power in the southern city-state of Isin. The enormous bureaucratic hierarchy, itself unproductive, could not be supported, or even fed, by Ur's local resources. Finally, an Elamite raider took the last king of the dynasty from his throne. From Isin, Ishbi-Erra attempted to reorganize a rump state on the model of Ur's imperial system, but the scribal formularies of the Ur III royal administration were only hollow bookkeeping techniques in the absence of real dominion.

The collapse of the Third Dynasty of Ur has been ascribed in some Mesopotamian and modern accounts to activities of tribal groups, the Amorites. In the *Myth of Martu*, for example, Amorites are described as uncivilized, for they "know not grain . . . , eat uncooked meat," and do not bury their dead (Buccellati 1966:92–93, 330–31). Furthermore, a "wall" (really a series of fortresses) was erected to the northeast of Sumer to protect the realm against groups of Amorites (Wilcke 1969; Michałowski 1976). Since, after the Ur III period, Amorites led rival dynasties in Mesopotamian city-states, these references have been interpreted to reflect a process of Amorite assimilation into Mesopotamian society. The data on Amorite behavior, however, are more complex than are reflected in the literary stereotypes and self-serving date formulas. Before and during the Ur III period, Amorites held royal commissions, appeared in military service to the crown, and acted as litigants in lawsuits. Amorites were interpreters, mayors, farmers, and weavers. Although some views of Amorites suggest they were rude, nonagricultural folk, other documents show them to be peacefully integrated within Mesopotamian society. Rather than apply a model of intrusion, conquest, and assimilation of Amorite foreigners into Mesopotamian society, one might understand the role of Amorites, and other such ethnic groups, within a larger pattern of social and political change in Mesopotamia (Kamp and Yoffee 1980).

If Amorites were not collectively ranged in hordes against Mesopotamians at the end of the Ur III period, being Amorite was not yet beyond usefulness, especially in the political arena. Amorite leaders contested with all comers after the fall of Ur, especially with other Amorites, for hegemony among rival city-states. Appeals to ethnic solidarity among the various Amorite groups were important in this struggle. Amnanum Amorites in Babylon and Uruk pledged mutual support, as the king of Uruk writes (Falkenstein 1963), in order to mobilize people from both city-states since the leaders were of "one house," presumably of one lineage. The ethnic denotation of Amorites seems justified, for being Amorite has little to do with a common subsistence pattern (pastoralists vs. agriculturalists), or a common residential pattern (nomads vs. city dwellers), or any common socioeconomic status. The term *tribe* or *tribal organization* does not seem at all appropriate in describing Amorite behavior, since *tribe* denotes a social organization without independent units of authority and in which surplus production and storage are discouraged through mechanisms of wealth and power leveling (Fried 1975; Sahlins 1968). The term *ethnic group,* however, which allows for the existence of more than one type of social and economic organization within the same bounded unit, seems to characterize well the range of Amorite activities.

Genealogies uniting groups of Amorites and others were constructed by the most successful of Amorite leaders in the quest to legitimize their claims to regional power (e.g., in "the Assyrian King List" and the "Genealogy of Hammurabi"). Amorites came to power in the Old Babylonian period, then, not as crude foreigners taking over power from defeated urbanites, but as relatively well organized forces whose leaders were fully urban (Ishbi-Erra was himself an Amorite) and able to take advantage of the flux in political leadership in the aftermath of the Ur III collapse. By using strong, traditional bonds of ethnic relationships, precisely because these bonds extended beyond the borders of particular city-states, Amorites were able to gain an advantage over their political competitors.

The Ur III dynasty typifies the apogee of centralization among early Mesopotamian states (Grégoire 1980) and is likewise the supreme example of an unsuccessful and short-lived attempt at pan-Mesopotamian political unity. To the brief span of time from about the last third of Shulgi's forty-eight-year reign to the first third of Ibbi-Sin's ill-fated years— about forty years in all—we owe tens of thousands of economic documents now found in museum collections or in private hands all over the world. These numerous data left by the massive bureaucracy in Ur and its subject city-states are forming the basis for new approaches to Mesopotamian economic history. Similarly, the Ur III royal court commissioned magnificent hymns to its kings which were faithfully copied in the scribal academies of subsequent periods as classics of Sumerian literature (Hallo 1962, 1963b). The quantity and quality of these sources from the royal house of Ur motivate scholarship today in roughly inverse proportion to the stability and normative character of the Ur III state.

The Old Babylonian Period (ca. 1900–1600 B.C.)

Emerging from this period of political rivalries among individual city-states following the collapse of Ur (Greengus 1979; Simmons 1959–61, 1978; Charpin 1978; Donbaz and Yoffee 1986), new coalitions began to form, eventually resulting in a northern core (Renger 1970) led by

Babylon and the sixth king of its "First Dynasty," Hammurabi, and a southern core headed by Rim-Sin of Larsa. Hammurabi's defeat of territories to the west and east of Babylon culminated, in his thirty-first year, in a decisive victory over Rim-Sin and in the consequent unification of "Babylonia" from the Gulf to Baghdad. Further conquests eliminated the remaining competitors to Hammurabi's sovereignty on the peripheries of this realm. Although many administrative documents, letters, and legal materials attest to the vigor of the royal administration in Babylon, Hammurabi's empire, formed during the last decade of his reign, was met by a serious rebellion in the south during the ninth year of his son and successor (Stol 1976) and, in fact, did not outlive that son's reign. The "First Dynasty" continued to hold sway in its old northern core for another four generations, after which time it was brought to an end by a raid of a Hittite king from Anatolia. Power was transferred to a "non-Mesopotamian" group of Kassites, who had previously been in control of territory along the middle Euphrates (Brinkman 1980) but who were also residing in Mesopotamian cities (e.g., Charpin 1977).

Evidence of economic and administrative documents written in the time of the last kings of the dynasty (Yoffee 1977) refutes the view that the royal house fell as if struck by "a bolt from the blue" (Postgate 1977:100; Oates 1979:84), specifically an attack by a marauding Hittite enemy and infiltration by Kassites. Indeed, the government imposed by Hammurabi on conquered territories was resisted almost from the outset. In spite of the proclamations in Hammurabi's so-called law code (see Finkelstein 1961, 1966) that all subject cities would prosper under his just reign, the provincial administration systematically by-passed local authorities and was geared mainly for the enrichment of the distant capital in Babylon.

It exploited the conquered territories not only by removing local authority, but also by abrogating traditional systems of land tenure in favor of the ultimate ownership of land by the Crown in Babylon. Greatly enriched by the initial success of the system, Hammurabi and his successor Samsuiluna engineered great feats of canal irrigation, both to open up agricultural land and to transport goods more easily. They glorified the capital by erecting temples and richly furnishing them. The loss of revenue accompanying the rebellion of the conquered territories, however, did not bring with it a change in these royal foundations. Building and waterworks projects were still undertaken and large pools of manpower had to be mobilized on a regular basis.

In order to fund these operations the Crown had to manage its diminished resources more prudently than before. Instead of maintaining squads of laborers at its behest year-round, the Crown now hired manpower seasonally. "Headmen" witnessed these contracts of hire or even acted as middlemen by supplying harvest laborers. In the late Old Babylonian period, new officials seem to have been created by the Crown precisely to negotiate these transactions with local authorities. Furthermore, the Crown became a credit institution, loaning its supplies of wool and grain on a short-term basis, perhaps in order to pay these laborers and new officials for whom its own estates were unable to provide sufficiently. In these loan contracts sometimes a clause was inserted so that the Crown could call for repayment at any point it chose. If, however, it exercised this option before the term of the loan, it lost whatever interest would have accrued.

The agricultural situation in Mesopotamia, in which salinization was an ever-present threat to productivity (Jacobsen and Adams 1958), became exacerbated in the aftermath of Hammurabi's centralization of the realm. In the period of the last kings of his dynasty, prices of agricultural products rose and seeding ratios per unit of land increased (Farber 1978; the same occurred in Ur III—see Maekawa 1984). There may well have been a decision to abandon or shorten the period of fallow on lands the Crown controlled, thereby providing short-term fiscal relief, since the lands would initially provide more grain, but ultimately there would result a loss in productivity. Although this process cannot be observed directly from available sources, we do see inflated prices, new methods of agriculturally intensive management, and an increased pressure to secure stores of grain that the Crown's estates were apparently producing insufficiently.

The archaeological reconnaissance surveys of Robert Adams (1981) have shown a progressive tendency during the late Old Babylonian period for nucleated settlement patterns to become dispersed into smaller communities that are more evenly spaced along watercourses. This settlement configuration is a predictable result of increased Crown reliance on traditional local authorities for manpower and the dissolution of vast Crown domains located in the proximity of urban centers. Also, at the end of the Old Babylonian period, many loans were issued by temples (Harris 1960), a situation that contrasts markedly with that of Hammurabi's time, when certain prerogatives of the temples, especially judicial ones, were "secularized" by the Crown (Harris 1961). In times of obvious fiscal and political uncertainty, the temple seems to have provided a refuge for unfortunate citizens of Babylonia—and managed as well, of course, to make a profit from the pious debtors.

Cipolla (1970:7, 11) has argued that

in the early phase of a decline . . . the problem does not seem to be so much that of increasing visible inputs—capital or labour—as that of changing ways of doing things and improving productivity. The survival of the political system demands such basic change. But it is typical of mature empires to give a negative response to this challenge. . . . since change hurts vested interests.

In these terms, the Old Babylonian political system could have changed to meet the new conditions of the loss of Hammurabi's conquests, but it typically sought not to do so. The results were environmental degradation, the collapse of the centralized political system, and the disintegration of authority into the traditionally organized local units and their elites. The character of the succeeding Kassite power structure has been called "tribal" (Brinkman 1980:464), because it was not highly centralized and because the bureaucracy may largely have been composed of personal clients of the new leaders. Thus collapse occurred not primarily as a result of externally applied pressures, but rather as a culmination of centrally inspired weaknesses that were easily exploited by foreign raiders and traditionally organized local power blocs.

The Old Assyrian Period (ca. 1920–1780 B.C.)

In the northern part of Mesopotamia, an Assyrian state rose and fell while Babylon was achieving power in the south. Situated in a dry-farming region and thus not dependent on irrigation for agricultural productivity, Assyria was not a land of many cities and its history was not as determined by urban interrelations as was the case in Babylonia. In the formative period of the Old Assyrian state, the prince of the city Assur, Ilushuma, relates his military expedition to Babylonia in order to "free" the citizens of several Babylonian cities. As plausibly interpreted by Larsen (1976), this campaign probably refers to Ilushuma's aim to open trade routes in the south to Assyrian merchants. Indeed, most of the sources for the Old Assyrian period are concerned with Assyrian mercantile activities. Overwhelmingly, these sources come not from Assyria itself, but from an Assyrian trading colony, Kanesh, located in the heart of Anatolia 470 miles northwest of Assur (see especially Larsen 1974, 1976, 1977; Veenhof 1972; Garelli 1963).

Mesopotamians were clearly familiar with Anatolian resources—obsidian, copper, precious metals (Yoffee 1981)—for millennia. Sargonic activity, in some accounts undertaken on behalf of merchants in Anatolia, is apparent in monuments of Akkadian kings found in southern Turkey (Lloyd 1978:138). During the Old Assyrian period this trade was not based on Assyrian political control of any strategic resource or territory. Rather, the trade attested in thousands of economic documents and letters was clearly entrepreneurial. Assyrian family firms moved textiles, some obtained in Babylonia, and tin (whose origin is still obscure) from Assur to Anatolia by means of donkey caravans. There the Assyrian merchants exchanged these goods for silver and gold, which they shipped to Assur.

Profit was made solely on organizational ability, Assyrians moving goods from where they were plentiful to where they were scarce. For example, in Assur, where silver was scarce, the silver-to-tin ratio was about 1:15, whereas in Anatolia, where silver was comparatively plentiful, the ratio was about 1:7 (for figures, see Veenhof 1972). If fifteen units of tin could be economically transported from Assur to Anatolia, two units of silver could be obtained. These two units of silver could then be brought to Assur and turned into thirty units of tin. Assuming a constant demand, the intelligence of where and how to get tin, and the technology of how to move the tin to Anatolia, great profit could be and was made by Assyrian merchants. Long-term business contracts were negotiated whereby joint capital could be amassed and continuity in business relationships assured for decades (Larsen 1977). In one such document, an Assyrian state official sanctions the proceedings, thus attesting to the interest the Assyrian government had in the trade. Indeed, according to Larsen, the leading merchant families of Assur held high government ranks in Assyrian councils. It is in this light that Ilushuma seems to have campaigned to open and/or keep open markets so that this system of international venture trade could function in one of its important nodes.

Why did this profitable mercantile system that supported the activities of the Assyrian state collapse? It should be noted that this trade continued through vicissitudes of Assyrian political change, most apparent in the seizure of power in Assur by Shamshi-Adad, an Amorite leader from the Euphrates area near Mari. Although problems with the succession of Shamshi-Adad's sons and the military activities of these kings must have affected the viability of the trade, other reasons for its failure seem important. Old Assyrian trade flourished during that period in Babylonia when there was no single political power in the land. Similarly, in Anatolia, governments consisted of local princes, although Assyrian merchants were obliged to obey the laws of the land and to remit taxes to the local palace. Less clearly, it seems that no power restricted Assyrian access to copper and tin. By the early eighteenth century B.C., however, this entire situation had changed. Babylonia was united by Hammurabi, and Anatolia was coming under the control of a new Hittite power. Old Assyrian trade, for all its immense prosperity, was extremely fragile. The Assyrian merchant colonies and the Assyrian political system that flourished on the profits of the trade were dependent on the relatively unrestricted passage of traders and goods over long distances. When constraints were imposed on this passage through the rise of strong centralized governments that attempted to control production and exchange, the foreign trade and the political system that was built upon it collapsed. The Old Assyrian political and economic system seems to have been reduced to the essentially rural countryside that was its original base. Only as a response to military pressures five hundred years later did a new centralized state rise in Assyria.

The End of the Cycle of Mesopotamian States

Philip Kohl has put the case for a Western Asian "world-system" in the third millennium B.C. (Kohl 1979) in which a Mesopotamian centrality in economic production influenced local developments from Syria to the Indo-Iranian borderlands. By the end of the second millennium B.C. this Mesopotamian preeminence had certainly broken down considerably; after 539 B.C. Mesopotamia was never again to be an autonomous political unit. The following brief remarks trace the course of this development.

In the fourteenth century B.C., Assyria experienced a political renascence, substantially in response to non-Mesopotamian forces, especially Hittites and Mittannians, that were threatening it (Gadd 1965; Grayson 1971; Garelli 1969; Machinist 1982). By creating an effective military regime to combat these enemies—and also to use against Kassite rulers in the south—Assyrian kings systematically began to centralize their power at the expense of the traditional Assyrian nobility that had shared power in the Old Assyrian state. After initial success a period of retreat and local consolidation began at the end of the thirteenth century and, apart from a brief burst outward (under Tiglath-Pileser I), continued for another two hundred fifty years, under the pressure especially of Aramean attacks from the west. The constant fighting with the Arameans, however, eventually created a tough Assyrian army core, and toward the end of the tenth century, under the leadership of several vigorous monarchs, this core became the basis of a new military expansionism inspired by the earlier model. The climax of this expansion came in the early seventh century with hegemony over Egypt, the Levant, and southern Mesopotamia. This climax, however, was rapidly followed by the loss of these dependencies. The Assyrian army was defeated in 614 B.C. by Medes and soon thereafter by a coalition of Medes and Babylonians. To all visible indications Assyrian political and social institutions ceased to exist in Assyria. The reasons for this collapse are remarkable.

The reforms of Tiglath-Pileser III in the eighth century marked the high point of the process by which the landed nobility was made subservient to the newly centralized royal administration (Garelli and Nikiprowetzky 1974; Garelli 1974). Also at this time, the policies of governing vast expanses of territory included mass deportations (as a last resort against recalcitrant provinces) to Assyria or elsewhere in the empire (Oded 1979). These deportees provided important labor in the foundation of lavish new royal capitals to mark administrative and dynastic changes and also to serve in military units.

One of the more interesting facets of Assyrian policy concerned its "Babylonian problem." This *Kulturkampf*, already detectable in the second millennium B.C. (Machinist 1976), preoccupied Assyrian affairs in the seventh century (Brinkman 1984). For the Assyrians, Babylonia seems to have been the heartland of Mesopotamian culture although, in Assyrian eyes, it was also politically chaotic and even decadent (most vividly portrayed in Vidal 1981). When an increasingly anti-Assyrian Babylonia was defeated by Sennacherib in 689, the carnage was considered an impiety in Assyria itself and, after the assassination of Sennacherib, his successor Esarhaddon rebuilt Babylon and restored its prosperity. Then an Assyrian prince, Shamash-shum-ukin, was installed as king of Babylonia, theoretically on a par (in the testamentary intention of Esarhaddon) with his younger but abler brother Assurbanipal, who took the throne of Assyria. In short order Shamash-shum-ukin led a revolt against Assyria that lasted four years and ended with a total Assyrian victory. The debilitating problems with Babylonia and especially the civil war severely diverted manpower and wealth from Assyria's other pressing foreign-policy needs. The temporary loss of taxes and tribute from the west could for the moment be overcome, but the opportunity afforded subject territories to consolidate their forces and resolution meant that the Mesopotamian civil war was very much a Pyrrhic victory for the Assyrians.

The growth of the new military establishment in Assyria in the first millennium B.C. implies an interest in securing foreign products as great as that characterizing the Old Assyrian regime. In the first millennium, however, Assyrian kings did not rely on international stability for the flow of goods, but rather attempted to seize the most important resources and to demand goods as tribute. With the defeat of the Assyrian army, therefore, the supply of products into Assyria disappeared rapidly. Meanwhile, the agricultural basis for the Assyrian economy had also been severely undermined by having to provide for the army's expeditionary ventures and to support the new capitals of imperial administration. The old rural estates, now worked by substantial amounts of unfree and non-Assyrian labor (Fales 1973; Postgate 1974), were increasingly granted to generals and bureaucrats for their services to the realm.

Clearly the maintenance of the Assyrian state was related to the success of its military machine. As long as the army could back up the royal demands, goods flowed from subject provinces to the agricultural heartland of Assyria. The new capitals and expensive monuments were dependent upon the continued effectiveness of the generals. The army, however, could not establish a functioning imperial system to integrate the conquered territories. When enemies struck a mortal blow at a weakened Assyria, not only did the empire dissolve, but the Assyrian heartland itself was reduced to its very basis of agricultural subsistence. The population of Assyria was no longer predominantly Assyrian and the traditional nobility had long before been systematically removed as a hindrance to royal centralization and military efficiency.

No reformulation from such a collapse was possible. Most of the people in the countryside and in what remained of Assyrian cities were Arameans and others who had been incorporated within the empire, many forcibly imported. These people did not think of themselves or of their culture as Mesopotamian, as is indicated by the increased use of Aramaic alongside Akkadian, which it eventually outweighed, in Assyria. One reason for the overt display of "Mesopotamianness" by the Assyrian warrior kings—for example, by gathering classics of Mesopotamian literature in vast libraries—may well have been the attempt to stress traditional ties with a past that they themselves were undermining but that separated them from a subject population that had only partly shared those traditions. Furthermore, such displays of "Mesopotamianness" may have played important roles in the internecine power struggles within the Assyrian ruling elite. After the collapse of Assyria only a few relics of Assyrian culture remained in Babylonia (Zadok 1984), meager reminders of the proud imperial history of the land.

As Assyrian fortunes waned, those of Babylonia waxed ephemerally bright. From the Chaldean tribes, which had consolidated their power in Babylonia, partly in response to Assyrian intervention there in the seventh century, powerful kings governed the south in the aftermath of the Assyrian collapse. Of these, Nebuchadnezzar seems to have mimicked the Assyrian strategy of campaigning abroad and deporting large segments of rebellious populations to his homeland. The end of Babylonia, too, followed closely its greatest imperial success. The strange career of the last Babylonian king, Nabonidus (Garelli 1958; Michałowski n.d.), who spent his last decade at the Tema oasis in western Arabia (Eph'al 1982), was swiftly brought to an end by Cyrus the Great of Persia, apparently to the relief of important elements of the Babylonian population (Mallowan 1972). Once the hub of the Western Asian universe, Mesopotamia became now merely a province, albeit an important one, in a completely new form of imperial system.

After the fall of the First Dynasty of Babylon, the role of Mesopotamia on the stage of Western Asian history inexorably changed. Before about 1600 B.C. it can be argued that Mesopotamian culture, if not its economic or political systems, was dominant in this arena. The method of writing, the literature and school curriculum, and even basic elements of Mesopotamian belief systems were exported from the Mesopotamian core. Gradually, after 1600, however, and more obviously after 1200, external situations began to influence, more than they were influenced by, conditions in Mesopotamia. One effect of this change was to turn already existing differences between Babylonia and Assyria into fixed points of reference. Although Assyrian high culture seems to have become ever more Babylonian during the first millennium, this tendency may have only exacerbated the Assyrian sense of distinctiveness within the larger Mesopotamian culture and, if anything, galvanized military programs of action against Babylonia.

Outside Mesopotamia, new actors, such as Indo-Europeans, entered upon the Western Asian stage, new ideologies competed for political sponsorship against the venerable gods of Mesopotamia, and even a new method of writing (the alphabet) eroded the grip that Mesopotamian scribes had maintained over the sacred and the artful. Long after the Persian conquest, Babylonian priests continued to manage their liturgical academies (which were also landowners), and some unpersianized or unhellenized elites still composed their business affairs in the cuneiform script (Stolper 1974; Doty 1977; Cardascia 1951). The political fortunes of Mesopotamia, however, were now in the hands of Achaemenians, Seleucids, Parthians, Sasanians, and Arabs. The ancient Mesopotamian cities of the south were progressively abandoned as the new leaders built new capitals. Finally, at the end of the first millennium A.D., the region was environmentally devastated, the result of centralized demands and technologies that were unprecedented and unimaginable in the old Mesopotamian regimes (Robert Adams 1981).

MESOPOTAMIAN CONCEPTS OF UNITY AND COLLAPSE

Ideals of Political and Cultural Unity

The native historiographic tradition in Mesopotamia very clearly expresses an ideal of political unity. The "Sumerian King List," composed just after 2000 B.C. but based on earlier sources, portrays the earliest periods of Mesopotamian history as exemplifying this ideal (Jacobsen 1939a; Hallo 1963a; Michałowski 1983). In the beginning, "kingship descended from heaven" to five cities. Dynasties of kings from each of these cities ruled in order, kingship passing from one city to another down the list. The various kings ruled for long periods of time, in some instances thousands of years, thus indicating a record of the most distant Mesopotamian past. After kingship had passed to the fifth city, there came the Flood. Afterward, kingship again descended to other cities in the same orderly succession. Kings now ruled, however, for largely credible numbers of years and some of them can be identified in contemporary texts of the early third millennium.

It can easily be shown that this orderly march of single, dominant cities ruling all of Mesopotamia is no faithful reflection of historical events. Inscriptions show that some dynasties listed sequentially were in fact contemporary and that some powerful cities were simply omitted from the list altogether. In one of the latter cities, Lagash, scribes composed their own king list, which is interpreted by its modern editor as a satirical commentary on the spuriousness of the "canonical" version that had slighted it (Sollberger 1967).

Some observers have thought that the Sumerian King List not only represents an ideal of Mesopotamian political unification but actually reflects the existence of an early confederacy. Jacobsen (1957) postulates that a "Kengir [Sumerian] League" functioned as an amphictyony in the earliest historic periods, a confederacy joined through common worship of the paramount divinity Enlil at the seat of his cult, Nippur. Although Nippur was an important early settlement in Mesopotamia (Robert Adams 1981), much of the "amphictyonic" character of the city is derived from its later role as the center for which obligations were demanded by Ur III kings. Also, during the early Old Babylonian period, Nippur symbolized hegemony over all southern Mesopotamia and so became an object of contention for competing city-state princes (Sigrist 1984). Jacobsen also notes that the title "king of Kish" was held by some early dynastic rulers who were not in fact native kings in Kish (Hallo 1957). Use of this title, then, implies there was a period when kings of Kish were sovereign over all Mesopotamia, the title afterward claimed by kings of other cities who pretended to this power. Finally, Jacobsen considers that certain "city-seals," cylinder seals found mainly at Ur in Early Dynastic I/II times which were carved with the names of various Mesopotamian cities, point to the existence of a Sumerian league.

In all these arguments, however, the reality of a *political* center in early Mesopotamia seems unlikely. Indeed, the nature of conflict among city-states in the Early Dynastic period makes unlikely the previous existence of a single Mesopotamian state before the time of Sargon. Rather, Jacobsen's cogent analyses indicate a very strong and multifaceted conception of a Mesopotamian *cultural*, rather than political, unity. This Mesopotamian cultural identity is also depicted in the standardization of writing (Powell 1981; Green 1981), numerical and mathematical systems (Friberg 1978–79), belief systems, and "canonical" literature in Mesopotamian city-states. The formation of such uniform cultural institutions was the more remarkable precisely because these city-states were *not* held together in a political confederacy. The absence of such a pan-Mesopotamian political entity, however, did not preclude the conception that there should be a political domain to match and concretize the cultural ideal of a single Mesopotamia. In historiographic writing, therefore, it was natural and proper to convey that ideal, that only one king, from one preeminent city-state, should rule over Mesopotamia at any one time. The fact of Sargon's real conquest and union of Mesopotamian city-states, along with the brief hegemony of the Third Dynasty of Ur (so-called because it is the third time the city of Ur is recorded in the Sumerian King List), provided confirmation of the potential of this ideal.

A variety of later sources show the continued preoccupation with delimiting and/or symbolizing a single Mesopotamian political entity. For example, Sargon of Akkad installed his daughter Enheduanna as *entu* ("high priestess") of the moon god, who was especially venerated at Ur. The office of this remarkable woman, who is identified as the world's first attributed author (Hallo and van Dijk 1968; cf. Civil 1980:229), continued to function from that time through the early Old Babylonian period, thus becoming one of those symbols of Mesopotamian political unity. Only one ruler—namely, that one sovereign over Ur—had the right to install an *entu*-priestess when a vacancy occurred, and kings often commemorated this significant event in the official name of that regnal year. Like a Supreme Court judge, once in office, this *entu* could not be summarily replaced, even if her original patron was overthrown and a new lord of Ur came to power.

In the Old Babylonian period, control over Nippur also symbolized a wider claim of lordship over all Mesopotamia. Thus, the great scribal academy in Nippur apparently composed a royal hymn in honor of each new patron (Hallo 1963b; cf. Frayne 1981), although dominion over Nippur sometimes fluctuated yearly among early Old Babylonian rivals. Presumably, the ancient professors were well funded by the competing city-princes.

Expressions of the cultural boundaries of Mesopotamia were naturally restructured through time and across changing regional developments. Typically, though, such ideals of what was Mesopotamian culture were never directly stated (Machinist 1986). Nevertheless, the evolution of a "Standard Babylonian" literary language; the various systematizations of god lists; the epics in which the Assyrian national deity, Assur, was superimposed on the Babylonian model; and "the preservation, transmission, and revision of whole bodies of texts—or what Oppenheim called the 'stream of tradition'—which were assembled from all parts of Mesopotamia over many centuries" (Machinist 1986:2) demonstrate the existence of such cultural boundaries.

Mesopotamian Explanations for Political Collapse

In Mesopotamian literature there are a number of literary and pseudohistorical texts that portray the collapse of the Old Akkadian dynasty and that of Ur III. These seem to have become paradigmatic explanations for the failure of Mesopotamian political systems.

The *Curse of Agade* (Cooper 1983) tells how Sargon rose to power with the help of the goddess Inanna and the god Enlil. The capital of Agade flourished with this divine favor until such time as Naram-Sin was reluctant to accept the prescribed ordinances and plundered Enlil's holy city of Nippur (whose scribes probably wrote this account). In revenge, Enlil called forth the host of Gutium, people "with human instincts, but [of] canine intelligence and monkey's features" (Cooper 1983:57), from their Zagros Mountains home to devastate Agade. To pacify Enlil the remainder of the gods pronounced upon Agade a mighty curse.

Contemporary historical materials contradict this theological version. Naram-Sin began his career, as we have seen, by quashing a rebellion against the newly centralized government. He then campaigned to the north and east of Mesopotamia and justifiably proclaimed himself by the new titles "King of Sumer and Akkad, King of the Four Quarters of the World." Describing the time immediately after his rule, however, the Sumerian King List remarkably inserts into its litany of king's names the phrase "who was king, who was not king?" This gloss presumably indicates that anarchy prevailed, but in view of the bias of the document, "anarchy" should mean here only that there was no city and no king at that time who could even claim to be supreme ruler in the land. Following this phrase, the text lists a series of Akkadian epigones about whom little is known except that they ruled in Agade. The list then passes to a dynasty in Uruk and only then to a period of Gutian dominance. Local authorities, however, governed in their city-states, and in most of the land, the Gutians, whose monuments are conspicuous by their absence, were never a seriously disruptive force.

Lamentations over the destruction of Sumer and Ur and over the destruction of Ur (two different texts) continue the theological perspective on collapse (Krecher 1980). In these texts, however, impiety on the part of the sovereign is not mentioned as the cause of divine disfavor (Cooper 1983). The motives of the gods, who never granted everlasting kingship to a city, are simply not to be fathomed by humans. In accounts from the first millennium which portray these political collapses, however, the behavior of the gods in withdrawing support for a dynasty is explained consistently as the result of the impious deeds of kings (Grayson 1975: *The Weidner Chronicle* and *The Chronicle of Early Kings*).

In the native tradition, then, a succession of early Mesopotamian states, not just a congeries of competing city-states, is assumed to be the normal and appropriate political condition of the land. Dynasties rule with the approbation of the gods and fall because their kings lapse into impious behavior (Güterbock 1934) or, sometimes, because the gods change their minds. Outsiders are then brought by the gods to be the agents of destruction of Mesopotamian states.

We have seen, however, that regional Mesopotamian states were far from typical entities in the course of Mesopotamian political events. Rather, they were rare occurrences, unable to establish a legitimate and institutionalized method of governance over the various city-states that guarded their local autonomies. Furthermore, the role of ethnic groups in the collapse of Mesopotamian states, which is given such prominence in the native historiographic writings, is spurious. Indeed, the very continuity of Mesopotamian culture and the resilience of the concept of a Mesopotamian state may have depended on the participation of these ethnic groups as "carriers" of the idea of traditional Mesopotamian civilization.

OUTSIDERS INSIDE MESOPOTAMIA

The nature of ethnic groups and of their participation in Mesopotamian civilization is a vast subject that is becoming vaster. In one article, for example, Klengel (1982) notes that "foreigners" in the Old Babylonian period—that is, people who were explicitly glossed with ethnic labels such as Sutean or Turukkean—often had Akkadian personal names. The contexts in which they appear seldom differentiate them from their neighbors and they would not have been recognized as outsiders were they not identified in texts as $lu_2.sutû$ or $lu_2.turukkû$. Further, for the second millennium, Dosch and Deller (1981) and Maidman (1984) have discussed the presence of Kassites in Hurro-Babylonian Nuzi, and Brinkman (1981) has followed the careers of Hurrians in Kassite Babylonia. For the first millennium Zadok (1984) has demonstrated the presence of Assyrians in Babylonia after the collapse of Assyria and also of Jews, Egyptians, and Iranians in southern Mesopotamian city-states (Zadok 1977, 1979, 1981). The evidence shows that certain distinctively marked ethnic categories both persisted and were significant within Mesopotamia, but at the same time, outside the literary stereotypes, such categories did not in themselves denote specific non-Mesopotamian occupations or non-Mesopotamian social status.

Indeed, Mesopotamian civilization, from the first significant evidence in the late fourth and early third millennia B.C., was an amalgam of many interacting ethnic and linguistic groups. In the late prehistoric periods in the land roughly between the two rivers, there emerged from the close association among these various groups, in order to facilitate a secure and regular supply of important resources among them, a common set of cultural traditions that we call Mesopotamian civilization (Yoffee n.d.).

The cultural boundary was importantly reinforced by the development of a writing system through which traditions could be standardized and replicated across time and space. Those responsible for preserving and transmitting these literate Mesopotamian forms, mainly scribes, never formed an autonomous elite apart from the local temple and royal elite and community nobles in each city-state who employed them. Since scribes were not autonomous, but subservient to ruling elites, ideals of areal unity and explanations of political collapse (of which the scribes were "carriers") could never function as patterns of accountability independent of the ruling establishment. Thus, those political ideals hardly constrained Mesopotamian rulers by linking temporal authority to a cosmic order as, for example, was precisely the situation in Han China (see Hsu, this volume). This is not to say, however, that political symbols established by one generation of rulers could not serve as models for later generations, as the titles of Old Akkadian kings and the *entu* institution show. In the absence of such a political ideology, Mesopotamian rulers remained little more than victorious lords, representatives of one city-state who briefly exercised dominion over their fellows.

Further complicating the problem of effecting political unity in Mesopotamia was the process in which the amalgam of ethnic and linguistic diversity in Mesopotamia became more heterogeneous, not less so, over time. Indeed, it might be thought that the development of a political ideology of Mesopotamian unity was in contradiction to the growing ethnic heterogeneity in the land. Nevertheless, this increasing cultural heterogeneity is often extremely difficult to detect other than in the personal names of people, including royal personages. Although attempts have been made to match this or that bit of material culture or literary or religious or legal institution to one or another of the ethnic groups, the task has not been easy. To this date, although the presence of Amorites and Kassites in Mesopotamian history is important and undeniable, not one text in the Amorite or Kassite language has been found. Grammars of both these languages have been written exclusively from analyses of personal names (Gelb 1980; Balkan 1954).

In the historic record, spanning twenty-five hundred years, Mesopotamian culture, of course, was not sealed and static, but like any other culture had to be learned and transmitted, and be socially important to its members. It is important to understand how this culture was preserved so long, in some cases almost in ossified form (the last Mesopotamian texts were written partly in Sumerian, a language not spoken in the land for at least two thousand years before becoming extinct as a written language), over such diverse social orientations and over city-state and regional spheres of interaction. Only through such an understanding can we appreciate the conditions under which Mesopotamian culture was no longer transmitted and so investigate the reasons for the collapse of Mesopotamian civilization.

I argue that the culturally heterodox situation in Mesopotamia cannot, by itself, account for the demise of Mesopotamian civilization. Rather, it was just those ethnic groups, since they were not bounded within particular city-states or regions and whose leaders had gained measures of political control because their power bases were not localized, that were in a position to maintain and transmit characteristically Mesopotamian cultural institutions. The multiplicity of these groups, then, did not fractionalize the overarching Mesopotamian civilization, especially in the absence of any real political entity corresponding to that cultural boundary. Rather they served to stabilize Mesopotamian values and so retard the development of a new and autonomous political ideology. Amorites and Kassites, for example, having taken political power, adopted venerable Mesopotamian cultural institutions—indeed, conservatively preserved them—precisely because in so doing they could legitimize their participation in the society, especially in the arena of political struggle. While adhering to principles of their own ethnic distinctiveness (and here differences as well as similarities between Amorites and Kassites are clear), members of these groups were, or became, Mesopotamians. These ethnic groups, then, were not so much assimilated into Mesopotamian society as they actually became *carriers*, guardians of Mesopotamian cultural traditions.

The position of ethnic groups as insiders in Mesopotamia, however, changed drastically over time. In the first millennium, neo-Assyrian and neo-Babylonian policies of massive forced incorporation of ethnic groups in Mesopotamia were obviously and utterly different from those processes of interaction in the early second millennium. Systematically cut off from participation in Mesopotamian politics, members of these ethnic groups found little use in becoming Mesopotamian.

With the conquest of Babylonia by Cyrus, the many local social orientations in Mesopotamia (and in his other subject territories) seem all to have been equally and explicitly recognized by the new rulers as long as they did not come into conflict with the imperial Persian ideology. Although Cyrus apparently modeled his inscriptions on Assyro-Babylonian antecedents, and documents dated to Achaemenid kings look much like neo-Babylonian examples, subsequent reformulation of a Mesopotamian pattern of governance, in which the rulers attempted to promote their Mesopotamianness, was an impossibility. Thus, after the conquest of Cyrus, the meaning of Mesopotamian culture, as an avenue to legitimation of the roles of the various ethnic groups in Mesopotamia, was immediately reduced. Mesopotamian culture became only one of several available orientations, and one that proved useful only in progressively restricted contexts. Eventually, Mesopotamian documents dealt only with the atrophied Mesopotamian cult and its landholdings (Doty 1977).

Thus, although Mesopotamian civilization did not collapse in pace with the fall of the state in Mesopotamia, the demise of the Mesopotamian political system did mean that subscription to Mesopotamian cultural norms no longer provided any selective advantage in the spheres of official life or in economic activities that were now in the hands of Persian, Seleucid, and Parthian administrations. Mesopotamian culture had been demoted, in effect, to one among many social orientations. Progressively, under Seleucid and later administrations, traditional Mesopotamian institutions became only dim reflections of an antique past, especially for members of the various and newly incorporated ethnic groups who had little reason to identify with, much less actively preserve and transmit, the Mesopotamian heritage. The ancient languages survived, although in increasingly restricted contexts, and the perception of Mesopotamian history became increasingly garbled under Seleucid and later regimes (Klotchkoff 1982).

CONCLUSION

In considering the nature and meaning of Mesopotamian collapse, we need to focus sharply on the specific element or elements that were undergoing the collapsing, to perceive that collapse is not a holistic phenomenon, and to investigate the interrelationships, if any, among the collapsing elements. In this chapter, much detail has been passed over and some opinions have doubtlessly been too confidently expressed as conclusions in the attempt to outline the several trajectories of collapse in Mesopotamia, the very precocity of which made it subject, as Adams (this volume) notes, to Veblen's "penalty of taking the lead."

In the long prehistoric and historic course of Mesopotamian civilization, one can hardly ever speak of a single Mesopotamia in political terms. Rather, one can delineate only a set of continuing Mesopotamian cultural institutions and ideals of social and political action. In the evolution of Mesopotamian civilization, city-states were the primary foci of integrative forces in which the major aspects of political struggle were confined. Of course, competition among city-states over access to resources and therefore to political leadership did promote both social change within the city-states and a tendency toward areal unification. This areal unity was in fact realized by Sargon but it proved ephemeral. Mesopotamia-wide political institutions could not be legitimized over the many formerly autonomous city-states and diverse ethnic and linguistic groups in the land. Political struggle continued to be played out in those city-states, and later in north-south regional differences that became exacerbated into almost "national" differences within Mesopotamia.

The early Mesopotamian states were always what Simon (1965) calls "nearly decomposable." That is, the formation of areal Mesopotamian states was made possible by forces in which subassemblies of city-states were put together into confederacies that then became regional states. In the collapse of such systems, the products of dissolution would fall not to zero-grade, but into one or another of the layers of subassembly that constituted the larger whole. Usually this meant to the level of the city-state itself. The nature of collapse of such political hierarchies in early times therefore implied that the reformulation of subassemblies was predictable and so was the appearance of new states and new collapses. However, in the case of Assyria in the first millennium, when the state had systematically eradicated its own infrastructure, collapse proceeded to the level of the rural countryside.

When the militaristic Assyrian and Babylonian "national" states, themselves creative responses to changing circumstances in Western Asia, were vanquished in the seventh and sixth centuries B.C., no longer was any characteristic Mesopotamian political reformulation possible. In Babylonia, Cyrus defeated a weak and uncertain leadership, and the priests of Babylon seem—wisely—to have welcomed the new conqueror. The Persian imperial ideology, designed by Cyrus precisely to govern on an international scale, explicitly recognized all diverse cultural orientations as legitimate as long as they did not conflict with the Persian government. This ideology contrasted utterly with the traditional Mesopotamian pattern in which advancement and legitimation, especially for ethnic leaders, meant overlayering their own social group identity with a subscription to Mesopotamian cultural norms and becoming Mesopotamian rulers. Although the ideal of areal unification in Mesopotamia was seldom in fact realized, its very existence provided the justification for political action under which differing and competing cultural systems could be subsumed. In the elimination of the cycle of Mesopotamian dynasties, therefore, Mesopotamian civilization itself became a less viable option for the inhabitants of Mesopotamia and was so doomed to a slow but inexorable death.

In Mesopotamia, in sum, each of the many historical political collapses contained the possibilities of regeneration until the time when not only was the bare cloak of Mesopotamian political ideals rent, but also the once-vital civilization was reduced to a recondite and dying art. Finally, even the memory of Mesopotamia was barely kept alive, less by the peoples who had captured Mesopotamia or even by those who lived in it than by the peoples whom Mesopotamians once had conquered. Only with the remarkable discovery of Mesopotamian texts and material culture in the nineteenth century A.D. has the legacy of Mesopotamia again provided a political ideal and a source of pride to those peoples who, across millennia of time, differences in language, culture, and even genetic material, live in Mesopotamia today.

NOTE

Jerrold Cooper, Peter Machinist, Piotr Michałowski, and Matthew Stolper critically read one or more drafts of this chapter and contributed significantly to both its historical detail and its overall logic. I am grateful for their friendly and expert advice.

The Collapse of Classic Maya Civilization

T. Patrick Culbert

The Maya lowlands were the site of villages during the Early Preclassic period,[1] perhaps as early as 2000 B.C. (Hammond 1977), but this earliest occupation was very sparse and scattered. By the Middle Preclassic, small villages were widely distributed, and by the Late Preclassic most of the manifestations of complex society had been established. The Early Classic saw further cultural elaboration and the appearance of such typical Maya traits as hieroglyphic writing and polychrome pottery. Influence from the great Mexican center of Teotihuacan touched parts of the lowlands during the Early Classic and may have been a further stimulus to the development of social complexity. The Late Classic was a period of florescence, a time of feverish activity and population growth at almost all major sites. Then, beginning at some sites near the start of the ninth century and spreading rapidly throughout the southern lowlands, the Maya underwent their justly famous collapse. Everywhere the hallmarks of Maya elite culture were abandoned, populations declined remarkably, and within little more than a century huge sections of the southern sector of the lowlands were abandoned—never to be reoccupied.

The Maya lowlands include the Yucatán Peninsula of Mexico, northern Guatemala, Belize, and small sections of El Salvador and Honduras. The major division of the lowlands is into northern and southern sectors. This division is based upon architectural and artifactual styles, and throughout much of Maya prehistory represented a fairly distinct cultural boundary. The area can be further subdivided into thirteen zones, seven in the

Table 4.1
Periods of Maya Prehistory

Postclassic	A.D. 930–1500
Terminal Classic	A.D. 830–930
Late Classic	A.D. 600–830
Tepeu 2	A.D. 700–830
Tepeu 1	A.D. 600–700
Early Classic	A.D. 250–600
Late Preclassic	300 B.C.–A.D. 250
Middle Preclassic	1000–300 B.C.
Early Preclassic	2000–1000 B.C.

southern lowlands and six in the north. These zones correspond to less distinct ecological and cultural differences and serve as a convenient frame of reference, but their boundaries are quite arbitrary. This chapter will deal primarily with the southern lowlands, where archaeological research has been most intensive. The effects of the Maya collapse were much more profound in the south, and the northern lowlands proceeded to a healthy Postclassic period, a phenomenon outside the scope of this study.

The Maya lowlands are a vast limestone platform mostly below four hundred meters in elevation. Only a small volcanic intrusion that created the Maya Mountains in Belize interrupts the limestone shelf. Karstic phenomena abound, and because most drainage is underground, permanent streams and rivers exist only at the fringes of the lowlands. Rainfall occurs in a rainy season between May and November. The lowlands receive between 1000 and 3000 mm of precipitation annually with the smallest amounts in the north and highest in the south. Moist tropical forests cover the region, giving way to drier scrub forest at the far north.

CHANGING VIEWS OF MAYA SOCIETY

Ideas about the structure of Maya society during the Classic period have been revolutionized since 1960. The traditional picture that crystallized during the 1930s and 1940s (Morley 1946; Thompson 1954) and held sway through the 1960s made the Maya seem unique among early civilizations. The lower classes were visualized as swidden farmers who lived scattered through the rain forest at a low population density. Periodically, they congregated for great fiestas at "vacant ceremonial centers" that were otherwise empty shells inhabited only by a few elite, specialists in ritual and the arts, and servants. Since the rain forest supplied each household with all the daily necessities, there was almost no economic

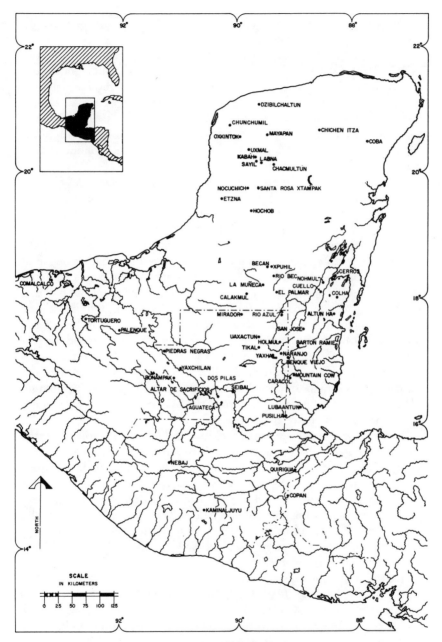

Figure 4.1 Maya lowlands sites.

specialization, and trade was confined to a trickle of exotica needed by the elite for prestige and ritual.

Those who ruled the ceremonial centers were gentle priest-kings whose principal occupations were conducting ceremonies and contemplating the stately procession of time that was commemorated in the hieroglyphic inscriptions. Without need to supervise the simple agricultural system and with little economic specialization, the priest-kings ruled through awe and the inherent piety of the peasants. Peaceful and philosophical, the elite were above the worldly concerns of taxes and conquests that beset rulers in other civilizations.

Looking back, it is hard to believe that archaeologists could have accepted such an idealized image. But we did. There had been almost no research on population or economics, the hieroglyphs could not be read, and visions of Tibetan theocracies danced in our heads.

The entire remarkable edifice came crashing down under the weight of archaeological evidence as data from the large projects that began in the 1950s and 1960s became available. The Maya had not been a scattered few but a dense population; the centers had not been vacant but had had thousands—tens of thousands for the largest sites—living within walking distance. Inferential evidence about the number of people to be fed and archaeological evidence about terraces and raised fields changed the picture of subsistence. Analysis of artifacts indicated specialization, even for everyday items such as pottery. Rathje (1971, 1972) demonstrated the need for long-distance trade in domestic, as well as elite, items. Population, subsistence, and economic structure of the Maya seemed more and more like those of other early civilizations.

Knowledge of elite life was revolutionized by breakthroughs in the interpretation of hieroglyphic writing. Proskouriakoff (1960, 1963, 1964) demonstrated beyond doubt that the inscriptions did not deal entirely with calendrics and ritual, but also contained historical information. The inscriptions soon began to tell of kings and dynasties, of royal marriages that tied great sites together, of combats and conquests. The kings who were revealed were more interested in their regal ancestors than in the gods; they schemed; they married for power and wealth; they fought battles like kings elsewhere.

Ideas about political structure changed under the impact of both historical and archaeological evidence. Maya sites had earlier been pictured as city-states, with the relatively egalitarian interaction between Greek city-states frequently posited as a model. The inscriptions indicated a world in which, at the very least, some sites were considerably more equal than others. Royal families from a few of the largest sites dominated elite interaction. They sent women (and sometimes men) to marry into the dynasties of smaller sites. They claimed capture of individuals from unnamed sites or sites of lesser size. By tracing the pattern of occasions upon which one site mentioned another site in its inscriptions, Marcus (1976) demonstrated that small sites tended to mention larger sites in their own regions but were not mentioned in return. She concluded that the hierarchical arrangements so indicated were the result of political domination of small sites by larger ones. All of this evidence pointed toward the formation of regional states by mechanisms ranging from alliance to conquest.

Archaeological evidence also provided indications of hierarchical organization within regions of the Maya lowlands. Although it had long been recognized that sites differed substantially in size, an objective measure of size-ranking was not achieved until Richard Adams (Adams 1981; Adams and Jones 1981) devised a method of counting courtyards (large paved spaces surrounded by monumental architecture). His results indicate a rank-size distribution centered upon very large sites in several different regions of the lowlands. This gave further impetus to the idea that the area was divided into regional states during the Late Classic. The sites that both hieroglyphic and archaeological data suggest are capitals of these states include Tikal, Copán, Yaxchilán, and Palenque. The spacing of these sites covers the southern lowlands quite evenly, with each of them at least one hundred kilometers distant from all the others.

Even granting the existence of regional states, the political structure of the Maya does not seem to have been highly centralized or bureaucratized. Adams and Smith (1981) have suggested that the Maya had a feudal organization, and Sanders (1981b) has posited the existence of patron-client states similar to those in some recent African kingdoms. Although differing in details, both models include a land-based aristocracy with a primary ruler who binds lower-level nobles to himself through weak mechanisms that involve such services as adjudication and military protection rather than economic benefits.

I see a somewhat stronger central authority with a firmer economic base. Agricultural intensification, specialization, and trade seem too evident not to have involved some administrative control. It also seems likely that the rapid development of raised fields in lands that had previously been unused may well have supplied an independent source of wealth that rulers could have used to undercut the power of local nobles. Thus, I suspect that by Late Classic times the largest sites were moving toward more tightly controlled kinds of organization than the feudal and patron-client models suggest. Nevertheless, my disagreements are only of degree. Compared to the highly centralized governments that arose sporadically in ancient Mesopotamia and China or to the large manufacturing-trade enterprise of Teotihuacan, the Maya were certainly less centralized both politically and economically.

THE COLLAPSE

Most facts about the collapse are clear. The Late Classic period, between A.D. 600 and 830, was a cultural climax in the Maya lowlands. Most southern lowlands sites experienced population peaks then, including some that had had little previous occupation. The indicators of elite activity show equally impressive peaks: monumental construction was at an all-time high; elaborate burials were commonplace; and the famous dynasties of the lowlands sang their own praises incessantly upon carved stelae.

In the Terminal Classic period, beginning at A.D. 830 and lasting for about a century, the signs of cultural success disappeared with striking suddenness. By A.D. 830, most sites had stopped carving dated inscriptions. By itself, this need not signal the death of a civilization, but the archaeological evidence clearly shows an equivalent loss of other elite activities: major construction slowed, then ceased; tomb burials became fewer and less elaborate; and in many sites the rapid process of decay had begun. Most importantly, the commoners as well as the elite were affected. Population declined drastically and there are clear signs of cultural impoverishment.

Tikal (Culbert 1973) is typical of the period. There, monumental construction slowed toward the end of the Late Classic and the inscriptional records of rulers became incomplete and hard to follow. By the Terminal Classic, major construction had come to a halt. The most striking feature, however, is the fate of commoners. Terminal Classic population dwindled to one-third its previous level, and the survivors clustered in the remains of masonry structures, discarding their garbage in rooms and over once-carefully swept courtyards, and occasionally suffering from the collapse of roofs that were no longer being maintained. The remnant populations attempted to maintain old ceremonial patterns, hauling ancient stelae hither and yon and resetting them in total disregard for the rigid Late Classic rules for stela erection. After a century, the survivors disappeared as well, leaving the site to the encroaching forest.

The pattern is repeated at the majority of large sites tested by archaeologists. Greatly diminished Terminal Classic populations persevered for a time in seeming poverty but left before the Postclassic. Abandonment was widespread and the loss of population very severe. There are hints, however, that not all smaller sites suffered so quickly; several dedicated their first, and usually only, stelae early in the Terminal Classic. They may have been centers less drastically affected by the initial impact of the collapse whose leaders seized the opportunity to proclaim their independence and grandeur as the authority of larger centers diminished.

The two known Pasión River centers, Altar de Sacrificios and Seibal, even underwent a brief florescence at this time. Both reached peak population during the Terminal Classic when other areas had already declined. At Seibal this was accompanied by a late flourish of monumental construction and the erection of dated monuments until A.D. 889. Shortly thereafter, however, these sites were abandoned as well.

In an important paper, Rice (1985) has focused attention on continuity of the Maya population and organizational system through the period of the collapse. He suggests that new centers, subject, perhaps, to some outside influence, emerged in the lake district of the central Petén during the Terminal Classic. These centers continued such traditional practices as the erection of stelae and led eventually to the Postclassic centers of the area as part of a continuous cultural heritage. Although I have emphasized disjunction rather than continuity, I think Rice's formulation is an apt counterpoint. The Maya tradition did not die and there were some Postclassic centers in the southern lowlands.

In fact, positing the existence of such persevering organizational centers solves what has always been a vexing problem: the reason why the reduced Terminal Classic populations eventually abandoned the major sites. If new centers of organization were emerging in nearby areas, the remaining populations might well have chosen, for reasons such as defense or greater availability of trade goods, to move closer to them. These aspects of continuity, however, do not negate the evidence of drastic changes in size and location of population.

Explanations of the Collapse

The participants in a 1970 School of American Research seminar on the Classic Maya collapse (Culbert, ed., 1973) reached a series of conclusions summarized by Willey and Shimkin (1973). Not surprisingly, there was general agreement that a phenomenon of such complexity could not be satisfactorily explained by any single cause but must relate to a conjunction of factors. Willey and Shimkin posit two major sets of stresses within Late Classic Maya society. One is a set of subsistence-demographic stresses in which, under pressure of increasing population, the agricultural system expanded from prime lands into more marginal areas, where greater technological efforts were necessary at the same time that risks were increased. Concomitantly, a shortening of fallow cycles led to problems with grass invasion, insect pests, and plant diseases. The system became ever more tenuous, and the need to counteract local failures demanded ever-greater shipment and storage of foodstuffs. As food shortages became a problem, both malnutrition and diseases related to increased population densities reduced the labor capacity just when labor demands were heaviest both to maintain subsistence production and to satisfy the wishes of an increasing number of elite.

The second set of stresses is social. Due to differential reproduction and survival, the elite segment of Maya society increased more rapidly than the lower-class segment. At the same time, the gulf separating the social classes increased as the elite became ever more exploitative. Under the stressful circumstances of the Late Classic, competition between the elite from major centers increased—a competition that took the form of labor-consuming investment in architectural splendor.

The Maya collapse seminar provided a kitchen-sink model that pointed fingers simultaneously at almost every aspect of environment and society. This was, in fact, the intention—to portray a society in which variables were so tightly interwoven and under such general stress that almost every juncture was vulnerable. Such may be reality for a society on the brink of collapse. If this is so, the most interesting causes of collapse may not be the specific factors that initiate the process, but the structure that allows perturbations to amplify throughout the system.

What has happened since the publication of the results of the 1970 Maya collapse seminar? Not surprisingly, archaeologists have not fallen silent but have continued to attack the topic, sometimes echoing and elaborating upon the themes of the seminar, sometimes arraying new data relevant to the questions raised, sometimes emphasizing directions little explored previously.

Three papers have elaborated, using new methodologies, upon the theme of interconnectedness that is at the heart of the seminar model. Although very different in method and content, they come from different directions to the same important point—that the collapse of Maya civilization was the result of the very processes that had been responsible for its success.

Hosler, Sabloff, and Runge (1977) explicitly test the Willey and Shimkin formulation by means of a computer simulation. After constructing a richly interwoven feedback model of the sort pioneered by Forrester (1961, 1969), they demonstrate that simulation does indeed lead to a sudden collapse. Such simulations, of course, demand quantification that for some variables must be based upon outright guesswork. The results, therefore, do not "prove" that the collapse followed the pathway suggested, but simply demonstrate that the outcome is plausible given the assumptions with which the simulators worked. Simulation makes it possible to test which variables in the system (as constructed) are so sensitive that changes in them will drastically alter the behavior of the entire system. In the Hosler, Sabloff, and Runge simulation, a change in managerial policy (demanding less labor for construction) results in a system that does not collapse.

As described in Chapter 1, Renfrew (1978) has approached the issue from the viewpoint of catastrophe theory, which gives a topological explanation of the way in which gradual change in control variables can lead to sudden transformations in the state of a system. Using the Maya as a test example, Renfrew proposes that the state variable, the degree of political centralization, was a function of investment in charismatic authority (public display, such as monumental architecture) and net rural marginality (a sort of balance sheet of lower-class benefits and costs). As charismatic investment increased and the balance for the lower class worsened, the system reached a point at which it tripped over a cusp (regrettably, the closest I can come to describing topological intricacies) and fell to a much lower level. Although Mayanists would not object to this model, which stresses the gulf between elite and commoners, catastrophe theory deals with so few and such highly aggregated variables that it does not seem of much practical utility. The importance of catastrophe theory seems to me to reside in the demonstration that sudden drastic changes in the state of complex systems may result from small and gradual changes in key variables.

In a 1977 paper I approached the Maya economic system from the standpoint of general systems theory. I posited that the existence of very large regional centers in the relatively homogeneous lowland environment was the result of a positive feedback chain in which the centers supplied goods and services to a regional area in exchange for subsistence support. The reaction would have been successful throughout much of Maya history, but could have become destructive when the point was reached at which food production could no longer be increased.

These three papers converge upon a very important idea that is inherent in the diverse new ways of conceptualizing complex systems. The Maya never attained equilibrium. They were a growth system, changing continually and subject to the possibility that the very processes that generated growth might lead to disintegration if the trajectory continued. This viewpoint contrasts sharply with most traditional ways of conceptualizing the Maya. In most older approaches the Maya were visualized as a stable equilibrium system capable of continuing indefinitely had it not been overwhelmed by some catastrophic change.

Other papers have dealt with the way in which more specific variables—social variables in most cases—contributed to the Maya collapse. The hypothesis that has received the most attention is that the collapse was related to a competitive battle for long-distance trade between the Maya and better-organized traders with roots in Mexico.

Both Rathje and Webb offered trade hypotheses in the volume from the 1970 Maya collapse seminar. The chief mechanism in Rathje's (1973) model is competition between the core area of the Maya lowlands and the surrounding buffer zone. With the growth of trading capabilities of buffer-zone sites, centers in the core were outcompeted and cut off from vital resources. The buffer zone in turn was outcompeted by Mexicanized groups that had the advantages of techniques of mass production and more efficient transportation by sea. In Webb's (1973) version, the Maya achieved a secondary state as a result of an influx of wealth derived from contacts with a primary state in Mexico. At the end of the Classic, the emergence of commercial trade changed the economic environment, and the Maya, mired within the limits of their organizational structure, were cut off from the vital external sources of wealth. Jones (1979) agrees with Webb's evaluation of the Maya as a secondary state whose role was to funnel trade goods to the more highly developed polities of Mexico. Unlike Webb, he envisions the basic change as one in the mechanisms of transport rather than in the nature of the trade system. At the end of the Classic a more efficient sea route around the Yucatán Peninsula replaced the previous overland route through Tikal to cause a collapse of the support system in the southern lowlands.

Considering trade in a different light, Freidel (1985) proposes a highland-lowland symbiosis upon which both partners were dependent. Cartels were formed in which partners merged their political economies around sets of shared symbols. Freidel believes that the southern lowlands Maya were ideologically ill-adapted to cartel formation because of an obsession with the purity of royal bloodlines. The northern lowlands Maya, who had taken a different developmental path less tied to royal lines, were better able to make the commitment to a shared ideology that is at the heart of cartel formation. Consequently they outcompeted the Maya of the south, and their success led to the southern collapse as well as to a vigorous Postclassic period further north.

Diverse though they are, these trade hypotheses share two important premises. The first is that the southern lowland Maya system proved less effective than some competing system. The second is that long-distance trade was so critical to the structure of Maya society that a restriction of trade caused the collapse. I find the latter premise worrisome. Given the size of the Maya lowlands and the considerable organizational abilities of the Late Classic polities, I find it difficult to believe that the rulers could not have found alternate sources of goods and wealth. Moreover, even if a loss of trade caused decline of the elite class, I do not believe that it could have been responsible for the population loss that occurred.

Hamblin and Pitcher (1980) have combined curve-fitting techniques from quantitative sociology with the old hypothesis of Maya peasant revolt. Their curves for the appearance and decline of dated inscriptions match curves for outbreaks of collective conflict in modern society. Hence, they conclude that rebellion of the lower class occurred among the Maya and escalated to the point of triggering the collapse. Although the techniques are very interesting, the curves are generated by simple mathematical relationships among a few variables, and I join Lowe (1982) in not believing that insurrection was necessarily one of the variables involved.

Cowgill (1979b) suggests that warfare aimed at territorial aggrandizement was a destructive factor in the Maya Late Classic. He believes that increasing militarism may have evoked policies that stimulated population increase and led to a critical overpopulation. The paper provides an important hypothesis about a possible connection between social and demographic variables, although I am not convinced that population levels can be directly influenced by social policies.

Foreign invasion is a possible cause of the Maya collapse that merits discussion. The idea of invasion has suffered a curious fate in Maya studies. With the discovery in the 1960s of the intrusive Jimba phase at Altar de Sacrificios (Richard Adams 1971) and of the vigorous Terminal Classic development at Seibal that included stela depictions of individuals who were not Classic Maya (Graham 1973), a number of researchers (Adams 1971, 1973; Sabloff 1971, 1973; Sabloff and Willey 1967) posited that an invasion from either the Gulf Coast or Yucatán had been a cause of the collapse. The issue was hotly debated at the 1970 collapse seminar and the majority of the participants seemed to favor the hypothesis. In the summary paper, however, Willey and Shimkin (1973) downplayed the role of invasion, seemingly convinced that it had been a result rather than a cause of Maya disintegration. Since then, the theme of invasion has been almost completely absent from treatments of the collapse.

This rejection of outside interference in the southern lowlands is due for reconsideration. New data from the site of Colhá, Belize (Hester, Shafer, and Eaton 1982), show an apparent slaughter of the elite at the end of the Terminal Classic followed by a new phase with connections to Yucatán. Río Azul, sixty kilometers from Colhá, may present a similar situation (Richard Adams 1984). In addition, Yucatecan influence of Terminal Classic or Early Postclassic dates has been suggested at Quiriguá (Sharer 1980) and at Nohmul (Hammond 1982; Chase and Chase 1982). Rice (1985) has even suggested Yucatecan influence in the Late or Terminal Classic in the lake district at the heart of the lowlands. All of this evidence points toward some kind of northern thrust into the southern lowlands—or perhaps to two separate ones, as the Chases (1982) suggest—that was more substantial and earlier than previously recognized. Although I will uneasily maintain my previous position that such influence was a result of collapse-related weakness in the south, the possibility that a shifting political balance between the northern and southern lowlands might have been a factor in causing the collapse seems greater than it did before.

DEMOGRAPHIC-ECOLOGICAL STRESSES

Most of the post-seminar articles that have focused on the Maya collapse have brought social factors to the fore. It is not that demographic-ecological stresses have been forgotten, for a number of authors (Richard Adams 1977; Sharer 1977; Hammond 1982; Sanders and Murdy 1982; Rice, Rice, and Deevey 1984) have noted their importance in general summaries. What has not been done is a reassessment of the situation in the light of new data—in spite of the fact that research in Maya demography and ecology has been very productive since 1970.

Demography

Demographic data about the Maya have accumulated very slowly. Settlement-pattern survey is difficult in tropical forest and is limited to the recognition of architectural features. With the near impossibility of surface collection, dating depends upon excavation. On the other hand, Maya archaeologists have the advantage that their prehistoric subjects constructed a majority of their structures upon low masonry platforms, the remains of which form the ubiquitous "house mounds" that everywhere dot the lowland landscape.

The difficulties of lowland survey have limited coverage to much smaller areas than the whole regions sampled for some early civilizations. Nevertheless, a substantial segment of the Central zone, the area stretching from the site of Yaxhá in the Central Petén lake district northward through Tikal to the site of Uaxactún, has sufficient surveys of both site and rural areas to make possible population reconstructions for this key area. Elsewhere, there are mapped areas in the Río Bec zone to the north, in Belize to the east, in the Southeastern zone, and along the Pasión River to the south. Unfortunately, there are as yet no population data for the Usumacinta and Northwestern zones, and the far northern sector of the lowlands provides only the surveys of Dzibilchaltún and Chunchucmil.

Three issues involving population are important for the purposes of this chapter. The first is relative changes in population densities over time. The second is the estimation of absolute densities during the population peak that immediately preceded the collapse. Finally, the question of whether the Maya collapse was a "demographic disaster" must be reexamined in the light of data acquired since 1970.

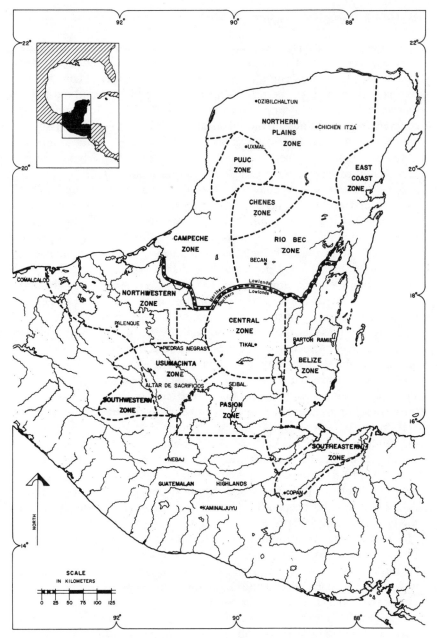

Figure 4.2 Maya lowlands archaeological zones.

Settlement Density Through Time

Mound samples have been dated at eleven Maya lowland sites. These include seven samples from the Central zone of the lowlands and one sample each from the Pasión, Belize, Río Bec, and Northern Plains zones.

I have suggested (Culbert, Kosakowsky, Fry, and Haviland n.d.) that most considerations of population change in the Maya lowlands have suffered from a serious methodological error. The crux of the issue is whether population figures must be adjusted to take into account the differing lengths of the ceramic phases upon which dating is based. Most earlier studies have simply compared mound counts at face value regardless of the lengths of phases. To consider one hundred mounds dated to a century-long Late Classic phase to represent the same relative population as one hundred mounds occupied at some time during a four-hundred-year Preclassic phase assumes an unrealistically lengthy period of mound use in the earlier phase. Consequently, I advocate adjusting counts for longer phases downward by a factor representing the proportional difference in time between the phases. For many sites, this has quite drastic effects upon relative populations of the Preclassic and Early Classic periods, which usually have long ceramic phases.

Table 4.2 presents the relative populations in the surveyed areas—after adjustment for lengths of phases—as a percentage of the population during the phase of maximum occupancy. The earliest populations reported at any of the sites date to the Middle Preclassic. Population densities at this time were low, less than 10 percent of eventual maxima at most sites. Populations rose almost everywhere during the Late Preclassic and Protoclassic periods, but generally remained at less than 25 percent of their eventual peaks. Early Classic population figures are extremely variable. The site of Dzibilchaltún and all of the Central Petén lakes except Yaxhá-Sacnab had very low populations, less than 10 percent of maxima. At other sites, relative populations ranged from 19 to 55 percent. At none of the sites was Early Classic population much greater than half the population maximum.

Rapid population growth in the Late Classic was general, and all but two of the sites in Table 4.1 showed Late Classic population maxima. At those sites for which chronological subdivisions of the Late Classic were used, most showed dense populations in both the Tepeu 1 (A.D. 600–700) and Tepeu 2 (A.D. 700–830) phases.

Two of the surveyed areas did not reach their population maxima until the Terminal Classic period (A.D. 830–930). At Altar de Sacrificios, the Terminal Classic Boca phase population was almost double that reached during the Late Classic. A similar situation prevailed at Seibal, the other Pasión River site, where the Terminal Classic Bayal phase was

Table 4.2
Relative Population Densities at Maya Archaeological Sites (as Percentages of Maximum Population)

Period	Altar de Sacrificios	Barton Ramie	Becán	Central Tikal	Tikal Sustaining Area	Macanché	Salpetén	Quexil-Petenxil	Yaxhá-Sacnab	Tikal-Yaxhá
Postclassic	0 / 27.8	84.5		3.4	1.1	10.6 / 18.2	1.5 / 5.9	0 / 0	0	0
Terminal Classic	100.0	59.1	20.0	14.2	21.4	21.2	44.1	22.9	15.7	100.0
Tepeu 2	60.6	100.0	49.7	100.0	98.6	97.0	100.0	100.0	100.0	54.1
Tepeu 1	30.6	100.0	100.0	94.9	100.0	100.0	52.9	94.3		
Early Classic	19.4 / 38.9	45.5	28.6	33.5	49.6	6.1	4.4	2.9	31.9	38.8
Protoclassic or Terminal Preclassic	34.7	68.1	33.2	18.8	12.9	18.2	0	0	12.2	29.5
Late Preclassic	25.9	16.4	12.5	14.2 / 19.9		10.6	1.5	5.7		
Middle Preclassic	8.3 / 5.5	13.6 / 16.4		2.3 / 0		23.7 / 6.8	8.8 / 6.6	15.7 / 5.3	9.1	22.4

SOURCES: Altar de Sacrificios: Willey (1973a); Barton Ramie: Willey et al. (1965); Becán: Thomas (1981); Central Tikal: Culbert, Kosakowsky, Fry, and Haviland n.d.; Tikal Sustaining Area: Fry (1969); Macanché: Rice and Rice (n.d.); Quexil-Petenxil: Rice and Rice (n.d.); Salpetén: Rice and Rice (n.d.); Yaxhá-Sacnab: Rice (1978); Tikal-Yaxhá: Ford (1981).
NOTE: Where two complexes occur within a given period, results for both are given and separated by a dotted line. When the temporal unit spans two or more periods, the periods are bracketed.

a period of major architectural and sculptural activity as well as the time of maximum population (Sabloff 1973). The second sampled area with a Terminal Classic population peak is the survey strip of the rural area between Tikal and Yaxhá (Ford 1981), an area that seems an anomaly in light of other Central zone population figures. At all other sites there were substantial decreases of population during the Terminal Classic with densities that generally were in the range of 15 to 45 percent of Late Classic populations.

With the exceptions of Barton Ramie, which maintained more than half its population into the Postclassic, and of the short-lived Jimba phase at Altar de Sacrificios, all sites had very low Postclassic populations, even those sites where Terminal Classic populations had been heavy.

The most important fact that can be derived from these figures is that at all sites the population peak was reached by a period of explosive growth during which population doubled from earlier levels.

Absolute Population Densities

Despite the methodological hazards involved, it is impossible to avoid the vexing problem of converting counts of Maya house mounds to absolute population densities. I have marshaled in Table 4.3 the mounds/km^2 counts from available surveys. Since some of the surveys were restricted entirely to the upland terrain in which the vast majority of house mounds are located, I have adjusted figures downward for those surveys so that they reflect mounds/km^2 of *total* terrain rather than just uplands.

Surveys from intersite or site-peripheral areas are quite consistent in suggesting densities between about 40 and 80 mounds/km^2. The only notable exception is the mound count for Thomas's (1981) survey in the Becán region which produced the astonishing figure of 222 mounds/km^2. Thomas's figures are an anomaly, particularly in view of the fact that Turner's (1974) data from the same areas indicate only 80 mounds/km. The possibility that there was an unusually high population density in the Becán region, however, is also suggested by the extreme development of both terracing and field walls in the vicinity (Turner 1978). Such features are absent in the Yaxhá-Tikal-Uaxactún strip, where rural population densities are much lower.

Housemound counts from surveys within the immediate environs of sites are expectably higher. Although at first glance the figures vary greatly, they can be interpreted in a manner that seems sensible and consistent. The lowest figures, at somewhat over 100 mounds/km^2, come from Seibal, Uaxactún, and Puleston's (1974) survey of 12-km strips radiating from Tikal. Such densities probably represent average figures for smaller sites in the southern lowlands and the outer reaches of very large sites like

Table 4.3
Small Structure Counts at Maya Archaeological Sites (Mounds/km²)

Site	Mounds/km²	Source
Intrasite		
Uaxactún	112	Puleston (1974)
Seibal	113	Tourtellot (1970)
Tikal (12-km strips)	119	Puleston (1974)
Tikal (7 km² outside central zone)	145	Carr and Hazard (1961)
Tikal (central 9 km²)	235	Carr and Hazard (1961)
Copán (estimated)	192	Willey and Leventhal (1979)[a]
Dzibilchaltún	442	Kurjack (1974)
Chunchucmil	400	Vlacek, Garza de González, and Kurjack (1978)
Intersite		
Tikal-Uaxactún	39	Puleston (1974)
Tikal-Yaxhá	76	Ford (1981)
Rural Yaxhá	59	Rice (1978)
Lake Macanché	82	Rice and Rice (n.d.)
Lake Salpetén	51	Rice and Rice (n.d.)
Lakes Quexil/Petenxil	40	Rice and Rice (n.d.)
Becán (Turner data)	80	Turner (1974), cited in Richard Adams (1981)
Becán (Thomas data, partly intrasite)	222	Thomas (1981)

[a]Estimate obtained by multiplying number of plaza groups by three

Tikal. The higher figures for more central parts of Tikal based upon Carr and Hazard's (1961) map of the central 9 km² of the site (235 mounds/km²), surrounded by a less carefully mapped outer 7 km² (145 mounds/km²), suggest a concentric pattern with decreasing mound density as one moves away from the site center. Puleston's data, which sampled an even larger area than the Carr and Hazard map, would fit well as an outer ring. The density of Copán matches the higher Tikal figures to suggest that the central parts of major sites reached mound densities around 200 mounds/km². The mound density at Dzibilchaltún (442 mounds/km²), confirmed by comparable figures from Chunchucmil (400 mounds/km²), has always amazed (and sometimes outraged) archaeologists whose work has been confined to the southern lowlands. There seems to be no valid way to avoid the conclusion that sites in the Northern Plains zone were twice as densely settled as even the largest of the southern sites.

To convert mounds counts to absolute figures at the time of maximum population requires estimating a series of variables, often without much basis in archaeological data. The first step is to estimate the fraction of total mounds occupied residentially at the moment of peak population. This step requires a series of adjustments of the raw counts. First, there must be a downward adjustment to allow for mounds that served functions other than residential. Second, another downward adjustment must be made for mounds that were not occupied during the *phase* of maximum occupation. Third, still further downward adjustment is required to account for lack of contemporaneity: that is, an estimate must be made of the number of mounds that, although dating to the *phase* of maximum population, were not occupied at the specific *time* of peak population. Finally, mound counts must be adjusted upward to take account of residential sites that were missed during survey, either through survey error or because they have left no surface indications.

With sampling by careful excavation, it is possible to arrive at factually based estimates for the first and second adjustments. The two final adjustments are much more enigmatic. Although they have been frequently debated (Haviland 1970; Sanders 1973), it would be unrealistic to say that Mayanists can do much better than make educated guesses about their magnitude. I have chosen to adjust mound counts downward by 50 percent as my educated guess at what these factors might total if it were possible to measure them exactly. This is a conservative estimate, and a number of my colleagues would argue for a smaller reduction, especially at large sites.

The final element in reaching absolute population figures is to estimate the number of people who inhabited each house. Estimates of family size range from Sanders's (1973:356) figure of 3.3 based upon Colonial data from Central Mexico to Villa's (1945) 6.3 for the modern X-Cacal Maya. I will accept the most commonly used figure, 5.6 inhabitants per house, derived from modern Maya households in Yucatán.

An average density for house mounds in rural areas of the southern lowlands would be 60 mounds/km² (Table 4.3). Reducing this figure by 50 percent and multiplying by 5.6 gives a rural population density of 168 persons/km². Intrasite densities probably ran about 300 persons/km² for smaller sites and may have exceeded 500/km² at major sites. Given the large areal extent and the frequency of sites, overall population densities for the southern Maya lowlands may well have been 200 persons/km² at the time of peak population. Northern lowland populations are harder to estimate. In the Northern Plains, densities within sites probably approached 1,000 persons/km², but there are no rural surveys to complement this figure. Given the poor soil cover of the Northern Plains, it is not unlikely that these higher intrasite densities were accompanied by rural densities substantially lower than those in the south.

Such population densities are exceedingly high for Neolithic farmers. Only a few of the more productive regions of the world, such as relatively recent Java and parts of China, had comparable populations. One might argue, as Sanders (1981b) has, that there were large, nearly unpopulated "no-man's lands" between sites that would have reduced overall population density, but since such unpopulated zones have never been discovered, it seems time at last to face the available archaeological evidence squarely. The Maya lowlands seem to have been one of the most densely populated areas in the preindustrial world.

Combining absolute population figures with the evidence for population growth explored in the previous section, one can project approximations for earlier periods in Maya prehistory. Occupation during the Middle Preclassic period almost certainly averaged fewer than 20 persons/km². By Late Preclassic times, population may have risen to 50/km², and Early Classic growth may have doubled the figure to 100 persons/km².

Postclassic Population

As work in Postclassic sites has increased, scholars have questioned whether the magnitude of the Maya collapse has not been overemphasized. The "so-called collapse" (often complete with quotation marks) is a phrase that has appeared with increasing frequency in the literature (Chase and Rice 1985; Sabloff and Andrews 1985).

In some ways this reaction is justified. The fact that Postclassic remains of the southern lowlands were frequently ignored in earlier publications implied that the Maya cultural tradition had died with the collapse. Some of us were even guilty of flamboyant language that could hardly fail to provoke a reaction from an archaeologist working in a very real Postclassic site.

> The ravaged land offered little potential for repopulation and the rain forest home of the Maya still remains an unpopulated wilderness with only the silent remains of the vast temple centers to remind the visitor of its once great past. (Culbert 1974:116)

The Maya cultural tradition in the southern lowlands did not die, of course, and it is important to emphasize that fact, as Rice (1985) and others have done. Centers of population persisted in some areas through Postclassic times. None of those centers, however, approached the size and complexity of Classic sites or of Postclassic sites in the northern lowlands. This fact implies a different level of organization in the southern Postclassic.

A point that I maintain as strongly as ever is that the scale of population decline at the time of the collapse was enormous. Some disagree. Sidrys and Berger (1979) reaffirm J. Eric Thompson's conclusion (1967) that the collapse largely affected elite populations while the commoners simply fled into rural areas. Assembling all of the radiocarbon dates from the southern lowlands, Sidrys and Berger point to the fact that dates from commoner contexts for the Postclassic are nearly as numerous as Classic dates from lower-class contexts—a possible indication of continuing high population levels. Their study, however, suffers from serious methodological defects. In addition to very small samples of commoner dates, the conclusions rest upon the assumption that the number of radiocarbon dates is a direct function of prehistoric population densities. Since it seems far more likely that the submission of radiocarbon samples is a function of archaeological problems rather than prehistoric population, I cannot accept the results as demographically meaningful.

We do, in fact, have solid archaeological evidence indicating where Postclassic populations lived and some idea of their magnitude. The area known most precisely is the central Petén lake district, where a series of small lakes following an old fault line extends seventy kilometers across the heart of the southern lowlands. Postclassic occupation was island-oriented (Rice and Rice n.d.; Rice 1985); eight islands and an isolated peninsula have dense Postclassic settlement. Even around the same lakes, however, mainland occupation of Postclassic date is spotty (see Table 4.2). The shores of Lake Macanché show moderate occupation and there are several Postclassic sites on the mainland near the large Lake Petén Itzá. The mainland areas surrounding the other four lakes show very sparse Postclassic remains.

Postclassic sites in the lake district have higher densities of structures than Classic sites. Sacpetén, a site on a peninsula in Lake Salpetén, has 819 structures/km² (Rice and Rice n.d.), several times the density of even the largest Classic sites. The total area of all the sites, however, is quite small, and it seems unlikely that more than a few thousand structures were represented by all the Postclassic sites of the lake district.

To the east in Belize, Postclassic populations seem to have been even more widespread than in the lake district. At Barton Ramie, the Postclassic New Town phase has a population level that amounts to 58 percent of the Classic period maximum (Willey et al. 1965). Even more importantly, Barton Ramie is not an isolated case; a significant number of other Belizean sites are reported to have Postclassic artifacts and architecture. Although there are not enough data to derive a quantitative estimate, it is clear that Maya populations throughout Belize continued to be sizable in the Postclassic period.

Throughout the rest of the southern lowlands, the story is quite different. Tikal provides a typical example: some of the ceremonial structures were used occasionally, for there is scattered Postclassic debris and evidence of incense burning in rooms and on stairways. Elsewhere at the site, Caban phase Postclassic ceramics at eight locations suggest the possibility of residence, probably no more than a single household at each location. Compared with the hundreds of locations that show Late Classic debris, it seems fair to say that Tikal was nearly deserted in the Postclassic.

The situation is similar at Uaxactún, Becán, Altar de Sacrificios, Seibal, and Palenque, all investigated in large archaeological projects. Moreover, Postclassic ceramics and architecture are distinctive and easily recognized, as attested in the numerous reports of Postclassic occupation in Belize. Consequently, the lack of reports of Postclassic settlement at the many Petén sites that have been subject to mapping or minor testing clearly indicates that the abandonment of at least the central precincts of Classic sites was very widespread. There have not been enough rural surveys to rule out the possibility that large Postclassic populations lurked in the hinterlands in areas yet to be discovered by archaeologists. But the few surveys in rural areas (see Table 4.2) have found them as barren of Postclassic populations as the centers of sites. To posit large populations hidden "somewhere out there" requires an act of faith of which I am incapable.

The present evidence, then, suggests that the southern lowlands between the Río Bec area on the north and the Pasión zone on the south and within the borders of Guatemala to the east and west was very sparsely populated in Postclassic times. Considering the hundreds of Classic period sites known from this same region, I continue to maintain that the Maya collapse was a demographic disaster in which a population loss that must have numbered in the millions occurred during the ninth and tenth centuries.

In summary, the population of the southern Maya lowlands seems to have risen gradually through the Preclassic and Early Classic to an explosive Late Classic climax. The maximum population density may have reached 200 people/km^2 over the entire region, a remarkable density for a Neolithic people. During the Terminal Classic and shortly thereafter, population declined to very low levels except for fairly small, quite well-defined areas.

SUBSISTENCE

Ideas about the subsistence base of the prehistoric Maya have been revolutionized since 1970. (See Harrison and Turner 1978 for an excellent treatment of this issue.) The traditional assumption that the Maya supported themselves entirely by long-fallow swidden agriculture has proven untenable, and archaeologists have been forced to conclude that the Maya relied upon other and more productive subsistence alternatives. Among these are shortened fallow cycles (Sanders 1973), root crops (Bronson 1966), double cropping in moister areas (Culbert, Spencer, and Magers 1976), infield-outfield cultivation with intensively cultivated kitchen gardens juxtaposed with swidden areas (Netting 1977; Wiseman 1978; Sanders 1981b), and terracing (Turner 1978). These agricultural alternatives are essentially more productive variants of the traditional Maya subsistence system. They involve use of the same lands as those presumed to have been used for swidden farming and achieve an increase in productivity by either more frequent cropping or more productive crops.

The last two alternatives suggested differ more fundamentally from the traditional system. Dennis Puleston (1971, 1978) has argued that the prehistoric Maya increased production by cultivation of the *ramón*, or breadnut, tree. The tree grows in the same upland terrain used for agriculture and would have created too much shade for other crops, so lands put to *ramón* orchards would have been removed from farming. But the *ramón* tree is a more productive crop than corn and the nutritional values of the *ramón* nut are impressive. Despite these advantages, the Maya seem not to have turned to *ramón* cultivation. Such cultivation would leave clear evidence, and as Turner and Harrison (1978:348–49) and Miksicek et al. (1981) have pointed out, there is absolutely no pollen or macrofossil evidence for *ramón* orchards. In addition, Puleston's arguments for a dependence upon *ramón* are inferential and easily challenged (Lambert and Arnason 1982).

The most revolutionary of the alternative agriculture systems proposed for the Maya is the use of raised-field agriculture in the low-lying swampy areas (*bajos*) that dot the southern lowlands (Siemens and Puleston 1972; Turner and Harrison 1981; Adams, Brown, and Culbert 1981). Such areas constitute as much as 50 percent of the land in some parts of the lowlands and are assumed not to have been used by the agricultural methods discussed above. Consequently, the use of *bajos* for farming would have represented a huge increase in arable land.

The rethinking of subsistence possibilities has led to a profusion of new, but still largely hypothetical, models for Maya agriculture. Since most of the suggested alternatives are not currently being practiced in the area, Mayanists are faced with the difficult task of reconstructing an extinct system. Few solid data are available about such variables as labor, yield, and risks, and research on even those parts of the system that leave tangible remains, such as terraces and raised fields, is still in its infancy. Despite these problems, there are five key questions about subsistence that must be faced if we are to understand the development and collapse of Maya civilization.

1. At what time did more productive agricultural alternatives become important?
2. What degree of centralized management was stimulated by or needed for the newly suggested subsistence methods?
3. How large a territory was necessary to provide food for major sites?

4. What was the ultimate support capacity of the agricultural system?
5. What amount of risk was involved in the intensive subsistence mix?

The Date of Agricultural Intensification

There can be no doubt that some of the most sophisticated techniques used by the Maya for agricultural intensification were already known in the Late Preclassic period. A complicated system of water management at the site of Cerros in Belize dates to the Late Preclassic (Freidel and Scarborough 1982), and some raised fields were constructed at Pulltrouser Swamp at a similar date (Turner and Harrison 1981). Although no agricultural terrace systems have been dated so early, they were certainly within the technological capabilities of the Preclassic Maya.

It is much more difficult to estimate the date when intensification techniques reached a point at which they were fundamental to the subsistence of substantial areas of the lowlands, because none of the really large-scale terrace or raised-field systems has been securely dated. The population figures suggest that the Maya reached the support capacity of long-fallow swidden by the end of the Preclassic, so intensification must have begun during the Early Classic. Until there is more concrete evidence, it seems most reasonable to infer that intensification paralleled the population curve and escalated rapidly to a Late Classic peak.

Subsistence Management

Two questions are involved in considering the amount of centralized management necessary to achieve and maintain productivity in the new, more intensive subsistence system proposed for the Maya. The first is whether construction and maintenance demanded the large labor crews Wittfogel (1957) envisions in his hydraulic hypothesis. Of the new Maya systems, only terracing and raised fields involve construction and both need only small-scale labor to produce usable results. Individual households could, over a period of years, construct substantial terrace systems. Similarly, small raised-field systems could have been constructed slowly, as Turner and Harrison (1981) suggest for Pulltrouser Swamp, with new segments added by accretion to ones already in use. The much larger raised-field systems in major *bajos*, however, may have demanded more sophisticated feats of hydraulic engineering. If major canals controlled water levels over large areas, such systems might be comparable to large irrigation projects that must be completely finished before any part becomes usable. The fact that some of the largest areas of raised fields are near major sites is probably significant (Richard Adams 1980). In maintenance, as well, only very large raised-field systems would pose a need for a substantial labor force. The need would have been even greater when heavy rains inflicted damage severe enough to require substantial repairs.

In sum, most Maya agricultural techniques do not presuppose the management of large labor forces. Whether large raised-field systems are an exception remains to be determined when their hydrological characteristics are better understood.

A more pertinent relationship between centralized authority and agriculture in the Maya lowlands involves the difficulty of maintaining the high productivity needed to feed the escalating population. Most of the segments of the new subsistence mix were more labor intensive than swidden agriculture. Increased labor intensity creates a potential conflict between the farmers, who must be motivated to maintain high productivity, and the central authorities, who must obtain a greater total yield out of a fixed amount of territory. Even a minor relaxation of effort on the part of individual farmers is a cumulative process, so continual vigilance and administration are necessary to keep production high.

The problem of management would also have depended upon the distance over which food was exchanged. If Maya economies by Late Classic times reached a scale at which major sites had to import food from some distance, administration would have been even more difficult. Problems of transportation, timing, and storage would have increased, and the systems would have involved distant producers who were hard to control or to involve in the exchange sphere. Increasing coercion might well have been necessary as stress within Maya society grew.

Regional Exchange of Foodstuffs

The high population density and complex subsistence system of the Late Classic make regional movement of large volumes of foodstuffs seem likely. In 1977 I suggested a process in which major sites became dependent upon importing food. Such sites gave up subsistence self-sufficiency early in favor of investing manpower in manufacturing goods to exchange for food from surrounding areas. Once begun, the process would have been deviation amplifying; it would also account for the immense size of some centers in an environment that favored a more even distribution of population. This process seems even more likely in view of increasingly clear indications that the Maya lowlands were divided into regions headed by very large regional capitals.

The mechanics and problems of large-scale food exchange have been little discussed. Two issues are important: the size of the area from which food could economically be imported and the location of sources of surplus food.

The major limitation for food transport in the Maya lowlands is the cost of porterage. Sanders and Santley (1983) estimate that a porter can transport 40 kg 25 km a day, consuming about 1 kg of grain. Allowing food for a return trip and a day of rest at the point of destination, the equivalent of 16 percent of a load would be consumed in moving food 50 km. A distance of 100 km between points of origin and destination would cost 33 percent of the load. A one-third cost is excessively high in terms of modern peasant economies (Clark and Haswell 1964), but cost is relative to the economic and cultural situation. At a time of food scarcity but abundant labor, such as one might picture for a major Maya site in Late Classic times, food transport might provide a better return than investing more manpower in an already overstrained, local subsistence economy. Sanders and Santley (1983) estimate that in times of maximal economic complexity in Central Mexico, food was imported into the Aztec centers from distances of as much as 150 km at a cost of 50 percent.

To estimate resource areas for one Maya center, I have drawn circles of 50-km and 100-km radii around Tikal. The 50-km circle encompasses only one area likely to have provided food for exchange, the lake district of the central Petén, an area of good farmland with few large sites. On the east, the 50-km circle barely touches the flank lands (Turner 1978) on the western slopes of the Maya Mountains, a zone of extensive terracing and possible food surplus. Elsewhere, the 50-km circle reaches only areas that were densely populated or that were not agriculturally rich.

The 100-km circle around Tikal is much more effective in reaching zones that might have been food reservoirs. To the east, the circle fully includes the terraced areas along the Maya Mountains and reaches areas of raised fields in northern Belize. Perhaps more importantly, the circle reaches several of the Belize rivers at points where they would surely have been navigable, opening an even larger zone by means of water transportation. To the southeast, the 100-km circle covers the Dolores-San Luís zone, an area of rich soils and double cropping with a light prehistoric population (Culbert, Spencer, and Magers 1976). To the southwest, the great bend of the Pasión River falls within the circle, opening a larger zone by means of canoe. This area is important because iconographic evidence suggests Tikal relations with the site of Dos Pilas just south of the Pasión. Chances for major support from the west do not appear very good, both because of poor soils and because the spheres of Tikal and Yaxchilán overlap at this point. There are good conditions for raised fields northwest of Tikal (Turner 1978) but potential competition between Tikal, Yaxchilán, and Calakmul. The area north of Tikal offers little potential for support. The large terrace and raised-field systems lie outside

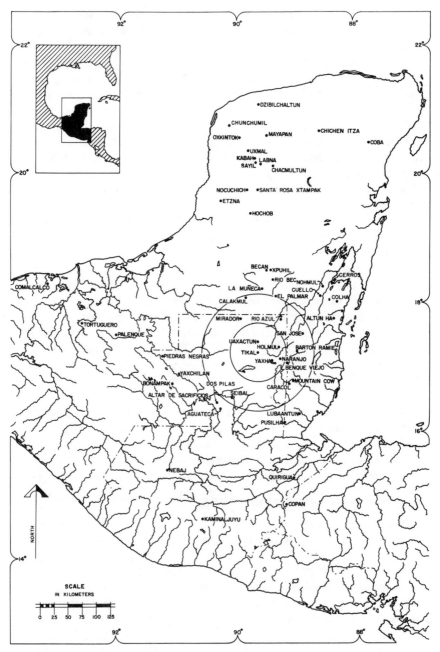

Figure 4.3 Areas within 50 and 100 km of Tikal.

the 100-km circle. More importantly, there were already such dense populations in the area that a food surplus is unlikely.

In the foregoing discussion, I have made allowance for canoe transport only in areas some distance from Tikal where rivers are easily navigable today. In fact, the upper reaches of rivers come much closer to Tikal on the east and northwest (Jones 1979; Siemens 1978). In addition, the raised-field systems in major *bajos* may have included canals large enough for canoe travel and might have interlocked in such a manner that substantial distances could be traversed. I suspect, in fact, that food transport was partly canoe-aided. Even without allowing for water transport, however, the importation of food from the whole area of the likely Tikal realm was a feasible enterprise.

Maximum Support Capacity

The key question in relating subsistence to the Maya collapse is whether Late Classic populations would have strained even the more productive subsistence mix now being proposed. The answer, I fear, is that we can only guess. Too many critical variables still cannot be quantified. We do not know what the sustainable yield of either bush or grass fallow would be. We cannot say how large an infield system would be possible at a Maya site nor how much food it might produce. We have no notion of average losses due to drought, insect infestations, or plant diseases, especially for short-fallow or continuous crop areas. These caveats should be sufficient to indicate that the calculations that follow will not be gems of precision.

The figure most commonly used as the maximum support capacity of long-fallow swidden agriculture in the southern lowlands is 77 persons/ km², a figure derived from Ursula Cowgill's (1962:277) estimated range of 40 to 80 persons/km² based on a study of modern *milperos* around Lake Petén Itzá. This estimate is certainly optimistic [see Reina's (1967) much more conservative one for the same area and Turner's (1974) criticisms]. I will begin with the more conservative estimate that, at best, swidden agriculture might support 60 persons/km² over a large area. Sanders (1973:342), who has excellent control of comparative data, estimates that shortening the fallow cycle to a 1:1 grass fallow might double the yield. If one adds the potential contribution from kitchen gardens, the judicious use of some root crops and *ramón* trees, and some terracing and double cropping, it would seem likely that the average support capacity of an intensified subsistence mix using only upland terrain might be three times that for milpa or roughly 180 persons/km².

The use of raised-field agriculture in the low-lying swampy areas between ridges would add substantially to the support capacity. Since the first report by Siemens and Puleston (1972) of raised-field patterns along the Candelária River in the northwestern lowlands, the evidence for extensive use of this system of agriculture has escalated. That such fields were, in fact, intentionally constructed has now been demonstrated by Turner and Harrison (1981) for the river-connected system at Pulltrouser Swamp in Belize. The first convincing evidence of much larger systems in the *bajos* of the interior came from the work of Peter Harrison (1978) in Quintana Roo. Here, aerial photography shows very clear grid patterns in the vegetation, and excavation indicates that the features are man-made (Gliessman et al. 1983).

Even higher estimates of the extent of raised fields have been made on the basis of radar imagery obtained from high-level flights by NASA (Richard Adams 1980; Adams, Brown, and Culbert 1981). The imagery shows faint canal-like patterns to be almost ubiquitous in Guatemalan *bajos*. Adams estimates that they may cover a total area of 2,475 km². Ground checking is still very preliminary, but the confirmation of the Quintana Roo system makes it more likely that the radar estimates are correct. In summary, then, the Maya certainly used raised-field agriculture and the verified instances are widely enough distributed to indicate that the system was known throughout the southern lowlands. Positive evidence is accumulating rapidly, and it seems quite possible that very extensive areas of *bajos* and riverine land were farmed using raised fields.

In calculating the maximum support capacity in the southern lowlands, then, one must include the possibility that almost all low-lying areas were converted to raised fields. The extent of such areas varies considerably from one part of the lowlands to another: in some areas seasonal swamps fill half the land surface; in others they are almost nonexistent. For the entire southern lowlands, one might guess that 20 percent of the land is usable for raised fields.

The productivity of raised-field systems is difficult to estimate. Denevan's (1982) estimate of a support capacity of 1,900 persons/km², based upon Central Mexican chinampas, and Gómez-Pompa et al.'s (1976) figure of 1,000 persons/km² for modern experimental raised fields on the Mexican Gulf Coast seem very high. Turner and Harrison's estimate (Turner, personal communication) of a support capacity of 666 persons/km² for the Pulltrouser Swamp system is based upon an actual Maya lowland system and will be accepted here. If an average of 20 percent of the land could be used for raised fields supporting 666 persons/km², the total support capacity would be raised by 133 persons/km². Adding this to the 180 persons/km² for upland agriculture gives a figure slightly in excess of 300 persons/km².

These estimates of agricultural support capacity can be combined with the previous estimates of population change over time to permit consideration of the changing population-subsistence balance. Late Preclassic population densities below 50 persons/km² were still within the limit of long-fallow swidden agriculture. In the Early Classic, areas of denser population reached 100 km², a level that would have demanded some intensification but not the full range of techniques. It was not until the general rapid growth of population in the Late Classic that the full panoply of Maya agricultural innovations would have been necessary throughout the area.

A crucial question in relation to the collapse is whether intensified Maya agriculture might have been so productive that subsistence stress was no longer a problem. Some researchers (Jones 1979; Freidel and Scarborough 1982) conclude that intensive agriculture was so productive and stable that outright subsistence failure should be dismissed as a factor in the collapse: "As interest in Maya agriculture grows we strongly suspect that . . . it will become apparent that the Maya were at no time straining the productive capacity of their resources in terms of subsistence" (Freidel and Scarborough 1982:153).

I cannot agree with this conclusion. Although my estimated support capacity of 300 + persons/km² may seem well above the maximum estimated population of 200 persons/km², the calculations made no allowance for either short- or long-term agricultural risks, a topic to which we now turn.

Agricultural Risks

The more intensive systems of agriculture now considered characteristic of the Classic Maya would have been subject to greater environmental hazards than a long-fallow swidden system. Since the systems themselves are largely conjectural, however, the risks to them are even more so. The sources of risk can be discussed, but they cannot be quantitatively estimated.

Some of the techniques proposed would have been sensitive to variations in rainfall. A second annual crop would have been affected by shortfalls in winter rain, the amount of which is, at best, marginal. Raised fields could have been flooded by excessive precipitation. It is suggestive that several of the experimental raised-field systems in Mexico reported by Gómez-Pompa et al. (1982) were destroyed by heavy rains.

Whether or not at risk from climatic variations, most of the new agricultural systems proposed involve short fallow cycles or continuous cropping. Raised fields may even have been farmed year round. Frequent planting of the same crop in moist tropical areas involves greatly increased dangers from insect pests and plant diseases (Janzen 1970; Brewbaker 1979). Although these problems can be partially controlled by careful crop rotation, the potential for losses, sometimes of a catastrophic nature, must have been much higher than for long-fallow swidden.

The foregoing hazards are unpredictable and short term and their effects would pass within a season or two. They might have contributed to stress within the Maya system by causing a reduction of yields as the system intensified. In their more catastrophic manifestations, such as severe inundation of raised fields, or insect infestations or plant diseases of epidemic proportions, they could have served as a trigger mechanism to touch off collapse in an already overstressed system. Brewbaker (1979), for example, has suggested that a chance introduction of maize mosaic virus into the Maya lowlands in the eighth century might have precipitated the collapse.

A more likely cause of subsistence failure might have been longer-term problems of environmental degradation whose effects could not be rapidly reversed. Two potential hazards are grass invasion and fertility loss, both long discussed as possible limiting factors for Maya agricultural productivity. As fallow cycles are shortened, competition between crop plants and weeds, especially grasses, increases. According to Sanders 1973, this competition can be overcome by weeding, although the labor involved would be very intensive. The magnitude of the problem caused by soil fertility is still an unresolved issue. There is agreement on the fact that shortened fallow cycles result in lower levels of plant nutrients and declining crop yields, but little quantitative information is available about the magnitude of the problem. Although the Maya could have used such measures as soil-restorative crops or green mulching (Turner 1974) to counteract fertility loss, there is no means by which to estimate the effectiveness of such measures or whether they were actually practiced.

Of even greater potential severity, as Sanders (1973; Sanders and Murdy 1982) has long maintained, is the problem of erosion. The Maya counteracted erosion with extensive terrace systems in some zones (Turner 1978), but did not do so in other key areas such as the central Petén, where heavy accumulation of sediments in Lakes Yaxhá and Sacnab (Deevey et al. 1979) suggests erosion on a destructive scale.

Finally, the Maya faced the problems associated with large-scale deforestation. If all of the agricultural measures being discussed were in use simultaneously, primary forest would have been nearly eradicated over large areas. Researchers concerned with modern deforestation have generated apocalyptic, if highly debated, predictions about the dangers involved. If some of the suggested consequences, such as soil destruction on a large scale (Goodland and Irwin 1975) or decreased rainfall (Lovejoy and Salati 1983), took place in Classic times, they would have had disastrous consequences for the Maya.

Thus, there seems ample reason to believe that the shift to intensified agriculture imposed increased risks of both a short-term and long-term nature. If some of the more drastic events that have been suggested actually took place in the southern lowlands, environmental degradation could have been a major factor in the collapse. At the very least, those who would argue for the stability of Maya intensive agriculture must deal with the issues involved.

AGRICULTURAL STRESS AND THE MAYA COLLAPSE

Research in the Maya lowlands since 1970 seems to me to indicate more strongly than ever the potential dangers in the population-subsistence balance in the Late Classic period. All available data show that populations in the southern lowlands rose rapidly to a Late Classic peak. Not only was the population unusually dense for a preindustrial civilization (200 persons/km²), but it covered an area too large to allow adjustment through relocation or emigration. At the time of the Maya collapse, population fell dramatically, even allowing for the pockets of population known to have persisted into the Postclassic. The magnitude of the population loss between A.D. 800 and 1000 was such that I do not believe that social malfunction alone can account for it. Consequently, any explanation of the collapse that does not include subsistence failure seems unsatisfactory.

Maya agriculture became increasingly intensive as the population rose, and the scale of the subsistence economy was much larger than previously realized. Both terrace and raised-field systems in some parts of the lowlands covered territories of great size. The support systems of the largest sites probably involved transportation of large volumes of foodstuffs from substantial distances (50 to 100 km). I believe that large-scale intensification occurred late, probably as a response to population growth. In the short term the system was successful enough to maintain dense populations for a century or two before the collapse.

The scale of the subsistence system, however, was such that it may not have had much potential for long-term stability. To continue functioning effectively, it would have needed management to ensure that farmers did not relax their efforts in any of the labor-intensive routines. But there is no evidence, as Willey and Shimkin (1973:391) note, that the Maya made any change in a management system that had developed in a time of considerably less complexity. Manpower demands for agriculture must have been very high, perhaps even high enough to stress the large population pool of the Late Classic. Nevertheless, the lavish use of labor for public construction continued until the point of the collapse. In addition, military competition between sites may have been a drain upon manpower, and there is increasing evidence that the southern low-land Maya may have been under military pressure from the north. Finally, agricultural risks must have been greatly increased by intensification. These would have included both short-term risks such as year-to-year climatic variation, insects, and plant disease, and cumulative long-term effects such as erosion and declining soil fertility. The Late Classic Maya, in other words, had committed themselves to an agricultural system whose long-range results and security were unknown.

Given the tight interconnections of all these factors and the paucity of precise data, one could construct almost any scenario of agricultural failure that suited one's fancy. I prefer to emphasize long-term environmental degradation as a critical factor. It seems quite possible that even had the Maya turned to more adaptive management and labor policies, they might still have faced disaster. The Maya system of intensification may be one in which short-term productive increase may simply be incompatible with long-range ecological stability.

Agricultural intensification in ancient Mesopotamia may have resulted in a similar contradiction between short- and long-term results. In discussing the decline of agricultural production at the end of the Ur III period, Robert Adams (1981) concludes that an abundance of water provided by an expanded canal system led to overirrigation, shortened fallow cycles, and salinization. Using almost the same words that I (quite independently) have chosen to describe the Maya case, he writes, "Thus long-term agricultural decline was in some ways a direct consequence of its earlier apparent 'success' " (1981:152). Although Yoffee (this volume, Chapter 3) sees organizational problems behind collapses of the various Mesopotamian states, the key point for my purposes is that increases in agricultural intensification in the Mesopotamian alluvial plain may, beyond a certain point, be inherently unstable. So, I maintain, was Maya agricultural intensification.

Lest I be accused of believing that all collapses are ecologically derived, I should note that the situation at Teotihuacan seems quite different. There (Millon, this volume) population stabilized at a level well below the potential support capacity of the Basin of Mexico and remained stable for several centuries before collapse occurred from causes that seem to have been largely social. In fact, most of the other cases of collapse discussed in this volume seem to have been the result more of social than of ecological instability.

This leads me, finally, to a conclusion that may be of some utility in the case of other collapses. Overextension—*overshoot* in systems terminology—often afflicts complex systems during periods of expansion. The success that occurs early in a period of expansion may lead to the construction of systems that are dependent upon continual growth or, put another way, upon the continual infusion of new capital. In the Maya case, the overextension was ecological and consisted of a population system dependent upon maximal results from a subsistence system that made no allowance for long-term hazards. More often, however, it seems to me that overextension tends to be political and administrative. Conquest empires that are expanding rapidly build bureaucratic structures that can live only off the capital provided by fresh conquests. When expansion reaches the point at which it can no longer produce new wealth, the administrative structures begin to feed off internal resources, a process that cannot long continue without inducing collapse.

NOTE

1. The chronological scheme used by Mayanists is a simple division into Preclassic (or Formative), Classic, and Postclassic periods. The period designations were originally intended to have cultural meaning, but the meaning has long since slipped so far from reality that the terms are no more than chronological indicators. Each of the periods is further subdivided as indicated in the figure accompanying the text. I have used detailed subdivisions only for the Late Classic, a period of great importance for the topic of the collapse. The Terminal Classic is the time of the collapse itself. In the early literature this period was treated as the final part of the Late Classic, but modern practice has been to designate it with a separate label.

The Last Years of Teotihuacan Dominance

René Millon

Teotihuacan is located in the Valley of Teotihuacan, a subvalley of the Valley of Mexico, twenty-five miles northeast of Mexico City, in the central Mexican highlands, a semiarid region of temperate climate at an altitude of over seven thousand feet (2275 meters). At its height in the middle centuries of the first millennium A.D. it was a city without equal in its world (Figs. 5.1–5.3). No contemporary city was at once so large, so populous, so densely settled, and so important to so many beyond its boundaries. It was a city that must have held a great attraction for outsiders—for traders and for potential buyers of their wares and the wares of the city's multitude of craftsmen; for pilgrims and the pious drawn to the city's shrines, monuments, and rituals and to the city as the seat of a religion that transcended the city's boundaries; for persons ranging from foreign dignitaries and hangers-on to the interested and the curious responding to the city as power center and as metropolitan cultural center.

Teotihuacan's estimated population of one hundred twenty-five thousand circa A.D. 500–600 (R. Millon 1970) is not high when compared with that of nonindustrialized cities in the Old World. Nevertheless, in the seventh century A.D. only five Old World cities are thought to have been more populous (Chandler and Fox 1974:368). But population is only one dimension of Teotihuacan's complexity as an urban center. It was in fact a remarkable city in many ways. Its great size was in part the product of an initial depopulation of most of the Valley of Mexico

Figure 5.1   The center of ancient Teotihuacan. Pyramid of the Moon, foreground; Pyramid of the Sun, left. In middle distance, Ciudadela, left, and Great Compound, right. At upper right, the irrigated plain of the lower Teotihuacan Valley.

and of the concentration of this population in Teotihuacan (Sanders 1981a:176–78; R. Millon 1981:221–22). This concentration was maintained throughout the rest of the city's history as a major center in what surely must have been deliberate policy. What resettlement subsequently occurred was in parts of the valley where population had not been concentrated previously. Most of the city's population came from the households of people who cultivated lands within walking distance of the city in the nearby irrigated floodplain of the Valley of Teotihuacan and beyond. But since the Valley of Teotihuacan is in the northeastern part of the Valley of Mexico (Fig. 5.3), this meant that the policy of population concentration left major parts of the Valley of Mexico, especially in the south and west, underutilized during the city's ascendancy, compared to the periods both before and after Teotihuacan was dominant (Sanders, Parsons, and Santley 1979:128). The political advantage of keeping most of the Valley of Mexico's population under direct control in the city appeared to have outweighed the economic advantage of making better use of the Valley's agricultural potential.

Members of most of Teotihuacan's households seem to have engaged

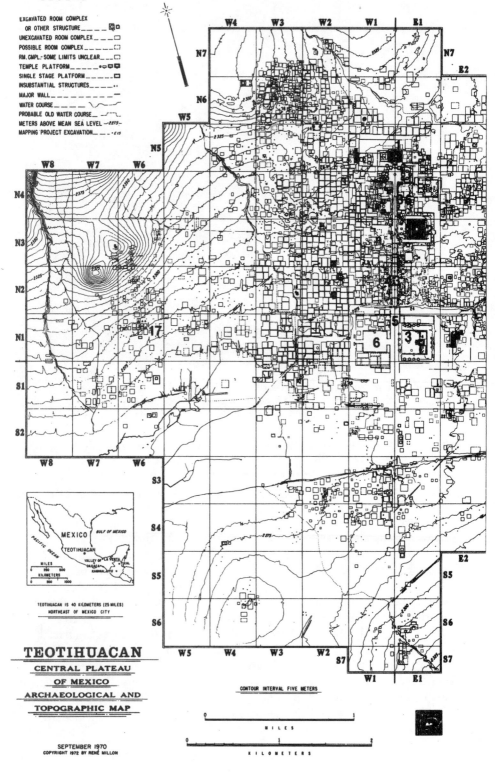

LEGEND

EXCAVATED ROOM COMPLEX
OR OTHER STRUCTURE ____

UNEXCAVATED ROOM COMPLEX ____

POSSIBLE ROOM COMPLEX ____

RM. CMPL.- SOME LIMITS UNCLEAR ____

TEMPLE PLATFORM ____

SINGLE STAGE PLATFORM ____

INSUBSTANTIAL STRUCTURES ____

MAJOR WALL ____

WATER COURSE ____

PROBABLE OLD WATER COURSE ____

METERS ABOVE MEAN SEA LEVEL ____ 2875 ____

MAPPING PROJECT EXCAVATION ____ E15

MEXICO

GULF OF MEXICO

PACIFIC OCEAN

TEOTIHUACAN

VALLEY OF
OAXACA
KAMINALJUYU

LA VENTA / TIKAL

MILES
0   250   500
KILOMETERS
0   1000

TEOTIHUACAN IS 40 KILOMETERS (25 MILES)
NORTHEAST OF MEXICO CITY

TEOTIHUACAN

CENTRAL PLATEAU

OF MEXICO

ARCHAEOLOGICAL AND

TOPOGRAPHIC MAP

SEPTEMBER 1970
COPYRIGHT 1972 BY RENÉ MILLON

CONTOUR INTERVAL FIVE METERS

MILES
0   1

KILOMETERS
0   1   2

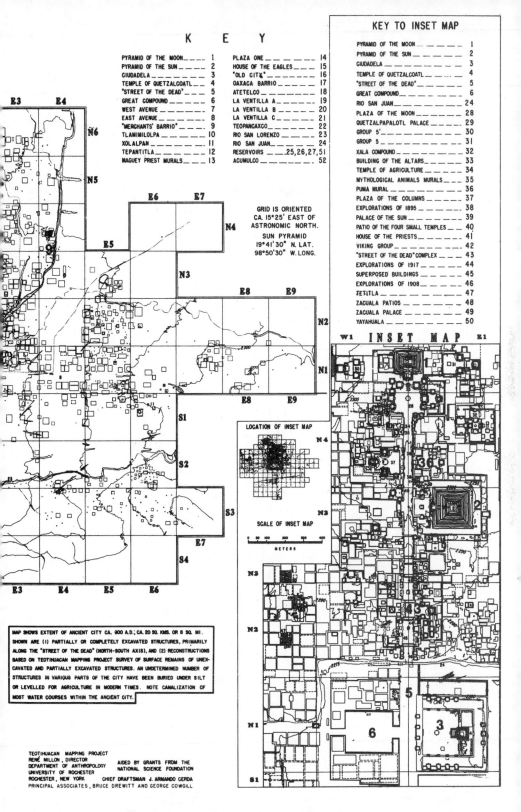

Figure 5.2 Map of ancient Teotihuacan. Most buildings shown are unexcavated apartment compounds.

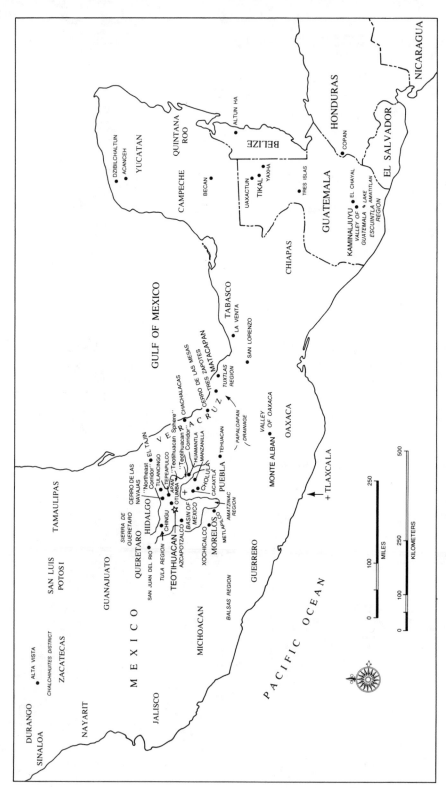

Figure 5.3 Map of ancient Mesoamerica showing locations of places referred to in the text.

in agricultural activities, but a significant fraction of the population appears to have lived in households where craft activities were practiced.[1] Obsidian was the major material used for cutting and piercing in craft and domestic activities and in weapons. A major source deposit of gray obsidian lies in the Valley of Teotihuacan; the best source in central Mexico for making prismatic blades is in a green obsidian found in deposits a short distance north of the Valley of Teotihuacan.

Many obsidian workshops have been found in the city (Spence 1967, 1981; but see also the critical analysis by Clark 1986). The location of some of them suggests an interest on the part of the state in the procurement, production, and exchange of obsidian and obsidian implements. From the fragmentary evidence we have, this interest seems to have fallen short of direct control of production and exchange (Spence 1981), although some temple workshops existed.

Pottery workshops also appear to have been numerous. Evidence also exists for lapidary workshops (where both shell and fine stone, such as jade and serpentine, were worked), for the manufacture of mold-made censer ornaments, for the making of both hand-made and mold-made ceramic figurines, and for the working of ground stone and chipped stone implements. Other craft activities, for which archaeological evidence is fragmentary, ambiguous, or incomplete, include carpentry and cabinet making, paper making, feather working, and the weaving of cloth and mats. The city's several thousand permanent structures, most of them of large size, attest to the activities of craftworkers involved in construction—in stone cutting; woodworking; the making of a distinctive concrete used to cover walls, floors, and ceilings; and the preparation and application of lime plaster to most concrete surfaces. The walls of some structures bear paintings with predominantly religious themes, frequently didactic in nature. Artists worked in workshops like other craftworkers. Significant advances have been made in the study of Teotihuacan iconography (for example, Barthel 1982; Berlo 1983a, 1984; Caso 1936–39, 1958–59, 1967; Kubler 1967; Langley 1983, 1986; C. Millon 1973; Pasztory 1973, 1974, 1976a, 1976b, 1978; Séjourné 1966; von Winning 1948, 1961, 1968, 1977, 1979a, 1979b, 1979c, 1984; and many others); much still is poorly understood.

The standard residential architecture in Teotihuacan is a walled compound, varying greatly in size, within which access ways lead to open patios around which rooms, often with porches, are disposed. In the score or so of such compounds excavated, it is usually possible to group most rooms and patios into definable units. For this reason I have called these structures apartment compounds. There are some two thousand in the ancient city, and they housed almost the entire population for hundreds of years. Except for the two palaces with similar ground plans in the political center, each excavated apartment compound has its own distinctive plan. That is, excavated compounds are not built to a uniform plan and do not have the appearance of state-directed construction.

The patios were connected in a system of underfloor drains built before floors and walls were constructed. This had the effect of requiring the construction or reconstruction of most, if not all, of an apartment compound in a single building operation, save for minor changes.[2] Unlike compounds in nonindustrialized cities in other parts of the world, the Teotihuacan apartment compounds so far known were not built up slowly through accretion to meet the changing needs of the people living in them. They were largely built and rebuilt all at once; and since they were occupied continuously for hundreds of years, and sometimes not rebuilt for a century, were relatively inflexible residential units, not well suited to meet the changing needs of those living in them. Excavated floor plans range from highly centralized to highly decentralized, from what appears to be well ordered to seemingly disordered.

The social composition of the apartment compound population is not known, of course, but inferences may be made from several lines of evidence. One interpretation hypothesizes that apartment compounds tended to be occupied by groups of biologically related males (Spence 1974); another, that they were occupied by a core of cognatically related kin with a bias toward males (R. Millon 1981:208–9).

The city also seems to have been divided into neighborhoods, or barrios. In some cases these coincide with clusters of craftworkers (for example, obsidian workers, potters, lapidaries). We found at least one barrio of foreigners in the western part of the city occupied by people with a cultural tradition from the Valley of Oaxaca in the southern highlands (Fig. 5.2, no. 17, Oaxaca barrio; Fig. 5.3) (R. Millon 1973:41–42). On the eastern side of the city there is another barrio where foreigners who may have been merchants from Veracruz lived (Fig. 5.2, no. 9, "merchants' barrio"). A barrio where people of relatively high rank in the hierarchy may have lived was found in 1983. It may have been where high-ranking military officers lived. Located in the southwestern corner of square N5E2 on the Teotihuacan map (Fig. 5.2), it has been provisionally designated the "barrio of the looted murals" because of the many fine mural paintings from two of its structures that have found their way into private collections and museums in the United States and Europe (R. Millon 1983). Other barrios have been isolated because they are spatially distinct from their surroundings or because of the distinctiveness of surface collections from them. It seems probable that the barrio and the apartment compound served as nodes in the administrative structure of the city, perhaps through barrio leaders and compound heads. What

ʼwe know of the hierarchy of settlements in the Valley of Mexico and surrounding regions that formed the nucleus of the Teotihuacan domain suggests their subordination to the metropolis through an administrative structure centered in the city.

The religious and the political dimensions of Teotihuacan's urban society are what strike scholars and others who visit the site. The scale of the monumental architecture, extending for a mile and a half (2.5 km) on the northern half of the city's principal avenue, the "Street of the Dead"[3] may be surpassed in some, but not many, nonindustrialized centers in the Old World. It is unequaled in the aboriginal New World. Much of this public architecture is religious architecture. This and other evidence leaves no doubt that the political realm was sacralized and that the boundaries of the political and the sacred were conceived and meant to be perceived as coinciding from the start. Through most of its history as a major urban center, the political and the religious appear to have remained *formally* undifferentiated at the highest levels, despite a de facto process of secularization that surely began relatively early.

The military arm of the state must have developed into a powerful force during the first century B.C. prior to the population concentration that transformed Teotihuacan into a metropolis at the beginning of the first century A.D. Dramatic evidence of the importance of the military in the third century A.D. was uncovered by a Mexican government archaeologist in 1983 and 1984 when a great burial pit containing eighteen sacrificed males, most with their hands tied behind them, and two associated burials in other pits, were uncovered by Saburo Sugiyama (n.d.) on the south side of the Temple of Quetzalcoatl in the Ciudadela, the city's religious and political center (Figs. 5.1; 5.2, no. 3). Most of the sacrificed males in the burial pit (15 of 18) were accompanied by obsidian projectile points and many other objects of shell, bone, and stone, some of which also had military associations. In 1986 a burial pit containing eighteen other sacrifices (seventeen male, one possibly female) corresponding to the pit on the south side of the Temple of Quetzalcoatl was uncovered on its north side by Mexican government archaeologist Enrique Martínez (Sugiyama n.d.; Mercado 1987). Here also hands of sacrificed individuals are reported to have been tied, and offerings featured obsidian projectile points.

This incontrovertible evidence of the importance of the role of the military in Teotihuacan early in its history, before its impact had been felt in most of Mesoamerica, is not reflected in the art of the time in the city. Teotihuacan-related armed figures appear in the art of centers in the southern Maya lowlands in the latter part of the fourth century A.D. but have not been found at Teotihuacan itself until the fifth century.[4]

Moreover, military figures are not common in Teotihuacan art until the century preceding its abrupt end as a major urban center in the eighth century. Although this surely does not accurately mirror the relative importance of the military in the state during this span of eight hundred years, it may more accurately reflect the official and traditional ideological view of a hierarchy predominantly perceived in religious terms.

Teotihuacan was above all a religious center without equal in its time. We see this manifested in its great pyramids, in the multiplicity of its temples, in the monumentality of its principal avenue that overwhelms viewers today and that anciently must have induced religious awe in believers. Teotihuacan has the unmistakable aura of a sacred city. On or adjoining its main avenue more than a hundred temples and shrines with their various grades of priests and attendants must have served believers from both within the city and beyond its boundaries. Like sacred cities elsewhere it was likely regarded as the center of the cosmos and, it can be argued, the place where time began (R. Millon 1981:230). If the latter were the case, whether or not celebrated in ritual, the very existence of Teotihuacan would have been a perpetual commemoration of the coming into existence of the present cycle of time. It must also have been the setting for ritual celebrations in accordance with both the solar calendar and the 260-day Mesoamerican ritual calendar. It also may have been the place to which foreign rulers came for investiture after acceding to office (Heyden 1975). These are some of the reasons why we must not lose sight of the religious importance of Teotihuacan in considering the economic impact it may have had or the political influence its state may have exerted.

The antecedents of Teotihuacan are the early settlements in the Teotihuacan Valley in the first millennium B.C. and the earliest settlements on the site of the later city in the last few hundred years before Christ. During the last century and a half before Christ, Teotihuacan grew to be a settlement of many square kilometers. It was then that the social, economic, political, and ideological changes occurred that, around the time of Christ, provided the basis for the transformation of Teotihuacan into a metropolis, with an explosive growth achieved by concentrating most of the population of the Basin of Mexico within its boundaries. Early urban Teotihuacan enjoyed many advantages. But what we know of the religion of its people prior to this population concentration does not prepare us for the mammoth undertaking represented by the building of the Pyramid of the Sun at the beginning of the next phase (Tzacualli) (A.D. 1–150) (Fig. 5.4).

On the center line of the Sun Pyramid on its west side is the entrance to a cave, a natural formation more than one hundred meters long, running in a generally easterly direction from its entrance. During the

VALLEY OF TEOTIHUACAN CHRONOLOGY
Table of Concordances

Horizon / Period	Date	Phase Names [1]		Phase Numbers [2]	Period
LATE HORIZON	A.D. 1500	Teacalco		Aztec IV	
	1400	Chimalpa		Aztec III	POST-
	1300				
	1200	Zocango		Aztec II	CLASSIC
SECOND INTER-MEDIATE PERIOD	1100	Mazapan		Mazapa	
	1000				PERIOD
	900	Xometla		Coyotlatelco	
	800	Oxtoticpac		Proto-Coyotlatelco	900 A.D.
	700	METEPEC		Teotihuacan IV	CLASSIC
	600	XOLALPAN	Late	Teotihuacan IIIA	
MIDDLE HORIZON	500		Early	Teotihuacan III	
	400				PERIOD
	300	TLAMIMILOLPA	Late	Teotihuacan IIA-III	
			Early	Teotihuacan IIA	300 A.D.
	200	MICCAOTLI		Teotihuacan II	TERMINAL
	100	TZACUALLI	Late	Teotihuacan IA	PRE-CLASSIC
	A.D. / B.C.		Early	Teotihuacan I	
	100	PATLACHIQUE	Chimalhuacan *		PERIOD
				Proto-Teotihuacan I	
FIRST INTER-MEDIATE PERIOD	200	Terminal Cuanalan; Tezoyuca	Cuicuilco *		LATE
	300	Late Cuanalan	Ticoman III *		PRE-CLASSIC
	400	Middle Cuanalan	Ticoman II *		PERIOD
	500	Early Cuanalan	Ticoman I *		
	600	Chiconauhtla	Middle		MIDDLE PRE-CLASSIC
	700		Zacatenco *		PERIOD
	B.C. 800				

Vertical label (left of Phase Names): TEOTIHUACAN

[1] Phase names used by personnel of Teotihuacan Mapping Project (Millon and others) and by personnel of Valley of Teotihuacan Project (Sanders and others).

[2] Phase numbers used by personnel of the Proyecto Teotihuacan, of the Instituto Nacional de Antropologia e Historia (see Acosta 1964: 58-59).

* Pre-classic phases elsewhere in the Valley of Mexico.

NOTE: The absolute chronology shown is that used by the Teotihuacan Mapping Project. Terminology for the Teotihuacan phases is based on the Armillas classification (1950) with modifications.

TEOTIHUACAN MAPPING PROJECT
UNIVERSITY OF ROCHESTER

J. A. Cerda.

RENÉ MILLON
9/64
REVISED 5/79

Figure 5.4 Chronological chart for the Teotihuacan Valley. The absolute dates for Teotihuacan shown at left represent the author's view on how best to reconcile conflicting radiocarbon dates and other evidence bearing on Teotihuacan chronology.

Tzacualli phase this cave was the locus of many rituals (R. Millon 1981:234–35). The placement of the axis of the Sun Pyramid directly over the entrance to the cave makes it evident that the Sun Pyramid is where it is because of the cave. Why should this have been? There are many beliefs associated with caves in Mesoamerica, including myths associating caves with origins—of people, gods, and heavenly bodies (Heyden 1975; Taube 1986). The cave also may be associated with Aztec beliefs held at the time of the Spanish Conquest relating Teotihuacan to the beginning of the present cycle of time. Teotihuacan's distinctive east-of-north orientation has been related to "the day that time began" in the present cycle of time (Malmstrom 1978). Was Teotihuacan oriented to the *day* that time began because it was believed that Teotihuacan was *where* time began? Was the cave the focus of origin myths concerning the birth of the sun and moon in the present cycle of time? Or to the origin of humankind? Or to both?

Are beliefs such as these, or related beliefs placing Teotihuacan in the center of the cosmos (M. Coe 1981:168), among the motivations that led to the decision of Teotihuacan's leaders to build the Pyramid of the Sun? Was the project to build the pyramid conceived to commemorate events of cosmic significance? Did the decision to concentrate most of the population of the Basin of Mexico in Teotihuacan coincide with the decision to build the pyramid? Was the project to build the pyramid self-consciously used by Teotihuacan's leaders to mobilize the population to labor in an enterprise under their direction that would have been seen as desirable and worthwhile? Was the project to build the Pyramid in effect a consolidation of state power, whether or not it may have been so conceived or perceived at the outset of the process? Even though they cannot be explored further, these are some of the questions raised by evidence bearing on the rise of the city that deserve mention here.

Beginning in the third century A.D., permanent residential structures in stone and concrete, surfaced with lime plaster, began to be built throughout the city. These often large, one-storey, walled apartment compounds became the standard Teotihuacan residential architecture for the remainder of the city's history. These are the structures shown on the Teotihuacan map (Fig. 5.2). The map shows that the city was divided into quadrants and clearly demonstrates that the city was planned. The "Street of the Dead" is its north-south axis; East and West avenues form its east-west axis. At the center of the Teotihuacanos' *axis mundi* was the immense Ciudadela compound, which housed many temples, including the spectacularly carved Temple of Quetzalcoatl, and twin palaces on the north and south of it (Fig. 5.2, inset). This was the city's political center, a political center in a sacred setting that must have been highly charged with meaning for the Teotihuacanos. It has been suggested that the Temple of Quetzalcoatl carvings may have celebrated "the creation of the universe from a watery void through a series of dual oppositions" (M. Coe 1981:168). If such were the case, it need imply no contradiction with beliefs relating to the cave and the Sun Pyramid. The two could have been viewed as complementary dimensions of the same process. The cave as sacred place and the Sun Pyramid above it probably had temporal priority over the Ciudadela—certainly the reverse was not the case—so that when the city took on its quadripartite form, with the Ciudadela as its center, the legendary creation account, perhaps the early focus of a cult associated with an older shrine on the site, may have been chosen deliberately for emphasis, raised to hitherto unprecedented prominence, and embodied in the Temple of Quetzalcoatl. The city's rulers were occupying the Ciudadela palaces by the third century A.D. Whether this represents a shift in residence by existing rulers from the residential area on the west side of the Sun Pyramid or the passage of power from an older line of rulers to a newer one is one of the issues involved in the interpretation of this evidence (for one interpretation, see G. Cowgill 1983b).

Teotihuacan was the most important prehispanic urban center in central Mexico before the rise to dominance of Tula and Tenochtitlan, the later capital cities of the Toltecs and Aztecs, respectively. The fall of the Teotihuacan state from its position of preeminence probably took place in the eighth century A.D., around A.D. 750. When the city was at its height, circa A.D. 350–600, a widespread network of ties beyond the core area of the Teotihuacan state in central Mexico (Fig. 5.3) directly or indirectly linked the city to many parts of the Maya area, to Monte Albán in the Valley of Oaxaca, to many centers in coastal Veracruz, and to parts of Guerrero and northern and western Mexico, to name those areas about which we know most. What happened to those ties? How and why did some of them weaken or break down? What happened in the core area?

The core area of Teotihuacan appears not to have been great (Fig. 5.3) (R. Millon 1981:228), probably no more than twenty-five thousand square kilometers, or ten thousand square miles (the Basin of Mexico and adjacent areas). The total population of this core area probably did not exceed five hundred thousand and may have been closer to three hundred thousand. It was somewhat larger than El Salvador or Belize or the state of Massachusetts, somewhat smaller than Belgium. Its "inner hinterland" (Hirth 1978) was the Basin of Mexico; its "outer hinterland" (Hirth 1978) included the Tula[5] region in the northwest (Cobean 1978; Cobean et al. 1981; Diaz 1980, 1981; Crespo and Mastache 1981; Mastache and Crespo 1974); parts of southern Hidalgo north of Teotihuacan, including the valuable green obsidian deposits of Cerro de las Navajas (Fig. 5.3); southeastern Hidalgo and northern Tlaxcala to the northeast and east (García Cook 1981; Matos et al. 1981); the Río Amatzinac region in the eastern half of Morelos (Hirth 1974, 1976, 1978; Angulo and Hirth 1981) south of the Basin of Mexico; and to the west, parts of the Valley of Toluca east of the Río Lerma (but apparently not Teotenango, which evidently was not an important center during Teotihuacan's dominance (Piña Chan 1972; Vargas Pacheco 1980; Sugiura 1981).

At the southeastern end of the area in northern Tlaxcala that García Cook (1981; García Cook and Trejo 1977) names the "Teotihuacan Sphere," he distinguishes a "Teotihuacan Corridor" that extends to the southeast (Fig. 5.3), passing through and dividing the Tenanyecac region, an area of distinctive culture.[6] At Huamantla, in southeastern Tlaxcala, the corridor split, one branch turning east toward Veracruz, the other turning south into southern Puebla, probably toward Tehuacán (García Cook 1981:Fig. 8–27). Another such "corridor" appears to have extended to the northeast (Fig. 5.3), from the eastern end of the Valley of Teotihuacan to Tepeapulco and Tulancingo in Hidalgo (García Cook and Trejo 1977; Litvak 1978). The latter "corridor" follows the most direct route to El Tajín, in north-central Veracruz on the Gulf Coast, and may have been the principal access route to that great center, with which Teotihuacan had close links.

TEOTIHUACAN'S TIES BEYOND CENTRAL MEXICO

For various reasons the ties of Teotihuacan with peoples outside its core area are not easy to define. Beyond the core area of the Teotihuacan state there is no agreement on the nature of the ties that linked the city at its height to so many other parts of Middle America. This makes it that much harder to examine what had happened to those ties by the time of Teotihuacan's last years.

When objects from Teotihuacan, disseminated by Teotihuacan, or otherwise related to Teotihuacan are found in centers beyond its domain, contexts that may imply high-level political and/or ritual exchange are not consistently distinguished (sometimes because of ambiguity in the evidence) from those that may imply economic interchange in marketplace or similar contexts. When this is coupled with ambiguities concerning the quantitative importance of Teotihuacan-related objects found in foreign contexts, it makes it very difficult to evaluate the economic importance of long-distance exchange (Ball 1983; Drennan 1984).

Because of such questions, in this section I attempt to consider some of the problems in interpreting evidence bearing on the relations of Teotihuacanos with peoples beyond their central Mexican domain, as an aid in understanding what had happened to that domain by the time of the final years of Teotihuacan dominance. Largely because no historical texts from Teotihuacan have come down to us, the most detailed and specific information on the relations of Teotihuacan with foreign centers comes from discoveries in those centers. I begin with the case for which there is the most evidence—the ties linking Teotihuacan to the great Maya city of Tikal—and follow this with a consideration of the related problems of the ties with centers in the Guatemalan highlands and the Pacific coastal regions to the south. Thereafter what I have tried to do, not entirely consistently, is move closer to Teotihuacan with each successive region examined, and in the process to consider most of the regions surrounding Teotihuacan's central Mexican domain. Partly because of the changing nature of the evidence as we move, in general, to the north and west, this procedure leads to an interplay between the evidence from a region and Teotihuacan itself, in which Teotihuacan plays an ever-increasing part. This has the effect of gradually setting the scene for consideration of what happened to the city proper in its final years.

Tikal and the Southern Maya Lowlands

Teotihuacan's ties with Tikal (Fig. 5.3), the largest and most important lowland Maya capital and perhaps the gateway to many others, probably began late in the fourth century. Ties with nearby Uaxactún appear to begin at roughly the same time (Coggins 1975), followed by ties with other Petén centers. Teotihuacan's relationship with Kaminaljuyú in the Guatemalan highlands probably began this early or earlier, as suggested by lowland-highland cross-ties (Kidder, Jennings, and Shook 1946; Coggins 1975), but the Kaminaljuyú chronology is insufficiently precise on this point (Sanders and Michels 1977; Cheek 1977a). Coggins (1975, 1979) suggests that the close ties with Teotihuacan manifest at Tikal from A.D. 378 to 457[7] were mediated through Kaminaljuyú. This depends, of course, on a prior Teotihuacan "presence" at Kaminaljuyú, suggesting that the period of most intense contact between Teotihuacanos and Kaminaljuyú occurred about one hundred years earlier than Cheek's (1977a: 443) chronology proposes, that is, from A.D. 400–450 rather than A.D. 500–550.

Tikal's relationship with Teotihuacan, however it may have been mediated, appears to have been relatively intense. In A.D. 378 a man known to epigraphers by the nickname "Curl Nose" became the ruler of Tikal (Jones and Satterthwaite 1982:13–16, 42–43, 64–74, 124–28; Mathews 1985:54, n. 6). Since the texts relating to Curl Nose and others associated with him in the fourth and fifth centuries A.D. are "highly ambiguous" (Mathews 1985:54, n. 7), they are subject to differing interpretations. In one influential interpretation, Coggins (1975, 1979) argued that although Curl Nose may have had kinship ties with the Tikal ruling family, he was clearly an outsider, probably from Kaminaljuyú but with strong links to Teotihuacan. Even though he was an outsider, he does not appear to have come as a conqueror, nor was he regarded as a usurper, Coggins argued. Curl Nose was succeeded by Stormy Sky, who was probably his son (Jones and Satterthwaite 1982:68). One of the monuments depicting the latter (Stela 31) bears a long text. How this text is to be interpreted is at issue. Curl Nose is mentioned more often than any other individual in the text (six times)(Jones and Satterthwaite 1982:64–74). Also occurring several times in the text is a glyph that appears only in this text, and in the interpretation put forward by Coggins (1975, 1979), it refers to people from Teotihuacan. Flanking Stormy Sky on the sides of the stela are two helmeted figures in Teotihuacan-style dress carrying spear throwers and shields such as those carried by Teotihuacan soldiers. On one of these shields is the head of a personage wearing the tassel headdress worn by the Teotihuacan Storm God (C. Millon 1973; Pasztory 1974). The subject of another stela (Stela 32), from which only the head and part of the upper torso remain, is the same personage with the same tassel headdress.

In foreign contexts the tassel headdress appears to be a symbol of the Teotihuacan polity, and it functions, in effect, as an emblem glyph. When worn by human figures, it signifies the presence of Teotihuacanos acting in an official capacity for the state (C. Millon 1973). The headdress and its contexts at Tikal may imply both a political and a religious connection with Teotihuacan. The economic connection between the two centers, which would have had a great potential, still is being explored. Santley (1983:93, 99–103) stresses the potential of Tikal as a major distribution point for obsidian in the southern Maya lowlands, with Teotihuacanos in Kaminaljuyú assumed to be in control of the distribution of the products of the gray obsidian deposits at nearby El Chayal (Santley 1983; Moholy-Nagy 1975; Moholy-Nagy, Asaro, and Stross 1984:105–11; but see also Stross el al. 1983:333–35).

The tombs of the two Teotihuacan-related rulers appear to have been identified (Coggins 1975:146ff., 187ff.; 1979; Jones and Satterthwaite 1982:68). Their offerings include objects with artistic, ceramic, and other links to Teotihuacan; they are Teotihuacan in style but were not made there.

There are ten other fourth- and fifth-century burials at Tikal that are not in the Tikal tradition (Problematic Deposits, or PDs). These burials manifest customs and practices found at Teotihuacan as well as some practices characteristic of Tikal burials (Moholy-Nagy 1987).[8] They are found only in two parts of Tikal: in the North Acropolis, Tikal's main temple and civic center at the time and the locus of the tombs of Stormy Sky and Curl Nose; and "in a loose cluster up to a kilometer west and south" of the North Acropolis (Moholy-Nagy 1987). Who were these people? Moholy-Nagy (1987) hypothesizes that they were high-status Teotihuacanos residing in Tikal in a relatively restricted area that also included local Tikal residents—that is, they did not live in a barrio "with well defined borders" like the Oaxaca barrio and the "merchants' barrio" at Teotihuacan. The area south and west of the North Acropolis where some of these burials were found is the part of Tikal where Teotihuacan-related *tablero-talud* temples have been found in both public and domestic contexts (LaPorte 1985; Moholy-Nagy 1987). At least one of the Teotihuacan-related persons who resided at Tikal must have been of very high status and politically important, for he was buried on the center line of the North Acropolis (PD22). He was accompanied by Stela 32, bearing the carved figure with the tassel headdress that may have been his portrait (Moholy-Nagy 1987; Schele 1986).

Coggins's interpretations of the artistic and textual evidence linking Teotihuacan and Tikal are disputed by Mathews (1985) and Schele (1986). Mathews argues that the early stelae and inscriptions relating to Curl Nose and Stormy Sky concern relations between Tikal and Uaxactún, an important Maya center a short distance northwest of Tikal that Mathews believes was dominated by Tikal through a large part of its history. He makes no mention of Teotihuacan in his discussion. Mathews's analysis was restricted to the monuments and inscriptions of the Maya Early Classic period (defined as extending from A.D. 238 to 593) and did not encompass any of the other evidence considered by Coggins.

Schele (1986) interprets the Teotihuacan dress, weapons, and symbolism in the fourth and fifth century A.D. Maya monuments at Tikal, Uaxactún, and elsewhere as representing the adoption by the Maya of Teotihuacan rituals involving war and sacrifice (including both self-sacrifice and captive sacrifice), which she calls the "Tlaloc Complex." These rituals were adopted by the Maya because they were consonant with ritual practices and beliefs with a long history in the Maya area, Schele argues. She sees the first appearance of this complex on Stela 5 at Uaxactún, which Mathews (1985) interprets as commemorating the domination of Uaxactún by Tikal. Schele observes that in subsequent iconography in Maya centers this Teotihuacan ritual complex was associated with conquest, of Maya by Maya.

In Schele's analysis, only one of the figures on Maya monuments bearing Teotihuacan symbolism, dress, or arms is a foreigner (the personage represented on Stela 32 interred on the center line of the North Acropolis in PD22, commented on above). All the others are said to represent Mayans—Mayans who bore or displayed Teotihuacan elements because of what these elements symbolized. We shall return to Schele's interpretation at the conclusion of this section.

Five of the ten Teotihuacan-related Problematic Deposit burials included in their offerings objects of green obsidian from Cerro de las Navajas, located immediately to the north of the Basin of Mexico and controlled by Teotihuacan (Moholy-Nagy 1987).

Of the 56,000+ pieces of obsidian recovered in excavations at Tikal, an estimated 98 percent were associated with prismatic blade production (Moholy-Nagy, Asaro, and Stross 1984:105–7). Most of this obsidian was found in associations dating from the A.D. 250–850 period and is thought to have been worked at Tikal from polyhedral cores that, from A.D. 250 to 700, appear to have been imported predominantly from El Chayal. The El Chayal gray obsidian deposits may have come under Teotihuacan control in the fourth century.

Approximately 1 percent of the obsidian found at Tikal (556 pieces) is green obsidian from the Cerro de las Navajas quarries near Teotihuacan (Moholy-Nagy, Asaro, and Stross 1984:Table 1). Some, perhaps most, of this obsidian was worked at Tikal to produce blades from imported cores during the A.D. 250–600 period. Some blades were found in burial offerings; most (450) were found in the course of general excavations "in contexts that indicate utilitarian function" (Moholy-Nagy, Asaro, and Stross 1984:116).

Most of the rest of the green obsidian was in the form of points and knives (77) of central Mexican types thought to have been made at Teotihuacan. These, too, were recovered for the most part in "general excavations." Points and knives of gray obsidian are more numerous than green (183) and also were found for the most part in "general excavations." Although predominantly of the same central Mexican types, they might have been expected to be copies that were locally made from El Chayal obsidian. Tests of 14 of these artifacts revealed instead that half of them had come from the gray obsidian deposits near Otumba in the Valley of Teotihuacan (Moholy-Nagy, Asaro, and Stross 1984:111–15). Though the sample is small, it suggests that 50 percent or more of the points and knives of gray obsidian at Tikal also may have come from Teotihuacan.

It is not surprising that the overwhelming majority of the obsidian used at Tikal was in the form of prismatic blades made from the gray obsidian of El Chayal, a relatively nearby source. What is interesting is that objects of obsidian most commonly found in ceremonial contexts (eccentric and incised forms) also were made of obsidian from El Chayal, as by-products in the basic process of prismatic blade production. In contrast, the rare obsidian from far-off Teotihuacan (ca. 1 percent of the total), whether in the form of cores or finished artifacts of the exotic green variety or in the form of finished artifacts of the more familiar gray, is found for the most part not in ceremonial but in utilitarian contexts

(Moholy-Nagy, Asaro, and Stross 1984:115–16). This suggests that if the central Mexican obsidian reached Tikal not primarily through marketplace exchange but rather, because of its rarity, largely through ceremonial gift exchange among persons of high status (Spence n.d.), it was not so highly prized as to be conserved primarily for use in offerings, but instead tended to be used for utilitarian purposes by the original recipients or by others who may have received it from them.

Although the highest frequency of central Mexican obsidian falls in the period from A.D. 250 to 600, its proportion was "always very small"; nevertheless, it continued to be imported in small quantities to the end of the Middle Horizon and beyond (Moholy-Nagy, Asaro, and Stross 1984:116). We do not know how long after the fifth century Teotihuacanos might have continued to control the distribution of El Chayal obsidian to Tikal. But if the continued importation of central Mexican obsidian is any guide, a "Teotihuacan connection" might have continued in attenuated form until the dominant role of the Mexican metropolis was ended in the eighth century.

The evidence from Tikal is the most detailed and specific we have for a relationship with a major foreign center. Although there is considerable evidence from other centers, especially Kaminaljuyú, even more ambiguities and uncertainties exist because no texts survive. The evidence from Tikal is only partly analyzed; much remains unclear. But principally because of the associated texts, we can be more specific about this relationship than we can about others that must have been much closer. Teotihuacan did not conquer or otherwise dominate Tikal. At the same time it is surely significant that representations of persons in Teotihuacano dress with characteristically Teotihuacan arms appear on monuments there and at nearby Yaxhá (Fig. 5.3) (Stela 11) (Greene, Rands, and Graham 1972:342, Pl. 163) during this period (see also the carving from Tres Islas to the south—Greene, Rands, and Graham 1972:208, Pl. 97). Stela 5 at neighboring Uaxactún, is also related to these events. Its date translates to A.D. 377 (Mathews 1985) a year before the accession of Curl Nose at Tikal. It depicts a figure recalling the armed men on Tikal Stela 31 carrying a spear thrower and a club with inset blades (Greene, Rands, and Graham 1972:308, Pl. 146). The spear thrower is said not to have been a weapon associated with the Maya prior to this time (Greene, Rands, and Graham 1972:308). Yet only one of these figures need have been Teotihuacano if we accept the interpretations of Mathews and Schele. Schele (1986) argues that, with one exception, all of these are Maya figures in Teotihuacan dress who had adopted ritual practices from Teotihuacan centered on war and sacrifice that were brought to Tikal by Teotihuacanos who lived and died at Tikal and were buried there. If Schele is right, the rulers of Tikal in the fourth and fifth centuries

A.D. would have been Maya who had been so taken with Teotihuacan war and heart sacrifice ritual that they adopted it to the point of adopting Teotihuacan dress, Teotihuacan arms, and Teotihuacan symbolism. For example, Stormy Sky holds aloft a headdress bearing the Teotihuacan war emblem—a shield with a hand in it, a spear crossing it, and a bird above it, in this case apparently devouring a heart (Jones and Satterthwaite 1982:Fig. 51d; von Winning 1948).

Schele's interpretation implies that Teotihuacanos were physically present at Tikal for many years. This is consonant with the Teotihuacan-style burial evidence analyzed by Moholy-Nagy and with the increasing number of Teotihuacan-related *tablero-talud* temples that have been found at Tikal in the restricted area referred to previously. There thus would have been strong ideological ties between Tikal and Teotihuacan that would have helped to legitimize any economic activities in which resident Teotihuacanos were engaged.

Who would these Teotihuacanos have been? Very likely they would have come to Teotihuacan from Kaminaljuyú. It is enough at this point to observe that the prominence given the tassel headdress is an indication that they likely would have been agents or representatives of the Teotihuacan state headed by persons of ambassadorial rank and would have served in this capacity in diplomatic rituals involving gift exchange at the highest level of Tikal society. Some may also have acted in economic activities and exchange on their own behalf.

Still to be done and potentially of great importance is the analysis of the physical remains of the individuals in the Tikal Problematic Deposit burials to determine, if possible, how likely it is that any of them were from Teotihuacan itself, using techniques such as those employed by Spence (1974).

In addition to the Teotihuacan-related evidence from Tikal, Uaxactún, and Yaxhá, there is also Teotihuacan-related evidence at two more distant cities in the southern Maya lowlands—Altún Ha in Belize, and Becán in southern Campeche (Fig. 5.3). The connection with Altún Ha is highly specific, involving objects from the Teotihuacan region in a ritual context that appear to date from the early part of the Tlamimilolpa phase (ca. A.D. 200–300). It consists of an offering of green obsidian artifacts from Cerro de las Navajas, along with locally made Maya and Teotihuacanoid ceramics (Pendergast 1971; R. Millon 1973:55–56, Pring 1977:147–48).[9] The Belize evidence appears to antedate the evidence for close ties with Tikal. Because it is a single, apparently isolated offering, the relationship with Teotihuacan which it appears to reflect may have been of very limited duration (Ball 1983:136–37).

The evidence from the fortified site of Becán is also highly specific but is said to be somewhat later, roughly coeval with the time Teotihuacan and Tikal were most closely linked (i.e., fifth century A.D.). (Sabucán phase at Becán). It consists of a cache that included a cylindrical tripod pottery vessel decorated in Maya style, in which a large, two-part, hollow figurine was placed. Within it were ten solid, miniature, mold-made figurines (Ball 1974a, 1974b). Hollow figurines with smaller figurines within them were made at Teotihuacan; they also exist in private collections with a presumed Teotihuacan provenience. Most of the miniature figurines found at Becán closely resemble Teotihuacan figurines but do not appear to have been made at Teotihuacan. Small quantities of green obsidian thought to be from central Mexico were also found in deposits of this phase (Ball 1974a, 1974b; Rovner 1974; Spence n.d.). The significance of this has been subject to differing interpretations. For example, Ball (1979) sees the earlier evidence as implying no more than indirect commercial interchange; Spence (n.d.), stressing the small amount of green obsidian involved, suggests that it probably reached Becán in a political context of ceremonial interchange. However one interprets the obsidian evidence, the ritual connotations of the figurine cache in the later phase (late fifth century) suggest a connection with Teotihuacan via Tikal or an action by Teotihuacan-influenced Tikaleños that involved primarily political and ceremonial intercourse rather than economic exchange (Ball 1983:135); possibly, Ball (1979:277) suggests, the military domination of Becán by Tikal was being memorialized.

Kaminaljuyú and Highland Guatemala

Was the Teotihuacan "presence" in Tikal initiated by local representatives of the Teotihuacan state based in Kaminaljuyú? Did it result from actions taken by Teotihuacan merchants in a Kaminaljuyú enclave? Was it the product of stimuli from merchants with military backing from Teotihuacan in a port-of-trade enclave at Kaminaljuyú? These differing possibilities stem from differing interpretations of the Teotihuacan "presence" at Kaminaljuyú expressed by three of the archaeologists who have worked there and in contemporary centers in the region—Cheek (1977a), Sanders (1977, 1978), and K. Brown (1977a, 1977b).

The first possibility—action by local representatives of the Teotihuacan state in Kaminaljuyú—implies a more substantial relationship to the Teotihuacan state, even if mediated and buffered, than any of the others. I am inclined to favor this interpretation, pending more intensive contextual analysis of the Tikal evidence. A loose alliance may conceivably have existed between Tikal and Teotihuacan, during parts of the fourth and fifth centuries A.D., through ties with Kaminaljuyú.

Necessary to this interpretation would be the judgment that there was a takeover of Kaminaljuyú and part of the region around it by representatives of the Teotihuacan state backed by military force by A.D. 350. An impetus for the takeover may have been prior entry by Teotihuacan merchants (acting as agents of the state?) attracted to the raw materials obtainable from a base in the Valley of Guatemala—obsidian deposits in the valley itself; cacao and marine shell from the Pacific coast; jade, quetzal and other tropical feathers, and copal (for incense) from the mountain slopes and lowlands to the north. Among these goods some, like shell and copal, were indispensable ingredients in the cultural life of the Mexican metropolis, their use not confined to upper strata. The takeover may have been designed to ensure the uninterrupted flow of goods to and from southern Guatemala, as well as perhaps to gain control of the distribution of the output from the El Chayal obsidian quarries nearby (Santley 1983). Although I favor the interpretation of a takeover by Teotihuacanos,[10] it is an interpretation subject to the many ambiguities and uncertainties in the evidence.

The work of Sanders and his associates at Kaminaljuyú (Sanders and Michels 1977) has placed the evidence of the Teotihuacan "presence" in a context absent in earlier investigations. The latter consisted primarily of excavations by Kidder, Jennings, and Shook (1946) in two mounds with Teotihuacan-style temple architecture near the southeastern edge of the city, and of unpublished excavations sponsored by the Guatemalan government and directed by Gustavo Espinoza in the late 1950s and early 1960s, exposing Teotihuacan-style temple and public architecture in an area in the northern part of Kaminaljuyú known as the Acropolis (Cheek 1977b:99–100). The Pennsylvania State University Kaminaljuyú Project involved both excavation and surface survey. Cheek (1977a, 1977b) excavated parts of a complex of Teotihuacan-style public architecture known as the Palangana, southeast of the Acropolis. He also restudied and published a description of Espinoza's excavations, together with modified versions of Tatiana Proskouriakoff's 1962 drawings of the ar-chitecture exposed and consolidated by Espinoza. The Sanders survey and testing program established that residential settlement in most of the rest of the city, although concentrated as it had not been before, apparently remained largely unaffected by Teotihuacan household ritual and other cultural practices (Sanders 1978). Population during this period is var-iously described as not substantially increasing (Sanders 1978:39) or decreasing (Michels 1979:296).

Arguments for intervention by the Teotihuacan state at Kaminaljuyú—which are far from unequivocal—are the abruptness with which Teoti-huacan-style religious architecture is described as appearing and disap-pearing, together with the number of constructions undertaken, using building materials and construction techniques closely resembling those at Teotihuacan (Cheek 1977a:447, 1977b:127–41). Teotihuacan-style religious architecture covers two extensive areas and is the only public architecture known from Kaminaljuyú at this time. This can be taken to indicate that the religion of Teotihuacan either had supplanted, or had been superimposed on, the local Maya religion.[11]

Intervention by Teotihuacan does not imply any large-scale military operation. It could have been carried out by a relatively small force, perhaps numbering a few hundred soldiers. Only part of the Valley of Guatemala would have been under their control (Cheek 1977a:448; K. Brown 1977a, 1977b). I am not persuaded by the argument of Sanders (1978:40–41) that the demographic base of Teotihuacan was insufficient to provide logistical support for a takeover of Kaminaljuyú by representatives of the Teotihuacan state such as suggested here. The small garrison supporting the Teotihuacanos based in Kaminaljuyú would have been locally provisioned, and in any case, control was maintained over a relatively brief span of time, perhaps less than one hundred years. The principal problem would have been the maintenance of effective lines of communication over so long a distance through territories most of which were not under Teotihuacano control, as others have pointed out (e.g., Sanders 1978). Although this would have been difficult, it would not necessarily have been the insuperable problem it has been made out to be.

The Escuintla Region

A relationship also existed between Teotihuacanos and people in the Pacific coastal region of Guatemala, especially in what is now the Department of Escuintla (Fig. 5.3). Presumably two attractions for Teotihuacanos in the region would have been cacao and marine shell, as noted above. The relationship is poorly understood because most of the evidence for it is without provenience, coming from an abundance of ceramic material in private collections, including many cylindrical tripods and composite, Teotihuacan-style incense burners (Hellmuth 1975, 1978; Rattray 1978; Berlo 1983a, 1984; von Winning 1979c). What Edwin Shook reports from his excavations in the region, as recounted in Berlo (1984:77–79, 138), suggests that the Teotihuacan "connection" appeared in few sites, was extremely localized within sites where it did appear, and represented a relatively narrow time span. Specific sites mentioned were Río Seco and Rancho Tolimán (see also Shook 1965:185–86, Fig. 2). It was also reportedly Shook's opinion that the Teotihuacan-related material he examined from Río Seco was made of the same local clays as other ceramics of the region (Berlo 1984:78, Plates 75, 77–79).

Whether what has been found in the region represents provincial outposts of Teotihuacan, as suggested by Berlo (1984:136–38, 199–201), is not clear, given the limited evidence from controlled excavation. The timing is even more problematic. Berlo (1984:201) suggests that it began in the fourth century, coeval with presumed Teotihuacano incursions into Tikal, perhaps providing a base of operations for Teotihuacano penetrations to the north.[12] On stylistic grounds this seems doubtful, since the type of mold-made decoration that appears on the Teotihuacan-related cylindrical tripods in these sites is found at Teotihuacan late in its history as a major center in contexts that seem to be two hundred years or more later than suggested by Berlo. In addition, excavations by Bove (1987) at Balberta, a major Early Classic period site on the Pacific Coast of Guatemala, argue against Berlo's suggested fourth-century settlement in the region. He finds no evidence there of a Teotihuacan "presence." Only controlled excavations in other parts of the Pacific coast of Guatemala promise to clarify whether Teotihuacanos actually were in the region and, if they were, when they arrived, what they were doing there, how long they stayed, and whether they were acting on behalf of the Teotihuacan state.

Matacapan

Teotihuacan appears to have had a base outside central Mexico at Matacapan in the Tuxtlas region of southern Veracruz (Fig. 5.3) which could have served in support of operations in Guatemala to the south and east (Valenzuela 1945; M. Coe 1965:683, 704–5; Parsons 1978:29; Krotser 1981; Santley 1987). Matacapan is one of the few sites besides Kaminaljuyú outside the domain of Teotihuacan where Teotihuacan-style *tablero-talud*[13] temple architecture has been found (Valenzuela 1945). Matacapan is a large site of more than seventy mounds "regularly laid out on an orientation slightly east of north, which is typical for Classic sites in Mexico" (M. Coe 1965:683; Valenzuela 1945). Teotihuacan has an east-of-north orientation of 15°30'.[14] Michael Coe's (1965:704–5) observation on Matacapan is often cited: "If this site is ever investigated with the thoroughness bestowed on the mounds near the Roosevelt Hospital at Kaminaljuyú, it seems highly probable that evidence would indicate Matacapan was an important way station on the road that the Teotihuacanos took to the highland Maya area."

Investigations to determine the nature of the Teotihuacan "presence" at Matacapan were begun in 1982 by Robert Santley (1987). In addition to the Teotihuacan-style temple, Valenzuela (1945:94–97) found Teotihuacan-style ceramics that included household religious objects (figurines and *candeleros*—small, usually twin-chambered objects probably used as personal incense burners), as well as much more common cylindrical tripods and ring-base bowls. Santley's investigations also have yielded Teotihuacan-related *candeleros* and figurines, as well as many Teotihuacanoid cylindrical tripods—the latter coming from all parts of the site (Santley 1987).

During the 1962 survey for the Teotihuacan map, *candeleros* and figurines were sometimes found in association in cultivated fields beyond the borders of the ancient city. At the time we thought they might have been used in agricultural rituals in the fields. Otherwise, *candeleros* seem primarily to be associated with domestic ritual (see, for example, R. Millon 1973:62). The same seems frequently to be true of figurines (Barbour 1976). Barbour and George Cowgill have suggested that the *candeleros* and figurines at Matacapan may reflect the long-term presence there of Teotihuacanos of lower status than usually are found in sites far from central Mexico (Barbour and Cowgill, personal communication, 1983). The presence of a Teotihuacan-style temple at Matacapan also suggests the presence of Teotihuacano priests or other ritual specialists.

Santley (1987) concludes that Matacapan was a Teotihuacan enclave with evidence for two levels of Teotihuacan-related ritual-ceremonial activity. The first was public, centering on the zone of civic-ceremonial architecture where the Teotihuacan-style temple was found; the second was domestic, centering on household ritual activities involving not only figurines and *candeleros* but also distinctively Teotihuacan-like burial practices. Evidence from excavation suggests the existence of "dwellings of the Teotihuacan type" and Teotihuacan-like domestic practices such as the use of distinctive portable ceramic stoves (Santley 1987). After the establishment of this enclave in the fourth century A.D. Santley (1987) suggests that Matacapan came to dominate other settlements in the Tuxtlas region (Fig. 5.3) through "colonization" and economic control, including control of exchange, one manifestation of which was the establishment in Matacapan of a large-scale "ceramic production-distribution system" involving mass-produced standardized fine-paste wares using local clays rich in kaolin. The implication of Santley's analysis is that Teotihuacan benefited economically from the establishment of the Matacapan enclave and the subsequent development of its "special resource base" (Santley 1987).

Looking at Santley's evidence from the vantage point of central Mexico, what does the relation of Matacapan to Teotihuacan appear to have been? The most likely interpretation at this point is that an enclave was established at Matacapan in the fourth century A.D. by Teotihuacanos acting as representatives of, or on behalf of, the Teotihuacan state. The enclave would have served primarily economic and political ends, both locally and as a base of operations for activities to the east, including the support of the Kaminaljuyú enclave (Parsons 1978:29). The Teotihuacanos who lived at Matacapan appear to have included both people of high rank and people of more modest status. It seems likely that with the passage of time there was an attenuation of the control exercised over Matacapan by representatives of the Teotihuacan state, with the relationship perhaps coming to an end in the sixth century.

The "Merchants' Barrio" in Teotihuacan

We found exceptionally high concentrations of foreign pottery (primarily from the Gulf Coast but also from the Maya lowlands) both on the surface and in excavation in a localized area near the northeastern limit of Teotihuacan (TE4, TE11).[15] When we were excavating, I thought the area might have been a base of operations of Teotihuacan merchants, so I named it the "merchants' barrio" (R. Millon 1973:34, 40) (Fig. 5.2, no. 9). I put the term within quotation marks, however, because other interpretations of these concentrations are possible, and in any case we could not be certain merchants were involved.

Ball (1983:137–38) has raised the question of a possible Maya enclave in the "merchants' barrio" on the debatable grounds that little Maya pottery has been found elsewhere at Teotihuacan and therefore that the Maya pottery (primarily food vessels) found in the "merchants' barrio" may represent vessels used by the inhabitants of the barrio for domestic purposes.[16] He sees a possible parallel to the situation in Teotihuacan's Oaxaca barrio, mentioned previously. As noted earlier, the parallel probably exists but with Veracruz rather than with the Maya area. Excavations in the barrio undertaken by Evelyn Rattray in 1983 and 1984 uncovered the foundations of many round structures seven to ten meters in diameter with associated burials (Rattray, personal communication, 1984). They are unlike most other Teotihuacan constructions known. Rattray (personal communication, 1986) commented that any ties to other parts of Mesoamerica that may exist in the barrio are more likely to be with Veracruz than with the Maya.

Fine paste orange, cream, and gray foreign wares, of which we found many sherds, came mainly from the Tuxtlas region and Matacapan (Rattray, n.d.b). Many of these sherds, as well as the greatest concentration of other sherds from the Gulf Coast and the Maya lowlands, were found in what we thought was a multiroom structure of adobe with earth floors which we excavated only partially (TE4) (Mezquititla). We found no in situ evidence of domestic activities in the excavation. More extensive excavations by Evelyn Rattray in 1984 in the same site (Mezquititla) established the presence there of large circular structures such as those referred to previously.

Another construction a few meters south of Mezquititla in which we placed two small excavation pits (Xocotitla) had appeared to be a standard Teotihuacan apartment compound (TE11) and yielded many foreign sherds (Rattray 1981a, n.d.b). However, Rattray's 1983 excavations at the eastern and southern end of this site uncovered the round construction referred to previously (Rattray, personal communication, 1984).

Rattray's discoveries in the "merchants' barrio" have significant implications. If this was another foreign barrio, occupied by people from the Gulf Coast, as the architectural evidence suggests (round structures, at least some of which were domestic), could its inhabitants have come from Matacapan? This is possible but unlikely. Santley (1987:Fig. 10) reports that domestic architecture at that site appears to be rectilinear. A more northerly source in Veracruz seems likely, and Rattray (personal communication, 1986) is investigating that possibility.

Is there reason to believe that the inhabitants of the barrio are likely to have been merchants? The main evidence that they may have been is the concentration of foreign sherds there from various parts of the Gulf Coast and from the Maya area, mainly from the northern Maya lowlands. This is hardly conclusive evidence, but it sets the barrio off from the rest of the city and as noted, it led to my naming it the "merchants' barrio." If merchants did live in the barrio, most likely they were members of a Gulf Coast ethnic group. Merchants who were Teotihuacanos would have lived elsewhere.

What do we know about merchants in Teotihuacan society? Not much. As we have seen, how we interpret the evidence for the widespread extension from Teotihuacan of networks of exchange to so much of Middle America, beginning early in Teotihuacan's history, depends in large part on how much was political and ceremonial interchange and how much was marketplace or similar kinds of exchange. Closely related to this is the question of the ties of Teotihuacano merchants to the state. To what extent was long-distance exchange stimulated by the activities of merchants motivated to act for their own gain while at the same time acting as agents of the state? Most likely, the "mix" changed according to circumstances. Testing such an assumption continues to be difficult, however.

The Northern Maya Lowlands

Most of the Maya pottery found in our excavations in the "merchants' barrio" appears to come from coastal areas of the northern Maya lowlands, extending on the east as far south as northern Belize in the southern Maya lowlands (Fig. 5.3) (Rattray, n.d.b; Ball 1983:137–38). None of this necessarily implies the movement of Teotihuacanos east of Matacapan, for all of this pottery could have been brought through various intermediaries to Matacapan. Recent finds from Dzibilchaltún (Fig. 5.3), the great Maya city in extreme northwestern Yucatán, along with older evidence from nearby Acanceh, raise other questions, however.

In the Mirador group, seven kilometers west of the center of Dzibil-chaltún, Andrews (1979) reports finding a small platform (9 by 10 meters) that in its second construction phase was faced with Teotihuacan-style *tablero-talud* construction dating to circa A.D. 600. This was before Dzibilchaltún had become a major urban center and when there was no other major Maya center in the area. Nothing else associated with Teotihuacan was found, and Andrews (1981:325) describes it as a "short-lived Teotihuacan architectural intrusion." More than a century later, in the center of rapidly growing Dzibilchaltún, a small one-room structure on a low platform was built with *tableros* around the upper part of its four facades, much like the *tableros* that decorated the upper parts of the facades of temple superstructures at Teotihuacan. Andrews dates this structure to circa A.D. 750. It was covered in the ninth century by a multiplatform structure, the lower terrace of which bore a modified *tablero-talud*. The latter two structures were built too late to be related to Teotihuacan.[17] The earlier platform is an isolated structure without any cultural context in the Mirador group relating it to Teotihuacan, making it difficult to evaluate. Andrews (1981:339) suggests that the builders of the platform "may have been encouraged" to make this "intrusion" because there was then no large Maya site nearby, making it possible for them to control the salt-producing areas a few kilometers to the north. Cotton is another raw material that might have been sought (Andrews and Andrews 1980:69, 74, 76, 153–63, 303–4; Andrews 1979, 1981:325–26, 331–32, 335, 339).

As noted, the Mirador group evidence at Dzibilchaltún is not the only evidence relating northern Yucatán to Teotihuacan. There is also the extraordinary and long-known stucco facade of Structure 1 at Acanceh (Seler 1915; Andrews 1942, 1965; Brainerd 1942; Marquina 1964:800–805; M. Coe 1980:77–78). Many stylistic elements on the facade seem to be derived from Teotihuacan and could reasonably be described as Teotihuacanoid.[18] The early dating of this structure (fifth or sixth century A.D. (Andrews 1942, 1965:298–99, 303, Figs. 4, 12; Brainerd 1942) appears to eliminate the possibility that these are late derivations transformed over time into the Teotihuacanoid forms and details we now see. If, as appears to be the case, the decoration of this facade is approximately contemporaneous with or slightly earlier than the early Mirador group *tablero-talud* temple at nearby Dzibilchaltún, the two together would suggest a closer relationship with Teotihuacan than either separately. Freer (1987) also points to evidence of the architectural use of the *tablero* and *tablero-talud* forms at Oxkintok and Aké in western Yucatán. In addition he argues that at Uxmal many central Mexican motifs and designs date from the sixth century A.D. rather than from several centuries later, the latter being the standard interpretation. If Freer is correct, this would mean that the Mexican connections would derive ultimately from Teotihuacan rather than from the later Toltecs.

The foregoing evidence would not necessarily imply direct intrusion by Teotihuacanos into western and northern Yucatán, however. The architectural and artistic evidence of connections with Teotihuacan could be the product of actions by a Gulf Coast group culturally closely related to Teotihuacan, for example. As a result, until it is possible to place this evidence in a wider social and cultural context, it must remain tantalizingly ambiguous.

Monte Albán and the Valley of Oaxaca

I have suggested that Teotihuacan and the powerful Zapotec center of Monte Albán in the Valley of Oaxaca, four hundred kilometers (250 miles) to the southeast (Fig. 5.3), had a "special relationship" (R. Millon 1973:42) very different from any so far discussed. Evidence of this relationship at Monte Albán is comparable in part to the evidence we have from Tikal, but it reflects a different kind of connection. The most dramatic difference is that Teotihuacanos represented on Monte Albán monuments are not armed or escorted by armed men. We also have evidence at Teotihuacan itself of an enclave of Oaxacans who lived in the city for at least four hundred years.

The Oaxacan enclave was established circa A.D. 300. The newcomers lived in their own barrio near the western edge of the city in standard Teotihuacan apartment compounds in one of which we exposed a standard *tablero-talud* temple structure (TE3) (Teotihuacan Mapping Project [TE3, 3A] and University of the Americas excavations). The offerings they placed in their burials consisted predominantly of locally made Teotihuacan pottery. But the people in this ethnic group also maintained many of the customs and beliefs from their homeland, including the use of Oaxacan or Oaxaca-style funerary urns, tomb burial in Oaxaca style (TE3A), and Oaxaca-style utilitarian and ritual vessels (R. Millon 1967, 1973:41–42, Figs. 58, 60; see R. Millon 1981:241n for other citations). The people of the Oaxaca barrio ethnic enclave were not of high status. We still do not know what kind of work they did. It is possible that some of them moved to small village sites in the lime-producing area of the Tula region after it was taken over by Teotihuacanos (Crespo and Mastache 1981).

Joyce Marcus (1980, 1983) has examined representations at Monte Albán of persons who appear to be Teotihuacanos and has analyzed their contexts. Eight named individuals appear on four stelae and another on a carved stone slab. What Marcus takes to be the Teotihuacan tassel headdress is worn by several figures on one stela and is separately represented several times on another.[19] Unlike similar figures at Tikal, the figures depicted on these stelae are unarmed. They are shown leaving what appears to be a Teotihuacan temple and arriving at Monte Albán, where they are being met by "an official wearing a typical Zapotec headdress." Marcus concludes that the visit is intended to memorialize "peaceful foreign relations." The stone slab known as the Lápida de Bazán depicts two personages, a Teotihuacano on the left and a lord of Monte Albán on the right, with both figures facing to the right. Each is accompanied by a column of glyphs. After analyzing these glyphs, Marcus tentatively concludes that the text of the Lápida de Bazán constitutes "a record of an agreement between representatives of the two cities." Marcus suggests that the "special relationship" between the two centers was maintained through "diplomatic encounters" of this kind (see also Marcus 1983). The major route used for such occasions, as well as for more mundane transactions, probably followed the south branch of the "Teotihuacan Corridor" to the vicinity of Cholula (Hirth and Swezey 1976), then south to Tehuacán (Noguera 1940; Drennan and Nowack 1979), and from there perhaps through the upper Papaloapan drainage to the Valley of Oaxaca. Teotihuacan-Monte Albán contacts may have become less frequent after A.D. 500 (Bernal 1965:806; Winter 1979), when Monte Albán reached the height of its power (Blanton and Kowalewski 1981).

Monte Albán was in decline during Teotihuacan's last century as a metropolis, and by A.D. 700 it was no longer a major urban center (Blanton 1978; Blanton and Kowalewski 1981). Flannery and Marcus (1983:184) comment that the declines of the two centers "were so suspiciously close in time" that it seems likely they were related. The inference is reasonable. It may be in fact that Monte Albán was significantly affected by some of the circumstances discussed below that presumably contributed to Teotihuacan's decline.

Central and Southern Veracruz

We know little about the political relationship of Teotihuacan to most of the major centers on the Gulf Coast. Aside from the presumed enclave at Matacapan, there is little that can be interpreted as evidence of the presence of Teotihuacanos in central and southern Veracruz or Tabasco. This lack of evidence may be misleading, however. Veracruz provided a major route to other regions to the east but was also important in itself to the Teotihuacanos. Cacao and marine shell would have been only the most obvious resources of interest in the region (R. Millon 1981:226–27). The evidence for ceramic interchange no doubt reflects, however imperfectly, significant interchange in other, more perishable products.

Teotihuacan ceramics are found widely in southern Veracruz, especially in such sites as Cerro de las Mesas and Tres Zapotes (M. Coe 1965:700–705), and in central Veracruz in such sites as Chachalacas (García Payon 1971: 526–32, and personal communication, 1970). In addition, a great many potsherds from Veracruz have been found at Teotihuacan, many of them, as we have seen, in the "merchants' barrio"—several times the number of Maya sherds found (Rattray, 1981a; n.d.b).

Quantities of fine pottery called "Lustrous Ware" were imported from the El Tajín region beginning in the Early Tlamimilolpa phase (A.D. 200–300) and continuing into the sixth century (Rattray 1979a:302; Harbottle and Sayre 1979), perhaps more than from any other region. This ware is widely distributed throughout the city, but no special concentration of it was found in the "merchants' barrio," suggesting that that barrio was involved neither in its importation nor in its distribution in the city. Lustrous Ware appears at Teotihuacan roughly a century before elements of the El Tajín art style appear in Teotihuacan art.

The relationship between the two centers seems to have been long lasting. The "northeast corridor" via Tepeapulco and Tulancingo is the most direct route between them and probably was favored. No signs of a Teotihuacan "presence" exist at El Tajín, and there is no reason to believe that Teotihuacan ever dominated El Tajín even briefly. Nor, to look ahead, is there any reason to believe that El Tajín was involved in the overthrow of Teotihuacan. Nevertheless, the increasing growth and power of El Tajín in the seventh century may have deflected to it goods and materials that formerly flowed to Teotihuacan (Litvak 1978:120). As we shall see, competition of this kind would have contributed to the problems faced by Teotihuacan in its last years, and so have contributed to its "fall."

Guerrero

Mineral resources and marine shell from the Pacific Ocean were among the attractions of parts of western and northern Mexico for the Teotihuacanos. Shell was highly prized, above all for personal adornment and for use in ritual. Pacific varieties of shell seem to have been favored (Starbuck 1975:112–59). Müller (1979) suggests that the presence of Teotihuacan ceramics at many sites in Guerrero (Fig. 5.3) (in central Guerrero, along the Río Balsas, especially near its mouth, and along the Pacific coast, as well as in neighboring parts of Michoacan) (see also Lister 1971:622–27; Chadwick 1971:673, 676) is attributable to demand for marine shell. She comments on Starbuck's (1975:144, App. V) evidence that exchange networks in the region for the export of shell to central Mexico were disrupted after the "fall" of Teotihuacan, noting that in post-Middle Horizon Cholula (i.e., after ca. A.D. 800) marine shell analyzed by Starbuck came largely from Atlantic species. Surface evidence suggests that the same was true of shell imported to a now greatly diminished Teotihuacan (i.e., post–A.D. 800)[20] (Starbuck 1975:144). Müller suggests that the route taken by the Teotihuacanos followed the "Teotihuacan Corridor," then moved through southwestern Puebla into Guerrero, following the Río Balsas drainage. Cacao also may have reached Teotihuacan through this or another more westerly Balsas route through central and western Morelos under the control of Xochicalco (Fig. 5.3) (Litvak 1978:120).

Paradis (1987) argues that the two regions of Guerrero most closely connected with Teotihuacan were the Pacific coastal region around Acapulco (where shell and perhaps cacao could have been obtained) and the north central part of the state, where there was an ancient tradition of lapidary craftsmen in the Mezcala area. North central Guerrero was also the probable source of Granular Ware, a ceramic ware in wide use at Teotihuacan for hundreds of years (Paradis 1987; Rattray n.d.b). Paradis suggests that Mezcala craft workers probably made the famous Teotihuacan stone masks and that some of these lapidaries may have worked at Teotihuacan itself. In the course of such journeys they may have brought Granular Ware to the ancient city. The Mezcala area is the one region of Guerrero that Paradis believes was economically and perhaps politically dominated by Teotihuacan.

Northern and Western Mexico

The major attraction for Teotihuacan of regions to the north seems to have been mineral resources. The San Juan del Río section of southern Querétaro may have been linked to Teotihuacan relatively early (ca. A.D. 400), judging from the abundance of Teotihuacanoid ceramics there. Perhaps San Juan del Río formed part of a "northwest corridor" to Querétaro and San Luis Potosí that began in the Tula region. Cinnabar may have been the attraction in the Río Verde area of south central San Luis Potosí ca. A.D. 400–500 (Michelet 1984). But, judging from ceramic evidence, the intensive exploitation of the cinnabar mines of the barren and isolated Sierra de Querétaro, two hundred kilometers to the north, began somewhat later (in the seventh century A.D.). (Cinnabar was highly prized as a pigment for funerary and other ritual uses.) All supplies for the support of the miners during periods of mining activity in this area would have had to have been brought in (Secretaría del Patrimonio Nacional 1970; Franco 1970a, 1970b). The mines may also have been exploited by a Gulf Coast state at times, since it seems unlikely that Teotihuacan mining operations were continuous, year-round operations.

Evidence of other Teotihuacan connections farther north and west in Guanajuato also seems to be late (end of Xolalpan phase and Metepec phase, post–A.D. 600) (Bejarano 1979).

Hundreds of kilometers to the northwest, mining operations were undertaken on a large scale in the Chalchihuites district of Zacatecas (Fig. 5.3) by the fifth century A.D. or earlier (Kelley 1980, 1985; Weigand 1968, 1978, 1982). Weigand (1982) argues that the scale of the mining operations in this region at that time is understandable only if what was being mined was destined for use in populous central Mexico and the exploitation of the mines "sponsored" by a power such as Teotihuacan. The mines yield cinnabar-bearing sands, hematite, limonite, malachite, chert, and other minerals. The area also provides "blue-green stones" that may be the source of the name Chalchihuites (the Nahuatl word for jade or green stone was *chalchuiutl* in the sixteenth century) (Weigand 1982). The Teotihuacanos used hematite in enormous quantities as a pigment, but as Weigand points out, it is a very common mineral known to have been exploited elsewhere. Malachite is another matter, however, since it was the mineral used to prepare the green pigments used in Teotihuacan mural and ceramic painting (Armillas 1950:53, 55; Torres 1972:24–25). Cinnabar might also have been sought, perhaps before the exploitation of the Sierra de Querétaro mines had begun. The same could be true of the "blue-green stone." These are questions that presumably will be answered by trace-element analysis, as was done with turquoise sources (Weigand, Harbottle, and Sayre 1977). Turquoise was imported from New Mexico to the Chalchihuites area and may have reached central Mexico from this "port-of-entry" (Kelley 1980:54–55). Although turquoise may have been used at Teotihuacan, it appears to have been quite rare.[21] We found none, for example, in surface survey and only one tiny fragment in our small excavation in a barrio of lapidaries (TE18) (M. Turner 1981, 1983; personal communication, 1983).

Alta Vista was the major center in the Chalchihuites area. Alta Vista is very close to the Tropic of Cancer, and Kelley (1976:31–32) suggests that its location " 'where the sun turns' . . . where [its] apparent northward movement stops" was deliberately chosen, perhaps by central Mexican ritual specialist astronomers. More recently, on the basis of additional evidence relating it to Teotihuacan, Aveni, Hartung, and Kelley (1982:316) have argued that Alta Vista "was deliberately located and oriented astronomically by people of the Teotihuacan civilization." They date its construction to circa A.D. 500 (Aveni, Hartung, and Kelley 1982:330–34). The site is now 4.2 km north of the Tropic of Cancer. They calculate that in A.D. 650 it would have been 14 km south of the Tropic (Aveni, Hartung, and Kelley 1982:318). Whether the new evidence argues for the presence of Teotihuacanos at Alta Vista, either long-term or short-term, and for direct or indirect political intervention by Teotihuacan in the economic development of the region remains to be determined. Results of analyses in process should provide a better basis than now exists for evaluating the role of Teotihuacan in the exploitation of these far-off mines. The question is clearly of potentially great significance to our understanding of the scope of Teotihuacan enterprise and of the reach of its economy and polity.

Although it would be unwise not to leave open the possibility, what is now known does not suggest that peoples from any of the regions discussed in the west and the north, or other parts of northern and western Mexico where connections with Teotihuacan have been reported, such as Jalisco (e.g., Corona Nuñez 1972), contributed directly to the "fall" of Teotihuacan. Dislocations in the north may have affected events in central Mexico indirectly, however (Armillas 1969). Even so, it appears that Teotihuacan was either still expanding in the north or had done so recently at the time of the "fall."

The Special Case of Cholula

Cholula differs from the other major centers so far discussed because, in addition to being on the borders of Teotihuacan's domain, it was culturally closer to Teotihuacan and had close ties with it for a longer period of time. It appears to have become an important center before Teotihuacan (Noguera 1956) and may have been a source of enrichment for religious traditions in the Valley of Mexico prior to Teotihuacan's rise. Its architectural, artistic, and ceramic traditions are closely linked to Teotihuacan from circa A.D. 200 on, although the Cholula tradition grows more and more distinctive with the passage of time. It appears to have maintained its independence throughout the period of Teotihuacan's ascendancy. It was a major commercial center with strong links to the Gulf Coast; as a religious center it was second only to Teotihuacan in central Mexico. And if bigger is better, the final stage of its great pyramid was both higher and covered a larger area than Teotihuacan's Sun Pyramid (Marquina 1970a, 1970b). It was evidently built sometime during the Xolalpan phase (but see the interpretation of Sanders, Parsons, and Santley 1979:134). Even if built late in that phase, its construction would have been more than a hundred years before the destruction of Teotihuacan. But soon thereafter, Cholula appears to have entered a long period of decline (Müller 1970:131; 1978:223, Lám. 3; Acosta 1970:Fig. 20; Dumond and Müller 1972; Hirth and Swezey 1976:13).

The fact that Cholula and a small domain around it were culturally closely related to Teotihuacan but remained independent of it is an indication that it was a power in its own right that Teotihuacan apparently chose not to challenge. Cholula may have grown too powerful too early for Teotihuacan to absorb it without a full-scale struggle. So long as Cholula did not directly threaten its neighbor, as it does not appear to have, the Teotihuacan hierarchy may have decided that it was safer to have Cholula outside its domain.

The long period of decline Cholula apparently underwent beginning circa A.D. 600, from which it evidently did not reemerge until circa A.D. 800, seems effectively to eliminate it as one of the possible sources of invading peoples who may have participated in the destruction of Teotihuacan. But its very decline seems likely to have contributed to that of Teotihuacan. Cholula had been very prosperous and would have been a major contributor to the economic well-being not only of its own domain, but also to that of neighboring regions of the Valley of Puebla and Veracruz, for whose populations it must have been a major focal point of exchange. As Cholula began to fade, Teotihuacan could have moved in to replace it in those areas. But as we shall see, there is said to be evidence of trouble for Teotihuacan in the "Teotihuacan Corridor" at about the same time. Both may be aspects of the same process of breakdown and fragmentation in networks of communication and exchange. There is some evidence that subordinate centers formerly under Cholula's control began to assume increasing importance and independence at this time—at Manzanilla (Hirth and Swezey 1976:12–13) and Cerro Zapotecas (Mountjoy and Peterson 1973:136). Nevertheless, we do not know what were the circumstances in Cholula itself that set off the process of its decline in the first place. That is a subject for another investigation.

Teotihuacan Abroad Near the End of the Middle Horizon

Having now completed our examination of Teotihuacan beyond its domain, what can we say of these relations in the seventh century, as we reach the last hundred years of Teotihuacan's existence as a major power? By this time, whatever role Teotihuacan formerly had played in the Maya area must have been sharply attenuated, with the possible exception of the Escuintla region on Guatemala's Pacific slope. The special relationship with Monte Albán also must have been weakened. Ties with Veracruz seem more likely to have remained stronger, but confirmation of this must await further work. To the north and perhaps the west the situation appears to be different. There, as we have seen, evidence exists of Teotihuacan expansion in the sixth and seventh centuries. Expansion to the north did not balance retrenchment to the south, however, and as we shall see, this lessened involvement coincides with evidence of growing economic and political problems for Teotihuacan in its "outer hinterland" and in areas immediately adjoining it, problems that may have contributed to the city's collapse. In considering this question, we must look at what was happening in city and countryside in the Teotihuacan domain during the course of the Middle Horizon.

ADMINISTRATION AND EXCHANGE IN THE TEOTIHUACAN DOMAIN

As noted previously, early in the Tzacualli phase (ca. A.D. 1) most of the people in the Valley of Mexico were removed from or otherwise persuaded to leave their homes and lands and resettled in Teotihuacan (R. Millon 1981:220; Sanders, Parsons, and Santley 1979:105–8, Maps 12 and 13; Sanders 1981a:177, Figs. 6-13, 6-15) (see also Robert Adams and Nissen 1972:9–33 for a partially comparable process at Uruk in ancient southern Mesopotamia that may have taken place over a longer period of time). During the Tzacualli phase (A.D. 1–150) 80 to 90 percent of the estimated population of one hundred thousand in the Valley of Mexico lived in Teotihuacan. Thereafter what appears to have been a planned resettlement of circumscribed parts of the valley seems to have occurred during the Middle Horizon (Fig. 5.4):

> During the succeeding . . . Middle Horizon there was a modest return to the countryside, but a return that resulted in a pattern of settlement so distinct and different from that of First Intermediate phase 3 [the Patlachique phase, preceding the Tzacualli phase concentration] that we are convinced that it was the product of a process of planning, engineered by the rulers of Teotihuacan in response to the needs of the city. The population of our survey area doubled from First Intermediate phase 4 to the Middle Horizon, and virtually all of this growth occurred in the countryside. In comparison to phase 3 [Patlachique] there was a major shift in geographic distribution of population. (Sanders 1981a:177)

The reason for this pattern of resettlement, Sanders, Parsons, and Santley (1979:116) suggest, was to relocate people in areas where agricultural production and resource exploitation could be maximized, while at the same time avoiding resettlement in older local centers where loyalties might be divided. The result in an extensive area in the south was the "disappearance of the upper two or three levels in the local settlement hierarchy" (Sanders, Parsons, and Santley 1979:115).

Throughout the Middle Horizon (ca. A.D. 200–750) at least 50 to 60 percent of an estimated valley-wide population of two hundred thousand lived in Teotihuacan. Why did this population concentration persist so long? The administrative advantages for the Teotihuacan hierarchy are evident in the short run. But the long-run consequence of this policy of concentration and of the limited resettlement in the countryside apparently was considerable underutilization of the resources of large parts of the valley, compared to prior and subsequent patterns of utilization (Sanders, Parsons, and Santley 1979:128).

Did the hierarchy fail to react adequately to changing circumstances? Is this seeming inflexibility an instance of the kind of rigidity and incompetence Cowgill (this volume) says we should expect in such a polity, and of the kind of contradiction that Robert Adams (1978:333) comments on in analyzing conditions in Sasanian Mesopotamia in the sixth century A.D.?

> An essential—perhaps almost a diagnostic—feature of large-scale, complex but pre-industrial societies like that of Sasanian Mesopotamia was that short-term and long-term success were antithetical. Political stabilization and economic maximization were achieved only with a progressive weakening of the capacity to adapt to unforeseen challenges and changes.

Did this kind of inflexibility and apparent inability to react to changing circumstances have its consequences late in Teotihuacan's history? We shall return to this question.

A major impediment to our understanding of Teotihuacan social structure both in city and countryside is the difficulty of recovering data on the system of land tenure and on the social composition of the groups that controlled and worked the land. We may postulate that when the population resettlement occurred circa A.D. 1, those with rights to exploit lands in the Teotihuacan Valley, especially the highly productive irrigated lands, would have had economic and social advantages over the newcomers, many of whom must have had to find new lands in previously unsettled areas to the north and northwest (Sanders, Parsons, and Santley 1979:Map 13).[22] This would have provided a base for persisting social divisions between "old families" and "new families," between established settlers and newcomers. We may also postulate that an earlier "layer" of internal division would have developed *within* the Valley of Teotihuacan prior to the resettlement, given the wide disparities in access to water that exist among the valley's cultivable lands, those with "the best assured access to water" having the advantage. Describing what may have been an analogous situation in southern Mesopotamia, when state and urban institutions were coming into being, Robert Adams (1981:245) writes of the advantages that "accrued to those with the best assured access to water," seeing in such differential access "an inconspicuous, slowly developing, but very powerful source of internal social and economic stratification." Such a process must have occurred in the Teotihuacan Valley before the resettlement, for the successful execution of the resettlement policy implies the prior or concurrent development of state institutions (R. Millon 1981:221). The two processes of stratification postulated—one internally generated, the other the result of resettlement—may have provided the basis for persisting internal divisions in Teotihuacan society. (See also Hoffman 1976, 1983, for possibly analogous processes of resettlement of Nekhen in Upper Egypt shortly before the unification of Upper and Lower Egypt; also Sanders, Parsons, and Santley 1979:392–94.) Was labor service on public lands a major source of revenue before the population resettlement? At the time of the Spanish Conquest such service on state lands formed the primary source of revenue in agricultural produce in central Mexican states and in many other New World states (Carrasco 1982). In a much earlier time at Teotihuacan would labor service have been associated with temple lands? Fundamental as these questions are, it may be some time before we find satisfactory answers.

What was the administrative structure in the countryside? Judging from the Middle Horizon settlement hierarchy, it appears that administration and control of communities within the Basin of Mexico came directly from Teotihuacan for settlements close to it and from secondary centers for the others (Sanders, Parsons, and Santley 1979:Map 14). Azcapotzalco was a large secondary center on the western side of the Valley of Mexico's lake system, covering at least two square kilometers (Sanders, Parsons, and Santley 1979:60, 128, 193). Some half dozen other secondary centers were much smaller. The remainder of the population lived in villages of varying size (Sanders 1981a:178). Teotihuacan was a "primate city," overwhelmingly dominating its settlement hierarchy (Jefferson 1939; Blanton 1976). It was at least ten times the size of Azcapotzalco and more than twenty times larger than other secondary centers (Sanders, Parsons, and Santley 1979:128). Judging from the obsidian production system, there was administrative intervention by the state in the procurement of at least some resources and perhaps in distribution (Spence 1981:781, 785). The exchange network that centered on the city may have taken on aspects of a "solar" marketing system (Smith 1976a:36; 1976b:334), with the flow of goods and materials restricted and hierarchical, moving into and out of the city through its settlement hierarchy. This may have been the case in both the "inner" and "outer hinterlands." Obsidian production is thought to have been concentrated in the city or in areas under state control (Spence 1981; Charlton 1978), and the same seems to be true of at least some other activities. Administrative intervention in the exchange process may have been an important source of state revenues. What we believe to have been the city's principal marketplace was an immense plaza in its center (Fig. 5.2, no. 6, Great Compound, central plaza).

This appears to have been the pattern of administrative control and exchange in the "inner hinterland." So far as we know it was maintained until the end. Expansion into "outer hinterland" areas to the north, the east, and the south occurred during the Tlamimilolpa phase (fourth century A.D.). To the north, in the Tula region, which continued to be exploited through the Metepec phase, the settlement hierarchy was headed by the architecturally complex provincial center of Chingú (ca. 2 km²) (Díaz 1980, 1981). Many settlements were located in lime-producing areas (R. Millon 1981:222–23). Great quantities of lime were consumed in construction in the city and in food preparation. This region seems to have been more closely managed and more actively exploited than other "outer hinterland" regions, and its exploitation apparently continued without significant interruption until the collapse of Teotihuacan.

Early in the Middle Horizon the Plains of Apan region of southeastern Hidalgo and northern Tlaxcala (the "Teotihuacan Sphere") (Fig. 5.3) witnessed a great proliferation of settlements and more than a three-fold increase of population, sharply distinguishing it from the contemporary settlement hierarchy in the Basin of Mexico (García Cook 1981:269). There were more than eighty settlements in the region, divided into six clusters, each composed of provincial centers, towns, villages, and hamlets (García Cook 1981:266). This area played a major role in the provisioning of Teotihuacan, as well as occupying a strategic position for communication and exchange with areas to the south and east. Similar hierarchies of settlements were found in the "Teotihuacan Corridor." Most of these communities, both in the "sphere" and in the "corridor," were nucleated. Larger communities covered one to two square kilometers with impressive ceremonial and civic architecture faced with lime plaster. But it is important to note that no *tablero-talud* architecture has been found in any of the "sphere" or "corridor" sites. Nor are characteristic Teotihuacan orientations found (García Cook 1981:267, 269). This is true of even so "Teotihuacan" a site as Calpulalpan, and of San Nicolás el Grande, where temple platforms bear only *taludes* (sloping faces) (García Cook, personal communication, 1981). (Linné [1942] excavated at both of these sites.) Why then does García Cook think of these as Teotihuacan settlements? He does so because the pottery collections from these sites, both in the "sphere" and the "corridor," stand out as so different from the collections from the other Tlaxcalan sites around them. Their pottery was "either very similar to or the same as Teotihuacan ceramics" (García Cook 1981:267). Thin Orange pottery is found, as well as Teotihuacan-style figurines, objects used in personal and household ritual (García Cook and Trejo 1977). Apparently because of this García Cook sees these sites as culturally Teotihuacan.

The absence of characteristic Teotihuacan *tablero-talud* architecture from these settlements does not mean that the people who lived there were not closely related culturally to Teotihuacan. Early temple platforms at Teotihuacan lacked *tablero-talud* architecture; only the *talud* was used, not only on the great pyramids but on relatively small temple platforms as well (in the Plaza of the Sun, for example). Possibly people in the "Teotihuacan Sphere" and "Teotihuacan Corridor" settlements in Tlaxcala were conserving and maintaining an old Teotihuacan tradition in their temple architecture. The problem is that the earliest *tablero-talud* architecture known comes from Tlaxcala, where it is dated earlier than 200 B.C. (García Cook 1981:252–54, Figs. 8-8, 8-9, 8-10). After this initial early use in Tlaxcala, the *tablero-talud* apparently was not used there again. (*Tablero-talud* architecture was used thereafter nearby, at Tepeapulco [Fig. 5.3] in the modern state of Hidalgo, however, where it was in a context related to Teotihuacan.) The problem remains, then, of how closely related to Teotihuacan these settlements were. The nature of the tie is important, because García Cook sees it as weakening in the latter part of the Middle Horizon. Both in the "sphere" and in the "corridor," settlements "tried to gain autonomy . . . by fortifying themselves," which had the effect of "blockading and weakening Teotihuacan" (García Cook 1981:269).

The third major area of the "outer hinterland" about which we have detailed information is in eastern Morelos, south of the Valley of Mexico— the Río Amatzinac region. Near the beginning of the Middle Horizon, with "agricultural intensification" as a major incentive, "the valley was unified under a large administrative center, population was relocated into rural areas, and controlled by a highly structured settlement hierarchy" (Hirth 1978:332, Figs. 3, 4). Cotton probably was grown there for the city; this was a major cotton-producing area for the Aztecs (Hirth 1978:328).

The complex settlement hierarchy began to change in the latter part of the Middle Horizon, as population was nucleated into fewer and larger settlements. This may have been an attempt on the part of the Teotihuacan state to gain increasing control over the region, [23] to intensify production of its specialized resources, and so to meet predictably increasing demand in an urban population whose upper strata were becoming more prosperous.[24] It is likely, for example, that demand for cotton cloth would have grown not only in the upper levels of the hierarchy but among other groups in the city who were benefiting from its prosperous economy. Since population concentration had worked in the Valley of Mexico, it may have seemed a reasonable political solution to an economic problem.

Whatever the reason for the population nucleation, the result was a decrease in regional productivity, as specialized rural communities and their diversion irrigation systems were abandoned in the hot and dry south where conditions for growing cotton are best. In addition, Hirth (1978:331) argues, nucleation itself is likely to have produced a more top-heavy administrative structure, development of demands for new goods and services, and a net reduction in the flow of goods and materials to the center, with a corresponding reduction in the flow of goods from center to periphery. The result would have been an increasing decline in the efficiency and effectiveness of the distribution network emanating from Teotihuacan. In addition, the nucleation process itself would have increased the power of the local hierarchy and led to a de facto increase in its autonomy. Hirth (1978:331) believes that similar processes of change occurred in other parts of the Teotihuacan hinterland, and that these, along with a decreasing flow of goods and materials in the city's long-distance trade networks, eventually "would have effectively strangled the extensive resource procurement network upon which it relied for its very survival."

The process sketched by García Cook in the "Teotihuacan Sphere" and the "Teotihuacan Corridor" could have led to the diversion of resources in much the same way as suggested by Hirth. The consequences, with the passage of time, could have been severe, since the underutilization of resources in its "inner hinterland" may have made the city even more dependent on agricultural resources from other areas in its expanded sphere.

Litvak (1970) has suggested that an increasingly powerful and independent Xochicalco (in western Morelos) (Fig. 5.3), a growing rival of Teotihuacan, may have played a significant role in slowing the flow of goods and materials in long-distance exchange networks to the south, in western Morelos and the Río Balsas region of Guerrero, affecting the flow to Teotihuacan of cotton, cacao, and other traditional products of the region. He suggests that Tula, Cholula, and El Tajín may have played similar roles. As we have seen, Tula did not yet exist and Cholula was suffering a severe decline of its own. The possibility that El Tajín might have played such a role already has been considered. Xochicalco was a large city with a fortified acropolis which dominated Morelos for a time after the destruction of Teotihuacan. There was a real basis for rivalry between the two centers, given its strategic location (Litvak 1970:140). In fact, if Teotihuacan was overthrown by invaders, it is logical to suspect that Xochicalco would have been involved.

Reasoning in part on the basis of Hirth's evidence from Morelos and in part on the basis of evidence for increasing autonomy from Cholula at Manzanilla, Hirth and Swezey (1976:15) suggest that problems for the Teotihuacan state began with the "gradual regionalization" of its hinterland. Their argument might apply to Tlaxcala as well. "Diverting resources from ... the Teotihuacán-controlled market system ... may well have set in motion a cyclical process whereby scarcities increased throughout the highlands stimulating the growth of regionalism, and a greater degree of mercantile activity independent of Teotihuacán control" (Hirth and Swezey 1976:13). If this process did occur, it obviously would have had a direct bearing on the problem of Teotihuacan's decline. Even so, neither this process, nor others related to it considered above, need have been irreversible. Nor do they prepare one for the sudden and cataclysmic quality of the destruction at Teotihuacan, or for its permanent destruction as a major political power. We shall return to this question.

THE METROPOLIS IN ITS LAST YEARS

There is evidence in the last century before the center of the city was destroyed that could be taken to represent decline, as well as evidence of what appears to be economic well-being. The quality of some ceramics declined (Rattray n.d.b), including those used in burials (Sempowski 1982). At the same time mass production of both the most common utilitarian and fine wares continued (San Martín Orange and Thin Orange[25]) (Rattray 1979b). To be sure, continued mass production of utilitarian ware may not be an indication of prosperity, but neither is it evidence of decline. The city's widely disseminated fine ware, Thin Orange, appears to reach the peak of its production in the Metepec phase (ca. A.D. 650–750) (Rattray 1979b). In addition, large cylindrical tripods of Thin Orange often are adorned with new, complex, mold-impressed motifs and scenes in the Metepec phase. Despite the relative abundance of both plain and decorated Thin Orange, the ware may not have been reaching all who wanted it, for the most common form—the undecorated, ring-base hemispherical bowl—also was being made in local clays.[26]

As for the working of obsidian, the evidence we have is insufficient to indicate whether there was any significant change late in the city's history (Spence 1981:783). If a process of "gradual regionalization" was taking place (Hirth and Swezey 1976), and/or if "rival exchange organizations" were developing beyond the Teotihuacan domain (Santley 1983:111–12), the market for obsidian, as well as for other products, would have been adversely affected.

It has been suggested that environmental conditions deteriorated toward the end of the Middle Horizon (post-A.D. 600) (e.g., Lorenzo 1968). The evidence on this is equivocal (Sanders, Parsons, and Santley 1979:134, 406–9). But it seems unlikely that any deterioration that may have occurred was sufficient to have precipitated decline and collapse, particularly since the resources of the Valley of Mexico were underexploited so markedly during the Middle Horizon. If environmental deterioration was operative, it must have been in combination with other processes of economic, social, and political change (McClung de Tapia 1978).

The population of Teotihuacan appears to have reached close to its maximum rapidly early in its history, thereafter remaining on a long plateau (Cowgill 1979a, 1979b) until it began to decline in the Metepec phase, if we are to judge from our ceramic counts (Cowgill 1983a). It is difficult to estimate by how much, but decline of any kind would be significant.

An important study of burials by Rebecca Storey (1985) from an apartment compound in the potters' barrio of Tlajinga (33:S3W1) provides quantifiable evidence about the quality of life in Teotihuacan.[27] The compound is thought to have been occupied by people who as a group were "one of the lowest in status" of those so far investigated at Teotihuacan (Storey and Widmer 1982:56). The remains of at least 171 individuals were found in excavation, 67 of which were in recognizable burials (Storey 1985:524–25). This study suggests that Teotihuacan, like other nonindustrialized cities around the world, was not a healthy place for many of its inhabitants. The life tables Storey constructed show that "juvenile mortality [was] quite high." Only about half survived to age 15 (Storey 1985:532). Almost one-third of her sample (52) were perinatals (Storey 1985:525–26, Tables 4, 5). Paleopathological analysis indicated that childhood was subjected to significant growth interruptions and was "not very healthy," perhaps because of the "synergistic effect of poor nutrition and disease" (Storey 1983). Storey also found evidence of prenatal stress and growth disruption in the eighth month of pregnancy, resulting in a leveling off of growth in this critical period. This alone could account for a high infant-mortality rate, since Storey reports that low-birth-weight infants have a death rate thirty times higher than infants of normal birthweight (Storey 1983). Comparable Old World conditions existed in ancient Rome and in seventeenth-century London (Storey 1985:531–32, Fig. 1). Storey suggests that if her data are representative of lower-status levels in Teotihuacan, the city "was probably dependent on rural migration to maintain its numbers . . . for at least the latter part of its history." (Storey 1985:533).

Storey's data span most of the Middle Horizon, beginning with the Early Tlamimilolpa phase, but appear to end in the middle of the Metepec phase (Storey 1985:526). Her data are silent, therefore, on the question of possibly worsening circumstances during the city's last fifty years and therefore may not bear directly on the collapse. But if her data are in any way representative of the mortality rate of a significant proportion of the population, the population decline in the Metepec phase could be accounted for in large part or entirely if the city gradually ceased to attract outsiders in sufficient numbers to compensate for those lost because city dwellers were unable to reproduce themselves.

Evidence from several of our excavations could be taken to suggest a population decline in the latter part of the Xolalpan phase (ca. A.D. 550–650). We found no Late Xolalpan phase constructions in excavations in three major city buildings: two on its principal avenue, the "Street of the Dead" (the Palace of the Sun [TE14] and the Great Compound North Platform [TE17]), and the third, an apartment compound a short distance away, Tepantitla (TE23), in the northeastern part of the city (Fig. 5.2) (Rattray n.d.b). This evidence is put into a different perspective, however, when taken in context with other relevant data. Excavations in two other apartment compounds west of the "Street of the Dead" each disclosed a series of earth floors datable to the Late Xolalpan phase (Tetitla [TE24] and Yayahuala [TE26]). In still another excavation in the northwestern part of the city, on the west edge of the "Old City," a midden of redeposited construction fill yielded mixed deposits of the late Xolalpan and Metepec phases in enormous quantities (TE12) (Rattray n.d.b).

What this evidence *may* indicate is that during the Late Xolalpan phase, Teotihuacan entered a temporary period of decline reflected in the relatively few major constructions undertaken compared to the periods before it (Early Xolalpan) and after it (Metepec). Earth floors accumulated with use, but major constructions were not undertaken. We may be seeing the early consequences of some of the processes implying deterioration of economic and political conditions in the Teotihuacan domain and beyond, discussed previously. But if this did begin to occur, the process was reversed in the Metepec phase. It will be difficult to pursue the question of a possible early decline that was later reversed, because in much of our data we are not able to discriminate between the Early and Late Xolalpan phases.

Although none of this helps resolve the problem of population decline in the Metepec phase, it serves to emphasize even more strongly how much construction activity occurred then. A considerable amount of building activity on the "Street of the Dead" took place at that time—in the Ciudadela (TE25S), the city's political center; in its counterpart structure across the street, the Great Compound (TE17), probable site of the city's principal marketplace and probably where sections of its bureaucracy were installed; and in the Palace of the Sun (TE14), the probable residence of the uppermost levels of the priestly hierarchy serving the Pyramid of the Sun, the city's major pyramid. Many apartment compounds also were rebuilt at this time—Tetitla (TE24), Tepantitla (TE23), Teopancaxco (TE20), Yayahuala (TE26), the Oaxaca barrio compound (TE3), and others. Some of the finest mural paintings date to this phase. This kind of activity is one of the reasons I have said that the Metepec phase was not a time of obvious decline. It may even represent a resurgence, a conscious effort to "turn around" and to restore the city's appearance of prosperity.

At the same time, new construction may have been selective. For example, temples that were parts of complexes fronting the "Street of the Dead," but that were themselves removed from the avenue, may have been allowed to deteriorate. Such seems to have been the case with the main temple-pyramid (TE27) in the Puma Mural Group and the plaza floor in front of it. The latter was pitted with holes and its surface eroded away in many places. The *tablero-talud* on the lower platform of the temple-pyramid was badly in need of refinishing when it was burned in the final days of destruction. Structures may have undergone such cycles regularly, for an earlier plaza floor in the Puma Mural Group also was in a badly deteriorated condition when it was covered by a later floor. The upkeep of structures on the "Street of the Dead" must have been a formidable task (as it is today), requiring crews of full-time plasterers and masons whose jobs never ended. Even so, the poor state of repair of this important temple was notable. We do not know how unusual this may have been. It was not true of the back of another temple (TE21) we partially exposed, fronting the "Street of the Dead" much farther to the south, in the "Street of the Dead" Complex. That structure was in an excellent state of repair. But it was true of the main patio of an impressive palace in the "Plaza of the Moon," as we know from Acosta's account of the last melancholy years of the principal patio of the Palace of Quetzalpapalotl, when it went through a gradual process of being closed off, culminating in its complete closure after it had begun to collapse dangerously (Acosta 1964:63). Parts of the North Palace in the Ciudadela were similarly closed off in the Metepec phase (Jarquín and Martínez 1982a:126, Lám. 2).

We are left with evidence for a possible population decline of unspecified dimensions. But it has a context demonstrating that the city was not simply falling apart slowly in a generalized decline. Much more complex, contradictory, and conflicting processes were being played out, and there is no satisfactory, simple explanation for it.

Potentially the most significant evidence bearing on the city's last years is the evidence suggesting that Teotihuacan society was experiencing serious internal problems by that time. It was a time when differences in status in the middle ranges of Teotihuacan society may have been widening; a time of increasing prosperity for some, of increasingly difficult times for others, perhaps for most; a time when military men and military orders were prominently represented and honored in various media; a time of continued secularization of political roles in a still formally sacralized polity; and perhaps a time when the integrative bonds of the state religion were weakening. This sounds cumulatively more impressive than it is. The evidence for most of these changes is sufficiently tenuous and ambiguous that they should be viewed only tentatively as suggesting a trend.

The evidence bearing on the sharpening of social distinctions and on the widening of differences in economic well-being comes from an analysis by Martha Sempowski (1981, 1982) of seventy Xolalpan and Metepec phase burials from three apartment compounds in the western half of the city—Tetitla, Zacuala Patios, and La Ventilla B. The sample obviously is quite small and localized. Earlier analysis of architectural and artistic evidence demonstrated that there were wide ranges of internal variation in status within apartment compounds (R. Millon 1976, 1981). This has been supported and amplified by Sempowski's analyses[28]; however, she found less internal variation in the Metepec phase than there had been earlier. As for differences among the compounds, there was an increase in the average richness of offerings of those buried at Tetitla in the Metepec phase, not only over those buried in the other two compounds but also in relation to those buried in Tetitla itself during the Xolalpan phase. At the same time, richness of offerings for those buried in Zacuala Patios dropped sharply from the Xolalpan to the Metepec phase, bringing them much closer to the offerings of those buried at La Ventilla B (lowest on the scale earlier), where there was no significant change. Thus, there was a widening of the gap in relative richness of offerings between the group at the top and the other two groups in the Metepec phase. The "top" in this case means a point near the upper end of the intermediate range of status. It does not refer to people in the upper strata. Tetitla's walls are decorated profusely with mural paintings, some of which manifest strong artistic links with the Maya. Altogether the compound has the flavor of an "International House" (C. Millon 1972; Hall 1962), but the status of its occupants falls far short of those at or near the top in Teotihuacan society.

In addition to the widening gap in richness of offerings,[29] there was a significant decrease in the number of different kinds of objects in burial offerings in Zacuala Patios and La Ventilla B from the Xolalpan to the Metepec phase (for example, cylindrical tripods and shell no longer accompanied burials in either compound). These and other kinds of objects increase in number at Tetitla during this same period. As noted earlier, ceramic offerings in general are of poorer quality. What may have been the most precious of all substances—jade—is no longer found in any burials in any of the three compounds in the Metepec phase.[30]

Sempowski's sample is small, but her analysis is suggestive. Inequality may have been increasing to a critical point late in the city's history. At the same time, even if this analysis is borne out in further work, it is well to keep in mind that societies do not necessarily decline, let alone collapse, because of social inequalities.

Teotihuacan must have had a powerful, effective, and reliable army by the first century B.C. Yet, as we have seen, military representations do not appear at Teotihuacan until the fifth century. The reader also will recall the appearance of military personages in Teotihuacan dress at Uaxactún, Tikal, Yaxhá, Tres Islas, and Kaminaljuyú beginning in the fourth century. *Atlatls* (spear throwers) of wood have been found at a Teotihuacan or Teotihuacan-period site named Metlapilco in south central Morelos in a Xolalpan phase context (Cook de Leonard 1956). But artistic representations of military men become numerous only in the last century or so of Teotihuacan's existence.[31] When they bear military equipment, the most common items are spears, spear throwers, and shields; some figures, notably among figurines, wear cotton armor and helmets. Military men not only are portrayed in various media; they are honored. This is shown by the prominence of their representations and by the contexts in which they appear, as well as by the fact that deities are portrayed bearing weapons. Military orders also are represented. A military emblem most frequently represented in the city's last phase is a hand in a shield, accompanied by a bird, usually with a spear or crossed spears behind it (von Winning 1948). As previously noted, a form of this "war emblem" appeared hundreds of years earlier at Tikal in the headdress of Stormy Sky, the successor to the Teotihuacan-related Curl Nose, on Stela 31—the stela with the Teotihuacan-related military figures.

We do not know how the army was constituted. Membership in a military order may have been an achieved status, as it was among the Aztecs. The honor accorded the military in these representations late in the Middle Horizon may represent a shift in power in the direction of the military or, much more likely, the validation in art of a shift that already had taken place. The internal consequences of this for Teotihuacanos may have been an increase in the repressive face of the state and in its obtrusiveness, together perhaps with a gradual erosion of the legitimacy of its authority.

The prominence of the honors rendered the military is one manifestation of the extent of the secularization of political roles by the time of the Metepec phase. But even if military men eventually took over Teotihuacan society—and I do not believe the evidence argues that they did—it seems highly probable that the form of Teotihuacan's sacralized polity would have been retained. It is difficult to judge how far the de facto secularization of authority had proceeded late in the Middle Horizon. It is surely significant that the military representations themselves show iconographic connections to supernatural beings worshiped in the city (see, for example, the paintings in the White Patio of the Atetelco compound [Miller 1973:158–62] or the figure in cotton armor with the tassel headdress and the Storm God glyph [R. Millon 1973:Fig. 49c]).

Such representations might be interpreted as reflecting a military takeover for which divine sanction is claimed; there is a more likely explanation, however. The visible embodiment of Teotihuacan's sacralized polity was the Ciudadela compound, where palaces for the rulers were incorporated in and formed a small part of a great enclosure with sixteen temples, one of them a major temple-pyramid. Although it may not have continued to serve as the day-to-day residence of the city's rulers (Cowgill 1983b), the rebuilding of parts of it during the Metepec phase, followed by the thoroughness and fury with which it and some of its inhabitants were destroyed, demonstrates that it remained the actual as well as the symbolic seat of power and authority until the very end. For this reason it seems highly probable that however far secularization of authority actually had proceeded, the rulers of Teotihuacan in attempting to exercise their authority would have continued to present themselves more as sacralized guardians of the faith governing under divine protection rather than as military figures ruling with divine sanction.

The possible weakening of the integrative bonds of religion referred to earlier rests on the most tenuous evidence of all. The great proliferation in the manufacture and distribution of *candeleros*, the small ceramic ritual objects for burning incense, suggests that they may have been used in personal rites at the household level to take the place of ritual practices formerly carried out in temples. The argument is tenuous because the proliferation of *candeleros* may be due just as well to the intensification of traditional ritual practices and attendant beliefs as to their decentralization or attenuation.

In all of the foregoing there is much that may be symptomatic of decline. But one is still left with the impression that none of these deteriorating or aggravating conditions represented irreversible processes. To account for what, in hindsight, we know did not reverse itself, we may have to return to our examination of the administrative machinery of the Teotihuacan state and the management, or mismanagement, of the Teotihuacan economy and polity. It may be that a critical reason for the alleged deterioration of economic conditions in the Teotihuacan domain was long-term mismanagement (Robert Adams 1978)—rigid inflexibility toward what needed change and gratuitous interference with what was working (Cowgill, this volume). Policies that might have made sense when inaugurated (such as the population resettlement) may have been maintained long after they began to cause problems of their own (the underutilization of the valley's resources). Policies that seem to have been working (the exploitation of the cotton-producing lands in Morelos) may have been sabotaged by bureaucratic interference (restructuring the Morelos settlement hierarchy to nucleate it on the Teotihuacan model). The same combination of inflexibility and interference may have affected other dimensions of the Teotihuacan economy and polity. The impressive exercise in statecraft manifest in the formation and growth of the Teotihuacan domain hundreds of years earlier may have become transformed gradually into an inefficient, incompetent bureaucracy, with officials who were unable to refrain from tampering with productive enterprises or to react appropriately to changing circumstances. If this is what happened, we are left with the question of why it may have been possible to reverse this process once but not twice. Is this an example of what Robert Adams (1978:332) has called "loss of resilience"? If so, when does such a process become irreversible? Are we able to recognize it as such only because of its consequences? Is the marked "unevenness" in development we see in the Metepec phase—great activity and prosperity in some sectors, slow-down and deteriorating conditions in others—another common char-acteristic of the final phase of the process of collapse in any complex nonindustrialized society? Is it possible, as George Cowgill (personal communication, 1983) has suggested, that collapse was unavoidable, no matter how the state was administered? Is it possible that accumulating difficulties stemming from such processes of change as discussed above were sufficient to bring the city down? Even if this were so, the form taken by the final catastrophe would remain unexplained. It appears much more likely that such changes were necessary but not sufficient in them-selves to set in motion the planned, organized devastation that ended Teotihuacan's domination.

DESTRUCTION BY FIRE

The end of Teotihuacan as a major power was fiery and cataclysmic. The fire was very selective. Violent destruction and burning were confined largely to monumental architecture on the "Street of the Dead" and to temples and associated buildings in the rest of the city. Our initial mapping survey recorded a high concentration of evidence for burning in the center and little of it elsewhere in the city. Because of the importance of this question, between 1974 and 1979 we systematically resurveyed major parts of the city specifically for such evidence, both the structures along the "Street of the Dead" and the permanent structures in eleven of the remaining eighteen square kilometers of construction, including close to a thousand apartment compounds (42 percent of the total). On the "Street of the Dead" and for varying distances on either side of it unequivocal evidence of burning was found on 147 buildings, with an additional 31 possibly burned. This includes virtually all the buildings on the "Street of the Dead" on which judgment was possible, excluding only those so completely reconstructed or otherwise altered that no basis for judgment existed. In the rest of the city, of a total of 68 temples examined specifically for evidences of burning, 28 were burned and 8 were possibly burned, for a total of 53 percent, whereas 22 showed no signs of burning (32 percent), and 10 were so altered that no judgment was possible. Of a total of 965 apartment compounds similarly examined, 45 showed clear evidence of burning (5 percent), 85 others were possibly burned (9 percent), for a total of 14 percent as opposed to 53 percent for temples. It is clear that the principal targets of burning were temples, pyramids, and public buildings.

What were the circumstances immediately preceding this deliberately planned systematic destruction? What we now know of the city's last years does not seem to prepare us for it. In 1981 I speculated on the immediate antecedents of the city's violent end in the following passage:

> Accumulating problems and conflicts, internal and external, may have been met by more exercise of force than customary, exacerbating existing tensions and creating new ones, and precipitating rapid, convulsive social and economic deterioration—so rapid that it is not manifest in what we see. For Teotihuacan to have been destroyed as it was, the state apparatus must have been in a condition of near impotence. Except for one *possible* reference by Leopoldo Batres (1906:15), there is no evidence that the city's inhabitants were slaughtered. The data available imply that the destruction was relatively bloodless, whether carried out from within or by invaders. This must mean that it occurred at a time of internal crisis. In the face of growing crisis, a split may have developed within the hierarchy over how to meet it. The ensuing factional dispute could have grown so deep and bitter as gradually to paralyze the power of the state and render it unable to act effectively when the onslaught came, from within or without. (R. Millon 1981:236)

The location and intensity of the fires along the "Street of the Dead" point to an organized, planned campaign of ritual destruction. Destruction most frequently took the form of burning in front of and on both sides of staircases and on the tops of temple platforms. In the Ciudadela all temples have visible evidence of burning with one equivocal exception (1B':N1E1). The same is true of most of the other structures, including the two palaces (for example, Jarquín and Martínez 1982). The sides of the Ciudadela temple platforms fronting the "Street of the Dead" were intensely burned in addition to the fronts and sides of their staircases. Across the street in the Great Compound all but three of the apartment compounds that have not been heavily altered by modern land leveling show evidence of burning.

In the Plaza of the Moon the enormous stones that formed the balustrade of the great staircase of the *Plataforma Adosada* of the Pyramid of the Moon were "removed, stone by stone . . . and thrown a few hundred yards away . . . [in] . . . a huge effort of purposeful destruction" (Ignacio

Bernal in M. Coe 1968:72–73). Similar destruction was found in the southwestern part of the Moon Plaza, especially in the main patio of the Quetzalpapalotl Palace. But there, differing interpretations of what occurred are possible, because the sequence of events is partly masked by deep looters' pits that may not have coincided with the extensive dismantling and destruction (Acosta 1964; Bernal in M. Coe 1968:72).

In 1978 we excavated part of the south side of the principal temple of the Puma Mural Group (TE27) (Fig. 5.2, no. 36) and found it to have been violently destroyed and burned. Building stone and building blocks of carved *tepetate* hit the plaza floor with such force that they bounced, leaving yellow smudges. A green onyx sculpture was shattered and its pieces scattered. A thin layer of ash covered the plaza floor. Construction debris from the destruction of the temple seems to have fallen on the plaza floor while an intense fire was burning on it (Sempowski 1979). A burning beam fell on the base of the temple platform. Destruction here was violent and thorough.

Eduardo Matos (1980) describes similar evidence in excavations carried out in 1964 in the "Street of the Dead" Complex,[32] a large walled complex between the Sun Pyramid and the Ciudadela discovered in our survey (Fig. 5.2, no. 43) (110:N2W1, 13:N2E1, 14:N2E1). Matos reports evidence of destruction and burning on the preserved floor of one of the temples, along with associated looters' pits. He suggests that the rooms of all temples on the "Street of the Dead" were similarly looted and burned (Matos 1980:87).

Mexican government excavation in the Ciudadela in 1981 disclosed additional evidence of violent destruction. In excavating the central temple on the rear (east) platform of the Ciudadela, the most important temple in the most important of the temple clusters on its four platforms (1Q:N1E1), Ana María Jarquín and Enrique Martínez found the scattered fragments of a carved stone female figure sixty centimeters in height scattered about the base of the burned temple platform, as though it had been smashed on top of the temple and its pieces deliberately hurled in all directions (Jarquín and Martínez, 1982b).[33] Fragments of four other sculptures were found scattered around this central temple (Jarquín and Martínez 1982c:36–39).

Even more dramatic evidence of violence comes from the North and South Palaces of the Ciudadela, where dismembered skeletons were found. These were individuals who had been felled, their skulls shattered and their bodies cut to pieces. Articulated limbs and other skeletal parts of an individual in the North Palace (1D:N1E1) (Burial 65) were scattered from the west room of the palace's northwest apartment across a large part of its central patio (Jarquín and Martínez 1982a:103, 107, Foto 5; González Miranda and Fuentes 1982:plan ff. 426). The person cut down evidently had been richly adorned. Associated with the dismembered body were many plaques of jade, possibly from a mosaic, and beads of jade, black stone, and shell. Burial 72 was said to have been another dismembered individual apparently found in an access way south of the west room of the northwest apartment (L. González Miranda and E. Martínez, personal communication, 1983; González Miranda and Fuentes 1982:422, plan ff. 426). Still another individual was found dismembered near the northwest corner of the main patio of the South Palace (1E:N1E1) (Burial 91) (González Miranda and Martínez, personal communication, 1983).[34]

Evidence of burning on floors and walls was visible everywhere in both the North and South Palaces in 1983; a layer of ash and carbon[35] had rested on North Palace floors exposed in 1981. Such a layer was found throughout the North Palace in subsequent excavations (Jarquín and Martínez 1982a:101). Considerable looting was associated with this destruction throughout the North Palace, much of it from burials.[36] On the floors of patios, porticos, and rooms, broken sculptures and other objects of stone, pottery, and other materials were strewn about. Broken braziers of the Old Fire God were found on the floors of the east porticos of three apartments (Jarquín and Martínez 1982a:121). At least six smashed depictions of the Teotihuacan Storm God were found in or adjoining the patio of the northwest apartment—the remains of four mold-impressed Storm God faces from Thin Orange vessels were lying face up on thin layers of ash in 1981, and a smashed ceramic disc and a shattered, stucco, painted vessel bore effigies of the god in the area of the first-mentioned dismembered skeleton (Jarquín and Martínez 1982a:103). The same patio had fragments of *almenas*, standard Teotihuacan roof decorations for temples, shrines, and public buildings, some burned bright orange. More of these were found in other parts of the palace (Jarquín and Martínez 1982a:121).

The Temple of Quetzalcoatl was undergoing destruction at this time as well (Cabrera and Sugiyama 1982). The great stone heads adorning the temple facades were dismantled and sent crashing down to the north and south, where they fell into the passageways separating the palaces from the temple and onto the palaces themselves. Stone head fragments found by excavators in the southwest apartment of the North Palace had fallen only into its main patio or other unroofed spaces, demonstrating that this part of the North Palace had not yet been destroyed when the dismantling of the Temple of Quetzalcoatl took place (see, for example, Jarquín and Martínez 1982a:Foto 9).

All of this information on the destruction of the city's religio-political center is in accord with earlier evidence for the destruction of the center of the city. But it goes beyond that evidence, rendering explicit what before had been implicit, and singling out other dimensions of the process of destruction. There is a quality of excess in some of the newly uncovered evidence of violence in the Ciudadela—in the dismemberment of the slaughtered individuals in the palaces and in the dispersal over eight hundred square meters of the smashed fragments of the goddess sculpture. This manifest evidence of fury and rage so impressed the Mexican investigators that they singled it out for comment (Jarquín and Martínez 1982a:103; Jarquín and Martínez 1982b:126; L. González Miranda, personal communication, 1981). The quality of excess displayed in these acts has its counterpart in the excessive thoroughness with which the center of the city was destroyed. Temples, public buildings, and palaces were not merely destroyed—they were knocked down, torn apart, burned, reduced to rubble, time after time, building after building, for more than two kilometers. There is a Carthaginian quality to this destruction. More than an explosive flash of fury is represented in these ruins. The process of overkill was carried out not only in the Ciudadela, the seat of power, but in structure after structure along the full length of the "Street of the Dead" to the Moon Plaza and Moon Pyramid. Clearly, those who carried out this process of systematic destruction were well enough organized and motivated, possessed of objectives clearly enough defined, and passionately enough involved to persist for however long it took to carry through those objectives to completion.

The scores of temples demolished on the "Street of the Dead" were never rebuilt; most never were used again as temples. The city may have been abandoned, or largely so, for a time after this destruction. One burned apartment compound excavated in part near the eastern end of the city's East Avenue may show evidence of abandonment for a period estimated as fifty years (Rattray 1981b:216; but see also Scott 1982).[37] Thereafter a much diminished city grew up again on the site of the former metropolis with a total population that must have numbered in the tens of thousands and that played a dominant role in major parts of the Valley of Mexico.[38] But it never again was a major power. Moreover, the center of the former city never again was re-occupied intensively, and the once-sacred places in the center of the former metropolis were the foci of no more than sporadic religious activity until the time of the Aztecs (see, for example, E. Romero 1982). These transformations are directly related and serve to highlight the significance of the ritual destruction of Teotihuacan's monuments.

Data on the differential burning of parts of the city did not exist until the city was mapped. As a result, it was not possible to put into context the problem posed by the "fall" of Teotihuacan, nor to consider whether and to what extent its ritual destruction had a structured dimension that might be found in the histories of other Mesoamerican centers. The ritual destruction of monuments is a deeply rooted tradition in Mesoamerica.

We see it first in Olmec civilization at San Lorenzo, in the Early Horizon, circa 1000 B.C. (M. Coe 1968:47–55, 72–77; 1981:139–42; Grove 1981). We also see it in Teotihuacan itself in the fourth century A.D., hundreds of years before its destruction. At that time, both the front and sides of the stone staircase of the Temple of Quetzalcoatl in the Ciudadela were burned by a fire so intense it cracked some building stones and caused others to spall. A renewal followed in the form of a new construction in front of and resting against and on top of what had been ritually destroyed (the four-tiered temple platform called the *Plataforma Adosada*) (R. Millon 1973:Figs. 32b, 34).

The traditional interpretation of the "fall" of Teotihuacan—destruction by fire (Armillas 1950:69)—has been amply confirmed. But the destruction was a ritual destruction that cannot be understood purely in terms of pillaging, looting, and burning. It must be seen in its cultural context. When so viewed, the destruction of the city's temples recalls planned acts of ritual destruction at other times and places in Mesoamerica. Planned ritual destruction of monuments was sometimes followed by renewal and rebuilding, as at the Temple of Quetzalcoatl in the fourth century, and at other times by the abandonment of part or all of the center undergoing destruction. See, for example, the contrasting accounts by Michael Coe on San Lorenzo (1968:47–55; 1981:139–42; Coe and Diehl 1980) and by William Coe on the ritual destruction and rebuilding involving Stela 31 at Tikal (1965:34).[39]

The analysis by David Grove (1981) of the reasons for the destruction of the monuments of San Lorenzo (and other Olmec centers) is pertinent here because it points up differences between Olmec monument destruction and that at Teotihuacan. Grove (1981:54–55, 61–65, 67–68), arguing against explanations based on iconoclasm and revolt, suggests that those Olmec monuments that were destroyed (not all were) were seen as repositories of supernatural power associated with rulers or "chiefs" and that their destruction was undertaken primarily "to neutralize supernatural power" unleashed on the death of a ruler or "chief." In support of this view, he notes that many of the destroyed monuments at San Lorenzo were buried in straight lines after their mutilation and that not all of them were destroyed at the same time. The destruction at Teotihuacan manifests neither of these characteristics. The destruction *was* carried out at the same time, and as we have seen, destroyed images were given no special treatment after their destruction. Iconoclasm does seem to have formed part of the process of destruction represented by the systematic smashing, dismantling, and burning of central Teotihuacan. The supernatural power that may have been seen as embodied in images and temples was rendered impotent through systematic destruction and burning. Burning itself must have formed an important part of the process of ritual destruction.

The extent, intensity, and excessiveness of the destruction argue that, although its form was ritual, its purpose was political. The burning of a temple had a political purpose at the time of the Spanish Conquest—it symbolized the subjugation of a community by its conquerors and the subjugation of its god by the god of its conquerors. Those who destroyed Teotihuacan, whether Teotihuacano or foreigner, juxtaposed a tradition of ritual destruction of monuments, whose purpose was essentially religious, with a tradition of the destruction and burning of a temple to achieve a political end. The ultimate purpose must have been the destruction of Teotihuacan as a dominant political power. This was the reason for the seemingly excessive destruction. To accomplish this political end must have appeared to require more than the destruction of the palaces and temples in its political center. It also must have appeared necessary to destroy Teotihuacan as a religious center—so thoroughly to destroy its array of temples, their images and paraphernalia, that they no longer would be charged with the powerful religious meaning they had had for so many for so long. Because there were so many temples and public buildings in the heart of the city, this could not be accomplished easily. What was involved was a monumental undertaking—not merely to burn, but wholly to demolish images and temples in a process of ritual destruction unprecedented in scope before and since.

Those who carried out the destruction were so successful that the new Teotihuacan that later grew up around the ruins of the old never again approached the greatness of its predecessor. Its importance remained localized. It never again was a major religious center. The "Street of the Dead" would have been for the first time an apt description, and it remained so for hundreds of years. No longer did any of its temples function; no longer was it the pilgrimage center it had been. Most of the buildings on the "Street of the Dead" were never used again. Where reuse occurred, it appears primarily to have been sporadic, with some exceptions six or seven hundred years later in Aztec times.

The measure of the importance of religion and ideology in the rise to dominance of Teotihuacan is apparent in the form taken by its destruction. To destroy Teotihuacan and prevent it from ever again rising to a position of dominance, it was necessary to destroy all its sacred buildings and desacralize their sites through ritual destruction by fire. The religion of Teotihuacan must have been inextricably tied to place, either because this is where the world had been created and where time began, or because of similar if less cosmically elemental beliefs. The totality, scale, and intensity of the destruction must have been such that it no longer was possible to reconstitute in any viable form the belief system that had been shattered—either at Teotihuacan itself or elsewhere.

WHO DID IT?

Since 1976 I have been trying with little success to resolve the problem of who was responsible for the destruction of the center of Teotihuacan. The 1980–1982 work by Instituto Nacional de Antropología e Historia (INAH) investigators has added immeasurably to our knowledge about the attack. But evidence for the identity of the attackers is largely negative. No exotic or foreign persons or artifacts have been associated with it. No bodies other than those discussed earlier have been found (they may have been removed by the survivors, of course). The enigma remains. Nevertheless, it seems worthwhile briefly to reexamine the question, even though most of what I have to say is speculative.

It now seems to me more likely that Teotihuacanos rather than outsiders were responsible. I say this not only because of the recent discoveries in the Ciudadela, but also because the scale, intensity, duration, and sheer excessiveness of the destruction imply a sustained motivation and dedication that seems more likely to be the consequence of explosive internal pressures than of actions carried out by outsiders. The latter cannot be excluded, of course, nor can a combination of the two.[40] Obviously, we are far from understanding how and why a sufficient number of Teotihuacanos might have reached the point of embarking on the destructive course that was to end forever the city's preeminence. If the impetus for the destruction was internal, it is at least possible that the evidence we seek may exist in the city itself, if we are able to recognize it.

The previously discussed evidence suggesting deteriorating conditions in the exchange network of the state within and beyond the Teotihuacan domain would have posed increasingly severe political problems both within the city and beyond it. Very likely the military would have been called upon more often to maintain state control. Increasing stress may have exacerbated existing differences, resulting in divisions so profound as to shatter the structure of Teotihuacan society. Since the temples and palaces in the city's political center were subjected to especially violent treatment, the city's rulers must have been the major target of the assault. Nonetheless, this was not a case of usurpation; after the Ciudadela was laid waste, it never again served as temple-palace. If the original impetus for those who later were to lead the assault that destroyed the city was a change in leadership that would have been at most a coup d'etat on the part of a bureaucratic faction, the process, once underway, may have changed its character. Once set in motion, it may have taken on a life of its own, with consequences not foreseen or intended. This may account for the ensuing impotence and breakdown of the state referred to earlier.

The occasion for the beginning of the process that led to such total destruction may have been completion of an important cycle of time when ritual destruction and renewal were scheduled to take place. What perhaps started as scheduled ritual destruction to be followed by renewal in the form of rebuilding may have been transformed under the leadership of a faction in the ruling hierarchy into an attack on the temple-palace itself, an attack not only on the rulers, such as may have occurred at other times, but also this time on the gods themselves. Ritual destruction was assuming a different form.

The violence of the iconoclasm manifest in the evidence from the Ciudadela argues this, as well as supporting the earlier argument that the rulers of the city continued to the end to present themselves as sanctified. In demolishing the temples and shrines of the state religion and shattering so violently the images of the gods, the iconoclasts were attacking the ultimate values of the society. If no new unifying system of belief was at hand for the insurgents and their leaders, systematic organized destruction, albeit in traditional ritual form, may have been followed by a period of disorientation, exhaustion, and rootlessness, in which local groups would have shifted for themselves.

Even so, the foregoing still seems insufficient to explain the intensity, pervasiveness, and frenzy of the destructive process carried out with such thoroughness and perseverance over so wide an area. Here perhaps the abiding qualities of Teotihuacan as city and state may be relevant. The preponderating influence of the Teotihuacan state in parts of Mesoamerica beyond its central Mexican domain endured for hundreds of years. The paramount role assumed by the city in its immediate region in the first century A.D. persisted for some seven hundred years, an extraordinarily long period of time for a single community to maintain itself in a position of dominance at once political, religious, economic, and cultural. Other cities have had longer lives, but underwent periods of decline or eclipse between periods of dominance. Although Teotihuacan may not be unique in the length of time it maintained its dominance, it surely is unusual in this respect. The demonstrable continuity of the Teotihuacan polity does not imply, of course, an untroubled political life. The vicissitudes of political life over the 700-year span of its existence surely must have included palace intrigues and coups, depositions of rulers, coups d'etat, and other political upheavals, as well as changing fortunes for various cults and social groups. (Cowgill 1983b discusses some of these possibilities.) But whatever forms political change and overturns may have taken, however violently a coup d'etat may have been expressed, the objective seems not to have been to alter the basic structure of the Teotihuacan state.

It may be unreasonable to expect to find surviving evidence of ideological views differing from or transcending the prevailing ideology of the state, particularly when we have no textual evidence. Nevertheless, what we do know does not lead us to expect to find an intellectual climate hospitable to the expression of conflicting or competing ideological views. The possibility that the expression of such differences was effectively repressed for centuries may be a clue to the explosive frenzy with which Teotihuacan's monuments were assaulted in the convulsion that destroyed them.

The price paid for political continuity may have been the suppression of the potential for radical internal change and transformation—for changes analogous in scope to the transformational change that occurred when Teotihuacan first assumed a position of dominance in the Valley of Mexico, or, less comprehensively, for the transformation to a more secularized societal structure, such as we see later in central Mexico.[41] The ultimate consequences of long-term imposition of conformity and resistance to change may have been such that a process of change that might have transformed the structure of Teotihuacan society assumed an irreversibly destructive course, culminating in the cataclysm that destroyed it forever. What had been the ultimate source of enduring stability may have been transformed into a spectacularly calamitous instance of "pursuit of policy contrary to self-interest" (Tuchman 1984).

Establishing whether this or some other course of events is what happened will not be easy. Pursuing the question is clearly worth the effort, however, not only for an understanding of Teotihuacan, but also because it may help us better to comprehend analogous circumstances at other times and places. Also for future investigation is the question of what happened to the cultural tradition so strongly associated with the upper levels of the Teotihuacan hierarchy, both on the site of the former metropolis and elsewhere in central Mexico, after the process of destruction had run its course. The focus of this chapter has been on the process of collapse. But collapse is never without continuity, at least so far in human history, and we are likely to comprehend collapse itself more effectively as we gain a better understanding of the forms taken by continuity.

NOTES

Results from many different research projects are discussed in this chapter. Research under my direction was supported by National Science Foundation grants G23800, GS207, GS641, GS1222, GS2204, GS3137, and BNS77-08973, and was carried out with successive permits and contracts from the Instituto Nacional de Antropología e Historia (INAH) and the Secretaría de Educación Pública (SEP) in Mexico. From 1973 to 1979 our research facility at Teotihuacan was supported for varying periods by contributions from Brandeis University, the University of Rochester, the State University of New York at Buffalo, the University of Toronto, the University of Western Ontario, and the Ivey Foundation, London, Ontario, as well as by donations from individuals and corporations. Since 1979 the facility has been receiving support from National Endowment for the Humanities and National Science Foundation research grants to George Cowgill.

Those who read the first draft of this chapter will recognize how much it owes to discussions and interchanges at the School of American Research seminar in Santa Fe in March 1982. In addition, after the seminar George Cowgill made many searching criticisms of the draft that led me to make significant changes in it. Other changes were suggested by Martha Sempowski and Margaret Turner.

Clara Millon's contributions, as always, were numerous, substantive, and fundamental. She proposed many changes, often of basic importance; she suggested alternative approaches to difficult questions and issues; she aided in clarifying and resolving many problems; and perhaps most important of all, she helped bring to the text what balance it has.

1. Much of what is stated below that pertains to particular discoveries outside the city's center but within the city proper, or to a perspective provided by knowledge of the city in its totality, comes from the work of personnel associated with the Teotihuacan Mapping Project of the University of Rochester (R. Millon 1973; Millon, Drewitt, and Cowgill 1973).

2. Apartment compounds so far excavated were successively rebuilt two, three, four, or more times during the centuries they were in use.

3. This was the name given the avenue by the Aztecs at the time of the Spanish Conquest when the city's center had been in ruins for centuries. The Aztecs also gave the pyramids the names they now bear (i.e., Pyramid of the Sun and Pyramid of the Moon).

4. Existing data may be presenting a misleading view of the evidence, however. A major source, mural painting, is known primarily from later structures, since few of the earlier structures have been excavated. In addition, ceramic decoration is largely non-figurative before the Xolalpan phase (i.e., before A.D. 400).

5. Tula "didn't exist" at the time of Teotihuacan's collapse and played no role in it (Diehl 1981:293).

6. Throughout this period (the Middle Horizon, A.D. 200–750) (Fig. 5.4) the divided parts of the Tenanyecac area, forming the heart of Tlaxcala, apparently remained independent of Teotihuacan and of the immensely important, nearby central Mexican city of Cholula, which was culturally closely related to Teotihuacan. Cholula is south of Tlaxcala, in western Puebla, due east of the southern end of the Basin of Mexico (Fig. 5.3). Cholula and surrounding parts of the state of Puebla also appear to have remained independent of Teotihuacan throughout its ascendance. Tlaxcala was independent of the Aztecs at the time of the Spanish Conquest.

7. This date is based on the Goodman-Martínez-Thompson correlation of the Mayan and Christian calendars (see discussion in Lounsbury 1978).

8. One object from one of these burials (Problematic Deposit 50) was a large cylindrical tripod that depicts a procession of four armed Teotihuacan-related figures escorting two figures wearing tassel headdresses and apparently bearing gifts (Greene and Moholy-Nagy 1966). The temple away from which the figures are walking may represent Teotihuacan. The temple at which they are arriving, with its Maya figure greeting them with precious quetzal feathers, may represent Kaminaljuyu. A third structure, also with a Maya figure, resembles pyramids of the much later "Twin-Pyramid Complexes" at Tikal but, unlike the latter, has a temple on top.

9. Early Maya ceramics from the "merchants' barrio" at Teotihuacan, mentioned above, redeposited from an earlier occupation in that barrio, primarily date to roughly the same time period (ca. A.D. 250–550) and are "most closely comparable" in "paste variants" to pottery from "northern Belize and northwestern Campeche" (Ball 1983:137).

10. This is a modified version of the interpretation of Cheek (1977a:445–46, 448).

11. I am aware of the problematical basis of this interpretation. How problematical it is may be seen if we compare this evidence with the architectural evidence for a very different but perhaps in some ways analogous case, namely, the question of the influence of Sumer (or Elam) on the beginnings of civilization in Egypt (see summary in Frankfort 1956:121–37; also Smith 1981:35–37). However this architectural and other evidence is interpreted, there seems to be general agreement that it does not reflect any direct political intervention from the southern Mesopotamian region in the affairs of Egyptian states in the last years of the Predynastic period. I realize that my interpretation of the Kaminaljuyu evidence may be oversimplified. I put it forward only because I find other suggested interpretations overly complex for the evidence and even less satisfactory than mine. They also seem to me to rely much too heavily on analogies with the Aztecs. In addition, some of the arguments put forward against an interpretation based on domination by Teotihuacan (e.g., Sanders 1978) would seem to apply in many respects with almost equal force to alternative interpretations.

12. See also Berlo (1980:235ff., 331, and 1983b) for a discussion of the possible importance for Teotihuacan statecraft of Teotihuacan-related pilgrimage sites on the shores of Lake Amatitlán a short distance south of Kaminaljuyu.

13. The typical Teotihuacan temple consists of stepped platforms of one or more bodies or terraces decorated with horizontal *tableros* (rectangular tablets surrounded by projecting moldings) resting on sloping *taludes* (basal aprons).

14. For a discussion of Teotihuacan's distinctive orientation, possible reasons for it, and possible meanings associated with it, see R. Millon 1981:239–40n).

15. "TE" followed by a number refers to one of the University of Rochester Teotihuacan Mapping Project test excavations.

16. Ball examined more than 500 Maya sherds from our "merchants' barrio" excavations (1983:137). It should be noted that Evelyn Rattray (personal communication, 1984) disputes Ball's interpretations of our data.

17. These two structures bore east-of-north orientations approximating those of structures at Teotihuacan, whereas the earlier *tablero-talud* platform at Dzi-

bilchaltún was oriented to true north. (The basic Teotihuacan orientation was 15°30′ east of north.) Andrews points out that many other structures built at Dzibilchaltún at this time and thereafter bore east-of-north orientations (Andrews 1979, 1981:330–31; Andrews and Andrews 1980:295). The timing of this shift in structural orientations from circa true north to east of north rules out Teotihuacan as its direct source, but east-of-north orientations approximating those of Teotihuacan were widely followed in central Mexico and elsewhere after Teotihuacan ceased to be important.

18. Although the facade of Structure 1 does not have the *tablero-talud* form as recently reported (M. Coe 1980:77), the stucco-decorated upper facade has been considered a modified *tablero* (Freer 1987).

19. Hasso von Winning (1982) disputes Marcus's identification of the tassel headdress on these carvings and her identification of some figures as Teotihuacanos, excepting only the Teotihuacano on the left on the Bazán Stone. He does not dispute the closeness of the relationship; his argument is rather that the *adorno triple* on these carvings and in other contexts at Monte Albán is not the tassel headdress but rather a Zapotec design. In this he also disagrees with C. Millon (1973). His argument is weakened, however, by the fact that most of the contexts he cites seem at least potentially relatable to Teotihuacan.

20. After the collapse of the Teotihuacan state and the burning of much of the center of Teotihuacan, the city may have been abandoned, or largely so, for a brief period. The community that replaced it was of much diminished power, with an orbit that seems not to have extended beyond the Valley of Mexico.

21. The often-illustrated Teotihuacan stone mask with a mosaic overlay of shell and what appears to be turquoise (e.g., Meyer 1973:9, 169) is the best evidence for Teotihuacan use of turquoise. However, the mask, now in the Museum of Anthropology in Mexico City, is said to have come from Guerrero, and it is possible that the mosaic overlay postdates the Teotihuacan period.

22. Those living in the Río Papalotla area immediately to the south of the Teotihuacan Valley evidently continued to work (and control?) these lands after their resettlement in Teotihuacan throughout the Middle Horizon (Sanders, Parsons, and Santley 1979:393–94).

23. Following the model successfully used centuries earlier in the resettlement program in the Valley of Mexico?

24. Part of Hirth's argument was based on the assumption of increasing population at Teotihuacan during this period (1974:248–49), whereas population seems to have increased only slightly (Cowgill 1979a; 1979b:54–55), and then decreased. His argument is relevant, nonetheless, because as indicated, population increase need not be the only reason for increase in demand from an urban population.

25. Thin Orange is an imported ware whose place of manufacture has not been located but which may be in southern Puebla (Sotomayor and Castillo 1965). It is so abundant at Teotihuacan, and its distribution in so many parts of Mesoamerica is so closely connected with the city, that both its manufacture and its distribution must have been controlled from Teotihuacan.

26. This is a suggestion by George Cowgill (personal communication, 1983).

27. The excavation at site 33:S3W1 was carried out by Rebecca Storey and Randolph Widmer in 1980. See Sanders et al. 1982.

28. Similar evidence for internal variation at 33:S3W1 was reported by Storey (Storey and Widmer 1982:59–60).

29. The ring-base hemispherical bowls in local clays referred to above, possibly used as substitutes for their Thin Orange prototypes, may be a minor manifestation of the same process.

30. This is not necessarily an indication that sources of jade were no longer accessible to Teotihuacan; it may be just as well an indication of a widening of the gap between those at the top and the rest of Teotihuacan society. As discussed below, jade was conspicuously present in the Ciudadela when it was demolished; of course, we have no way of knowing whether such jade was newly imported.

31. See note 4. Figurines of military men date predominantly to the Metepec phase (Barbour 1976:140).

32. Major Mexican government excavations were carried out in 1981 and 1982 in the central part of the "Street of the Dead" Complex by Noel Morelos García. He found no burials in these excavations (whereas burials were found in excavations in process elsewhere) (Cabrera, Rodríguez, and Morelos 1982a, 1982b) and so speculated that this might mean that the "Street of the Dead" Complex was an administrative center where people did not live (Morelos García, personal communication, 1981). Unlikely as this may be, all but one of the 1980s and earlier excavations in the "Street of the Dead" Complex seem not to have yielded burials either—Excavations of 1917 and Edificios Superpuestos (Gamio 1922; Marquina 1964) and the Viking Group (Armillas 1944). The only exceptions are the problematic "sepulchres" reported by Charnay from his initial excavations at Edificios Superpuestos (1888:147–50), and a burial excavated by Instituto Nacional de Antropología e Historia (INAH) investigators that was apparently found in the same structure (González Miranda and Fuentes 1982:433, Plano 7).

The mound excavated by Matos (1980)(110:N2W1) may have been explored previously by Almaraz (1865:355) if the location shown in Gamio (1922:1:1:map fol. p. 106) is accurate. Almaraz, however, leaves the impression that the mound he explored was completely excavated. It is possible, therefore, that he excavated a mound in the center of what we now call the "Street of the Dead" Complex. Almaraz shows a mound there on his map (1865), whereas Charnay (1888:143) records no mound there, nor does Gamio (1922). Our map shows a slight depression on this spot (Millon, Drewitt, and Cowgill 1973:58–59, west of site 18:N2E1).

33. The sculpture, almost certainly clothed in perishable materials when in use, may have represented the "Great Goddess" of Teotihuacan, the female supernatural who was one of the triad of supernatural beings associated with the complexes of three temples found in the city; her presence is powerful and pervasive throughout the city. Representations of or related to this deity may have appeared on *tableros* on the *Adosada* of the Temple of Quetzalcoatl. An impressive carving of the "Great Goddess" (C. Millon's provisional designation) was found by Morelos García in the 1981 INAH excavations near the base of a temple (40H:N2W1) on the west side of the "Street of the Dead" in the central part of the "Street of the Dead" Complex (Cabrera, Rodríguez, and Morelos 1982b:311–12; erroneously identified as "Tlaloc" by Morelos García). The pres-

ence of a female deity, previously erroneously identified as "Tlaloc" or the "Rain God" (now termed the Storm God), first was discussed by Pasztory (1972 and definitively established in a 1973 paper; see also Pasztory 1976a, 1976b; Berlo 1980, 1983a). Pasztory's work constituted a major breakthrough in the study of Teotihuacan religion.

34. Burial 91 is incorrectly shown as having been found in the North Palace in Cabrera, Rodríguez, and Morelos (1982b:103, 422, and plan fol. 426) (Gonzaléz Miranda and Martínez, personal communication, 1983).

35. Also visible in this layer were fragments of *bajareque* burned orange. *Bajareque* is a mixture of mud, straw, grass, etc. used between beams in roof construction.

36. Except for Burial 91, the dismembered skeleton, no burials were found in the South Palace proper (González Miranda and Fuentes 1982: plan fol. 426). This may accord with architectural evidence suggesting that the South Palace was used more for public activities—such as audiences, judicial proceedings, state ceremonials, calendrical rituals—with the North Palace and its western adjunct (1C':N1E1) serving primarily private, residential, administrative, and other more narrowly secular ends.

37. There also may be evidence that the inhabitants of this apartment compound "fell victim to armed assault," as reported by Davies (1983:107–8).

38. For a discussion of this period with a different emphasis, see Sanders, Parsons, and Santley (1979:129–37).

39. Tula also underwent massive destruction and looting. Diehl (1981:292) writes:

Tula's destruction and looting is frequently associated with the final conquest of the city. I doubt this because the effort involved seems too great and too systematic to be the immediate aftermath of a conquest. Instead I think it was a planned, systematic treasure hunt directed by the rulers of Tenochtitlán [several hundred years later] or some other elite who claimed dynastic descent and attempted to validate it with bonafide Toltec art.

Diehl's observation might be reasonable if one tries to relate the scale of the destruction at Tula (far less than at Teotihuacan—there was far less to destroy—but still quite extraordinary) to the "immediate aftermath of a conquest." But if at Tula the destruction also was ritual destruction, especially ritual destruction with political objectives, his observation would not follow. The timing of the destruction at Tula is, of course, a critical question. Was the large-scale destruction and looting associated with the burning of the Tula acropolis or did it follow a period of abandonment? Although many of the buildings were excavated long ago, it still should be possible to find undisturbed evidence that could be excavated with this problem in mind. Whether Tula also was subjected to a process of ritual destruction is of major interest, given the evidence for the earlier ritual destruction at Teotihuacan.

40. Cowgill (personal communication, 1983) has suggested that a coalition of outsiders should be included among the groups that may have been responsible for the destruction of the center of Teotihuacan, outsiders from a number of different communities, including Cacaxtla. Cacaxtla is a site in Tlaxcala noted

for its post-Middle Horizon murals in Maya style featuring two groups in bloody combat (Foncerrada de Molina 1978, 1980; Kubler 1980; Quirarte 1983). Whatever the likelihood of such a coalition carrying out the kind of destruction found at Teotihuacan, it does seem possible that the Cacaxtla murals were thought by those who executed them to commemorate in some fashion a conflict associated with or otherwise related to the "fall" of Teotihuacan.

41. Or as the transformation described as occurring in some other early civilizations, as, for example, in southern Mesopotamia (e.g., Robert Adams 1966:120ff.).

The Dissolution of the
Roman Empire

G. W. Bowersock

No study of the collapse of ancient civilizations can avoid the Roman empire. Thanks to Gibbon, it is undoubtedly the best known candidate for decline and fall. The magnitude of the empire, its slow and complex dissolution, and the superabundant evidence make this case at once conspicuous and exceptional. Views of collapse that depend upon a loss of centralized control and political fragmentation themselves collapse before the cataclysmic restructuring and reorientation that took place in the Roman empire over several centuries. Ancient historians agree that the loss of centralized control took place in the Roman world in the third century A.D., but no one has ever suggested that the Roman empire collapsed until two centuries later at the earliest. Political fragmentation led to new seats of power closer to the periphery, and it redefined political and social boundaries in a way that facilitated the perpetuation of control from these new points.

Unlike the other civilizations considered in this volume, the Roman empire is fully documented in written sources of the period. The historians of antiquity, the inscriptions, the papyri, the coins all conspire to provide such details of the gradual dissolution of the Roman empire as are largely absent from the evidence for other ancient civilizations. Consequently, in the other cases the exploitation of archaeological data is often the principal foundation for inferences about the collapse of the civilizations they represent. Sophisticated procedures for interpreting those data have, to some extent, compensated for a lack of contemporary written evidence.

But it would be quite misguided to interpret the Roman empire solely on the basis of its archaeological evidence when we know so much more. In other words, the role of archaeology in understanding what has been called the decline and fall of Rome must inevitably be very different from the role it has elsewhere.

Accordingly, in trying to consider the Roman empire as an example of the collapse of an ancient civilization, we must be as clear as possible about the sense in which we understand collapse, the sources available for explaining it, and the historical confines of the empire itself. There was nothing homogeneous about the Roman empire. It was a shifting, coruscating, animate political system that can most profitably be compared with itself at different times. The notion of collapse need not even require a perceptible decline to explain it, although this is often presupposed. Teotihuacan collapsed after some seven hundred years because it was systematically destroyed in a ritual manner, as Millon has vividly shown in his chapter, and not—in any discernible way—as the result of gradual decay. Why it was destroyed, especially if by insiders (as Millon suspects), would be worth knowing, but there is insufficient evidence.

Furthermore, if we wish to look for a decline, we must likewise identify a peak, and that too is difficult. No historian would dare to tell us when Rome reached the pinnacle from which it began its decline. No one would wish to repeat Gibbon's mistake, and it is established by now that at the end of his life Gibbon himself knew that he had made a mistake (Craddock 1972:338). Not the Antonine Age, which he had originally seen as Rome's peak, or the Augustan Age or the Ciceronian Age or the time of the Punic Wars or, for that matter, the reign of Constantine can serve as the point from which Rome began an irreversible fall. Nor, regrettably, is archaeology of much help in this matter. The fundamental questions are still essentially those which Gibbon framed, and as a science archaeology had scarcely dawned upon scholarship in the eighteenth century. Nonetheless, had Gibbon been acquainted with the excavations of sites in Italy, North Africa, and Gaul, as well as the hellenized countries of Roman civilization, it is unlikely that these discoveries would have done more than fire his imagination, just as the antiquities he saw in Italy did before he undertook the history.

More serious than Gibbon's reappraisal of the beginnings of decline was his gradual postponing of the fall. The reader of his history at first feels that the increasing power of the military will lead to a moment of collapse, only to discover that it is the advent of Christianity that seems about to produce the fall we have been led to expect. Yet, after a certain time, it is not Christianity but barbarism that is presented as the harbinger of disaster. But even with the arrival of the so-called barbarians, the story of Roman civilization continues, and before Gibbon is done, he has carried his narrative well into the second millennium A.D. Gibbon offers no clear answer to the question of when the Roman empire fell. The most obvious answer is that it fell when the Ottomans captured Constantinople. But that is hardly a satisfying or meaningful response. Gibbon's title, which he chose at the beginning of his undertaking, invites us to ask: when did the Roman empire fall? His work, once completed, shows us that the question, like the title, is a misleading one. The proper question is, Did the Roman empire fall at all?

As heirs of Gibbon, western historians have repeatedly grappled with the ill-formulated question that he bequeathed them. In the twentieth century two of the most influential historians to have concerned themselves with the apparent collapse of the Roman empire were the Russian émigré Michael Rostovtzeff (1957) and the British economic historian A. H. M. Jones (1964). Rostovtzeff's views, though still discussed and admired, have long since been discredited. It became increasingly apparent that Rostovtzeff attempted to interpret the decline of Rome and its subsequent demise in terms that would explain his own experience of the Russian revolution. The role he assigned to a hypothetical bourgeoisie in the Roman empire and the theory of military anarchy in the third century A.D. cannot be substantiated. Nonetheless, Rostovtzeff's learned and provocative attempts to interpret later Roman history in economic and social terms had repercussions in the work of the next generation of ancient historians, notably that of Boak (1955) and A. H. M. Jones himself.

Jones's large work on the later Roman empire is a singularly scattershot interpretation that lacks a sharp focus and rests on a highly personal and selective reading of the ancient evidence, but it does provide a broad survey of the last centuries of antiquity (in traditional historiographic terms) as a whole. Jones lays stress on the bureaucratization of the post-Diocletianic empire, on the growing lack of participation of the municipal aristocracies in civic affairs, and on the worsening inflation of the third and fourth centuries. The Church emerges as somehow disrupting the equilibrium of civic life in the earlier days of the Roman empire. But all of this, while describing more or less the altered social and economic conditions of the later Roman empire, does little to indicate a state of decline, let alone demarcate a time of collapse.

There is simply no obvious reason why the court of Theodosius I was to be seen as any more in decline than the court of the Emperors Claudius and Nero toward the middle of the first century A.D. No eunuch was more powerful than Claudius' freedman Pallas, and no general overwhelmed the empire more effectively than Corbulo. In the time of Claudius and Nero, voices were raised against bureaucracy and corruption at high levels, but no one (so far as I know) has used this evidence to argue for the decline of the Roman empire at that date. Nor, for that matter, does anyone place the decline of the Roman empire precisely in the latter years of the fourth century A.D. The more one examines hypotheses of decline—not to mention fall—the more difficult it is to find exactly when any writer thinks that clear signs of collapse were to be found.

In a vast and complex political system that allows its centers of gravity to shift over the course of time, there is a resilience that defies disintegration or decline in the system as a whole while tolerating it in particular parts. This means that it is more reasonable to look for individual places at which decline or collapse can be observed than for a time of crisis in the entire political structure. It is possible to speak of the decline of Athens within the Roman empire after the Herulian invasion in the third century, or of the decline of Rome as a city after the fourth century. But the fate of these cities cannot provide the means by which to measure the health of the empire as a whole. In assessing the fortunes of places (cities or regions), archaeology is often the primary indicator. We can chronicle the collapse of Ephesus and Aphrodisias, of Italica and Merida, or of Palmyra and Petra on the basis of the surviving and uncovered remains. This is the kind of collapse inside the structure of the greater Roman empire that can be compared with what happened at Teotihuacan and Tikal. It is accordingly legitimate to investigate the collapse of places, but it would be an illegitimate move to treat a place name such as Tikal as also the name of a larger political system and then to invite comparison with other political systems such as the Roman empire.

Infections of a system can be more or less injurious, depending upon the time and place, and the harm that is done in one place at one time may be balanced by growth elsewhere. Potentially disrupting elements need not necessarily cause a disruption at all because of their presence. If this is the case, then it is incumbent upon an interpreter to discover why they should have an effect when they do. As far as the Roman empire is concerned, one often looks in vain not only for an explanation of why potentially disrupting elements disrupt, but also for an indication of when they do the disrupting. It is only when we direct our attention to particular places within the Roman empire that we can begin to speak with certainty about disruption. And localized disruptions may only turn out to be part of a broader restructuring through the mechanism of compensatory growth in other places.

In fact, what has been viewed by some historians as inimical to the health of the later empire as a whole has been construed by others as a source of strength: Rome's peculiar talent for absorbing foreigners from the far-flung parts of its empire into the central administration and the government of its provinces has been seen, along lines laid down by

Rostovtzeff, as the importation of alien elements that served in the long run to unsettle the stability of the Roman regime. But it was again the Emperor Claudius who formulated the policy of bringing in foreigners as a means of strengthening his government and winning a broad base of support for it.[1] On the whole, Claudius' policy was vindicated and sustained over precisely those centuries that were considered by Gibbon and others the greatest in Rome's history. Most ancient historians today would probably be inclined to support Claudius' opinion that it was the very exclusivity of Athenian policy that led to such vulnerability in the great civilization of classical Greece.

Accordingly, to compare features of the later Roman empire, such as its bureaucracy, its civic life, and its problems of inflation, or its welcoming of foreigners into the central government, with similar features in other great civilizations that have suffered some kind of decline or change (Ottoman, for example) seems less helpful than to make comparisons within the long and well-documented history of the civilization under review.

It has been suggested that the archaeology of the Roman empire has done relatively little to alter the problems and questions with which Gibbon was concerned. In the illumination of daily life, city planning, architecture, and art, as well as in the rich treasures provided by epigraphy and coins, Roman archaeology has provided immense gains for scholarship. But these have largely supplemented material that was already abundant and that is essentially different from the archaeological evidence for civilizations otherwise virtually unknown or undocumented. Before anyone sank a spade in the ground, we had the Arch of Constantine, the Colosseum, the Arch of Galerius, the Maison Carrée. Pompeii and Herculaneum were excavated during Gibbon's lifetime, but it is a fact that the central issues in his work were not seriously impaired by his disinterest in the results of the excavations. The discoveries at those two great sites illuminated local life in the first century A.D. but contributed almost nothing to our understanding of the disintegration, if such it was, of the empire as a whole. The excavated remains of Pompeii tell us no more about the decline of the Roman empire than the remains of St. Pierre on Martinique tell us about the decline of French colonialism. What the remains do tell us is how people lived at a certain moment in time that would otherwise have been lost to us.

It is important to stress the character of Roman archaeology in addressing the larger questions about the Roman state because, by contrast, archaeology has provided the principal information for the collapse of certain other ancient states. In Mesoamerica, we have been told, the great civilization of Teotihuacan came abruptly to an end after some seven hundred years of apparently uninterrupted splendor. No one knows what caused the destruction of the great city or—and this is much more important—whether or not the population moved somewhere else and continued from a different location to exert power and influence in the area of Mesoamerica. The ecology of the region appears to be such as to make indications of this kind very hard to determine. It is, at any rate, somewhat easier to talk about the fall of Teotihuacan, precisely because it is a particular place, than it is to talk about the fall of Rome (in the sense of the Roman empire). When Teotihuacan went, so apparently did its political system. When Rome went (or at least went into eclipse), its political system did not. In fact, it seems that the concept of decline and fall, which is so familiar from Gibbon's title (at least in the Anglophone community), has acquired, from the more visible and dramatic falls that are attested by archaeology, a vividness that not even Gibbon intended.

It is for this reason that recent historians of Late Antiquity have tended to step aside from the language of decline and fall. Notable among them are Alan Cameron and Peter Brown. In an important paper on the so-called struggle between pagans and Christians in the late fourth century, Cameron (1977) undertook to dismantle the view that the pagans in the Roman bureaucracy of that time coalesced in one final effort to prevail over the Christians. The notion of a pagan revival at the end of the fourth century is a familiar one to students of Late Antiquity and turns largely upon the role of Symmachus in opposition to the Christian emperor and, above all, the powerful bishop at Milan, Ambrose. But Cameron was able to point out, with a full array of documentation, that Symmachus and his friends, such as Nicomachus, were on excellent terms with the leading Christians of the day.

Christian aristocrats and bureaucrats were as unconcerned about religious differences as pagans were. It has long been recognized that much Christian iconography is directly related to pagan predecessors and that pagan festivals were cheerfully perpetuated by Christians. The pagan element in the Christian reverence for relics was a perfect theme for Gibbon's irony. But there is more to it than irony, as Peter Brown has emphasized in many writings (Brown 1972, 1978, 1981, 1982). The spiritual world of the Neoplatonists with their demons and angels was not far removed from that of the Christians with their own angels, saints, and martyrs.

What all of this implies is that the world of Late Antiquity can be seen not as a world in decline from some previously lofty standard, but as a world in transition. Social, political, and intellectual reorganization was accomplished entirely within the framework of what had been there before. Boundaries, physical and spiritual, were changing and being redefined. The centers were being moved; and the relegations of imperial authority from Rome to Constantinople, and ultimately to Milan, Aquileia, and Ravenna in the north and west, are also metaphors for the tendency to move toward the periphery. To call all this a decline or signposts on the road to a fall would be inappropriate. The right vocabulary is transformation, reformation, and relocation.

If the Roman empire as a whole did not collapse or fall in any fundamental way that might be comparable to the fate of Teotihuacan, then what happened to it? It is obviously not here today, and it is equally obvious that, at least in the West, by the seventh century the Arabs had taken over a large part of the former territory of Rome. The Arabs represent a terminus in the affairs of the Roman state in the West that is comparable to the Ottoman capture of Constantinople in the East. Both episodes provide a kind of authoritative disappearance that marks the end of an established political system. But there is no reason to assume that either of these events was inevitable because of decay within the existing state. On the contrary, the internal mechanisms had, up to that point, shown themselves uncommonly resilient and adaptable. Similarly at Teotihuacan there are few, if any, perceptible signs of decay before its sudden demise after seven centuries: Millon speculates that the exchange network of the state may have deteriorated and thereby created political and social strains. Or again he thinks that at the end Teotihuacan may have fallen victim to an excessive resistance to change or transformation. But the evidence is clearly not definitive.

It is nevertheless in the West that the concept of collapse has meaning in the history of the Roman empire. In former times the last emperor of Rome was identified as Romulus Augustulus, and the end of the empire was dated precisely to 476 A.D. (Momigliano 1973; Arce et al. 1980). The foundation of the Ostrogothic kingdom in Ravenna seemed visible proof that the old order had passed away. It is unlikely that anyone would wish to maintain this position any longer. Many leaders of Italian society before the Gothic arrival accommodated themselves easily to the service of the new dynasty and saw in it the heirs of the grand tradition of Roman imperial rule. As the emperor Claudius had seen at the beginning, Rome's strength depended on the absorption of people from the provinces into the administrative system. From this perspective the Goths were no different from the Spaniards, North Africans, Syrians, and Danubians who appear as Roman emperors in the course of the second and third centuries. We have been schooled to call these Gothic emperors barbarians, but they thought of themselves as Romans and, what is perhaps more important, so did their subjects. The career of Cassiodorus in the sixth century is a bracing illustration of the integration of Ostrogothic rulers into the framework of the Roman empire (O'Donnell 1979). Cassiodorus was able to praise them in the language of Cicero and Tertullian and to serve as a representative of the West in the court of Constantinople for a decade as part of the continuing diplomatic nexus that held the Roman world together.

As far as the internal functioning of the Roman empire in the sixth century is concerned—and the sixth century may be viewed in broad terms as the eve of the Arab conquest—there is no clear indication of any substantial instability or depression in the social, economic, and political life of the time. This is not to deny that there are periodic problems and complaints, but there is nothing that goes beyond the distress signals given by the affluent Pliny about the state of agriculture in the early second century A.D., or indeed the high-principled moralizing of a Sallust in the first century B.C.

This assessment of the situation in the century before the Arab conquest will undoubtedly strike many as surprisingly optimistic. But it is supported by an admirable study that has escaped most professional ancient historians.[2] Gerald Gunderson (1976), who labels himself a new economic historian, has attacked two traditional canards of late Roman history. He has argued with compelling ingenuity that there was neither a decline in the population of the empire in the final period nor a falling off in productivity. He begins by acknowledging the scarcity of labor in the late empire, a fact on which all historians would probably agree. But he then goes on to argue that a shortage of labor does not necessarily imply a diminished population. It could be instead the direct result of an increase in resources or in productivity, or in both. Gunderson notes that the behavior of the land market can provide evidence on income and production per capita. "If the marginal product of land rises or, at a minimum, does not fall," he writes, "it indicates that the labor scarcity is being created by increases in productivity" (Gunderson 1976:46).

Previous historians have often argued in a highly selective way from specific localized instances of abandonment of land or reduction in population to a generalized set of phenomena throughout the empire. After all, the Roman empire was a big place, and there was a tendency to move from the center toward the periphery: whenever land can be seen as being depopulated in the center of Italy, one can point at the same time to increased use of land and the probability of increased productivity in other parts of the empire. By a detailed study of land prices in those parts for which we have evidence, the new economic historian can show that land values did not fall in Late Antiquity and, accordingly, that high taxes should be seen not so much as the screw that squeezed the last drop out of the provincials, but rather as a conduit through which a share of increased productivity was made available to the imperial government.

I am persuaded that this view of Late Antique taxation as a response to improved economic conditions, rather than as an unreasonable demand on a shrunken economy, deserves serious consideration. The results of this new assessment of Late Antique economic history offer a theoretical justification for the implications of archaeological discoveries in both North Africa and Gaul, where there is, in Late Antiquity, every sign of enormous prosperity from the land (Goodchild 1976; MacKendrick 1971:127–49). It has been almost a source of embarrassment to historians and archaeologists alike that precisely in the time of alleged decline there seemed to be such affluence and growth in two of the principal regions on the periphery of the western Roman world.

In short, in the western Roman empire of the fifth and sixth centuries, changes are clearly apparent in the cultural and administrative boundaries. But these changes show a healthy, rather than an unhealthy, disposition to adapt to the availability of land and to the needs for communication. With the increased importance of Constantinople, it made good sense to establish western centers that were closer to the great roads that crossed the Balkans, linking West with East. Hence the importance of places like Ravenna, Aquileia, and Milan. And the land route across North Africa was essential not only for securing the southern shore of the Mediterranean but equally, as the Arabs recognized later, for the overland passage from the East into Spain.

Only in the most superficial sense, then, can the old Roman empire be thought of as declining or collapsing. It is true that by the end of the sixth century what existed in the Mediterranean world looked very different from what had been there in the time of Augustus. But the evolution had been a natural one, and Augustus himself, who was a master of change under the guise of ancient tradition, would easily have understood this Late Antique polity. Parts of it were soon to be disrupted violently by the Arabs in the seventh century. The warriors of Muhammad were very different from the Goths, who were Christian and proud to be assimilated into the Roman empire. That is why their arrival is in no way comparable to that of the Arabs. And that is why a Cassiodorus at Ravenna, or an Isidore at Seville, could so easily assume the mantle of a Seneca in the court of Nero.

Even with all the fresh thinking that has been going on in the 1970s and 1980s about the decline and fall of Rome, older opinions continue to thrive. In his vast and enormously stimulating work, *The Class Struggle in the Ancient Greek World*, Geoffrey de Ste Croix has devoted a substantial appendix to the decline of the Roman empire (de Ste Croix 1981:453–503). The casual reader might not suppose that a book of this title would be so substantially concerned with Rome, but such is the range of de Ste Croix's vision that he is actually more involved with the Greeks under Roman rule than he is with them in their Archaic and Classical periods. The book is a deliberate attempt to establish a Marxist interpretation of Classical Antiquity. As readers of de Ste Croix will be aware, he considers himself a more correct Marxist than almost anybody else and thereby provides an interesting illustration of the internecine strife that seems to afflict Marxist historians. Reviewers have pointed out that, despite his massive erudition (including a traditionally conservative marshaling of documentary evidence), de Ste Croix finds himself in serious difficulty with the notion of a class struggle (Millar 1982). He gets around this, as many have noticed, by claiming that exploitation of the lower classes is in itself proof of the existence of a class struggle. It is immaterial here whether or not that is the case (although it may be doubted), but the emphasis which de Ste Croix lays upon exploitation is directly relevant to his interpretation of the decline of Rome. It is, in fact, what makes his interpretation so fundamentally traditional. He sees the empire as disintegrating through the loss of individual freedom.

It is certainly true that by the seventh century some kinds of serfdom had arisen in parts of the western empire, but it is by no means clear that this constituted increased exploitation of the lower classes, since the transition to a feudal system is somehow linked to the disappearance of a slave economy. So, paradoxically, de Ste Croix is caught in the curious dilemma of blaming the collapse of the empire on the elimination of slavery. Now it is perfectly true that some elements of what de Ste Croix calls enserfment can be seen in the later Roman empire, but it is equally true that they can be seen at a relatively early stage. As Averil Cameron has pointed out in a perceptive notice of de Ste Croix's book, most of what he has to complain about is already in place by the end of the fourth century A.D., and it constitutes a response to the problem of labor supply which (it may be argued) is due more to increased productivity than the opposite. Cameron quite rightly observed, "There was a gap of several centuries between the completion of this process of enserfment by the end of the fourth century and the collapse to which de Ste Croix wants it to lead in the seventh" (Averil Cameron 1982:12).

The newer interpretations of Late Antiquity have accordingly not come apart as a result of de Ste Croix's arguments.[3] Averil Cameron (1982:12) writes with good reason of the sixth and seventh centuries, "It is in fact far from certain that the Empire was then on the verge of collapse." This is the old story: whenever one sets out to discuss collapse, one ends up by talking about continuity. It happened to Gibbon, and it has happened to most scholars who have addressed the issue with care. Arnaldo Momigliano (1976:125) commented with arresting insight, as he prepared in Spoleto an essay on Gibbon's history:

> There are few places in Italy where one is less aware that the Middle Ages were a barbaric parenthesis between the Golden Age of the Antonines and the Renaissance. ... Spoleto was exactly the sort of town in which a late

Roman aristocrat could turn up without feeling the shock of a conflict between the old and the new. The city absorbed Christian and pagan events without being much shaken by either.

S. N. Eisenstadt observes in this volume that in most cases collapse ought to be seen as the reconstruction of boundaries. It is intimately connected with continuity, and apart from cases of violent disruption, it is the rearrangement of boundaries that causes old forms to disappear and old structures to be altered without the annihilation of the system as a whole.

A system that did not have the capacity to adapt and to change, to respond to pressures and to blur the distinction between outsiders and insiders, would indeed be vulnerable to collapse. It is imaginable that the Teotihuacanos had such a brittle political system that it could snap under a single blow, perhaps even administered from within under ritual circumstances. But, although the archaeological evidence at Teotihuacan may suggest an abrupt type of collapse, we should ultimately be as reluctant to infer such an end for a civilization about which we know so little as for Rome, about which we know so much. After all, the political state of Teotihuacan lasted longer than the western Roman empire. To have managed this, it must have possessed a most remarkable capacity for adaptation and restructuring. It is, of course, more exciting to talk about total collapse, and some pundits would be speechless without such a concept. But change does not always mean decay. It is the task of a responsible historian to address himself to the complex process of transformation through which recognizable political and cultural systems ultimately cease to exist in the form by which they once were known.

NOTES

1. Claudius' policy may be seen in the speech given to him by Tacitus in *Annals*, Book 11, chapter 24. By a happy accident the text of Claudius' original speech, paraphrased by Tacitus, survives and may be seen in *Inscriptiones Latinae Selectae*, ed. H. Dessau, no. 212.

2. I should like to express my gratitude to Robert McC. Adams for drawing my attention to the Gunderson article at Sante Fe.

3. It is instructive to find that an article (Pelikan 1982) that begins with allusions to Marx and Gibbon on the decline of Rome is explicitly concerned with the *city* of Rome rather than with Rome as shorthand for the Roman empire. Of the decline of the city there can be no question.

The Roles of the Literati
and of Regionalism in the Fall of
the Han Dynasty

Cho-yun Hsu

The establishment of a unified China under the first imperial dynasty, Ch'in (221–206 B.C.), was the result of a long power struggle among seven former Chou vassal states. Each of these states had undergone domestic political consolidation in order to mobilize its resources for survival. Ch'in, the victor, therefore inherited a strong political authoritarianism (Hsu, Cho-yun 1965; Bodde 1938). The Han dynasty (the Western Han, 206 B.C.–A.D. 23, and the Eastern Han, A.D. 25–220), which inherited its governmental structure from Ch'in precedents, only briefly tolerated competing political factors. The first element to face suppression was the remnant of the aristocracy subjugated by the Ch'in. Its surviving members took part in the civil wars that eventually overthrew the imperial throne of Ch'in. Some actually allied themselves with Han and became meritorious generals of the new regime. Along with other local dignitaries, they filled the power vacuum during the civil-war years, and during the uncertain early decades of the Han government took local leadership into their hands (Chu 1972). Once well established, the Han government consolidated local leaders with wealthy and influential persons in the provinces and forcibly moved them into new settlements built around the imperial mausolea in the capital region, a practice followed in every imperial reign since the death of the founding emperor (Chu 1972; Hsu, Cho-yun 1965a:370).

The second group to be suppressed consisted mainly of the descendants of meritorious generals. For the first three reigns of the dynasty, these generals and their children enjoyed the enviable status of shareholders of the new dynasty and monopolized ranking offices in both the court and provincial governments. After a century of monopoly, during the reign of Emperor Wu (140–87 B.C.) this group was gradually edged out of its position, titles, and domains; many even lost their lives (Chu 1972; Hsu, Cho-yun 1965a:370). The reign of Emperor Wu also saw the decline of the influence of wealthy merchants and manufacturers. The laissez-faire attitude toward commercial activities of the early decades of the dynasty created such opportunities to achieve prosperity that some wealthy persons were virtually lords without titles. Accompanying economic prosperity was the momentum of urbanization that created sizable cities where entrepreneurship flourished (Chu 1972:113–22; Hsu, Cho-yun 1980:36–38, 152–54, 190). The foreign wars fought along the steppe land to fend off nomadic intruders, a constant threat since the founding of the dynasty, dried up the imperial coffers of Emperor Wu, who was determined to take the initiative in such campaigns. Opening up a thousand miles of navigable waterways in North China to facilitate shipment of grain from the east and the south and building flood-control projects along the Yellow River also drained the resources of the court. In response to the resulting fiscal difficulty, the court imposed heavy market and property taxes on the private sector. The worst blow delivered to the private economy was the introduction of government competition. By monopolizing production of the most essential items (such as iron and salt) and the most profitable commodities (such as wine), the government made huge gains. Staples, collected as taxes in kind, were transported to other regions and sold by the government for profit. Thus, the private sector faced such strong government competition that the survival of private traders was impossible. The Han dynasty crushed the third group, the well-to-do, by encouraging citizens to inform on tax fraud, the penalty for which was confiscation of property. Widespread imposition of this penalty ruined the entire upper-middle class of Han society (Hsu, Cho-yun 1980:39–43; Chu 1972:352 n. 10b; Gale 1931).

After these three groups were either destroyed or subordinated, Han imperial authority became almost monolithic. Yet it needed a pool of literati from which it could draw bureaucrats, an indispensable commodity for an empire. In the interval between Ch'in and Han and in the early years of the Han dynasty, intellectuals reemerged after a dormant period of anti-intellectualism during Ch'in. This new acceptance resulted from their ability to render pragmatic services, such as providing strategic advice and diplomatic manipulation, during a period of rivalry for power and position, but did not extend to less practical scholarly pursuits. Even Liu Pang, the founding emperor, who received great assistance from scholars, did not conceal his contempt for pure knowledge. Only that having immediate applicability drew his attention: Li I-ch'i, Lu Chia, and Chen Ping were diplomatic and military intellectuals. Chang Tsang was a mathematician who supervised the auditing of government accounting and set standards of measurement for public construction (*Shi-chi-hui-chu-k'ao-cheng* [SC][1]). The power struggle of the early Han dynasty raged until the victories of three generations of emperors who gradually increased imperial power and authority. During this period, literati were retained not only by the imperial court but also by feudal vassal kings who were either imperial princes or meritorious generals, and their roles closely resembled those of their predecessors in the Chan-Kuo or "warring states" period (463–222 B.C.). They served largely as military advisors and diplomatic strategists (*Han-shu-pu-chu* [HS] 45/1–5, 32/9, 32/22).

In the three reigns from Emperor Wen through Emperor Wu, as imperial authority was finally established and legitimized, the strategists were replaced by intellectuals whose literary skills were valuable to the court. The Han literary style, *fu*, was developed to its best form by Chia Shan, Mei Cheng, Yen An, Ssu-ma Hsiang-ju, and others (*HS* 44/8, 47/2, 51/1–30, 57A/2, 64A/1–21). Some of the literati ventured to criticize real politics, but their influence was minimal. It is no accident that much of the best *fu* expresses the frustration of the authors (Wilhelm 1957:310–19). As Ssu-ma Ch'ien pointed out, literati were retained essentially as entertainers, and therefore could not expect any better treatment (*HS* 62/21). Furthermore, the monolithic authoritarianism of imperial power must have created a feeling of impotence that the helpless literati could only lament (Hsu 1972:284 ff.).

The literati put their skills at the disposal of the political authority, rendering their services in the same manner as vendors of a marketable commodity. An old Chinese proverb describes just such a transaction: "One learns his literary or military skill in order to sell it to the household of the rulers." The salaries and positions allotted to the literati were far inferior to their value to the buyer, however. The Chan-kuo period was a sellers' market because there were numerous states competing to obtain the useful knowledge possessed by the literati. In the early years of the Han dynasty, autonomous principalities and feudal vassals posed a threat to the imperial government, so intellectuals still had some options and could choose a "buyer." Once imperial unification was complete, however, there was only one buyer. In this market the commodity faced a drastic fall in price. This situation was vividly depicted by Tung-fang Shuo, a humorist at the court of Emperor Wu, as he contrasted his chances of success with those of his Chan-kuo predecessors (*HS* 65/17; Hsu Fu-Kuan 1972:286–88).

Han literati needed to find a marketable function other than simply selling their knowledge. The early Han Confucians provided the court with useful services as well. Shu-sun T'ung codified court rituals with which Han emperors could rule with respectability (*HS* 43/15–16). Chia I broadened the regulated rituals to include a new dress code, a new calendar, and other reforms in order to symbolize the beginning of a new political authority (*HS* 48/1). The other concerns of Chia I, as evidenced by his political essays, related to current affairs. A commentator on strategy and politics, he was a worthy successor to the Chan-Kuo scholars. However, he never ventured to cast his eyes beyond contemporary events in order to place the Han regime in a cosmic system as did Ting Chung-shu. The pragmatic services rendered by Shu-sun Tung and Chia I could not raise the stature of scholars because they did not carve out an autonomous intellectual domain that commanded the respect of the imperial power. Not until the intellectuals undertook the development of a logical cosmological order did their status rise above that of political servant. An intellectual's concern is with providing guidance and seeking fundamental meanings and concepts, and his knowledge ought to be more than a commodity. Literati develop knowledge by organizing information into logical systems that society can use to create a predictable order. Even the value of human life hinges on intellectual order (Mannheim 1936:16–24, 79 n. 2, 80–83).

The unification of China, almost synonymous with the entire known civilized world of East Asia in ancient times, challenged the literati to unify knowledge under one system. By the eve of the Ch'in unification, Han Fei had achieved a synthesis of thought drawn from the Confucian, Legalist, and Taoist schools. A more ambitious attempt was made by a group of scholars sponsored by Lu Pu-wei. The voluminous *Lu-shih-chun-chiu* incorporated thoughts of all the major schools except the Legalists. This attempt involved a comprehensive interpretation of the cosmic order and heralded the Han cosmology of macro-micro-cosmic correspondence proposed by Tung Chung-shu (Hsu, Fu-Kuan 1975:5–69). After the Han dynasty was established, another effort was made to reach an all-inclusive synthesis in the compilation of *Huai-nan-tzu*. The preface of *Huai-nan-tzu* declared that the goal of this collective work was to establish an intellectual system that was not only universal but adaptive and responsive to all kinds of possible changes as well (*Huai-nan-tzu* 21/1, 8). A synthesis of Taoism, Confucianism, and naturalist Yin-Yang theories, *Huai-nan-tzu* attempted to build an organic relationship between nature and man (Hsu 1975:85–170).

Lu-shih-chun-chiu and *Huai-nan-tzu* reflected a goal of their own time, the creation of a gigantic system that could unify the world of nature and the order of man. A truly comprehensive cosmic order was developed by Tung Chung-shu, whose major contribution was the inclusion of a fourth dimension, time, in a previously three-dimensional universe, in his macro-cosmic and micro-cosmic theories. Tung drew on the Kung-yang new-text tradition and emphasized that history should render judgments on individual events and the responsibility of those who were involved. Tung, a Confucian scholar heavily influenced by the Yin-Yang school, became a leading figure of his time, and his interpretation became the theme of Chinese thought in the Western Han (*HS* 27A/2).

Liu Pang appointed himself emperor of the Han dynasty following victory in battle. Ironically, the problem of the legitimacy of the dynasty was not raised until it had become firmly established. In the court of Emperor Ching, a debate on the issue of legitimacy was held between a Confucian scholar and a Taoist scholar. The Confucian argued that the will of the people should be the ultimate source of legitimacy for a new regime, whereas the Taoist insisted that regicide should be considered a crime even if the ruler was evil. The debate was cut short by the personal intervention of the emperor, who preferred to cast no aspersions on the legitimacy of the Han regime (*HS* 88/18-19). In this debate the Taoist wanted to adhere to a static order that was universal and in equilibrium. Such an order would provide the Han regime with no claim to sovereignty. Meanwhile, the Confucian ideology permitting governmental change to be determined by the people did give the Han court a mandate, although at the same time it took away the regime's right to perpetuate its rule. The Confucian ideology therefore served as a foundation for Han legitimacy but also gave scholars the right to review the record of the Han court. Tung Chung-shu's system of correspondence between nature and man thus rendered a service of paramount importance to political authority while it gave intellectuals the latitude to exercise influence.

Tung Chung-shu's system had a theological structure, although he was not the first to attempt to build an all-encompassing cosmological order in the Ch'in-Han academic world. Tung thought that any unusual natural phenomenon such as an eclipse of the sun or a flood represented deviation from the normal pattern of constancy. His belief that there should be an idealized and constant order prompted him to define any deviation as abnormal, after the Kung-Yang tradition. He also attempted to establish a yardstick for social relations by comparing the social order to the natural, normative order. Any deviation was investigated, the degree of deviation measured, and a verdict on the deviant pattern rendered (*Chun-chiu-fan-lu* 5/4). Tung used an idealized yardstick to judge reality. He even elevated Confucius to the status of a hypothetical judge who assumed powers equivalent to those of a sovereign in order to render judgments and to reward or punish according to the idealized moral standard. Thus a moral orthodoxy was imposed along with political authority (*Chun-chiu-fan-lu* 7/3). In Tung's scheme, Confucian scholars had the power to judge and criticize the real world, and Confucian classics were established as the standard for moral judgment. Confucian scholars confirmed the legitimacy of the Han imperial authority and attained equal status with the imperial authority. Thereafter, Han literati were no longer mere retainers of the court; they gained acceptance as a result of developing their role as upholders of social conscience and social consciousness.

The elevation of Confucian classics to the level of canon in Tung Chung-shu theology had an impact on Han politics. In the biography of Chang T'ang, a professional judiciary who had no Confucian education, it is said that Chang was often dispatched by the court to consult Tung on major policy debates and that Chang subsequently requested that students of Confucian erudition in Chun-chiu and Shang-shu be appointed to positions on the judicial staff so that jurisprudential discussions could be based on Confucian principles (HS 59/1-2; Wallaker 1978:216–28). Therefore, the adoption of Confucian classics as the foundation for jurisprudence appears to have been institutionalized. The case of a pretender who claimed to be the crown prince, settled by Chun Pu-i on the basis of the Confucian ethical code included in the Chun-chiu, confirms the establishment of Confucian ethics as a constitution (HS 71/2-3).

Literati, especially Confucians, thus gradually obtained the power to make judgment, a power that could challenge and alter political authority. It is therefore not strange that a disciple of Tung Chung-shu suggested that the emperor should look for the most worthy person to succeed to the throne, as the heavenly mandate was to be handed over voluntarily from one worthy to another. This courageous and rather naive scholar was executed for his offense against the Han sovereign (HS 75/12). The tradition of calling upon politics on occasions of natural disaster and irregular phenomena was carried on nevertheless. Some Han scholars apparently had so much faith in the metaphysical theory of mandate alteration that they dared to cast doubt on the continuation of Han rule.

The strength of Han intellectuals, of course, was not derived solely from their theoretical and intellectual commitment. At least two other factors contributed to their power: the growth of the educated population and the literati's gradual domination of the bureaucracy that developed as regular channels of recruitment opened up.

The upper echelons of literati included imperial retainers and scholars of the Imperial Academy, specifically erudites and their students, as well as staff members from commanderies and counties who were recommended to take court examinations. There had been a small number of Academy faculty ever since the Ch'in period. They gained neither in numbers nor in influence during the early Han until the reign of Emperor Ching, although occasionally local staff members were dispatched from the provinces to receive higher education in the Imperial Academy (HS 89/2). The first increase in the number of intellectuals in the Han court occurred during the early reign of Emperor Wu (140–87 B.C.). In 135 B.C. Empress Tou, the last major anti-intellectual figure, died. The new administration under Prime Minister T'ien Fen brought hundreds of Confucian scholars into government service, among them Kung-sun Hung, who subsequently became premier. This change encouraged many to pursue scholarship as a short cut to power and glory (HS 88/3). In 126 B.C. Kung-sun Hung established a student body of fifty in the Imperial Academy. Meanwhile, provincial governors were granted the privilege of sending their local staff to receive higher education in the capital. The total number of regular and special students, estimating one person per province, or "kingdom," was probably about one hundred. From that time on, enrollment grew steadily. Emperor Chao (86–74 B.C.) increased the quota to one hundred, not including special students. At the end of the reign of Emperor Hsuen (73–49 B.C.), the regular quota was doubled again. Emperor Yuan (48–32 B.C.) granted a quota of one thousand. At the same time, provincial academies were established under the tutelage of local teachers who were considered members of the provincial administration. At the end of Emperor Ch'eng's reign (31–7 B.C.), more than one thousand students of the Imperial Academy gathered to protest the arrest of a popular official; the total student body must, therefore, have been far larger (HS 72/24).

In A.D. 5, scholars of Confucian classics as well as other specialties were summoned to the capital. Several thousand arrived (HS 12/9). This figure is probably representative of the population of established scholars in the provinces. At the conclusion of the Western Han, Wang Mang built an Imperial Academy campus with dormitories of ten thousand rooms. A description of the layout of the academy's campus mentions thirty divisions near a park of one hundred rows of elm trees under which students of different provinces gathered and even traded their staple products. The campus became very crowded as enrollment grew: "the buildings were so closely connected that students walking under the eaves did not need to worry about exposure to the rain or sun" (HS 99A/8–19). There were thirty departments, each of which had 366 students from which twenty-four teaching assistants were chosen. The total enrollment, therefore, was more than ten thousand.

The student body of the Imperial Academy thus increased two-hundredfold in 126 years, yet this sizable group represented only the tip of a gigantic iceberg. Academy graduates were assigned to secretarial and clerical work in central as well as local government, and very soon the entire government was staffed by intellectuals who had received higher education. It is said that after Kung-sun Hung presented his proposal to recruit the educated for government work, every level of the hierarchy was full of learned and educated persons (HS 88/4–6), and at the local level, staff were sent to the capital for higher education and provincial academies were established by imperial decree during the reign of Emperor Wu (*HS* 89/3).

Thus, the literati had grown into a system or, more precisely, a subsystem within the imperial system, which originally was essentially political. More important, during its growth this subsystem acquired an ideology that justified its existence, a structure of regeneration that coexisted with the political power structure.

At local levels educated youths were candidates for advanced education at the Imperial Academy. They constituted the base of a pyramid many times larger than the student population at the top. Elementary education served as the foundation, and the student population on this preparatory level must have been larger than at the provincial level. Altogether, educated people at all levels probably represented a sizable social group in the last decades of Western Han.

The influence of the literati in government was more formidable than would be expected on the basis of their numbers. Their greatest asset was their ability to serve in the expanding bureaucracy. In the first reigns of the Han dynasty, political power was monopolized by a small group consisting of imperial kinsmen and meritorious generals and their descendants. The absorption of literate men into government service was viewed as expedient for the discharge of archival and clerical tasks. The growth of government was an inevitable consequence of bureaucratization, which in time was associated with the institutionalization of charismatic authority. During the early reigns a recruitment system based on recommendation for merit was shaped in order to provide the government with competent bureaucrats. The reign of Emperor Wu witnessed the increasing influence of recommended bureaucrats, and during the following four reigns (86–7 B.C.), Han bureaucracy and the Han recommendation system were virtually inseparable. The entire government, from the central court to the local organs at the county level, was overwhelmingly dominated by recommendees who advanced along a meticulously designed course to become the prominent local elites in government (Hsu, Cho-yun 1965a:367–69; Ikeda 1976:319–44). The intellectuals therefore monopolized the machinery of governance and thereby shared political power with the emperor. Even though the outer court, the bureaucracy, often had to face strong interference from the inner court, which actually represented the personal authority of the emperor, it could nevertheless still maintain its own voice (Lao 1948:227 ff.).

The Han court claimed more courageous and righteous critics than any other Chinese dynasty. This phenomenon may be attributed to the unusual strength of the intellectual-bureaucrats as a subsystem of the political structure. An indispensable group with sincere faith in its political philosophy, it acquired so much influence on Han politics that Wang Mang was able to usurp the throne, partly due to the support of literati who considered him a fellow traveler. Wang Mang's revival of Confucian institutions thought to have existed in antiquity appears to have been his effort to implement Confucian symbols. Ironically, his failure to be recognized as a legitimate ruler and his final fall resulted from the intellectuals' loyalty to the legitimate heritage of the Han imperial household, a cardinal virtue in the Confucian value system. The establishment of Eastern Han therefore should be viewed as the success of an alliance of literati with the local powerful class (Yu 1956:226–44; Utsunomiya 1954:394–96).

During the Eastern Han period, recommendation was the sole channel for the recruitment of candidates for government appointments. The provinces annually recommended such candidates (*hsiao-lien*) according to a complicated quota system. On the average, each province annually recommended one candidate for every 200,000 persons (*Hou-Han-shu-chi-chieh* [HHS] 4/12–13, 37/12–13; *Hou-Han-chih* [in HHC] 28/4). When this quota system was decreed during the reign of Emperor Ho (A.D. 89–105), the entire population of 53,256,229 persons should have produced at least 266 recommendees a year. Since the forty less-populated provinces enjoyed a minimum quota, they should have produced an additional 40 recommendees with a resulting annual, national figure of no fewer than 300. During a thirty-year generation, a cadre of nine to ten thousand candidates would have entered the bureaucracy and obtained political and social influence (*Hou-Han-chih* 23B/31). The student body of the Imperial Academy increased, and its social status was enhanced by the personal attention extended to intellectuals by emperors. By the end of Eastern Han, there were more than thirty thousand students in the Imperial Academy, three times the largest total during Western Han (*HHS* 79A/1-2). The larger the top of the pyramid of educated men, the larger the base as well; thus it is only logical to assume that intellectuals of Eastern Han enjoyed greater influence than did their Western Han predecessors.

The Han literati, already influential in politics, also gained economic power. During the early reigns of the Han dynasty, the primary powerful class was landlords who were either descendants of pre-Ch'in nobility or rising Han aristocrats and members of the ruling group. These landlords, as a countervailing force for an expanding imperial authority, faced harsh suppression during the reign of Emperor Wu (Chu 1972:200–201). From that time on, neither local powers nor families that had built their fortunes by means of manufacture and trading had any chance of gaining power at the local level. Under the strong political authority that monopolized the means of accumulating influence and wealth, only members of the political structure were in a position to seize land, the principal productive resource in an agrarian economy. Landlords therefore mainly came from the groups close to political authority, such as imperial kinsmen, relatives, and ranking officials. The Han salary scale was very generous, and an official, middle-ranked or above, could normally accumulate sufficient savings to purchase land. Land under direct government control was easily transferred to government employees by means of a lease or other methods. Influential people could also obtain land with the assistance of their local governments. Emperor Wu confiscated real estate of the wealthy and promptly gave it to new landlords who were close to the politically powerful. Uneven distribution of land persisted; it merely changed hands. Imperial kinsmen and court favorites constituted a much smaller percentage of the landlord class than professional bureaucrats because the latter were much more numerous. Because the recommendation system had a built-in regional quota for recruitment, candidates were drawn from a wide geographical area, and those who became bureaucrat-landlords controlled land, the most valuable resource, in all areas. The book *Ordinance for Four People*, attributed to Tsui Shih of the Eastern Han period, depicted the control of manufacturing and marketing by landlords in a system of intensive agriculture. Tsui Shih probably represented many of the intellectuals who depended on farming for a living and held the role of intellectual-bureaucrat for social status (Hsu, Cho-yun 1980:51–55).

Literati also built up their social influence by organizing into groups with a sense of solidarity. During the Han period, especially the Eastern Han, the ties between a tutor and his disciples were very strong. A recommendee often regarded his recommender as a tutor and became his protégé or retainer. During the Han period, tutoring was the predominant form of education, and the relationship between tutor and student was so highly regarded that it was compared to that between parent and child. The Confucian ethic of filial piety therefore was expanded to include a strong sense of reciprocal obligation. Common interest as well as a closely knit network of social ties bound the literati into a well-defined social group with strong group identity (Jih-chih-lu 24/26–27; Hai-yu-tsung-kao 36/796; Ho 1956:76; Chu 1972:207). The most influential literati leaders were able to weld successions of leadership lasting several generations and actually constituting a form of hereditary nobility (*HHS* 32/4, 49/2, 61/20; Yang 1936:1007–63; Kamada 1962:450 ff.). Ironically, the recommendation system that had brought new blood into government service began to restrict and negate its very function during the late Eastern Han. The internal stratification of the literati social group not only weakened its solidarity but also undermined the respect it would otherwise have commanded from other social groups.

This subsystem became so autonomous that a conflict with the main system, the imperial authority, could not be avoided. The area ripest for collision was ideology, prompted by the literati demand that the political authority should be reshaped according to Confucian idealism.

Some idealistic, leading literati set up a normative model toward which the real world should strive. Tung Chung-shu espoused restraint of the exercise of imperial authority by a cosmic order governing every force including human behavior. Many espoused idealized Confucianism as a yardstick to measure and hence to sanction policy for the behavior of the Han government. Nevertheless, the Han secular order was based on the Han imperial system, and Tung Chung-shu and others had to accommodate to reality to a certain extent (Yu 1976:31–43). Pan Ku lamented that a long succession of renowned Confucian premiers indeed were concerned primarily with their own government careers and could not measure up to the criteria for an ideal minister (HS 81/23–24).

A second type was the critic who compared the real world to the standard of an ideal world. Such individuals were rarely found in the Western Han period, although the Discourse of Salt and Iron might be regarded as a collective criticism of this type. During Eastern Han, Wang Fu, Tsui Shih, and Chung-ch'ang T'ung were typical of those who expressed this harsh criticism of political, social, and economic faults of the time (HHS, chuan 49 and 52). The Eastern Han period did witness a prolonged social crisis due to the uneven distribution of wealth and abuse of privilege by the powerful; thus criticisms were often justified (Balazs 1964:213 ff.). Critics could not emerge until there was a convincing ideology and a sizable audience who would listen, debate, and communicate. They appeared in Eastern Han instead of Western Han, because literati during Eastern Han were more numerous and influential.

The third category was made up of the protesters who finally forced the collision between imperial authority and the scholars. The student movement during the late Eastern Han testifies to this role. In order to uphold an idealized monarchy, students of the Imperial Academy fought the eunuchs and imperial relatives who had the power to mobilize the state machinery in the name of the ruler to destroy the protesters. Yet the intellectuals defied the power of their enemy. Many died; more were jailed. Their courage was derived from their organization into a formidable social force, and they institutionalized their frustration concerning the government by publicizing their criticisms (HHS 67/1–3, 19, cf. chuan 68). They were organized, they had considerable support, and they were determined to express their conscience.

The fourth category, the eremites, were silent protesters. The prototypes of this personality type were the four legendary recluses who rejected the invitation to serve the new regime at the beginning of the Han dynasty.

Ssu-ma Ch'ien reserved the top positions for Po-I, Shu-Ch'i, and Lu Chung-lien, whom he rated historical figures, probably due to his admiration for dissenters who chose to live in retirement, an option permitted by Confucianism and insisted upon by Taoism. During Eastern Han many eremites were recognized. Some were frauds, but many sincerely chose to live in retirement after having been painfully convinced that the gap between an ideal world and ugly reality was too wide to be closed (*HHS* chuan 73; Kamada 1962:511–16).

In the course of their growth, the literati acquired intellectual autonomy by systematizing knowledge, which gave them the power to legitimize the regime. Self-regeneration through bureaucracy and control of economic resources such as land gave them sufficient self-confidence that they became indispensable to the state. Their demand that the political authority meet their standard, in addition to their obvious autonomy, was enough to alienate the throne from their intimidating influence. Therefore, almost as soon as the literati had replaced the meritorious generals in dominating the court, the throne began to rely upon imperial consort family members and other favorites to form an inner court. The usurper Wang Mang, who established a short-lived dynasty between the Eastern and Western Han periods, was able to do so because he was member of both the Confucian literati and the imperial consort family. The Eastern Han dynasty was essentially founded by a group of Confucian literati whose leader, a member of the Han imperial household, had a more legitimate claim to the throne than did the usurper (Bielenstein 1954, 1959). Fewer than two generations after its establishment, the Eastern Han throne once again drifted away from the influence of the literati-controlled court to form inner centers dominated by eunuchs and members of consort families (Chu 1972:210–18, 232–40). The final collision, between the eunuchs and the literati, occurred during A.D. 166–176 and brought an extensive purge of the literati. Both the dynasty and the literati were thus destroyed (Chu 1972:241–43; Balazs 1964:175).

REGIONALISM

Regionalism is another element that contributed to the fall of the Han order. Han China was a vast country consisting of several regions of distinct terrains and climates. The most obvious divisions from the north toward the south were the valleys of three great rivers: the Yellow River plain in the north, the valley of the Yangtze in central China, and the Pearl River drainage down in the deep south. From the west to the east, the rivers flowed from rugged mountains toward the alluvial plains. Thus in these three river systems were several regions in which livelihoods were determined by geographical conditions. People in each region had developed distinctive tongues, customs, and even religious faiths, although they were all members of the nation of China. Away from central China there were border regions where the Chinese and other ethnic groups mingled. For instance, along the transitional zone between the Eurasian steppe and China proper, pastoralism and agriculture formed a mixed economy in which Chinese and nomads encountered one another. In the southwest mountain areas, Chinese settlers lived along the valleys of rivers and lakes while the aborigines held the high land.

During the Western Han period, China consisted of 103 commanderies, intermediate-level administrative units divided into 1,587 counties. Thirteen inspector generals were dispatched by the imperial government to oversee the performances of the local administrators. The thirteen divisions or provinces assigned to the inspector generals coincided more or less with the territories of the warring states before China was unified in the third century B.C. The provincial divisions also roughly coincided with physical boundaries. It might not be a sheer coincidence that provinces, rather than commanderies, gradually became meaningful units of local administration. In the Eastern Han period, the provinces were formally established as the principal administrative units, superseding the commanderies. Meanwhile, the governors, who had much more authority than inspector generals, could exercise formidable influence upon issues at both the national and the local levels since the resources at their disposal were from an enormous area. An ambitious governor, if he wished, could afford to be independent. Thus, in the Eastern Han period, any lessening of centripetal forces would have resulted in disunity.

All these regions could be differentiated into core areas and peripheries. The east section of the core area was located in the mid-reach of the Yellow River Valley, which was the cultural and demographic hub of the Chinese world. Big urban centers were densely distributed to accommodate a prosperous economy. In the western section was the capital district, the seat of imperial authority. Wealth, talent, and military might were concentrated here.

Outside the core area were the Yellow River highland in the north and northwest, and the northern alluvial plain of the Yu-Chi region. The Huai and the Yangtze drainages in the southwest were known respectively as the Hsu-Yang and the Ching regions. The Szuchuan basin in the west was the I region. Beyond these regions of China proper were the borderlands in the mountainous south, the coastal provinces, and the transitional zones in the north stretching from Manchuria to steppe land in central Asia.

Intensification of farming in crowded core areas took place during the early reigns of the Han empire (Hsu, Cho-yun 1980:147–54). Intensive farming required sizable labor reserves that could also be used to produce manufactured goods. A national network for the exchange of commodities produced by cottage industries served the Han population. This network was hierarchical, as was the marketing system developed in premodern China (Skinner 1964:3–43). The Han exchange network was built upon the need for regional interdependence (Hsu, Cho-yun 1980:37–38, 134–35). It was delicately balanced and could be upset by disturbances such as war or natural calamity, which could break down the national network into several regional networks. Further breakdown could then occur, disintegrating a previously integrated system into a group of communities sustained by local self-sufficiency (Skinner 1971). The exchange network therefore was rather fragile to serve as the bond holding China together for prolonged periods, vulnerable as it was to foreign invasions, civil wars, and natural calamities. The network probably had only limited influence on the vast, less-populated peripheral areas in the south, southwest, west, and northeast. In these relatively underdeveloped and underpopulated provinces, often newly inhabited by migrants from the densely populated core areas, local and community-level self-sufficiency was more prevalent than participation in the integrated national network. The weak linkage between core and peripheral areas allowed populations outside of the core area to develop regional and local identities.

Circulation of local elites within the bureaucratic network was another unifying force. As discussed previously, the Han government recruited candidates for government services by means of a recommendation system. A quota of recommendees was assigned to each of the commanderies from which local elites were drawn to serve in the central government. The typical route for advance of a young intellectual within the bureaucracy began with education at a local academy or tutoring at home. In his early years he was employed by the county government, often as a junior scribe. He might be gradually promoted to the position of a secretary in charge of one department in the county government. Then he would be recommended to take a job in the commandery government. After his worthiness was proven, he would be recommended to taken an examination at the capital, where he was either enrolled in the Imperial Academy or appointed to the position of a court attendant. Having finished such training, he was assigned a job in the central government. In his career he might also be dispatched to govern a county or a commandery. He never, however, would be assigned to govern his native place. Therefore, each local government was administered by an outsider and a staff of native sons. Such a bureaucratic circulation of talents allowed the local people to participate in governance at both the national and local levels. Thus, regionalism could be counterbalanced by pulling the local elites into the power equilibrium, that is, the Han bureaucracy.

Such a system, however, still had to face a problem of conflict of loyalty. The Confucian ethic model was built on a graded differentiation of human relationships. The priority of loyalty was ranked according to the degree of personal intimacy. Loyalty to the local community was ranked higher than that to the state; gratitude to the recommender was more intense than to the imperial throne. Hence, regionalism never could be overcome by nationalism. Regionalism could be a significant factor in causing a member of the Han elite to place local interest above the national interest. Participation in local public affairs was thus often regarded as the hallmark of the local elite.

Before a bureaucrat entered government service or after he retired, he was often a recognized leader in his own community. Ti-wu Lun is an interesting example. He organized a militia for community self-defense in times of chaos and later served as a local bailiff. In the midst of his career, he retired to trade in salt. After the Eastern Han regime was established, he entered government service. As a ranking official, he was honest and sincere, a respected censor who never spared any wrongdoer (*HHS* 41/1–6). Peng Meng was a scholar included in the *Biography of Eremites*. When he made the decision to retire in silent protest against Wang Mang, police were dispatched to capture him, but the local people gathered to resist the arrest. He thus also appeared as a local leader (*HHS* 83/3–4). Liu I lived in seclusion until he responded to the invitation to enter government service. As an official, he resisted the pressure of the powerful in order to protect the well-being of the common people. At the time of the Yellow Turban uprising, he retired. At home, he gave relief to several hundred of the poor (*HHS* 81/22).

Han China was divided into the core areas, the peripheries, and the borderlands. This differentiation resulted in relatively uneven potentials for exercising influence upon the national power equilibrium. Distribution patterns of Confucian literati serve as an index to show that the elites were spread quite unevenly. Of the Confucian literati purged in A.D. 166–176, 188 of the most prominent victims can be traced in historical records. Chin Fa-Ken, analyzing their places of origins, found that 80 of these elites were from four commanderies (Junan, Chenliu, Yingchuan, and Shanyang) at the mid-lower reach of the Yellow River, just next to the eastern capital region, and the remaining 108 were scattered in other parts of the empire (Chin 1963). It should be pointed out that in the Eastern Han these four commanderies had lost 32 percent of their population, which constituted a little less than one-tenth of the national total.

Yet the concentration of Confucian elites there amounted to 43 percent of the 188 prominent scholars! If uneven distribution of Confucian scholars reflected uneven distribution of power in favor of the core area, resentment of the local elites of other regions who felt that they had been deprived of their share of power was inevitable.

Meanwhile, in the peripheral areas social power most likely would be concentrated within small groups of elites, since leadership tended to be monopolized by the local establishment. In the Eastern Han the restriction of triple avoidance meant that any candidate to a local administrative position could not be appointed to serve in his own home area or areas where he could find kinsmen and relatives, or the area from which his own local administrator originated. Such a restriction caused two regions in north China (Yu and Chi) for years to receive no regular appointment to fill up the administrative vacancies (HHS 60B/8–9). This incident reflected the fact that elites in the two peripheral regions were small in number and virtually all belonged to a network of personal ties and connections. The internal solidarity of local elites could be a logical consequence of small-group mentality. Strong local and regional identity therefore could well serve as a centrifugal force opposing the centripetal force essential to national unity.

Several peripheral regions were notable in their challenge to the core's dominance. One was the Yu-Chi region, which consisted of formerly underdeveloped provinces north of the Yellow River. By the end of the Western Han dynasty, however, population increase and economic growth had made this region sufficiently strong to pose its first challenge to the core area. In the first century A.D., Han loyalists and peasants rising against Wang Mang both raised armies in north and central China outside the core areas along the Yellow River. The major operations led by Liu Hsiu, who was to found the Eastern Han dynasty, were supported mainly by the Yu-Chi region, where large numbers of immigrants created sufficient local wealth to fight Wang Mang's army, which had been raised and sustained by the core area (Bielenstein 1954).

In A.D. 70 the Yellow River was first set on a regular course by Wang Ching. The Yu-Chi region greatly benefited. In the second century, frequent intrusions of nomads along the northern and western borders of China drove large numbers of people from northern provinces into the Yu-Chi region. Therefore, the demographic decline did not occur in the Yu-Chi region as much as in the core area. By the end of the Han dynasty a warlord had taken control of the court. The Yu-Chi region served as a base of resistance organized by a group of the old establishment. The leader of this operation, Yuan Shao, proclaimed himself the governor of Chi, from which he was able to raise an army allegedly one hundred thousand strong, supported by a ten-year supply of stored grain. Yuan Shao remained a major contender for hegemony over China in the last decades of Han (de Crespigny 1970; *HHS* 76/5–6; 74A/3–6).

Other regions notable in this struggle were in the rich land of south China along the Yangtze River, especially the mountain-circled Szuchuan Basin in its upper stream and the lake areas in the middle and lower reaches of the mighty Yangtze, known as the Ching and the Yang regions, respectively. Ever since the era of Neolithic cultures, these three southern regions had developed distinctive features. The crop was rice instead of millet; transportation was by boat instead of wagon; the houses were built with wooden structures instead of stamped earthen walls and foundations. During the early reigns of the Western Han, the southern provinces remained underdeveloped and underrepresented in the national power structure. However, the south, which contained much fertile land, became a refuge haven for a steady flow of immigrants from the frequently war-afflicted north. By the late Eastern Han, the demographic figures of the southern provinces generally showed double, triple, or even four or five times the Western Han statistics (Lao 1935; Hsu, Cho-yun 1980:137–39), yet they were underrepresented in the national elite community. Among the prominent literati who suffered from political purges, only ten were from the Ching-Yang region and four were from Szuchuan (Chin 1963). After the Han court lost its control over provinces between the second and third centuries, the Szuchuan, Ching, and Yang regions each produced contenders to take part in the internecine struggle over the dominance of China. In the following seven decades of tripartite division of China, A.D. 196–265, the Ts'ao family, which occupied the core area, had to face strong challenges put forth by the Liu Pei group, which occupied Szuchuan, and the Sun Chuan group, which occupied mainly the Ching-Yang regions in the Yangtze Valley. The combined strength of the Lius and the Suns was much smaller than that of the Ts'ao. Nevertheless, these two southern powers managed to maintain the struggle for a prolonged period, even after other northern powers had failed to resist the Ts'ao's claim of dominance.

Regionalism in the Han empire, as well as in other political orders of Chinese history, was a continual problem for the state. The assignment of regional quotas for recommending candidates to participate in the national bureaucracy had always been a necessary counterweight to prevent runaway centrifugal tendencies. As long as there was no disturbance in the system, an equilibrium of power-sharing and resource circulation indeed could be maintained by constantly recruiting elites from the provinces. Nonetheless, frequent redistributions of population created new regional strengths that were eventually used by the regional and local leaders to claim some kind of autonomy.

In summary, regional differentiation in the vast land of China has always supported centrifugal tendencies. The tradition of intensive farming often tied the population to the soil. During the Han dynasty, migration, always a slow process, took place in such a reluctant manner that much of the south and other peripheral areas remained thinly populated until the invading nomads drove the Chinese to the south beginning in the fourth century. Regional differentiation was strengthened by the difficulty of incorporating peripheral areas into the national resource-flow network and was further bolstered by the Confucian focus on local concerns, encouraged by the constant tension and frequent conflicts between the literati and the throne. As a result, China was torn to pieces by the previously dormant centrifugal forces, only to be reunited by the centripetal force of a shared cultural heritage and the reintegration of the national exchange network under a new political power. Even a brief unification could cement cultural and economic bonds, since time was required for tension to mount between a new regime and the Confucian elite and for regionalism to gather momentum.

In Han China by the beginning of the third century A.D., the Confucian elite had lost interest in participation in the national bureaucracy, and thus China remained disunited. Some Confucian intellectuals even questioned the validity of the whole system, including their Confucian beliefs (Balazs, 1964:187–255). In the following centuries the Chinese preferred to adopt a foreign faith, Buddhism, and to develop the indigenous folk faith, Taoist Millennialism. Confucianism was to remain at a low ebb for five centuries.

EXTERNAL FACTORS

Of course, the fall of the Han dynasty as a political order cannot be explained solely on the basis of the two factors presented here, which can be classified legitimately as social cleavages within the Han political order. There were also external factors, such as the constant raids by nomads along the steppe land between central Asia and northeast Asia, which drained Chinese resources.

Nomadic intrusions indeed constituted one of the principal exogenous factors that contributed to the fall of the Han empire. The disturbance created by the Ch'iang tribe along the western border has been regarded as fatal to the Han order. Considerable resources were drained to fend off the invading Ch'iang while revenues from the war-affected provinces were reduced (HHS 76/22). Yet the Ch'iang intrusions were usually localized ones, and the scale of battles hardly exceeded operations of ten thousand men to fight a few months. Truly large-scale war did not occur until there was a decade of continuous conflicts (A.D. 141–151). The whole population of the Ch'iang tribes was probably not much more than half a million persons, which was 1 percent of the Han population (HHS 87/21–23). On the contrary, the campaigns against the Hsiung-nu in the Western Han were on a much larger scale. The Hsiung-nu was initially a nomadic empire stretching across the entire north Asian steppe land. The effort to defend China from the Hsiung-nu invasions remained the primary concern of the Han court throughout the first half of the Western Han period (HS 94B/22–25). The magnitude of the campaign against the Hsiung-nu, as well as its total cost—including the opening of a silk route—far surpassed the efforts of those who deplored the fight against the Ch'iang in the mid-second century. Western Han was not exhausted by the Hsiung-nu problem. Had the Eastern Han been a strong coherent political order before the social cleavages reached a point of no return, Han resources would have been sufficient to handle the disturbances caused by the rise of the Ch'iang.

The peasant uprisings in the second century are often cited as significant in bringing down the Han political order, a theme especially favored by Marxist historians in modern China. The uprising itself might indeed have been a reaction against the polarization of the distribution of wealth, which was clearly recognized by social elites among the Eastern Han scholars (Balazs 1964:187–225). The revolt rose in the spring of A.D. 184; major campaigns took place in areas near the eastern capital area, in the peripheral provinces next to the core area. Remnants of the Yellow Turban forces fought sporadically in scattered localities for four more years until a warlord, Tung Cho, marched into the capital, the event that signaled the actual end of the Han (Levy 1956). The Yellow Turban revolt was a significant incident that coincided with the fall of Han. The general deterioration of Han effective rule, however, had started at the time of purges against the literati (A.D. 166–176). In A.D. 188 Tung Cho took advantage of the anarchy created by factional conflicts between the pro-literati bureaucrats and the anti-literati courtiers and eunuchs which was an extension of the cleavage between these groups (de Crespigny 1970). The Yellow Turban revolt was one of the symptoms of the loss of effective governance by the Han order. It was hardly a cause of the fall.

Both the Ch'iang disturbances and the peasant uprisings certainly aggravated the deterioration of the Han rule. Both, however, probably played triggering rather than determinative roles in ending the Han. The Han empire was terminated by internal dissension. On the one hand, the powerful literati, who served as cultural carriers and social critics as well as bureaucrats and community leaders, competed against the imperial authority for the control of resources and undermined the justification of the legitimacy of imperial rule by constantly demanding the fulfillment of the Confucian moral code. On the other hand, peripheral areas of the empire, as soon as they grew sufficiently in a general trend of demographic redistribution and economic development, tended to take a centrifugal attitude and even challenged the dominance of the core area. The institutional cleavage in the form of conflict between the imperial authority and the literati and the spatial cleavage in the form of competition between the core area and the provinces, compounded with the catalytic function of external invasions and internal uprisings, finally brought about the fall of the Han dynasty.

NOTE

1. Modern editions of historical sources or works of traditional scholarship used in the text are as follows:

Chien-fu-lun. (Wang Fu) Ssu-pu-pei-yao edition

Chun-chi'iu-fan-lu. (Tung Chung-shu) Ssu-pu-pei-yao edition

Hai-yu-tsung-kao. (Chao I) Commercial Press edition

Han-shu-pu-chu. [HS] (Pan ku) I-wen reprint

Hou-Han-shu-chi-chieh. [HHS] (Fan Yeh) I-wen reprint

Hou-Han-chih. [HHC] in Hou-Han-shu-chi-chieh

Huai-nan-tzu. (Liu An) Ssu-pu-pei-yao edition

Jih-chih-lu. (Ku Yen-wu) Ssu-pu-pei-yao edition

Lu-shih-chun-chi'iu. (Lu Pu-Wei) Ssu-pu-pei-yao edition

Shih-chi-hui-chu-k'ao-cheng [SC] (Ssu-ma Ch'ien) I-wen reprint

The Role of Barbarians in the Fall of States

Bennet Bronson

The collapse of ancient states and civilizations is a large topic. A few definitions and restrictions must therefore be imposed. First of all, I will confine myself to discussing the fall of states rather than of civilizations, which are a class of entities too incorporeal and susceptible of resurrection to be easily dissected. States, on the other hand, are real enough. They are also mortal enough. Although recoveries after seemingly fatal illnesses can readily happen, and though parts of the great traditions of some states seem able to survive almost indefinitely, one cannot reasonably doubt that all states do fall, just as prophets and social critics have always predicted.

Second, I propose to adopt a rather loose, minimalist definition of *state*. I will apply that term to any organization that exercises major political authority in a relatively centralized and institutionalized form over a relatively large and contiguous population. However, deciding where the exact boundary between states and nonstates lies is less essential to my argument than is determining the relative status of any pair of conflicting polities with respect to centralization and the institutionalization of power. Certain of what I have called nonstates will seem like states to some. Yet in all cases these will be found to be substantially less statelike than another polity in the immediate neighborhood, and the difference is what matters.

Third, there is the problem of telling just when a state has fallen: when it has undergone political destruction such that it can no longer be considered to exist. The fate of Carthage after the Third Punic War, with its rulers executed, its populace carried off, and its capital leveled and sown with salt, is likely to be called a "fall" by almost everybody. But controversy surrounds the ends of other states. As in the case of Rome, many dates have their partisans, and some might even deny that the state in question ever fell.

I have opted here for a commonsense definition. Coups and revolutions do not usually count as falls. Neither do simple changes of dynasty (although the continuation of a dynasty is a strong indication that the state has not fallen), nor gradual shifts in integrating institutions, organizational patterns, names and symbols, or ethnicity of the ruling class. However, when several of these elements change simultaneously, quickly, and substantially during or just after an interval of decreased centralization, I will presume that a fall has occurred. When a different government of equal or greater authority promptly picks up the reins, as in the case of the Roman conquest of the Greeks or the British conquest of Benin, the term *fall* is in some ways only a technicality. When, on the other hand, a government that is similar to the old one comes to power after an interval of rule by a disparate and less centralized government, as has repeatedly happened in China, I am inclined to think that the fall of the original is nonetheless real.

Such subtleties may be unnecessary in any case. The particular instances of political destruction I wish to consider are not ambiguous, and few will argue that the states in question are not states or that they failed to go through an experience very like a fall. The more serious questions are not of whether but of why.

Even if one takes the position that decline is inevitable, that it is intrinsic to the very idea of organizing society on a scale larger than that of the family or village, one still finds no obvious explanation for the apparent fact that in the long run states always fall. Are declines and falls causally related? Are they so closely related that the causes of the latter are just intensified versions of the causes of the former? Many believe so. On the analogy of a machine whose regulatory systems have gone awry, they would see the actual fall as simply that point on the spiral of increasing oscillation where the fabric tears and the machine of society flies apart. In this view, the causes of the fall are complex, of long standing, and essentially internal.

As I too am a believer in social phenomena caused by positive feedback, I do not doubt that states have often fallen for internal reasons. Yet I am uncomfortable with the partial circularity of the logic behind such explanations. How do we know that the symptoms we observe are those of decline? Because the state in question eventually falls. And how do we know that these symptoms of decline are causative agents? Either because we think we see them getting worse as the end approaches or because we have defined them that way. True, we can attempt to specify in detail the ways in which these symptoms could actually prove fatal to a state, and for the sake of simplifying our model of decline we can ignore the likelihood that some symptoms can be cured. But I am uneasy nonetheless. The internal causes we are prone to cite bear a resemblance to self-justifying prophecies even if, unlike Jeremiah and his many successors, we do not always ascribe the fall of states entirely to sin.

Internal versus External Causes of Decline

The symptoms of decline are rarely easy to recognize in spite of the folklore that tells us that things get worse as the end approaches. When a randomly chosen point in the lifespan of a state is viewed without foreknowledge, we tend to find abundant evidence that the state, though in reality perhaps newborn, is in precipitous decline. Observers agree that falling states have problems with restive local magnates and inefficient, corrupt bureaucrats. But is this not usually true of states on the rise? Consider the evidence of Pepys's diary on the state of officialdom in late seventeenth-century England—are many kingdoms in the last stages of decay more corruptly and inefficiently governed than England on the way to becoming a world power? Or look at Herodotus' description of Athens at the dawn of its Golden Age—did its bureaucracy, to the extent Athens had one, make any effort at all in those days to deliver services to Attica and its client states? Did it have less trouble then than afterward with independent tendencies on the latter's part? Were its leaders, who included individuals like the astonishingly rapacious Themistocles, more dedicated to organizational goals or less greedy for bribes?

As for places that had real bureaucrats and where we have solid data on them, what grounds exist for thinking that these were any less rigid and incompetent during rises than during declines? How about the British India of the 1800s in the dismally corrupt era of the East India Company, and of the 1930s, after the maturing of the outstandingly efficient Indian Civil Service? How about early and late Ch'ing China? Or if these examples are disallowed because the ends of the states in question entailed changes in government but not actual political destruction, how about China in the Southern Sung period, just before the Mongol conquest, or Byzantium in the dark days of the early fifteenth century? Were their governments then more incompetent or venal than in earlier and happier years?

Further, is there evidence that the per-capita cost of government does run significantly higher during declines than rises? The variants of manorialism-cum-feudalism, in which the average citizen may owe as much as two-thirds of his gross labor to his rulers, are surely the most expensive of all common governmental forms; numerous examples exist of such systems being either strengthened while states are on the rise (as in eighteenth-century Russia) or imposed in very severe form at the moment of state formation (as in sixteenth-century Mexico). Moreover, the careers of governments with substantially centralized revenues do not show a clear pattern of thrift at the beginning and wild profligacy toward the end. Justinian in sixth-century Byzantium can hardly have ruled more economically than the Comneni emperors of the twelfth century and the Palaeologi of the fourteenth, nor were the early Mongol and Ottoman rulers notable cheese-parers.

One in fact would be surprised to see that the decline of states correlates at all with waste in government, despite the prominence of this factor in the writings of ancient and modern social critics. After all, the main cause of budgetary fluctuations in early times was military rather than moral. Early governmental budgets were at least as dominated as our own by defense expenditures, and these varied sharply from year to year in response not only to perceived or pretended military need but to military success as well. Well-fought wars against easy and wealthy enemies clearly were profitable ventures, capable of supporting all governmental expenses for a considerable time. Likewise, a poorly managed campaign must often have been disastrously expensive even when it was not followed by an attack on the capital city and the looting of the national treasury. One questions whether nonmilitary inefficiency and corruption has much effect in loot-financed states of this kind. To be highly solvent—to extend the canals, expand public services, fill the capital with splendid monuments, and maintain the ruler and nobility in suitably decadent luxury—does not always require hardworking bureaucrats and upright administrators. As shown by Rome in the days of its greatness, all it takes is a successful army.

I am arguing not that bad government is irrelevant but that it is (1) difficult to measure and (2), whenever we look at strictly contemporary documents rather than the moralizing works of later commentators, not at all clearly associated with declines and falls. Explanations that focus on bureaucratic bloat are also (3) suspiciously relevant to modern partisan political beliefs and should be received with caution on those grounds alone. I quite agree that good government—that is, ungreedy rulers, intelligent bureaucrats, and a justified general perception that the citizenry gets reasonable value for its tax money—is conducive to stability. I even think that some of the more long-lasting states in history owed part of their success to the fact that they tended to be better governed in this utopian sense than the general run of known polities. However, there may be other routes to stability (simple terror, for instance), and there may be causes of instability more decisive in their effect than any amount of inefficiency and corruption.

I do not propose to consider the full range of destabilizing factors that might plausibly have been decisive in the falls of at least some states. They include intangibles such as losses of morale and momentum; internal factors such as economic recessions, revolutions, and civil wars; and external factors such as environmental or medical catastrophes and war with other states. One would be foolhardy to disbelieve categorically in any of these. I believe in the importance of epidemiology and demography in social explanation, and the overwhelming significance of interstate war has already been referred to. But nonetheless, the remainder of this chapter will focus on still another external cause, perhaps the oldest and most popular of all explanations for drastic political declines: conflicts with nonstates, or invasions by hordes of barbarians.

THE CASE FOR BARBARIANS AS CAUSES OF COLLAPSE

I will use the term here in a limited sense: a *barbarian* is simply a member of a political unit that is in direct contact with a state but that is not itself a state. Under this definition it is perfectly possible for a barbarian to be civilized insofar as he may be literate (like the Batak of Sumatra and the Irish in the Dark Ages), or technologically sophisticated (like those modern Pathans reputed to make automatic rifles in blacksmiths' shops), or appreciative of the great tradition of nearby states (like many of the neighbors of the Romans and Han Chinese). He is a barbarian not because he is uncultured but because he is on the outside looking in.

True, most of the barbarians of history have been not only outsiders but poor and aggressive as well, but this is a logical consequence of their outside status rather than a part of the definition. Although one can conceive of barbarians who are rich and on cordial terms with their state-organized neighbors, it is hard to see how the rich ones can have remained barbarians for long. In the absence of very substantial physiographic barriers, few states can be indifferent to potentially significant taxpayers living just beyond their borders, and the interest of poorer barbarians will be equally great. If the rich barbarians successfully resist both their state-organized and unorganized but poorer neighbors, it is probably because they have set up a state themselves.

Barbarians who remain barbarians are therefore poor. Their aggressiveness toward states, however, follows not from their poverty but from (1) the generally perceived advantages of predation as a way of getting rich and (2) the pattern in which riches are distributed within states. The essence of a state, after all, is its superior ability to concentrate resources. Its gross national product and income per capita may be no higher than that of an equivalent noncentralized area, but these will necessarily, because it is a state, be concentrated in a relatively few spots. These spots— the national and provincial capitals, the temples, the homes of the elite— are bound to be tempting targets to predators from nonstates. If they limit their raiding to the settlements of other barbarians, the risk may be lessened but the profits—because of the greater dispersion of wealth in nonstates—are, almost by definition, small. This must be clear to any thoughtful war chief. Sooner or later, acting on a possibly incorrect estimate of a favorable risk-profit ratio, he is bound to organize a border raid.

Thus, most barbarians as defined can be expected to be raiders, just as civilized tradition holds them to be. The real question is whether they are anything more than that. Many states have certainly learned to cope with ordinary borderland banditry through such proven methods as bribes to leaders, trade embargoes, punitive counter-raids, and occasional annexations. Is there reason to think, as many historians suppose, that a well-run state should not be able to cope indefinitely? Barbarians do appear to overthrow states, but in reality are these anything more than jackals, opportunistic minor predators feeding on victims that are already moribund?

The empirical frequency of barbarians' association with the fall of states might lead one to suppose that their role is not entirely negligible. Large numbers of barbarians are much more likely to be conspicuously present at the time of death than either natural catastrophes or demonstrably unusual levels of inefficiency and corruption. In fact, except for the special (because often not fragmenting in its effect, not because uncommon) case of states overthrown by other states at an equal or higher level of centralization, it is not easy to find a documented instance of a state that is destroyed politically, so that its former territory reverts at least temporarily to nonstate organizational modes, in which the immediate agents of destruction are not barbarians. The prima facie case for considering them causes in some sense appears quite strong.

However, the notion that barbarian attacks can be decisive causes makes most of us uneasy even if we do not reject it out of hand. In my own case, this unease is the byproduct of an indifferent classical education. Whatever I and my schoolmates learned about the decline of empires we learned from our Latin and ancient history textbooks, and these agreed that the causes of the fall of Rome were essentially internal and inordinately complex. Perhaps to counter our schoolboyish partiality for Attila the Hun, we were taught that barbarians in general and those who overthrew Rome in particular were (1) overrated as to military effectiveness,

(2) substantially romanized anyway, and (3) opportunists who could not have succeeded if Rome had not been enfeebled by insane taxation, growing unworldliness, and massive corruption. The textbooks dwelt particularly on the corruption, managing to give the impression that the Cincinnatan and Cordelian virtues had been rampant down through the end of Augustus's reign and that the excesses of Nero and Caligula typified most of the (greatly telescoped) Imperial Period. The barbarians we learned about were those of Caesar and Tacitus: fierce and incorruptible if resistant to discipline. It was perhaps inevitable that we joined the "more and better" school. Those who eventually pulled a terminally diseased Eternal City down were simply lucky. In its heyday, Rome beat more and better barbarians than the fourth and fifth centuries ever saw.

That this might be an incorrect estimate of the relative strength of the Goths and Vandals versus the earlier Gauls and Germans is less important than the fact that almost any serious young Latinist of the post-Gibbon period has been led to accept the corruption hypothesis as an axiom, and that this is bound to color his or her attitudes toward other historical declines and falls. One is surprised to learn that in the case of Rome the barbarian hypothesis has not been entirely discredited:

> It was only in the West that the imperial government broke down in the fifth century. Yet in the East Christianity was deeper rooted and more widespread, and monasticism was both more extensive and carried to greater extremes. The army in the East was fully as large and as expensive, and the bureaucracy as swollen and corrupt. Yet at the very time when the Western Empire was staggering to its fall, the Eastern was making a recovery. . . . These facts indicate that the Empire did not, as some modern historians almost assume, collapse from internal causes. It succumbed to persistent attacks by invading barbarians. (A. H. M. Jones in Eisenstadt 1967:159)

I will not speculate on the other emotional and intellectual sources of our general distaste for barbarians-as-cause hypotheses. It is enough to say that most western historians and anthropologists share it and that the historiography of other nonbarbarian peoples shows similarly strong predispositions to believe that empires fall because they are rotten, not because they are pushed. Moreover, I will not venture to claim that this prejudice has no validity. It is sufficient for the moment to indicate that the rational proofs for inner rot over outside push are not always overwhelming and that the contrary formulation continues to be semirespectable, even among students of the fall of Rome.

BARBARIANS IN THEORY

Assuming, then, that the destruction of states by nonstates is not empirically incredible, the next step is to consider how it is possible. What factors might allow a group of barbarians to overcome a state? Does the state not have an almost insuperable advantage as long as its strength remains unsapped by poverty and dissension? Is it conceivable that states in their prime as well as their senescence might be overthrown, indicating unambiguously that barbarian attacks are a primary cause? To answer, we must consider not only the nature of the state in question but that of the barbarians as well.

For one thing, it is evident that there were marked differences in effectiveness among those stateless peoples who had the opportunity to become barbarians—that is, who were historically in contact with states. The substantial percentage of the earth's surface held by states since antiquity indicates that numerous peoples did not do well in the barbarian role; a good many politically uncentralized groups must have succumbed to the blandishments or legionaries of civilization immediately, and many others can have held out for only a century or two. However, some evidently did better, and a few became real stars of barbarianhood: the Mongols of the thirteenth century, the Moros of the sixteenth to twentieth centuries, the Pathans and other Afghans during the whole of the present millennium. Such groups were consistently successful over the years both in attack and defense against a wide variety of state-organized enemies. That special skills were involved is clear. One can hardly doubt that being an effective barbarian took considerably more than a warlike disposition and a sincere desire to become rich.

The defensive successes of barbarians are often felt to be a simple matter of terrain. Many of the more notable barbarian strongholds—the Himalayas, Hindu Kush, Zagros, Atlas, and Alps—are daunting to even modern armies and must have seemed almost impregnable to their ancient counterparts. Yet (1) there are similar areas in the New World which, far from sheltering barbarians, were foci of state development; the barbarians of the ancient civilizations of the high Andes were lowlanders of the eastern rain forests and southern prairies. (2) Successful barbarians have existed—Manchurians, Mongols, Moros, Scythians—in places without extraordinary defensive advantages. And (3) the inhabitants of the best-defended terrain—Pathans, eastern Tibetans, Ghurkas, Caucasians, Albanians, highland Scots, Swiss—have often shown a marked aptitude for offensive warfare in environments quite different from their mountain homelands.

Explanations of barbarian success when on the offense tend to focus on hardiness, mobility, and the militaristic attitudes bred by a nomadic way of life. These explanations are undoubtedly true in a limited way but do involve a certain circularity of reasoning. Of course the barbarians that win are hardy, mobile, and militaristic. So are the victorious armies of state-organized societies—those are simply the qualities of good troops everywhere. It is not in fact obvious that the barbarian lifestyle is any more conducive to the military virtues than that of peasants, landlords, or tradesmen. Farmers do not necessarily lead easier lives than shepherds. Merchants may not be less skillful with ships and horses than pirates and bandits. And historically the best peasant infantrymen (e.g., the northern Italians of Republican and early Imperial Rome) and cavalrymen (e.g., the Isaurians of the Byzantine Empire) are claimed to have been at least the equals of any barbarian on a man-for-man basis, and the specialized military elites of a number of premodern states (e.g., the Samurai, Nayars, Mamelukes, Spartans, Normans) in their day appear to have been individually superior to most of their enemies, whether barbarian or civilized.

Several factors other than geography and psychology may help to explain barbarian successes. First, they enjoy a distinct advantage in military funding. Assembling an army is cheap for barbarians and expensive for states. Although war can indeed be self-supporting for any militarily successful polity, the front-end expenditures of a war conducted by a true state—enlistment bonuses, provisions, pay during the early stages of a campaign—are bound to be relatively high. This is so even when enlistees are induced to pay most of their own expenses by promises of loot once they have entered the war zone: not only are entirely unpaid soldiers, as all authorities agree, likely to start looting while still close to home, but the state's investment in military pay and provisions are what form the basis of its claim to keeping part of the profits of war for itself, whether in the form of outright booty or of taxes on a still-productive, and so only moderately looted, population of new subjects.

A barbarian war chief, by contrast, has none of these concerns. His initial expenses are minimal and the cost of maintaining his army nonexistent. If he is poor enough to start with, the profits from even a minor victory may be attractive enough to justify considerable risks. And importantly, the possibility of long-term losses is limited. Whereas the leader of an aggressive state must not initiate an attack before weighing the incalculably grave consequences of possible defeat, ranging from taxpayers' complaints and mutinous troops to conquest by a now-victorious enemy, the prospect of failure is less daunting to the leader of a barbarian raid. In most cases he should not have much to be concerned about besides personal safety. He can depend on the attacked state to be reluctant to undertake the expense of even a major punitive expedition, much less actual annexation of a poor and underpopulated barbarian territory.

Second, nonstates have certain built-in organizational advantages when in the defensive role. A number of observers have pointed to the military effectiveness of the unilineal "segmentary" kinship systems of Africa and southwestern Asia, which provide an automatic concentration of troops to match the size of attacking forces but have no vulnerable government center and no need for more than a rudimentary command structure. It is not in fact clear that kinship-based segmentary systems of the Afro-Asian sort are necessary. As is shown by the clientship-based chiefdoms of the bilateral Tausug and other Moro groups in the southern Philippines (see, e.g., Kiefer 1972), other nonstate systems are capable of similarly fast, semiautomatic responses to outside aggression. Successful defense may require little more than a warlike population and a degree of xenophobia. Coordination among the defenders does not seem necessary or even desirable: most theorists of guerrilla and counterinsurgency warfare agree that self-sufficiency and capability for independent action on the part of small units are the hallmarks of success in defensive wars against numerically superior enemies.

One also should not undervalue a further advantage of societies without generals and kings: if there is no authoritative leadership, there is no one who can offer an authoritative surrender. It has been suggested (e.g., Caroe 1976:337), for instance, that this is the main reason for the comparative success of the British in pacifying Baluchistan as opposed to the areas farther north on the Pakistan-Afghan frontier. The Baluchi may have been no less resolute and skilled in war than the Pathans, Kafirs, and Hazaras, but they had leaders who could in some degree persuade their followers to abide by the agreements they had signed.

On the other hand, the military advantages of acephalous organization are rather less evident when it comes to sustaining an offensive. Centralized organizations, all else being equal, can be presumed to have greater staying power: superior discipline, larger reserves of materiel, and greater ability to withstand tactical defeats in the name of strategic victory. Although barbarians could be expected to do well against states in raids or short wars within the territories of those states, the theoretical advantage might shift as campaigns drag on and the invaders begin quarreling or considering the advantages of taking their loot and going home. The defending state must of course be resolutely led and must take care not to leave an opening for a sudden knockout blow to its leader or capital. But it should otherwise perform effectively in such situations, as perhaps is shown by the celebrated tenacity of the Southern Sung in their defense against the Jurchens and Mongols or the spectacular counter-barbarian successes of the Byzantines in the centuries before the unexpected knockout at Manzikert.

This presumed advantage of states in protracted defense suggests that successful barbarians would have evolved institutions to counter it, but what these are is unclear to me. The exceptionally wide distribution of the idea of the raid chief, with substantial military authority but no civil powers, indicates that the need for offensive coordination is recognized in many military traditions. Raid chiefs appear even in acephalous societies that, like those of the Plains Indians of North America, are not oriented toward predation on states and are very common among both acephalous and chiefdom-level barbarians. Since the nature of the authority of the raid chief is clearly a key factor in sustaining an offense, one would expect to find significant differences among barbarian groups in the way he is selected and the kinds of agreements his followers make with him. However, the evidence on the subject is very scattered. The only generalizations possible at the moment are that selection is frequently based on achieved rather than ascribed criteria—hereditary raid leaders seem to be much rarer than hereditary priests or tribal chiefs—and that traditional law often grants special coercive powers to leaders of raids while these are actually in progress. One can readily conceive that two successive raids by one barbarian group will be organized quite differently, depending on such variables as the nature of the target, the charisma of the leader, and the length of time the raid is underway. Even deliberate innovation is not out of the question. The isolated, focused, and classless ad hoc society of a long-distance raiding party seems an excellent laboratory for organizational experiments.

Another institutional variable worth considering is that of the quasi-religious, elite military associations—the Dog Soldiers of the Plains Indians, the Jomsvikings of the Scandinavians, the *ribat* of North Africa, and similar warlike cults of the Middle East—which occasionally are known to have served as the cadres or shock troops of nonstate armies. The fact that analogous associations (e.g., the Knights Hospitaller and the Assassins) are also found in anarchical states but not in states under full centralized control suggests one of the reasons for their existence: they are a way of producing military units with the training and discipline of a national army in the absence of a nation, substituting a religious focus for patriotic esprit de corps and perhaps supported logistically by tithes rather than taxes.

Cultist shock troops are prominent in the histories of some barbarian areas and (as shown by the experiences of the American and British armies with Muslim "fanatics" in the southern Philippines and on the North West Frontier of India) can be excellent soldiers. They are one possible answer to the problem of persuading barbarians to press home an attack or carry out an offensive campaign with as much determination as a regular state army. Another possible answer may be mass, quasi-religious indoctrination of all armed forces, like that used by Shaka in forming the Zulu impis. And of course, such measures for stiffening troops under adverse conditions would not be needed when campaigns are going well. A string of profitable successes should often be enough to counterbalance any shortcomings of barbarian armies with respect to their willingness to continue a war.

One should not assume, incidentally, that nonstate armies are necessarily outnumbered by the armies of states. It is a familiar fact that the mountain tribesmen of northwestern Pakistan and eastern Afghanistan are individually capable warriors, considered by their former British enemies to be superior to most Indian (as well as British) soldiers on a man-for-man basis. It may come as a surprise, however, to learn that these archetypal individualists have not historically been averse to mass mobilization and large-unit military tactics. During the nineteenth century, virtually every tribe on the North West Frontier assembled at least one *lashkar* or raiding party of between five thousand and ten thousand men (see, e.g., Swinson 1967:242, 314; Barth 1965:61, 122); some, like the indefatigable Afridi, did it several times. And there is no sign that raids of this size were anything out of the ordinary in the context of the long-term history of the region. Through social mechanisms that are not quite clear (charismatic religious propaganda and cultist elite units played a part), a number of the Frontier tribes routinely fielded raiding parties that were equal in size to a Roman legion. When, as occasionally happened, several tribes formed an alliance, their combined forces were not inferior to the full armies of most known premodern states.

This is an exceptional case, to be sure. Yet it serves to give emphasis to the general point toward which the present arguments have been building: that barbarian military capabilities may in some circumstances be so formidable as to explain the fall of states without reference to those states' internal conditions. The conventional wisdom is erroneous: the theoretical advantage of centralized over noncentralized polities is neither invariable nor insuperable. Given the right barbarians in sufficient numbers, it is plausible that even the best-organized and least-senescent of states could be overthrown.

BARBARIANS IN PRACTICE

To establish empirically that this is so, one must be able to show in any given case that (1) the attackers were really barbarians, that (2) the attacked state had not been fatally weakened beforehand, and that (3) the result was true political destruction, not just a change in government.

A number of examples could be cited that seem to meet these restrictions: the Arab seizure and transformation of Byzantine Syria a bare decade after the stunning Middle Eastern conquests of Heraclius, the Mongol eradication of the young and vigorously expanding Khwarazmian empire, or the devastation of a whole spectrum of North African societies at the hands of the Banu Hilal and their kin. However, no such direct evidence can be altogether convincing. Definitions are bound to be disputed: some might feel, for instance, that the later state-building achievements of the Arabs and Mongols qualify them as protostates rather than barbarians even in the 640s and 1200s, in spite of their lack of bureaucracy, laws, taxes, currency, monopoly on the legitimate use of force, or most other statelike attributes. Moreover, an autopsy on any political body is likely to show the presence of potentially fatal diseases: for instance, the mutual exhaustion of the Byzantines and the Sasanians at the time of the Arab conquest, or the famously bad intelligence work that led the Shah of Khwarazm to imagine that he could murder a Mongol ambassador. And even if one accepts one or two such examples as valid (the early Mongol victories in particular are a little hard to explain entirely in terms of the internal problems of the vanquished, as it stretches credulity to claim that a quarter of the states in Eurasia had grown fatally corrupt at once), one can still dismiss them as freaks. Perhaps such phenomena are too rare to be included in a general theory of the decline of states.

Indirect evidence, however, suggests that barbarians with decisive power over the survival of states are not all that rare. The ability of the Mongols and Arabs to overthrow states almost at will is matched by a number of less well documented barbarian successes.

Consider the case of northern India. Observers have long been puzzled by the paradox of an area that contains one of the world's great civilized traditions but whose political history is unusually chaotic and surprisingly short. After a moderately early but abortive start in the Indus Valley and in spite of the apparently steady development of an extraordinary orally transmitted culture, the material trappings of centralized polities come late to the subcontinent—it is not always realized that the first archaeologically recognizable, large post-Indus settlements are not earlier than the fourth century B.C., or that the first substantial concentration of monuments and inscriptions is not much earlier than the time of Christ. Moreover, when solidly visible states do appear in sudden profusion in the late first millennium B.C., they lead curiously checkered careers. During the succeeding eighteen centuries, the entire northern two-thirds of the subcontinent produced exactly two moderately durable, region-spanning states: the Gupta and the Mughal. Neither of these nor any of the smaller northern states lasted longer than two centuries, and anarchical interregna were everywhere prolonged and severe. Yet the region was highly civilized. It was creative, populous, and rich. It had been that way for three millennia. It should have produced large, durable empires to rival those of China, the Middle East, the Mediterranean, and Peru. But it did not, and the question is, why?

Aside from possible idiosyncrasies of national psychology, one of the few obvious differences between all northern Indian states and most states elsewhere is the fact that all were within raiding range of unusually effective barbarians. In few other parts of the world have barbarian raids been as unremitting and as spectacularly successful. From the days of Alexander the Great down to the mid-eighteenth-century blitzkrieg of Nadir Shah, attacks by outsiders, sometimes organized as states themselves but invariably making heavy use of tribal soldiers, are a normal state of affairs. With the exception of an apparent intermission between A.D. 750 and 1000, not a century passes without a great raid that goes at least as far as the Ganges and probably not a decade when barbarians do not repeatedly pass the Indus. And it is noteworthy that the armies and often the leaders of these foreign attackers are usually from one area, the North West Frontier.

As I said earlier, the Frontier tribesmen have throughout their history been barbarians of barbarians, among the finest of all irregular soldiers. Their extraordinary talents as guerrillas can be measured objectively by their success against British armies during the nineteenth and twentieth centuries when, alone among the world's preindustrial peoples, they not only withstood frequent and determined pacification efforts by large western armies but retained the capacity to go repeatedly over to the attack. That the British barely broke even with the Pathans and their peers leads one to wonder what chance any army with premodern weapons would have had against the same opponents. And historically it is not clear that the armies of most North Indian states of the pre-British period did have a chance. Rajputana, with its small and highly militarized kingdoms, is the only exception. Over the past thousand years, the rest of the region has succumbed repeatedly and often to marauding armies composed partly or wholly of Afghans and Pathans.

This extraordinary situation is without parallel in the history of other regions: it is as if the fall of the western Roman empire had been prolonged indefinitely, with an endless supply of Attilas, Theodorics, and Stilichos, but with very few Charlemagnes and not even the possibility of a Belisarius or Justinian. This analogy may be overstretched. But the Indian data do at least indicate that we must be cautious about accepting the European-Middle Eastern-Chinese pattern of short dark ages and long imperial periods as normal. Cultural and political success do not always go together. In India, for all its cultural enlightenment, the barbarian-dominated dark ages are the political norm and the stable empires the rare exceptions.

The implications for the present argument seem clear. Although Indian historical documents are not detailed enough for one to prove that barbarians in any single case were solely responsible for the fall of a local state, the larger picture is such that one cannot doubt that barbarians were decisive causes of numerous events of this kind. Over the last two millennia many states in India must have fallen for reasons that had nothing to do with internal problems. As with kingdoms lying in the path of the Mongols, a contented citizenry and competent government was no guarantee of survival for a smallish state in North India faced with yet another incursion of Pathans. Diplomacy must often have been the only skill that counted on such occasions; other functions of government were entirely irrelevant.

In case this too is felt to be an extreme example that is not germane to our understanding of ordinary political processes, it is worth turning to a brief examination of two somewhat similar situations on a much smaller scale in Southeast Asia, in the Deli Plain around Medan in northern Sumatra and the Central Plain around Manila in Luzon. Both areas are flat and fertile—the rice-growing Central Plain is now the granary of the Philippines, and the soils of the Deli Plain, famous for its tobacco, are reputed to be among the richest in tropical Asia. Both have adequate seaports (Manila Harbor is notably good), are located on major trade routes (the Deli Plain lies along one side of the Straits of Malacca), and have easy access to resource-rich hinterlands. Both should have been prime locations for ancient states of the sort that in the early to middle first millennium sprang up in many of the other flat and fertile parts of Southeast Asia: the Kyaukse Plain on the middle Irrawaddy, the shores of the Great Lake and Tonle Sap in Cambodia, the deltas of the Salween, Menam/Chao Phya, Mekong, and Red rivers, and the intervolcanic valleys of central Java. Yet when Europeans first reached the Deli and Central Plains in the sixteenth century, these areas not only contained no states or cities but were virtually unpopulated. Archaeological evidence shows that the northern edge of the Deli Plain did support one short-lived citylike settlement, Kota Cina, in the thirteenth to fourteenth centuries (Milner, McKinnon, and Sinar 1978). The archaeology of the Central Plain has not produced even that much; as far as is known it had no settlement larger than a village or government more ambitious than a minor chiefdom at any point in its precolonial history.

Here again a plausible explanation can be found in the presence of raiding tribesmen. The Batak who inhabit the mountains behind the Deli Plain were notorious as predators and self-confessed cannibals; in spite of their possession of an alphabetic script and moderately developed chiefdoms, their reputation for ferocity extended over much of the region. Further, they were numerous. Their knowledge of wet rice farming and their control over extensive paddy and swidden land inside their mountain homeland made it possible to support a relatively large, dense population, most of it within one or two days' travel of the coast. A state located on the coastal plain would not necessarily have had even a numerical advantage over the Batak, and the narrow shape of the plain would have made it nearly indefensible against an attack from the interior. That under such conditions a state may have survived for a time—Kota Cina is large enough to imply some degree of political centralization—is noteworthy. But its extinction and the absence of other states seems almost inevitable in view of the hazards of the social environment.

The Central Plain of Luzon had similar liabilities as a habitat for kings and kingdoms. Its barbarians in the early Spanish period (Doeppers 1968)— who technically did not achieve that status until then, given the absence of previous states for them to interact with—were less concentrated than the Batak but were singularly varied and formidable, ranging from the powerful Moro chiefdoms of the newly islamicized Sulu area to swidden-farming mountain tribes like the Zambal and Ibaloi to headhunting bands of nonagricultural Negritos. All except perhaps the southern Moros were in fact headhunters, which may help to explain their interest in raiding settlements too small and poor to attract the kinds of barbarians who, like the Moros, were mainly interested in slaves and other conventional forms of wealth. The mountain tribes were also skilled at warfare. In spite of their marked technological disadvantage (the swiddening groups did not even use bows, much less guns), they were a formidable obstacle to colonial efforts at pacification. As late as 1760, two hundred years after the founding of Manila, exactly two Spanish-controlled settlements had been pushed beyond the margins of the Central Plain.

The point here is not that the Luzon barbarians destroyed any states but that they appear to have been powerful enough to prevent their rise, in one of the best locations for a state in all of Asia. The case is similar to that the Deli Plain: despite their apparent locational and ecological advantages, both areas suffered the disadvantages of a narrow indefensible shape and a very extensive and easily defended barbarian hinterland that reaches to within a few tens of miles of any point in either plain. In Central Java, by comparison, the mountainous areas between the state-controlled valleys are narrow; even at a fraction of carrying capacity, the populations of the valleys would have far outnumbered the maximum possible populations of the mountains. In the extensive mainland deltas, the populations of the early states were not only much larger than those of their potential barbarian enemies but much farther away; the nearest truly rugged terrain is several weeks' journey from the central parts of any of the plains.

On the basis of only two cases, it would be rash to offer generalizations about the connection between barbarian success and relative population size, relative defensibility of bases, and simple travel time. Although other examples exist of rich but narrow areas hemmed in by excessive numbers of potential barbarians, and though some of these (like the western plain of Taiwan and perhaps parts of the Maghrib as well) do show abnormal or aborted patterns of state development, there may be exceptions, and of course there are many instances of states in quite different settings that nonetheless had severe barbarian problems.

It may be more productive of generalizations to consider further those Southeast Asian states that were not geographically vulnerable to barbarians. Most were to some extent indianized, especially on governmental levels. Their kings had Indian names, built Indian-style monuments, used Indian gods in their state religions, read Indian literature in the original, and were at least familiar with, if not thorough appliers of, Indian theories of politics and government. However, the derived states of Southeast Asia differed from their Indian prototypes in one crucial respect: they tended to last much longer. The present Thai kingdom goes back, with substantial continuity of territorial boundaries and of many political and cultural institutions, to the thirteenth-century kingdom of Sukhothai. The Angkorean empire of Cambodia survived from 802 to about 1440, with its capital at Angkor itself for most of that time and without significant changes of identity despite its occasional defeats by other state-organized enemies and its gradual loss of large tracts of territory to the conquering Vietnamese and Thai. The kingdom of Champa in central Vietnam retained at least its name, language, and Hindu-Buddhist culture for more than a thousand years. Even the comparatively short-lived Pagan kingdom of Burma was ruled by a single dynasty for two hundred fifty years before being destroyed by the Mongol armies of Kubilai Khan.

This picture of relative stability is somewhat misleading—wars between state-organized polities were frequent and savage—and does not apply to most of the insular part of Southeast Asia, where the various coastal kingdoms and chiefdoms mutated with bewildering speed and where even the great inland states of early Java are too poorly known for one to say whether they were stable or unstable. Nonetheless, the contrast with northern India is striking. There, the kinds of major states whose names are known through inscriptions and histories tend not to last for more than a century without drastic changes in name, dynasty, capital city, structure, and even ethnicity of the ruling class; the longest-lived states, like the Gupta and Mughal empires, have lifespans of about two hundred years. In Southeast Asia, major states last two or three times as long.

This difference between the two regions cannot readily be explained in terms of consistent differences in the internal structures of the states involved. Both South and Southeast Asia contained a wide range of ethnic groups, economies, and basic cultural patterns. Their environments, resources, and population densities were broadly similar. They had closely related state ideologies as well as comparable government institutions.

Both may be presumed to have suffered from a similar number of organizational problems.

The fact that political life expectancies in the two regions differ seems to me susceptible of only one explanation that can apply to all states in the first and to none in the second. The states of northern India were open to attack by exceptionally able barbarians; the states of mainland Southeast Asia were not. Unless we retreat to vague assertions about Southeast Asians being simply better rulers and subjects than Indians, we are forced to consider the idea that it is a difference in vulnerability to barbarians that has halved the expected average lifespans of all states that have ever existed in North India, and thus that the presence of these barbarians may have had a lasting and decisive effect on fundamental political processes over an area as large and densely populated as most of Europe.

BARBARIANS AND THE FALL OF STATES

None of the foregoing should be taken as a claim that most falls of states are caused primarily by barbarians. They are in second place even among the external causes: as with tanks used as antitank weapons, states have always been the principal destroyers of states. Essentially internal factors must often have been decisively important: as suggested earlier, the normal instabilities of any social organization seem capable of sometimes becoming amplified to such a degree that they tear the system apart. The hostile outsiders who are almost certainly present during any political dissolution could in the case of an internally caused decline be no more than spectators or minor participants. On the other hand, they could be the main cause of the symptoms of decline. Altogether there are four possible causal roles that outsiders can play.

(1) They may be only vultures, scavengers that wait until their victim is thoroughly dead before starting to feed. In this case, their association with the death of states does not have causal meaning. (2) They may be jackals, predator-scavengers that finish off the already weak or sick. Because the victim might have recovered if left alone, the causal status of outsiders of this kind is real but still secondary. (3) They may be wolves, predators that not only prey on weakness but that harry healthy victims until they become weak. Such wolfish outsiders must be counted as primary but not exclusive causes of political death. And (4) the outsiders may be tigers, capable of bringing down the healthiest and strongest of prey without preliminary harrying. Where these exist, they are capable of causing the fall of a state without the assistance of other external or internal factors.

Earlier parts of this chapter have sought to show that barbarians as well as state-organized polities are capable of filling any of these outsider roles. The first, or vulture, role, perhaps exemplified by the relationship of the Scandinavians to the Roman empire, is not of interest from the standpoint of explaining political disintegration. The fourth, or tiger, role, represented by the Mongols of Jenghis Khan's period, is important but essentially uncomplicated in terms of the political processes involved. The second and third roles are more complex, however, and require further discussion.

A central problem is that of telling jackals and wolves apart, since barbarians of both classes can be expected to have made decades or centuries of probing attacks before the coup de grace is finally administered. The wolf scenario is a familiar one: (1) Barbarian raids call for military countermeasures. Taxes increase. (2) The raids continue. After several rounds of raid and response, taxes grow heavy enough to cause an economic slowdown and/or resistance by elite taxpayers. The defense budget is cut. A military coup occurs. (3) Improved military tax-collection methods produce more slowdown and/or resistance. Faced with mutiny by unpaid troops, commanders start collecting their own taxes and hiring cheap barbarian soldiers. The raids still continue. The commanders secede. The now-autonomous provinces are defeated in detail by outside attacks or subversion. (4) The state falls.

Unfortunately, a jackal scenario could look quite similar, with raids, tax increases, coups, secessions, and all the rest; the only difference is that the activities of the jackals are not a determining cause of later events, perhaps because, as in the case of the early Arab successes against a Byzantine empire hard-pressed by the Sasanians, the state regards another state as its real enemy, or even because the threat from barbarians has been inadvertently exaggerated or deliberately misrepresented. Soldiers and tax collectors have been known to inflate the strength of enemies even in our own society; there is no reason to think that ancient governments were always in as much danger as they said they were when it came time to persuade the taxpayers to respond to another emergency defense appropriation.

Jackal or wolf status also depends to a degree on the effectiveness of the ordinary counter-barbarian measures taken by a particular state. Just as there are barbarians who traditionally do well against states, there are states that, like Byzantium, seem to have evolved highly effective mixtures of strategies for dealing with barbarians, so that raids and raiders that might be highly dangerous to one state might be almost routine to another able to counter them with a minimum of expense and sociopolitical disturbance. Faced with two enemies, the same group of barbarians could be simultaneously jackals and wolves.

Although this kind of relativity is built into any causal formulation involving states and barbarians, we need not abandon all hope of assigning responsibility. The issue of whether the barbarians in a given case are truly dangerous can be partially resolved by considering the cost effectiveness of war and the nature of a government's revenues. It was already suggested that ancient government budgets were often balanced, and perhaps almost entirely sustained, by profits derived from military ventures—from loot, slaves, and more drawn-out methods of appropriating the property and labor of subjugated areas. It was also suggested that not only rich states but rich barbarians were liable to annexation: a fertile and well-populated nonstate on the borders of a militarily competent state, like Gaul in Julius Caesar's day, was less of a threat than a temptation.

The state seeking to defray the cost of its counter-barbarian effort should therefore in the short term seek to neutralize the poorer barbarians on its borders with inexpensive passive defenses while behaving aggressively toward nearby states and richer barbarians. As long as it does well in warring against its wealthy neighbors, it will be able to cope with the others even if this does mean occasional pacifying expeditions and perhaps limited annexations of unprofitable but dangerous tracts of territory. One can conceive that it is not even necessary for the state to win all of its wars with its peers; drawn contests might on occasion profit both governments by offering an opportunity to extract what amounted to extraordinary taxes from each other's populations. But no such balance can last long. Eventually the time comes when either interstate draws become unprofitable or there are no more rich neighbors to conquer as the state in question comes to be surrounded by states and nonstates against whom aggressive war is invariably a losing proposition. From this point onward, any barbarian attack involves a net loss to the treasury which can be made up only by a depletion of reserves or an increase in taxes. When the loss becomes intolerable—that is, when the budgetary drain reaches the stage of causing a general economic slowdown—the formerly unimportant barbarians are seen to have been wolves all along. The state will be destroyed in short order unless it manages a last-minute reform by pulling back to a shortened perimeter of defense and developing new sources of revenue.

Parenthetically, it should be pointed out that the unprofitability of wars against poor barbarians is not an absolute; it depends to a large extent on the administrative and technological abilities of the state or its entrepreneurs. Ordinary ancient states seem to have limited their conquest profits to mobiliary loot, domestic slaves, and agricultural land that was generally of a kind that could be farmed by methods very like those used at home. Some of the more successful states, however, appear to have been more imaginative exploiters. One of Rome's strengths was its highly developed system of market-oriented estate agriculture, which not only made it possible to absorb almost unlimited quantities of slave labor but also enabled its entrepreneurs to take over or develop from scratch a wide range of very un-Italian farm systems, from the flood-irrigated fields of Egypt to the heavy-soiled forests of northern Europe. Although we should not of course imagine that any ancient state could exploit its conquests with the efficiency and ingenuity of more recent colonial powers, we must nonetheless recognize ability as a secondary factor in the causal equation. All else being equal, states with good managerial skills and a flexible exploitative technology can afford to annex, and thus indefinitely to neutralize, much larger barbarian areas than can other states.

However, whereas annexation and subsequent conversion may be the only sure defense against a particular barbarian group, they are only a short-term solution to the general barbarian problem. Expansion increases the length of the periphery to be defended and brings new barbarians onto the scene as well. Unless most of the barbarian reservoir can be brought profitably under control (and one imagines this is possible for a preindustrial state only when the reservoir is small, or rich, or easily colonizable by the state's own citizens), the wolf pattern is bound to continue to develop and the state to decline toward its fall. The timing of this final event is indeed influenced by nonbarbarian internal variables: by military skill, public morale, relative prosperity, tax-collecting efficiency, administrative economy, and even, insofar as legal and illegal corruption do consume a substantial portion of state revenues, absence of bribe-taking and excessive greed in the ruling classes. Yet in such cases the barbarians are still the primary cause.

To distinguish wolves from jackals, then, it is sufficient to show that barbarian attacks are the chief reason for defense expenditure at the point when military costs begin to exceed military profits. In real cases this may not be easy to demonstrate. Most ancient states, one imagines, considered their main enemies to be other states and spent their defense appropriations accordingly; if this was so at the time the cost and profit curves crossed, then the other states are the primary cause of the decline even when the final kill is made by barbarians. There may also be early states (Tokugawa Japan might be an example) whose main military effort was usually directed toward suppressing internal dissidents rather than outside enemies; it is even possible that this might be the real reason behind a military budget that is ostensibly oriented to border defense. However, the fact remains that a substantial minority of ancient states did have severe barbarian problems but no excessive difficulties with other states or militarily organized internal enemies. The wolf scenario seems able to account for the declines and falls of many of these.

A last complication must also be mentioned. While conceding that barbarians of the tiger and wolf categories can conquer states and be the main determinants of their antecedent declines, one still might say that this does not explain the actual falls. Except in extreme cases like Jenghis Khan's complete eradication of Khwarazm and the Tangkut kingdom, why should a barbarian conquest be regarded as a fall? Was not Theodoric the Ostrogoth as ardent an admirer and defender of Rome as most of the preceding Italian-born emperors? What about the Manchus or the Mughals: were they not participants, respectively, in the Chinese and Indian civilizations—external proletarians, as it were—before the conquests, and did they not manage to run China and India successfully? Is the seizure of power by barbarians any more fatal to a state than a rebellion or coup d'etat?

I believe that it often is. Their "proletarian" status notwithstanding, conquest by barbarians can rarely be inconsequential from the standpoint of political continuity. We may properly be doubtful that the social consequences are always as drastic as Bury (1927:51) says they were at the time of the invasion of the Huns:

> The fate of the conquered populations was to be partly exterminated, partly enslaved, and sometimes transplanted from one territory to another, while the women became a prey to the lusts of the conquerors. The peasants were so systematically plundered that they were often forced to abandon the rearing of cattle and reduced to vegetarianism.

Moreover, the Manchu example shows that it is indeed feasible for a group of barbarians to take over the apparatus of a previous government in intact condition and to run it with efficiency and minimal disruption; their victory over the Ming dynasty resembles a rebellion rather than a conquest in terms of its systemic effects. The example of the Mughals and also the Vikings (in Normandy and the Ukraine; their later conquests are as rulers of states) shows that some barbarian leaders are capable not only of running large states but of establishing innovative administrative systems. It is clearly possible that some barbarian conquests might resemble the conquest of states by other states—that is, the administrative apparatus of the previous government could be replaced by a quite different but equally centralized administration so quickly that the "fall" becomes only a technicality. An interesting example is that of the Almoravid takeover of Muslim Spain, where a group with little previous contact with states of any kind managed to establish a successful governmental system with apparent speed and ease.

Nevertheless, it would be unrealistic to conclude that painless barbarian conquests are a general rule. One finds few other historical cases of outsiders who do not have states themselves being able quickly to master the art of national government. The mere fact that these outsiders are admirers of a civilization does not make them preservers of the polities that support that civilization, nor does extensive prior contact with a state mean that they have the vaguest notion of how it runs. As shown by the Spanish devastation of Peru and Mexico, even states may not appreciate or be capable of retaining previous institutional systems. As shown by the behavior of the Mongols in their early campaigns, barbarians may be quite uninterested in previous institutions or in preserving the previous culture and population. And, as shown by Theodoric's Ostrogoths and the various other invaders of Rome, a lack of administrative talent and/or will is to be expected in even the most ardently admiring of barbarian conquerors. This by itself is enough to explain the close empirical association between conquests by barbarians and the falls of states.

The Collapse of Ancient States and Civilizations as an Organizational Problem

Herbert Kaufman

Despite the ambiguities of the term *collapse of civilizations*, the common element running through all the cases in this volume is the dissolution of large-scale political systems encompassing many local groupings of people and institutions, and perhaps comprising numbers of regional collections of localities. (In general, dissolution was indicated by the disappearance of the boundaries of the overarching polities, so that only the less-inclusive institutions remained, if anything did.) Explaining the demise of these political organizations, and the occasional regeneration of systems seemingly well on the way to dissolution, therefore may identify the dynamics of collapse wherever it occurs.

That is not to say political disintegration is the sole indicator of the collapse of civilization. Usually, it is associated with a reduction in the capacity of the people in the afflicted polity to feed, house, clothe, and defend themselves, collectively and individually. Sometimes religious practices and institutions also declined. The quality of life, the material standard of living, the unifying bonds, the productivity and the security of the population all diminished. Populations fell sharply, and in one or two instances disappeared altogether from the areas affected. Political dissolution was not isolated from other changes in society.

Under these circumstances, it is difficult to determine whether decomposition of overarching governmental structures was the cause or the effect of the other misfortunes. But one thing is clear: whenever that cluster of changes ordinarily referred to as the collapse of civilizations occurred, disintegration of overarching governmental organizations was a prominent feature of the process.

For this reason, the process may be approached as an organizational problem. Students of organization have been concerned with the demise of many kinds of organizations, and their mode of analysis can be applied to this phenomenon as well. All organizations elicit contributions to their operations from their members and from the world beyond their borders. Understanding how they do this and why their efforts sometimes fail may illuminate the collapse of ancient civilizations.

GOVERNMENT SERVICES IN DAILY LIFE

In ancient states and civilizations the proportion of governmental services performed by local units of government (including regulation of behavior, which is usually regarded as an imposition by those who are regulated but as a service by those who are protected) was greater than those performed by regional or central units of government, and probably much greater than those performed locally in modern states. In ancient polities most regional and central officials were in all likelihood distant, dimly perceived figures, while community leaders were familiar, lifesized individuals.

Nonetheless, the impact of central and regional officials on local life was by no means insignificant. It stemmed from the critical character of the duties these officials performed rather than from their deliberate intrusion into the details of individual lives. As persons, they may have seemed shadowy to villagers, but the water the villagers needed for agriculture depended heavily in many cultures on central planning, mobilization of labor, and continuing oversight of operations to construct, manage, and maintain the distribution network. Materials and products not locally produced could be acquired by trading local surpluses only if routes between localities were made secure enough to permit trading parties to travel reasonably safely. Farms, local settlements, towns, and cities could produce items for subsistence and trade only if they were not continuously plagued by marauders, extortionists, and conquering armies from their own and other cultures. Shrines and temples and other monuments to deities could be on a grand scale, and safe from possible desecration, only if resources for their construction and maintenance could be gathered from areas and populations larger than those of individual localities. Only political and administrative institutions encompassing constellations of localities could establish and maintain the order, the coordination, and the security on which depended the activities essential to the existence of these complex social systems.

Thus, every farmer, every artisan, every merchant and trader, every town and city elder, and even every priest was to some extent a beneficiary of the overarching political and administrative structures above him. Most of these ordinary people and local leaders were doubtless ill-informed about the occupants of the key positions in those structures and about the tasks they did. Probably only a few had more than the haziest notion of how those tasks contributed to their daily lives. With the advantages of hindsight, however, we can see that the operations of these super-structures influenced the lifestyle of even the most humble inhabitants of those lands in numerous, fundamental respects.

That is not to say local institutions were of no importance. Central authorities did not act directly on the populace but issued demands and instructions to local leaders or field administrators who were part of the local scene. Even taxes were often collected through tax farming rather than by direct collection, and military commanders in the field often recruited local manpower to fill the ranks of their forces. So an individual would not usually see direct evidence of the central structures and might therefore have regarded most of the governmental services and constraints he encountered as local in origin. And indeed, local leaders may well have had broad discretion in spheres not of concern to the central au-thorities.

Nonetheless, although the superstructure may not have been salient to many people, it played an important part in their lives. The importance of this part was most vividly demonstrated when the overarching insti-tutions failed or even faltered, for reasons to be discussed shortly. Nothing defines the role of an element in a system as clearly as what happens when it stops functioning.

In the political systems reviewed in this volume, decline in the effec-tiveness of the central political and administrative organs was almost always accompanied before long by a decline in the standard of living of most of the people within the jurisdiction of those organs. Where irrigation was vital, reckless use of water could lead to salinization of fields, or inadequate maintenance of water courses could diminish the availability of water. Agricultural productivity would decline in either case. Lower productivity, in turn, cut the revenues of the central insti-tutions, which frequently responded by increasing taxes or drafting labor. If the central institutions were successful in these efforts, the heavier burden on the populace lowered living standards, thereby reducing in-centives to work vigorously and arousing resentment. If the central in-stitutions could not maintain their revenues despite tax increases (because of continuing drops in productivity and/or concealment of true harvests), management and maintenance of the irrigation systems would fall, further depressing productivity and setting off still more frantic attempts to keep up revenues. Things would spiral downward.

The downward spirals would set off chain reactions. If dependable supplies of water decreased, localities closer to the sources might withdraw larger proportions, depriving more distant localities of the volumes they had come to need and expect. Not only would such practices have depressed productivity still further, but they would have set off disputes between localities that the weakened central organs would have been unable to resolve. Disorder within the system would therefore have been added to the other impediments to efficient production.

The drop in agricultural productivity and the resulting relative shortage of the necessities of life would also have engendered higher prices for food, inducing artisans to demand more for *their* labor and products. In short, inflation was likely to set in, disrupting established patterns of trade both inside the afflicted societies and outside in their exchanges with other societies. To the extent that some of the revenues of the overarching political and administrative structures of the societies were derived from such exchanges, the position of those structures would have been rendered even more precarious.

Under these conditions, the central organs would have found it increasingly difficult to maintain adequate defense forces as well as to preserve internal order and maintain large-scale public works. Bandits, raiders, and other freebooters from beyond the perimeters of the polities could roam more freely, but most of all, adjacent political systems would be tempted to invade and seize territory, making war a normal state of affairs in the border regions. Several motives for attempts to expand the boundaries of any human organization may be surmised, with the quest for more resources and for glory often appearing on any list. At bottom, however, reduction of uncertainty seems to be a consistent driving force. What goes on outside a system is often unpredictable and potentially threatening; if such challenges can be brought within the system, they are more easily controlled. Outward thrust is therefore a common feature of organizations in all spheres of human activity. In the case of states, it is usually expressed as distrust of allegedly aggressive neighbors and as a desire for security, and frequently takes the form of preemptive strikes described as defensive measures. No matter how big a system gets, external uncertainties, both real and imagined, continue to plague it; rarely, therefore, does this impulse let up. It is one of the reasons why there is seldom surcease from warfare between states. Economic problems that weakened defensive capabilities were consequently virtual invitations to invasion.

Disorder and warfare, in turn, must have impaired productivity and trade still further. Farmers in many areas must have feared to work their fields, merchants and traders must have been reluctant to move their wares, and roads and irrigation works must have been damaged by all the violence and left in disrepair because of dangers to the repair teams. These disruptions doubtless contributed still more to inflation and resulted in still more frenzied endeavors by the central organs to acquire the wherewithal for defenses and restoration of public improvements. The production and preservation of religious monuments and pageants and services may also have diminished while the costs of providing fewer of them rose; unifying symbols would have been losing their power and perhaps even arousing bitterness over their expense. Alienation could well have spread throughout any polity so afflicted, possibly inducing people—especially the highly skilled—to migrate to more stable and congenial areas or even to join brigands, rebels, or invaders.

In short, what the overarching political institutions did was to provide the environment and the means for the people within their jurisdictions to function and prosper. The central organs themselves did not actually do the work that nourished and sheltered and secured the populace, but they made it easier for the populace to do those things for themselves. As a result, when the effectiveness of the central organs shrank, the quality of life of the people suffered, and the survival of their polity, economy, and social order was placed in jeopardy.

But every explanation gives rise to a new enigma. Even if this reading of the experience of ancient states is correct, the reason for the decline of governmental services in polities where they had been of a high order for long periods is not self-evident. It is all well and good to say that governmental dysfunctions and the quality of life are so intertwined that each sustains or depresses the other; however, the question to which this volume addresses itself is, Why did systems change from an ascending spiral, or at least from an equilibrium, to a descending spiral? Why did once-flourishing states undergo such difficulties?

WHY DYSFUNCTIONS OCCURRED

In the most general terms, it looks as though either of two sets of factors could have set such a train of events in motion. One is a group of exogenous events undermining the capacity of the central political and administrative institutions to maintain the level of activities that provided favorable conditions for the productive efforts of the populace. The other is a set of social cleavages within those institutions that, even in the absence of exogenous triggers, curtailed their ability to maintain their activities.

Exogenous Factors

Among the exogenous elements that could have impaired the functioning of the central organs of government in the polities under consideration are natural disasters such as prolonged droughts, repeated crop failures, cataclysmic floods, and epidemics that carried off large parts of the population. Any of these could have reduced state revenues drastically and thus slashed the capacity of the state's machinery to perform the services it previously provided. So could the exhaustion of mineral resources or of soil fertility. To maintain vital governmental services under these circumstances, the rulers and administrators of the overarching institutions probably did what most of us do under such pressures—they intensified their performance of familiar routines and tried, by means of carrots and sticks, by exhortation and command, to get everyone else to do likewise. In some cases, this strategy doubtless worsened the situation by tiring and disaffecting an already weakened and discouraged people and by deepening the resource problems that drove the leaders to desperate measures in the first place. Despite their labors, things probably deteriorated further.

The revenues on which the overarching state depended could also have been adversely affected by events beyond their borders. For example, if a polity's traditional trading partner discovered new sources of materials it had hitherto obtained from that polity, established trade patterns would have changed suddenly and dramatically, depriving the original supplier of the benefits of exchanges on which it had come to rely. Or if other states engaged in warfare against each other, patterns of exchange and regular trade routes of states militarily uninvolved and politically indifferent could have been unhinged. The concentration of military forces anywhere on the borders of a system probably would have persuaded leaders to divert resources from the satisfaction of their people's daily needs and aspirations to the strengthening of boundary defenses. Some polities were doubtless able to withstand such shocks because of the size of their surpluses, of their reserves, and/or of the alternative trading opportunities open to them. A good number, however, were launched on self-reinforcing cycles of increasing pressure on the populace and the land to offset shrinking collections, getting less rather than more as a result, and therefore squeezing still harder.

Conceivably, misfortunes of this kind could have impaired the functioning of societies even if the political and administrative institutions had been able to maintain the level of services they rendered before the exogenous mishaps occurred. Much of the time, however, they were the triggers for political and administrative disabilities, which in turn depressed economic and social vigor. Political and administrative institutions were vital links in an intricate chain of events that the exogenous factors could activate.

Endogenous Factors

Even if no exogenous factors triggered dysfunctions in the operations of the overarching political and administrative organs of the states under study, however, those organs occasionally still came apart as a result of the centrifugal forces built into them. These needed no independent stimuli to set them off; they were constantly thrusting toward fragmentation and from time to time outweighed the factors that had originally generated the overarching institutions and held them together. The institutions, in short, could be weakened or destroyed by internal dynamics that divided their ruling groups or shattered their administrative machinery.

Divisions within the ruling circles.   When the group with the greatest collective influence in the governance of a polity is cohesive and its members jointly hold and wield the implements of power, those implements strengthen and support each other. The implements include control of wealth, of military power, of symbols, of knowledge, and sometimes of popularity. If the inner circle is unified and its members relatively unspecialized, each member has a share of all the implements and none has a clear advantage over the others; the chances of their sticking together are then reasonably high, and the effectiveness of each implement is multiplied.

When each member (or subset of members) of this group separately gets almost monopoly power over one implement, the cohesion of the group undergoes great change. One probable reason is the narrowing of vision and interest that comes from looking at the world from a specialized viewpoint; people who see things from multiple standpoints would seem logically more likely to appreciate their colleagues' positions and therefore to reach a comfortable consensus than people who perceive and judge the world around them in the light of a single value and set of considerations. To be sure, even relatively unspecialized inner-circle members may have serious fallings out. But the cleavages doubtless become wider and deeper as the number of resources they hold in common decreases.

This seems to be exactly what happened in several of the polities examined in this volume. Occupants of the formally designated seats of civil authority, their staffs, high-ranking soldiers, the high-born and the wealthy, high priests, and, in some instances, intellectuals fell out with each other (even though there was some overlap in these categories). Perhaps each faction thought its moral claim to preeminence was superior to those of the others, or believed that its special skills better enabled it to unify the polity, or feared that its concerns were not receiving due emphasis in the decisions of the group. Perhaps several of the factions succumbed to the temptations of power when they concluded that their exclusive resources made them stronger than the others. Whatever their motives, the rivalries and struggles among them grew more rancorous, more difficult to compromise, and sometimes more violent. Shifting alliances formed and broke up, and splinter groups within factions defected from one coalition to another. Occasionally, the outcome was full-fledged civil war. At any rate, energies that had once gone into the maintenance and advancement of the system, to the benefit of most of the people in it, were increasingly consumed by intramural battles and maneuvers.

Consequently, decisions were delayed or undone, and confidence in the firmness of policies could not have been high. The solidarity with which the polities confronted challenges to order and security and productivity must have been weakened, and the resulting failure to cope with the challenges may well have provoked new disputes and strife in the inner circle. Accusations and recriminations probably flew thick and fast. The decline in revenues that seems frequently to have accompanied a rise in disorder, insecurity, and unproductiveness doubtless added to the tensions within the ruling groups. The overarching political mechanisms thus needed no independent outside forces to explode them, their internal divisiveness being enough not only to atomize them but also to *generate* external forces that would add impetus to their own tendencies toward fragmentation. Without any external triggers, the downward spiral described earlier could have started and gained momentum.

Indeed, the very symbols and doctrines that at one stage integrated the polities became, in many instances, instruments helping to shatter their unity. In each of the societies considered, a transcendent philosophy of some kind served the populace as an explanation of the relationships between their social entity, the natural and social world in which it was embedded, and the awesome, mysterious, and overwhelming forces that sometimes buffeted it and sometimes heaped blessings on it. The philosophy usually provided the rationale for personal submission to the occupants of the officially designated seats of power and justified the exercise of authority by individuals not very different from those over whom they held sway. The prevailing body of belief thus buttressed the established political order. But it turned out to be a double-edged sword in several of the overarching states.

The reason for its double-edged character was that beliefs vindicating the power of rulers also became limits on their power. If they ruled because they enjoyed the approval of forces greater than they, or because they were wiser or more virtuous than their fellows, it followed that evidence of supernatural disapproval, or of folly or vice, vitiated their claims to general obedience. Gradually, the doctrines that conferred on them the ability to elicit obedience came in some cases to justify insubordination and even rebellion. Indeed, in time, the doctrines not only *permitted* such resistance to undeserving rulers; they were sometimes held (as at various periods in China) to *mandate* it. The security and power of the inner governing circles were thus weakened by the very principles that had once blocked challenges to their ascendancy.

In every society, there were people who claimed plausibly to be as well-versed in the prevailing transcendent doctrines as the ruling circles. Specialization of labor sometimes produced a group outside the dominant clique with great expertise in the lore and symbols having special status in the society. At other times, dissidents from *within* the inner circle challenged their erstwhile colleagues. Occasionally, a charismatic figure would arise from the rank and file to win widespread support for condemnation of rulers' transgressions against basic principles.

Custodians of overarching political power then found themselves embroiled in struggles to *retain* their authority instead of giving their undivided attention to the constructive *application* of their authority. What might have been minor exogenous problems were neglected. The unattended small difficulties became great vexations. The vexations increased the pressures on and within the ruling circle. The divisions reduced the rulers' ability to cope. Internal and external forces thus joined and strengthened each other.

Yet this was not the whole story. Troubles with administrative machinery added to the plight of the polities.

Runaway field administrators.   Decisions reached by the central officials of the overarching polities would have been nothing more than statements of aspirations and intentions if they had not resulted in appropriate action on the part of large numbers of people in the countryside and the cities throughout each realm. To produce such action, the central officials set up hierarchies reaching out into the field. Through the hierarchies the wishes of the center were communicated to local officials and to the populace at large, resources were mobilized, public works were directed, information was gathered, and noncompliance was detected and corrected. To a considerable extent, as we have seen, the central organs and their field officers were stimulators and coordinators rather than operators; much of the actual physical toil in the systems was performed and supervised by local people, and as noted earlier, even tax collection was farmed out to locals. Nevertheless, all of the polities developed bureaucracies, both civil and military, with numerous field stations run from the center. The reach of these field structures is a major indicator of the political boundaries of those systems.

Throughout history, keeping administrative field officials loyal and obedient to central authorities has been one of the persistent problems of government. Field officers have always exhibited a strong tendency to act independently. Often, it was because they came to identify with the local interests of their region and turned into spokesmen for their neighbors instead of representatives of their hierarchical superiors. Sometimes it was because they were not sure what their superiors wanted—officials at the center were not always coordinated or in agreement with one another and sent conflicting directives, or their directives were ambiguous. At times, central officials were so uninformed about conditions in the field that they issued orders nobody could carry out. But it was also true that field officers found they could enrich themselves and satisfy their egos by running their areas as virtually personal fiefs. Whatever the motivation, the upshot was that things went on in the field that central officials did not know about, would not have approved, never intended, and would have overruled had they been sufficiently aware and powerful. (Sometimes field administrators, including military commanders, attained so much power that they could actually defy their nominal superiors.) Whatever the forms of governmental authority, some systems were in fact almost totally decomposed as a result of administrative fragmentation.

The dangers of such fragmentation were evidently recognized by the rulers of many of the overarching polities with which this volume is concerned. The rulers employed a standard set of techniques to avoid them. These included rotation of field officers to numbers of localities (so as to prevent the formation of strong commitments to any single place or group), intensive training and indoctrination of bureaucrats (to the point in some polities of turning them into an elite corps totally identified with, and sometimes dominating, the center), careful weeding out of bureaucrats showing evidence of less than total allegiance to their superiors, promotion of only the most loyal to higher positions in the field and headquarters, and sometimes the posting of field officers' family members to the capital (where they were hostages in effect even though they lived very comfortably).

Despite such efforts, field officers still carved out little empires for themselves in many places. And although such developments did not necessarily impede the mobilization of resources and the coordination needed to maintain systemwide defenses and construct regionwide public works (decentralized aggregations of units can achieve a great deal by cooperation), they tended to make such concerted action more difficult. With no higher authority to settle disputes, quarrels festered and intensified. Competition between provinces and the exaction of tribute from trade passing through each region imposed burdens on commerce. Regional officials must have vied with each other to divert the costs of security and construction to other areas, with the result that both kinds of public service suffered. Similarly, each area probably tried to skim off as many benefits for itself as it could, without regard to the effect on the entire system, so that economic activity and living standards and local public services in many parts of the polities declined, disparities between areas increased, and tensions straining the overarching polity rose.

Thus in any polity the administrative system itself, without any other precipitating factors to set it off, could have broken up and started the sequence that led to the self-reinforcing drop in activity described above. In an inherently centrifugal state of affairs it is hardly surprising that centripetal forces are occasionally overcome.

The Merging of Cause and Effect

From this discussion, despite all the disclaimers, one might form the impression that each cause and consequence of governmental dysfunctions is in a discrete, watertight compartment of its own. It is only the inability to discuss everything at once that creates this impression. In practice, the factors constitute a single, indissoluble mass. The categories are purely analytical.

For example, the factors that operated within the boundaries of each political system were inextricably linked with those that operated outside. If a faction feeling threatened by another political system came to power and made preparations for war, the preparations themselves could have moved the other system to similar action even if it had originally had no intention of attacking. If the local leaders and the population of a peripheral district, unhappy with their experience within a given polity, elected to make common cause with a neighboring overarching system, the secession could provoke a war between the two systems. If traders nervous about internal disorders in other polities declined to take the risk of crossing their borders to effect exchanges, the economy of their own polities would feel the effects. It would be purely arbitrary to classify such factors as internal or external; internal events have external consequences, and external events are internalized. Anticipations of events inside and outside the boundaries of a system often stimulate actions whose origins cannot reliably be fixed on one side or the other. Indeed, even in the case of organisms, much of what is "inside" then comes from "outside"—including their genetic heritage, their physical substance (through what they eat), and their learned patterns of thought and behavior—blurring the difference. It is many times more blurred in the case of political systems. Governmental dysfunctions that seem superficially to originate from within can often be traced to things that happened elsewhere, and dysfunctions that look as though they came from beyond will often turn out to have some roots within.

By the same token, the discussion above treated seriatim things that occurred almost simultaneously because reactions were often so swift that they fed promptly back into the stimuli until the two events were virtually one, at least from the standpoint of the analyst centuries later. It is hard to determine whether destructive use of land preceded ecological problems or followed from rulers' efforts to keep up production after ecological misfortunes, but the two phenomena were probably so closely associated as to be one, for all practical purposes. Weakness at the political center might have brought on the contumacy of field officers, but the contumacy of field officers could just as well have caused the weakness at the center, and the two could have gone on at the same time. Falling tax yields probably accounted for failures to maintain irrigation projects, but inadequate maintenance due to squabbling in the political and administrative structure of the state may have reduced tax revenues. It would be a mistake to think that such events were neatly separable just because we are forced to take them up sequentially.

So the initial, precipitating factor that started the fall of living standards, the deterioration in the quality of life, and the breakdown of the functions performed by the overarching governmental institutions in the systems examined is difficult to isolate even when we understand the way these features of those societies interacted. Any of the factors could have occurred independently in the first instance, but once one did, its effects rippled through the polity in question, tripping other factors until they were all activated and reinforced each other. Since modern observers are alerted to this process in ancient civilizations only by evidence left when the process was already well underway, we can merely guess at the specific cause in particular instances; first causes become pure conjecture. All we can do with confidence is identify the circumstances that *could* have been the triggering events and piece together reasonable reconstructions of what happened after the triggers were pulled.

This explanation of the many ways in which the routines of daily life and the functioning of governmental institutions could be started on a downward spiral that would gain momentum as the two factors aggravated each other presents us with new mysteries. If the overarching systems were so vulnerable and fragile, how was it possible for so many of them to endure for centuries? How was it possible for some of them to reverse, at least temporarily, what seem to have been severe downward slides? And how did a few reestablish boundaries approximating their old political borders after severe declines that left their political systems splintered compared to what they had been at their zeniths?

TWO REDEEMING FACTORS

Two factors seem to have forestalled or reversed, for a while, the onset of the downward spiral to which the polities examined were so susceptible. One was the acquisition of new resources. The other was the emergence of extraordinary leaders. The occurrence of either was usually associated with an improvement in living standards and an increase in governmental services. The two together frequently meant a dramatic rise in both.

Once again, cause and effect are hard to disentangle. The acquisition of new resources by discovery of previously unrecognized reserves within a polity, for example, could have stimulated economic activity, providing more revenues for public services, thus making possible still more economic advances. All of this would make a ruler look good. On the other hand, an energetic leader might have spurred the search for new resources or gone out to conquer them, which could account for the prosperity of particular polities in given times. In this sense, a leader could make the rest of the system look good. It is not easy to determine which way the causal arrow pointed.

Still, these factors, acting independently or in tandem, were apparently the reason for the long duration of some of the polities observed, and for the regeneration of others, notwithstanding the frangibility of such overarching political systems.

Resources

Labor, arable land, water, wood, metals, and minerals (building stone, precious stones, and semiprecious stones) were the major resources of the polities reviewed in this volume, though draft animals and horses for warfare were also important in some cases. Where these were in plentiful supply, economies prospered, sustaining government activities that assisted and facilitated productivity. The political systems that lasted long, or that displayed great recuperative powers, were usually well-endowed in many of these respects and were therefore able to acquire by trade or intimidation or conquest what nature did not bestow on them. Food and housing and clothing were in adequate supply, ceremonial practices and structures flourished, governmental revenues were ample, and essential public services were effective.

This may be one of the main reasons for the expansion of these polities over large areas. Their needs may have begun to press on the supply of resources, especially as the resources were depleted; in any event, urbanization probably put a strain on the resource base. Some of these problems could be solved temporarily by more intensive exploitation of whatever was at hand. Eventually, however, the leaders of these polities would doubtless have been tempted by rich areas beyond their borders. Occasionally, expansion might have been accomplished by mutual accommodation between the growing polity and its neighbors; often, it was achieved by military conquest. The quest for additional resources was not the only incentive for expansion; as noted above, uncertainty about the intent of neighbors and uneasiness about dependence on supplies not under the control of the dependent but powerful polities must also have played a large part in the drive outward. Nevertheless, there is good reason to infer that the drive was also animated by an urgent need for more resources to fuel the prosperity and growth of vigorous systems and thus to fend off the prospect of painful contraction.

Resource problems or opportunities should not necessarily be regarded as taking precedence over all the other factors contributing to economic and governmental hardships of polities, however. After all, what is defined as a resource and how accessible it is depend on the state of technology, the availability of substitutes, willingness to invest in its development, and the effectiveness of governmental services required to protect and encourage its use, among other things. Poverty and wealth of resources are results of many conditions besides natural endowments. In other words, resources as a variable affecting the fate of polities should be seen as dependent on other variables in much the same way that other variables are dependent on it.

Nonetheless, when we try to explain why some political systems, despite all the dangers of disintegration described earlier, survived for long periods and even made comebacks after suffering serious declines or political dissolution, the abundance of resources, however it comes about, clearly must be assigned great weight.

Leadership

From time to time, in some of the polities, leaders appeared who seemed to have the ability to determine the course of events almost single-handedly. Some, it is true, probably made things worse; the ones who are remembered are usually the ones who allegedly turned things for the better. In either case, they were the exceptions, not the rule. But to explain the survival of shaky political systems, the contributions of successful leaders cannot be denied.

Of course, the evidence is never free of ambiguity. An observer looking back over time cannot be sure that the reputedly extraordinary leaders were not the beneficiaries (or victims) of forces that would have produced the same results no matter who was in office. People frequently get credit or blame for things over which they have little control. Yet even after discounting for this possibility, we can see leaders in the past who were in all likelihood responsible for rescuing overarching political orders that gave every indication of being on the downgrade.

In some instances, the extraordinary leaders proved to be the founders or rejuvenators of dynasties that lasted for generations. Chances are that reversing the downward trend in the system started an upward spiral from which their successors benefited. At any rate, the positive effects continued past their lifetimes.

Such cases were probably unusual. Often the achievements of dramatically successful leaders were undone soon after they passed from the scene; their accomplishments were purely personal rather than institutional. Indeed, their very success might have contributed to the undoing of their work after their deaths. For one thing, they left such an attractive legacy that later aspirants would fight long and hard to succeed them. For another, their achievements doubtless rested in part on their talent for choosing vigorous, assertive, confident aides, and each aide may well have seen himself as the only worthy successor of the charismatic chief. (On the other hand, strong chiefs may have attained their dominance by eliminating all possible rivals, leaving the system vulnerable because it was denuded of strong personalities in a position to pick up the reins.) The outcome would therefore have been division, bitter controversy, and possible civil war in the inner political circle, with all the paralysis, ineffectiveness, and destructiveness entailed by fragmentation of this sort. Although these hypotheses about the reasons for the short life of systemic renewal by great leaders are largely conjectural, there is not much doubt that the accomplishments of exceptional leaders seldom outlived them very long. Their contributions were more or less ephemeral in most cases.

Consequently, as a factor in the long duration or the salvaging of political systems, leadership probably did not figure as prominently or as frequently as resources did. But it entered into the fate of polities often enough to make it a significant element all the same.

THE ROLE OF CHANCE

It is difficult to escape the conclusion that the overarching polities with which this volume is concerned were in a much more delicate balance than the size of the populations they encompassed and the extent of the areas they governed might lead one to suspect. Their equilibria could be easily upset and sent upward or, more frequently, careening downward by any of many factors. Anything as large and powerful as the political systems in this volume's purview looks superficially as though only earthshaking events could have much of an impact on it. Because the unifying forces were offset by deeply rooted tendencies toward fragmentation, however, even modest shocks could start the process of decomposition into smaller groups and social structures. Although many of the component *parts* were highly unified and durable, the overarching political entities into which they were assembled were comparatively easily disrupted. That is why the list of disturbing factors just set forth is so long, and why forces of modest proportions could work great effects on the polities examined. It did not take much to set things off.

Because there were so many possible origins of such intricate processes of change, it was virtually inevitable that each system would trace a unique historical trajectory. A common experience for all would have been astonishing under these conditions; it is far more plausible that some would have risen to great heights and plunged to utter oblivion, in contrast to others that went through repeated cycles of growth and dissolution and regeneration. It is to be expected that success over a long period would not necessarily guarantee immortality or even continued good fortune. It is not surprising that peoples adjacent to flourishing civilizations and sharing many attributes with their neighbors fared poorly. One would anticipate that a society seemingly in the doldrums might suddenly have come to life and begun to thrive. A variety of historical patterns rather than a single one would be thoroughly in keeping with the dynamics to which the systems were subject.

Chance obviously played a large part in the success or failure of states. More or less random distribution of resources, climatic shifts, outcomes of battles, emergences of great leaders, technological developments at home and abroad, natural disasters, and other things profoundly affect the fortunes of political systems and the people in them. Accidents of geography and history might confer on a society great natural wealth, runs of good harvests, great leaders, freedom from external challenges because neighboring states are weak or involved with other foes, and other blessings. Bad luck might inflict drought, dearth of natural supplies, continual wealth-draining warfare, epidemics, or other destructive burdens. A combination of favorable circumstances could catapult one system to the summit and keep it there for a long time; a sudden misfortune might drag a system from its day in the sun after a short interval. That is not to say that the people in positions of responsibility in the overarching polities had *no* influence on their own fate; their actions could certainly exacerbate difficulties or take advantage of opportunities. But it is still true that adventitious factors could, and probably did, overwhelm their efforts, especially since there is a tendency for people to continue doing what they did in the past even when changing conditions make their old patterns of behavior decreasingly efficacious. Success and failure of encompassing political systems consist in substantial measure of luck.

Chance does not mean events are inexplicable. Clearly, a chance event can be accounted for after it occurs—at least to the extent of narrowing the causal factors to a small number of possibilities, if not to a strictly determinate set. And chance does not mean there is no pattern in the course of events. There is often a distinct and measurable pattern in aggregations of chance events even though nobody can predict what will happen in any individual case. In other words, when events are governed by chance, probability theory is often the means to understanding, which is quite different from the incorrect inference that chance is beyond understanding.

Until the stochastic patterns are identified, the experience of every overarching political system of the kind discussed in this volume will seem to be in a class by itself. On the other hand, so many factors enter into the experience of each system, and the universe of such systems is so small, we may never be able to assemble enough data from this universe alone to detect the patterns. Only if the systems are part of a larger universe—perhaps the universe of all large-scale organizations—would the prospects of success be brighter.

Nobody can say with justifiable confidence that broadly encompassing political orders are unquestionably special cases of large-scale organizations, and that organization theory can therefore be fruitfully applied to the analysis of their dynamics. But cross-comparisons between these polities and other large organizations seemed to the members of the seminar on which this volume is based to suggest fresh insights into both fields. Thus, the seminar closed on a note of hope that interaction between the fields could continue and expand.

NOTE

For the substantive evidence on which the argument of this chapter is based, I depended almost entirely on the papers of my colleagues in the seminar on the collapse of ancient states and civilizations and on their lively discussions of those papers. I should like not only to acknowledge my debt to them, but also to thank them for their patience and kindness in sharing their knowledge and wisdom with a member of a different guild. It was an illuminating and exhilarating experience. Most of them, I am sure, disagree with parts of my interpretation, but I think we all felt the cross-fertilization of specialties was fruitful.

The section on "runaway field administrators" is taken from the work of James W. Fesler, Cowles Professor Emeritus of Political Science at Yale University, the leading authority on headquarters-field relations in administrative organizations.

Beyond Collapse

Shmuel N. Eisenstadt

The central problem of this volume—the collapse of ancient states and civilizations—may be illuminated by viewing it from the perspective of a comparative study of civilizations and how sociological analysis and theory bear on this study. In reviewing the findings of the seminar on which this volume is based, I find ten major points to be especially noteworthy.

1. The so-called collapse of ancient states and civilizations is one example, possibly the most extreme one, of the larger problem of how social boundaries are restructured and reconstructed, with particular reference to the boundaries of political systems.
2. The construction of boundaries of social groups, collectivities, and institutions is a continuing aspect in the life of human societies and not an anomalous response to some sort of irregular or periodic stress.
3. Social systems and organizational boundaries do not exist, contrary to some assumptions in sociological, anthropological, and historical analyses, as natural, closed systems. Rather, such boundaries are continuously constructed, open, and very fragile.
4. No human population is confined within any single such system, but rather people belong to a multiplicity of only partly coalescing organizations, collectivities, and systems.
5. The division of labor in such systems includes that of special social actors, the "carriers" of the ideologies of the systems. Aspects of

"power" are always closely interwoven with the identity and character of these social actors.

6. Although the delineation of definite organizational boundaries in social systems implies the existence of an "environment," such environments are not given by "nature"; these environments, rather, are themselves constructed by the process of establishing social boundaries.

7. The construction and maintenance of organizational boundaries involves the creation of various mechanisms of social integration and control; the viability (or lack of it) of these integrative mechanisms is crucial in the maintenance or change of the societies in which they are embedded.

8. Such integrative mechanisms become more important and more autonomous the more complex social and political systems and civilizational frameworks become.

9. Such complexity is manifest not only in the different levels of structural differentiation, such as the division of labor, in an organization, but also in other important, but less hierarchically neat dimensions; for our topic the most salient is the degree of overlap or coalescence among different circles of ideology and power that fall within the same overarching societal boundaries.

10. Finally, in such systems change is almost never total; rather, it usually entails differential change in the various subsystems or components. Thus, we return to our starting point, namely, that collapse is only an extreme case of the restructuring of boundaries of social and political systems.

THE CONSTRUCTION OF SOCIAL BOUNDARIES

The construction of human social life is a matter of defining social interactions and the division of labor in a systemic way. A crucial aspect of any social organization is the process of delineating its institutional boundaries, including their important symbolic components, how these boundaries are continuously related to those of other systems, and how the environments encompassed by these systems are structured. It should be stressed that all social entities, or systems, are in the process of being constructed, that is, social systems are not "natural," with change to them occurring only irregularly. On the other hand, it is important to recognize that within social boundaries, human interaction continuously takes place, although the rules and parameters of such interaction should not be understood as self-limiting and mutually exclusive enclosures.

Human populations are, in fact, not organized in only one way, in a single "society" in a tightly-structured "system." Populations are institutionally distributed in political systems, economic collectivities, ascriptive social organizations, and ideological frameworks. These different institutional structures may evince different patterns of organization, overlap in different degrees, and change within the same society in differing ways and paces—although the organizations themselves are obviously not unconnected.

All such collectivities, organizations, and systems tend to preserve ("homeostatically") their boundaries and also to extend them, particularly in the face of both external and internal "stresses." These two tendencies are particularly visible in the way such systems maintain their environmental settings and seek to alter them. The environments are not "given" but themselves are created and selected by social activity. Even in the simplest forms of human societies, such as Australian bands, we can see how subsystemic boundaries are continually constructed. In comparison to such complex societies as those in Mesopotamia (Chapter 3, this volume), these boundaries are not as distinct or explicitly articulated, but even in very simple societies the dynamic construction of organizational boundaries can be observed.

Different types of boundaries are constructed in societies according to the presence of different types of social actors, different carriers of the rationales of the various types of boundaries. These different kinds of social actors, or social elites, have to be distinguished: first, there are carriers who structure the division of labor in a society, the variety and amount of economic and ecological differentiation; second, there are carriers who articulate ideologies and political goals; third, there are those concerned with structuring the integration of different ascriptive social collectivities; and fourth are those who articulate the basic cultural visions and models predominant in a society or in a sector thereof.

Among these different institutional actors or carriers there develops a very complex and extremely important set of interactions. The study of such interactions among the carriers of institutional boundaries has received, however, comparatively little attention in sociology, history, or anthropology.

This point is critical for the study of collapse (and reformulation of boundaries from collapse) because it is necessary to specify in such studies what kinds of social boundaries are failing and how these are related to other organizational boundaries. In this volume, of course, we are referring mainly to the boundaries of political spheres, but even in these examples we see clearly that interaction among political and other kinds of boundaries such as cultural or economic are crucial for understanding the causes, amount, and institutional products of political collapse.

It has been highlighted in this volume that it is fallacious to assume that there exists a natural environment for any society. The environment is never "out there" but is, within obvious constraints, constructed by a society and can be understood only in relation to other boundary-defining processes of a society. Thus, environmental choices are made, by social actors, and these choices form the boundaries of the environmental system and so condition or generate possibilities of environmental change, including environmental degeneration. Temptations to view environmental boundaries as independent of social ones (as is sometimes found in anthropological studies or in theories of "oriental despotism") must be strongly resisted.

The processes of constructing organizational boundaries involve continuous struggle among the different carriers of the division of labor, ideological visions, and power mentioned above. Furthermore, different coalitions of these social actors structure and articulate those various system boundaries.

The fragility of social structures and their organizational boundaries in very complex societies such as in ancient states and civilizations requires special mechanisms of control and integration, regulative systems that try to overcome the inherent instability in the construction of such boundaries. Among the most critical mechanisms are those concerned with processing information, settling disputes, and establishing public symbols and their ritualization (various ideological institutions and occasions).

Social control is established by a combination of organizational structures (e.g., bureaucracies, legal symbols) and systematic restructuring—through processing of socialization, communication, and public and semi-public rituals.

In more complex organizations (such as ancient states and civilizations) those mechanisms of integration become more autonomous (Simon 1977). Thus, both the structure of various social systems and the control mechanisms of those systems have built-in levels of both stability (in the process of constructing the systems themselves) and instability (the boundaries of the systems must be continually remade). Understanding the dynamics of collapse requires not only analyzing the boundary relationships among social organizations, but also investigating the network of control of mechanisms within and among the various organizations.

Social Order and Social Control

The complexity of organizational structures and their relationships, the difficulty in maintaining their overarching boundaries, might lead one (perhaps correctly) to the conclusion that it is very difficult to talk about their dynamics, as was attempted. Nevertheless, this conclusion goes against an important strain in sociological and anthropological theory, especially evolutionist theory. It might be worthwhile, therefore, to make our criticism of these approaches explicit, and at the same time to point out some possibilities of such systematic analysis.

The classical evolutionary view of social systems has been informed by the assumption that cultural spheres of behavior were by and large subsets of the social division of labor. This emphasis, apparently derived from utilitarian ethics and classical economics, is that the mechanisms governing the social division of labor, and in particular the market, assured the maintenance of those social formations or systems. It was one of the insights of the "founding fathers" of sociology (Marx, Durkheim, and Weber), however, that organizational aspects of the social division of labor were unable to explain the nature and continuity of any specific social order. Each of them stressed, in different degrees, three aspects of the social order that are not determined by the social division of labor itself.

The social order, first, as stressed by Durkheim and to some extent by Tönnies, depends on the construction of trust and solidarity; second, as enunciated above all in the works of Marx and Weber, it depends on the continuous regulation of power in order to establish legitimacy for the exercise of power with its possibilities of exploitation; third, explicit in all, but especially in Weber, the social order must provide a meaning for and legitimation of social activities. The very construction of the social division of labor generates uncertainties with respect to these three dimensions of social order: no concrete division of labor can be maintained without establishing trust and solidarity, regulating power legitimately, and giving meaning to organizational activities. The founding fathers further stressed the great tension that existed between the organizational division of labor and construction of trust and meaning and the regulation and legitimation of power. The recognition of this tension, however, has had the unfortunate result of segregating, after the founding fathers, analyses of the social division of labor and of social evolution (put in terms of structural differentiation) from those analyses of how power is regulated, trust constructed, and meaning established in the social order.

Consideration of the stability or instability in overarching societal structures of ancient states and civilizations must bring these investigations together again. First must be examined the amounts and mechanisms of distribution of resources among the different groups in a society, that is, its division of labor; second must be identified the "institutional entrepreneurs," the elites, the various carriers analyzed above, who compete to articulate the interests of the various groups and so to mobilize their resources; third must be included the nature of the "visions" that inform the activities of those elites and that are derived from the major cultural orientations or codes prevalent in a society. The institutionalization of these visions provides the arena in which the quest for meaning in the social order is supplied and enables the concretization of "charismatic" authority.

These elites, the different carriers, include, as we have seen, those political leaders who establish the regulation of power in a society, articulate models of cultural order that supply social meaning, represent the solidarity of the major different groups, and must address the problem of social trust. However, just as there are different types of cultural orientations in different societies, there arise different types of elites who tend to exercise different modes of control over the allocation of basic resources in the society. Coalitions of these elites develop in order to facilitate the flow of resources, both in their production and distribution, beyond the boundaries of local groups. These elites are especially concerned with structuring the perceptions of members of society in general and the relationship of local groups to the newly integrative institutional (economic, political, and cultural) markets.

The crystallization (rise) and reproduction (maintenance) of any collectivity, organization, political system, or civilizational framework is shaped by the different forces and factors enunciated above. In turn, these processes generate systems of conflict, change, and possible transformation.

Conflict, Collapse, and Continuity

Conflict is inherent in any setting of social interaction, especially in those political and civilizational frameworks that are discussed in this volume, for two basic reasons: first, because of the plurality of actors in such settings; and second, because of the multiplicity of principles of cultural orientation within ancient states and civilizations. Accordingly, there exists within any society the possibility that "antisystems" may develop. The existence of potential antisystems is evident in themes and orientations of protest and of social movements and heterodoxies, often led by secondary elites. Although such dissident tendencies, orientation, and organizations may remain latent for very long periods of time, they may also constitute, under propitious conditions, important foci of systemic change.

Such antisystems may be activated and transformed into agents and processes of change by several processes connected with the maintenance and continuity of the differentiated settings of social interaction within the macrosocietal order. The most important of these processes are shifts in the relative power positions and aspirations of various categories of people; second, the potential rebelliousness and antinomian orientations inherent in the process of socialization and of cognitive control can become activated among members of new generations, especially in the upper classes; third, differential rates of biological reproduction may result in demographic shifts that may restructure the reproduction of social settings; and fourth, interactions between a society and intersocietal elements (e.g., "barbarians," in Bronson's chapter, this volume) or those resulting from problems of conquest can end in internal social restructuring. Such social change is brought about usually through the activities of those secondary elites who challenge the shape of the social order controlled by the ruling coalition of elites.

Thus, the possibility of the failure of the integrative and regulative mechanisms of any society is inherent within that society. Every civilization, or every type of political system in a civilization, does, on the one hand, construct some specific systemic boundaries within which it operates. On the other hand, the very construction of social, economic, or political systems and of their boundaries generates within them various contradictions and conflicts that may lead to change, transformation, or decline—different modes of restructuring their boundaries.

Although potentialities of conflict and change are inherent in all human societies, the directions of change, including collapse, differ greatly according to the specific constellation of institutional forces outlined above. That is, different coalitions of elites, the social divisions of labor, and the specific international and ecological settings of societies allow us to see some regularities in social change. "Collapse," thus, is likely to be one possible kind of change, particularly plausible in those societies in which the differentiation among social groups is relatively small and the major elites are embedded in ascriptive groups. In contrast, in ancient states and civilizations the degree of differentiation is relatively large and the major elites do not owe their status exclusively to their position within any single ascriptive group. Indeed, as the chapters in this volume stress, ancient states and civilizations do not collapse at all, if by *collapse* is meant the complete end of those political systems and their accompanying civilizational frameworks. Thus, the investigation of collapse in ancient states and civilizations really entails identifying the various kinds of social reorganization in these types of societies and so viewing collapse as part of the continuous process of boundary reconstruction. One of the major aims of a comparative study of collapses of ancient civilizations is precisely to distinguish between those conditions that result in irreversible—total or partial—declines and those in which possibilities of regeneration ensue.

Of special interest in this regard is the distinction between the older "ancient civilizations" (e.g., Mesopotamia, Maya, Teotihuacan, as represented in this volume) and those called by Karl Jaspers "Axial Age" civilizations (Eisenstadt 1986 and the Roman and Han China examples in this volume). In the former, pre-Axial civilizations, there was a relatively weak distinction among the boundaries of the major institutional collectivities (that is, the carriers of religious and political institutions were not separate and autonomous), and sectarian and heterodox visions did not develop as active elements of change. Consequently, there was more of a tendency in those ancient states to disintegrate (at least partially, especially in the political system) and to lack the ability to reformulate those centralized political institutions. In the great civilizations of the Axial Age (especially the Greek, Roman, Jewish, Christian, Chinese, Hindu, and Buddhist ones), however, collapse contains within it the seeds of likely reconstructions.

Thus, in reviewing the various cases of collapse presented in this volume, we see a very interesting relation between modes of collapse and continuity. That is, the reason there are so very obvious differences between the collapse of Teotihuacan and that of Han China, for example, is that there are very different modes for ensuring continuity. The characteristics of what happens beyond collapse depend on levels of hierarchical organization, types of ideological carriers, systems of social controls, and integrative mechanisms. Collapse, far from being an anomaly, both in the real world and in social evolutionary theory, presents in dramatic form not the end of social institutions, but almost always the beginning of new ones. Investigating collapse, therefore, leads to a better understanding of the past—and the roots of the present.

Onward and Upward with Collapse

George L. Cowgill

TROUBLES WITH LANGUAGE AND CONCEPTS

It is a common observation that the social disciplines suffer from serious and deep-seated problems. Various authors have their lists (e.g., Blalock 1984) and I have my own ideas about what most needs attention, which I will discuss briefly here. The seminar on which this volume is based assuredly did not solve any of these problems, and we did not directly talk about some of them at all. Nevertheless, it is important to review these pervasive difficulties, both as a basis for discussing some results of the seminar and to encourage further work on these problems.

Adequate conceptualization of sociocultural phenomena is a task still in its infancy. It is quite unsporting, like shooting fish in a barrel, to ridicule social scientists for turgid, obscure, or pretentious jargon. However, their prose often reflects a real effort to break free of the bonds of the categories, conceptions, and misconceptions of everyday plain English (or plain French, or whatever). These efforts have achieved limited success so far, but they are of the highest importance.

Trying to think effectively about social phenomena calls to mind the fable of the blind men and the elephant. We are all groping. When someone "sees" a part of the beast we are trying to comprehend, it is only a partial and limited insight. So far, the different insights are incommensurate and we do not see how to put them together. A central point about the great successes of the physical sciences in the past few centuries is that people found good ways of "seeing" the phenomena they studied. It became reasonably clear what was important and also what was unimportant, which concepts of everyday thought had to be drastically redefined (e.g., energy) and which had to be discarded altogether (e.g., thinking of fire or heat as substances). To be sure, as Kuhn (1970) has emphasized, ways of seeing physical phenomena that were highly effective for a time eventually broke down and generated paradoxes that led to crises and revolutions, and to new pictures of the physical world. But the old pictures would not have generated crises if they had not been so clear and, up to a point, so effective, detailed, and accurate in their predictions. This kind of clarity and detail remains sadly lacking in the social disciplines. We have the specious clarity of the grand abstract schemes, clear because so bare of detailed and differentiated implications for different specific sets of circumstances. These schemes contrast with analyses of specific episodes that are detailed, subtle, and often persuasive, but hard to see how to generalize effectively. We do not yet have schemes that are simultaneously clear, able to handle rich content, and reasonably effective at prediction, or even able to persuade a majority of scholars that they offer satisfying understanding.

A debate exists between advocates of approaches modeled on the physical sciences and promoters of an "interpretive" approach, whose most prominent advocate is Clifford Geertz (Shankman 1984). Perhaps it is futile and misguided to try to achieve significant nomothetic insights into social phenomena. It must be admitted that efforts along these lines still leave much to be desired. However, too many social scientists have an impoverished view of the content, methods, and style of the "hard" sciences. It is not that there is something about a scientific approach that makes the richness of phenomena thin and dry, it is that too many people have an excessively thin and dry idea of what it is to do science. I believe we can make nomothetic generalizations that do justice to the idiographic richness of individual cases and that the best way to make progress is to continue to seek explanations that have a logical shape similar to explanations in the physical sciences. The last thing I advocate is that we should borrow specific concepts from, or seek close analogies with, physical or biological sciences. But I urge that we strive for models that achieve high outputs of usefully accurate predictions and postdictions of significant phenomena in return for relatively economical inputs of relevant data and parsimonious theory.

To make my arguments clearer, I will list several major problems in thinking and talking about social phenomena.

Solid-looking Concepts that Dissolve

If one examines a commonsense concept closely, it often turns out that "there isn't any such thing." An acquaintance who launched a major study of power reached the conclusion that there is no such thing as power. It is like the episode in Lewis Carroll's *Through the Looking Glass* in which Alice is in a toyshop whose shelves are obviously fully stocked, except that, exactly wherever one is looking directly, there isn't anything. Our daily lives are replete with concepts (and words for these concepts) that are perfectly clear and unproblematic to all of us, except the persons who have studied them. A good example is the concept of "collapse of a civilization," which, as the chapters in this volume show, is a far less simple idea than we have been accustomed to think.

What should be done about this? We cannot do everything at once, and it seems necessary to begin any investigation of social phenomena by taking for granted a number of terms that are, one hopes, peripheral or background concepts, and to concentrate on developing clear and nontrivial meanings for some limited number of key concepts. The strategy is to expand cumulatively the number of incisively defined concepts that are connected in a network of mutual relevance. To judge by experience in the physical sciences, there are some everyday concepts that are best done away with entirely. Often, however, a meaning is found that is related only remotely to everyday thought, but which plays a well-defined and useful role in technical thought. For example, quantum mechanics gives a picture of "matter" that is strikingly different from our everyday thought and experience. This has not led physicists to say that matter doesn't exist. Instead, they say we have to think about matter in a way that, although it leads to highly accurate predictions, is disturbingly different from the way we grew up thinking about it.

Unperceived Miscommunication

A closely related problem is a tendency toward hairsplitting in some semantic domains, while casually using other terms that conceal semantic quagmires. It is hard and frustrating to clarify and make precise our thought and language, but it is vital work. We must beware of starting with a set of terms and then seeking meanings for them. We should try, instead, to identify genuinely different concepts and then assign names to each. Also, we should look for sets of phenomena that seem more than superficially similar, look for what seem to be recurrent kinds of relationships among them, and give clear names to each of these kinds of phenomena and relationships. Logical clarity in conceptual schemes is also important, but mere clarity is not enough if the schemes are too abstract to help when we try to understand specific instances in any depth. We may find the polysyllabic tongue-twisters of the organic chemists ugly and unintelligible, but we do not ridicule them for the excellent reason that, to initiates, these chemical terms convey very clear and precise information. They are essential for investigations that are obviously highly effective.

While we focus on trying to develop clear, precise, relevant, and rich ideas about one topic, we necessarily use many other terms in an offhand and unexamined way, as if we all knew what they meant and as if we all understood exactly the same things by them. In fact, the amount of covert misunderstanding and miscommunication that goes on among students of human societies is hair-raising. The fallacy of arguing about words rather than ideas, of using different words for the same concept, is well known. But there is also the fallacy of *failing* to argue about different ideas because the differences are masked by shared use of the same words.

The main things to be done about these semantic problems are to be watchful of one another and to try to catch ourselves when we use words vaguely, or contradictorily, or with two or more confusingly different meanings. This is not to say that there is no proper use for ambiguity. On the contrary, we need some words whose meanings are broad, and we need others whose meanings are a bit fuzzy, with slightly indistinct semantic borders. However, and I intend no paradox, we must be *precise* about the broadness or fuzziness of these terms, and they must be complemented by other terms that are as nearly razor sharp and crystal clear as we can get them.

In later parts of this chapter, I have tried to put these exhortations into practice. I hope I have had some success, but readers will have missed the point if they do not think about how my terms and concepts could be improved.

Imitating for the Wrong Reasons

Another persistent source of trouble is aping the shadow rather than the substance of fashionable terms that have proven genuinely useful in other fields. As long as the social sciences remain intellectually underdeveloped, they will be subject to "cargo cults" and messianic enthusiasms. The only remedy is to develop indigenous theory that is rich and successful enough to prevent our being easily seduced or bamboozled by clever, ambitious, and energetic persons spouting half-baked or half-digested versions of something that has become popular (often for good reasons) in some other discipline.

Our susceptibility to these fads is a major way of failing to communicate miscommunication. The fact that words such as entropy, information, homeostasis, energy, and force have very well defined and useful technical meanings in other fields means that it is easy to bootleg them into human studies without noticing that our use of them is, at best, extremely vague and is often only metaphorical. Some of us may be afraid to admit that we don't quite know what they mean (the "emperor's new clothes" syndrome), but I believe that more often the semantic murkiness is simply not noticed.

As an example of obscurity, consider the phrase, "This was due to the operation of the law of. . . ." The wording suggests that scientific laws commonly are agents that cause certain phenomena. However, laws are not agents; they are generalizations about relationships among entities that hold over some usefully wide range of circumstances. We may say, "This apple fell because of the operation of the Law of Gravity." But we know that what is meant is that the apple moved toward the center of the earth because there is a physical force between any two masses, described by the Law of Gravity, and because motions of masses are affected by the forces acting on them in ways described by simple laws of motion. When social phenomena are said to be due to the operation of some law, it is far less clear that either author or reader appreciates that the explanation, if it is not simply fallacious, must be a treacherous shorthand for the effects of phenomena whose behavior is believed to be described by the law in question.

Difficulty in Making Generalizations Simultaneously Valid and Interesting

One style in the study of human affairs is the formulation of grand, sweeping, general theories. Many people find them quite pleasing. Some of these theories are grandly wrong. Others, however, are not especially wrong, as far as they go, but they have remarkably little empirical content. They are very limited in their logical implications about just what should or should not be observed in specific circumstances. Such theories are resistant to falsification (it is hard to find evidence that is clearly counter to expectations), and they offer some people a satisfying sense of having explained much because they can be invoked as applicable in so many instances. But they have very weak predictive power and tend to be unfruitful; they fail to generate critical problems that could guide further research.

A contrasting style is the rich, meticulous, and often fascinating ex-amination in depth of the detailed particularities of events in a certain time and place. Between these styles is a wide gulf. It is scarcely seeing the forest versus seeing the trees. Often users of the first style have trouble seeing the forests because of the continents, whereas followers of the second have trouble seeing the trees because of the twigs. We urgently need studies that lie between these extremes, that deal with particulars but do not assume that facts somehow speak for themselves. These studies should look beyond isolated examples at a reasonable number of instances in sufficient detail and with sufficient understanding so that they can arrive at insights that, though generalizable to a useful extent, have less than cosmic pretensions and can claim to explain fairly specific aspects of specific situations. This is, of course, exactly what we hoped to achieve in this volume.

Entities at Diverse Levels

Another problem in social studies is the diverse levels at which entities are conceived. Sometimes the objects of attention are individuals or households, sometimes they are communities, sometimes they are institutions, and sometimes they are entire states. There are many levels, but we can speak roughly of a "micro" versus "macro" contrast. Some scholars tend to explain changes by the decisive acts of heroic individuals; others deny that specific individuals make any difference at all. It is platitudinous to say that neither extreme can possibly be the whole truth or even most of the truth. Merely saying this, however, does not get us very far. How can we effectively conceptualize explanations that accept the relevance of phenomena best described on diverse levels, some in terms of individual actors and some in terms of larger social units? It simply won't do to think that if one grossly inadequate model explains a little bit of the whole thing and other grossly inadequate ideas explain other bits we can just add them all up and, collectively, they will amount to a pretty good explanation. This "additive" strategy for improving theory, which some writers seem to favor, is painfully misguided. We should be looking for theory that integrates diverse things in some structured way. But how do we do this? How do we formulate theory that takes account of individuals and also takes account of "emergent" phenomena that refer to no specific individuals, but to things generated by interactions of many individuals?

It is helpful to keep in mind the difference between proximate (or immediate) causes and ultimate causes. We can always give an account in which the macrolevel outcome is viewed as the immediate consequence of the myriad microlevel details of what happened before. But can we give a more parsimonious account in which the microlevel details don't matter, and the important parts of the macrolevel outcome are explained solely with reference to previous states of phenomena also described on the macrolevel? This doesn't solve the problem, but I hope it formulates one aspect of it a bit more clearly.

What's in People's Heads

Some people regard ideas, attitudes, and individual character (either of a few key actors or of large segments of society) as decisive for explaining sociocultural change. Opposed to this is the narrowly materialist view that ideas have no causal relevance, that changes in ideas are merely consequences of changes in material circumstances and do not play any independent role in causing further changes. I wish we could quickly dismiss both extreme idealism and extreme materialism. However, unhappily, examples of both continue to be common in scholarly publications (as Flannery 1972:400 notes).

It is important to distinguish two styles among materialists. Some simply tend to ignore mental phenomena. They explain material phenomena entirely in terms of other material phenomena and they just don't talk about anything else. This approach is wholly inadequate for two reasons. First, mental phenomena are an exceedingly important category of social phenomena, and an account of a social situation is grossly unsatisfactory if it leaves them out or assumes that, if they are understandable at all, they are to be explained by some quite unrelated discipline. Second, it makes the unwarranted assumption that mental phenomena are not relevant for the explanation of material phenomena.

Many materialists, notably Marx, have known better than simply to ignore ideas altogether. Even such an extremist as Marvin Harris (1979) recognizes that people think and have feelings, that they are concerned about codes of behavior, that their actions are shaped by mental as well as physical needs, that they pursue strategies intended to achieve certain outcomes and avoid others, and that what people do is affected by what they believe. However, Harris argues that ideas rarely change spontaneously in any way that in turn causes significant changes in material circumstances. Causation flows overwhelmingly from the material to the mental. Changes in ideas that are, themselves, consequences of changes in the material realm may, in turn, have an influence on further material changes. However, these mental phenomena only mediate between one set of material circumstances and another set of material circumstances. Mental phenomena play an autonomous causal role only rarely and to a limited extent.

It is unlikely that the role of mental phenomena is really as small in good explanations of sociocultural change as Harris argues. Nevertheless, we cannot simply dismiss this variety of materialism. In any case, material circumstances are tremendously important for understanding sociocultural change. To underrate them is just as obtuse as it is to ignore mental phenomena.

There is, however, a serious error of method in Harris's brand of cultural materialism. He advocates treating as a last resort explanations that assign to mental phenomena some autonomous role in causation. Such explanations are to be entertained only if every imaginable explanation in purely material terms has been tried and found wanting (Harris 1979:56). The fallacy here is that what might be defended as a good strategy for *discovery* (although I would not defend it myself) is applied in the context of *confirmation*. If cultural materialist explanations are really better than other kinds (as evaluated by the accuracy of their predictions and the diversity and importance of the phenomena to which they apply), the best way to establish this is to compare them on an equal footing with other explanations, including explanations that allow mental phenomena to be causes as well as consequences.

I emphasize this because it brings us to what continues to be the key problem in understanding sociocultural change. Ideas can be both causes and consequences, but we cannot just "add" ideas and material circumstances or tack on transfers of information as an extra feature of models that began by dealing with transfers of matter and energy. How, then, can we put ideas and material circumstances together in an effective and unified theory? The essays included in this volume should help to improve theory that tries to integrate the mental and the material. The interplay of materialist and idealist concepts was a recurrent theme in our seminar. There has been a surge of archaeological interest in this problem (e.g., Hodder 1982), but Millon (personal communication) reminds me that we should familiarize ourselves with what earlier thinkers such as Max Weber (1978) had to say on the matter and with criticisms and elaborations of their ideas.

Evolution

One borrowing from other disciplines that has been especially problematic in social studies is the concept of "evolution." Attempts to apply this concept effectively to human societies have been extensively criticized by others, notably Yoffee (1979), and they receive further attention in the first chapter of this volume. I will add only that I think social evolutionists are especially prone to invoking the "operation" of the Law of This or the Principle of That as pseudo-explanations.

Systems Preconceptions

A second problematic borrowing is systems theory, especially "General Systems Theory." This approach has also generated strong feelings, both positive and negative. Merrilee Salmon (1978) offers a levelheaded appraisal (cf. Doran 1970 and Spaulding 1973). It is hard to quarrel with the general notion that many of the entities we want to think about are systemlike. That is, they have reasonably distinct and differentiated parts (subsystems), and the parts tend to be interrelated. A change in one part is likely to have consequences for other parts, and the connections between parts form a more or less complex network with many reciprocal (two-way) relationships, rather than unidirectional, unbranching chains from prime causes to initial effects, secondary effects, tertiary effects, and so on. We *must* look at social phenomena in this broadly systemic way if we are to understand them. But we must also specify clearly and effectively the entities we are trying to think about, how we should think about their differentiated parts, and, especially, specify in some detail just how the different parts affect and are affected by one another. Above all, these specifications must be rich enough in logical implications about real-world instances to make it easy to imagine evidence that would falsify them and, if they survive repeated attempts at falsification, to carry us interestingly beyond what we already knew. One of the banes of "systems-talk" is the use of complex diagrams, full of boxes and arrows. Too often the arrows show only that a change in one part is *somehow* relevant for another part or, at best, a symbol is added to show whether a positive change in one part tends to cause a positive or a negative change in another part. Such diagrams have been described as "less than meets the eye." Several archaeologists who have attempted computer simulations have suggested that, in the current state of the art, one of the greatest benefits of such efforts is the salutary experience of being forced to think harder about exactly how the different parts affect one another (e.g., Aldenderfer 1981).

Two major problems arise in many recent uses of systems concepts in studies of societies. First, the rather well developed systems vocabulary encourages us to think that we are much further along toward effective theory than we really are. It gives us a specious sense of clarity and understanding, because we have so many new labels to apply. However, many of these terms, such as "homeostasis," "linearization," and the like, have been either applied loosely or used, at least so far, as synonyms for more familiar expressions. They are useful to the extent that they call attention to things that might otherwise be overlooked. But they are no more than initial orienting concepts for beginning the hard thinking. However, people tend to define these systems ideas rather vaguely, then erect increasingly elaborate structures that are abstractions built out of abstractions. The language flows most satisfyingly, diagram follows diagram, and one has the sense that something is being talked about. There is far too strong a tendency to take the terms and concepts of systems theorists as relatively unproblematic building blocks and to think upward from them. Instead, we should take them apart, look at them more critically, and think down, as well as up, so that the systems concepts are better connected to rich bodies of actual data.

The second major problem with systems thought is that it lends itself to begging a central question. It encourages us to assume that sociocultural entities are normally highly integrated (highly "systemic") with well-developed mechanisms for self regulation. It is remarkable that aggregates of individuals of the species *Homo sapiens* have been able to establish state societies at all, even problematically and for short times. Most writers about states assume that there was a time when humans had no states, and they feel compelled to account for the beginning of states. They rarely feel a comparable need to account for the persistence of states. But our psychological and social propensities evolved under the selective pressures prevailing in bands of rarely more than twenty-five to fifty persons, with population densities rarely higher than a few people in every hundred square kilometers. It seems extraordinary that, with nonindustrial technology, humans have created social systems incorporating ten thousand to a hundred thousand times as many individuals as the societies that shaped the evolution of ancestors biologically similar to us. This is an astonishing example of the plasticity of human behavior, of the cultural options that our biological substrate permits. My wonderment about this underlies all that I have to say about large-scale societies.

In fact, probably most states *don't* work very well. Many analysts, Marxists and others, have emphasized conflict, especially between classes in stratified societies. They have also argued that societies may experience contradictions—for example, between means of production and social relations of production. Sometimes the extent of conflict or the seriousness of the contradictions has been exaggerated and the amount of counterbalancing cooperation and compromise underrated. After all, cooperation and compromise are important in bands of twenty-five. Morton Fried (1967, 1978) and Elman Service (1975, 1978) have emphasized opposite sides of this issue. Both have seen some parts of the elephant (to return to my earlier simile). It is time to move beyond this particular debate.

The point I am more interested in emphasizing is that there are many sources of trouble for states besides the conflicting interests of diverse groups and the contradictions that arise when the social system and ideology are incompatible with the technology and organization of production. Other problems include technical difficulties in getting and properly analyzing important information, mistaken beliefs about the likely consequences of policies and actions, bungling, and everything implied by Parkinson's (quite seriously intended) Law (Parkinson 1957). I strongly suspect that the notion that *any* state has *ever* functioned really smoothly is just one of the myths of ruling elites. Even in their best days, nearly all states have probably been quite ramshackle contraptions, at best half-understood by the various people who made them, maintained them, coped with them, and struggled against them. Probably states avoid failure as long as most of them do, not because they function smoothly, with truly effective self-regulating devices, but because most of their people do not perceive rebellion as a realistically appealing option and feel that the best they can do is to put up with their state. It is instructive to read Goubert's (1966) account of affairs in France during the reign of a king as strong and given to putting things in order as Louis XIV.

Many readers may feel that I have just repeated a number of truisms. Perhaps so, but when one gets absorbed in systems talk, it is much too easy to lose sight of these truisms. We get tricked into the assumption that states are normally well supplied with well-working mechanisms for self regulation until a "system pathology" comes along to upset things. I propose something closer to the opposite assumption: that large-scale human societies are *normally* not working quite the way they are supposed to, not wholly under anybody's control, and at least somewhat misunderstood (in diverse ways) by everyone. This is not to say, of course, that all states are in equally bad shape. Obviously, at some times states are in much worse condition than at other times. Furthermore, what is "good" for one segment of society may be "bad" for another segment, and vice versa.

Thus, it is surprising that states have come into existence at all, and the problem of how and why they fail is an aspect of the problem of how and why they ever exist. By pointing out that humans do not "naturally" live in large societies and that we cannot smuggle in the assumption that states normally have highly effective homeostatic control mechanisms by labeling them systems, I want to call attention to the thought and effort required to create states and to keep them going. Eisenstadt also emphasizes this (Chapter 10, this volume). Statecraft is a human invention (or, rather, many related inventions) that commands respect, although possibly grudging respect. In certain contexts and in some scholarly traditions, people have known this for a long time. Most of the early great Chinese thinkers (Confucians, Legalists, Mohists, and others) were explicitly concerned with proper management of states. In this volume Hsu (Chapter 7) describes how it became accepted in Han China that good statecraft requires close attention by a large and highly schooled body of carefully selected officials. In classical Greece, politics were also a major object of philosophical discussion, and theories of statecraft were explicit.

I have the impression that China and Greece are exceptions, and that in other early civilizations there was much less reflection about statecraft or, at any rate, much less that was made public and recorded. Of course, even though officials tended to be more literate than most people in ancient societies, a good deal of practical development of techniques must have taken place and been transmitted without much systematic reflection or written discussion. Just as states differ in the material technology available to them, they must differ in the lore and techniques of statecraft at their disposal. Are there significant differences between Chinese and other early states that can be related to the apparently much stronger tradition of self-conscious statecraft in China? I return to this question in connection with Bronson's views (Chapter 8, this volume) about South Asia.

POLITICAL FRAGMENTATION AND THE EXTINCTION OF CIVILIZATIONS

Phrases such as *collapse of civilization* and *decline* or *fall* of empires are examples of the troubles with words that I have discussed above. They have been used to mean a variety of things. Often they are used more or less interchangeably, or without much thought about differences in their meanings. We need to make these terms more precise.

One important distinction is that between the decline or deterioration of something and its actual termination. Judgments about moral or aesthetic decline are defensible if we take pains to make explicit the standards of quality and recognize that not all reasonable people need share these criteria. Nevertheless, I feel surer talking about decreases and increases in quantity or quality of more material phenomena, such as volume of long-distance trade, income per capita, social mobility, political centralization, security of life and livelihood, disparities in the distribution of income, and the like. We can speak fairly clearly about changes in primarily economic, political, technological, and demographic aspects of societies, and our discussions can often be phrased in terms of increase or decrease, elaboration or simplification, expansion or contraction. Admittedly, we often lack the data to infer much more than the direction of the change, and even this much can often be debated by reasonable persons. But at least we can understand fairly well what we mean by a change in one of these aspects of a society.

Contemporary views on what was happening, to the extent that they are available to us, are also relevant data. We need not, of course, agree with any of them. It is also important to remember that persons in different social positions may have had very different views, not all of which have been transmitted to us with equal clarity. Certain themes seem chronic, especially complaints that things are not as good as they used to be and dire predictions that they will get much worse. It is impossible to evaluate these without some idea of changes in their frequency and intensity and the extent to which, at any given time, there were others who took a brighter view of things.

In turning to phrases that refer to the termination of something, rather than to its decline, it is useful to distinguish two broad categories. One set refers to the end or transformation of a civilization, whereas the other refers to the political fragmentation of a large state or empire. This distinction is often blurred. One source of confusion is that *civilization* and *society* are often used nearly as synonyms, and *society* in turn is not sharply distinguished from *state*, so that it is not clear if *the collapse of Rome* means that the Roman great tradition was no longer being practiced; that Roman society was in a condition of acute disruption and, in important senses, had ceased to function; or that the Roman state had fragmented. Very often, of course, more than one of these is meant. Nevertheless, they are distinct, and we need to have distinct terms that mean precisely one thing or another thing, but not more than one thing.

We should clearly differentiate between *state*, *society*, and *civilization* and use the last term in a specifically *cultural* sense, to mean what Redfield and Singer (1954) call a "great tradition." To speak of the collapse of a civilization, then, should be to refer to the end of a great cultural tradition.

In contrast, the collapse or fall of a state or an empire is a concept with obvious political reference. However, the coming apart of a large political system into a number of smaller, politically autonomous units is more accurately described as *political fragmentation*. I urge that we avoid using *collapse* or *fall* as synonyms for political fragmentation.

In this scheme the breakdown of a society is not synonymous with either the collapse of a civilization or the fragmentation of a state. Social, political, and cultural troubles tend to exacerbate one another and are often systemically interrelated. However, it is possible to have acute social problems (if not a complete social breakdown) without political fragmentation. It is also probably possible that some kinds of large states can break apart without incurring severe social troubles.

As Yoffee observes in Chapter 1, the complete termination or even the rapid drastic transformation of a civilization has been a rare event, at least so far. Political fragmentation is more common. For example, the great traditions of Mesopotamia and Egypt lasted for about twenty-five centuries, and the Chinese has endured nearly as long. But each has seen several cycles of political fragmentation followed by reconstitution of empires. And, although the Roman empire assuredly came apart politically, Bowersock (Chapter 6) argues that the civilization of Classical Antiquity did not perish, but was transformed in Late Antiquity and the early Middle Ages.

We asked seminar participants to focus mainly on political fragmentation, partly because this would provide us with more instances. Another reason, as is suggested by the Roman example, is that it can be difficult to decide when it is best to say that a given civilization is no longer practiced by any society and when it is better to think of the civilization as surviving, but in a drastically altered form. This is an important problem, but we feared that if we encouraged participants to emphasize it we would be led too far from questions that interested us more. We hoped that if we concentrated on political fragmentation we would have a theme large enough to be important but specific enough to enable us to make substantial progress within the scope of the seminar. We suggested that the central topic should be successes, failures, and problems of statecraft. We asked participants especially to discuss specific episodes in which large, nonindustrialized states fragmented and were succeeded by smaller states that did not immediately reunite politically.

At the same time, we did not want to discourage participants from discussing anything but political matters in the narrowest sense. In order to understand how and why large states fail it is necessary to understand the connections between politics and all sorts of economic, social, technological, and environmental phenomena, as well as the connections between politics, ideologies, and the modes by which people believed, thought, and felt. Our principal goal was to gain a better understanding of how all these things influence one another. However, we did not want especially to look at instances of termination or transformation of great traditions; we wanted mainly to examine instances of political fragmentation. We hoped that participants would bring up whatever seemed relevant for understanding these instances. This, naturally, involved us in discussions of great traditions, among other things.

Political fragmentation is only one of the kinds of troubles that beset governments. When we were planning the seminar, a colleague at Brandeis suggested that one of our instances might be the fall of the French ancien régime in 1789. That was a time of political and social crisis. Many holders of high office and/or high status lost their positions and often their lives. The old political system was abruptly ended and replaced by a series of very different systems. There was much more than a rebellion, that is, the attempt forcibly to replace one set of officeholders with other people. In 1789 there was a true revolution: the introduction of a new system of government, with new ideologies and new bases for claims to legitimate political authority. However, this revolution was not followed by any significant political fragmentation. In fact, later French governments allowed less regional autonomy than had existed under the ancien régime. What fell in 1789 was not a state, but a system of government.

In the first century B.C. the Roman republic suffered a long series of political crises, not resolved until Augustus established the imperial system of government. He took pains to preserve many republican forms, but the changes he made amounted to a transformation of the Roman political system, and for all practical purposes the Roman republic ceased to exist. But as in the French example, the fall of a system of government was not followed by political fragmentation. As these instances show, the collapse of empires, in the sense of political fragmentation, should not be confused with the fall of specific administrations or even the breakdown of systems of government.

All these vicissitudes of political systems are important kinds of sociocultural change, well worth study. However, we were not being arbitrary by concentrating on fragmentation. Political troubles that do not lead to fragmentation, especially troubles that lead instead to changes that facilitate *greater* political centralization, are often connected with expansion, increase, and/or elaboration in technology, population size, production and exchange, and the like. I have taken pains to make a distinction between political fragmentation and cultural, social, economic, or environmental troubles, but the fact remains that such troubles are often concomitant with fragmentation.

Some seminar participants stuck rather closely to the theme of political fragmentation, whereas others paid more attention to civilizational aspects. Thus the seminar turned out to be less tightly focused than we had expected. However, the rise, transformation, decline, and fall of great traditions, although less easily dealt with, are of deeper significance than the persistence or disintegration of states. It is just as well that they insisted on finding their way into our discussions.

THE MAIN KINDS OF TROUBLES STATES HAVE

In Chapter 10 Kaufman sketches general kinds of troubles that occurred repeatedly in many different states. He does not describe any specific state but provides a very good synthesis of states in general. Kaufman sketches a typical trajectory. We should try to usefully disaggregate this ideal trajectory. Can we identify distinct types of states that have different kinds of troubles or, at any rate, different troubles to different degrees? Can we develop theory connecting kinds of states with kinds of troubles, or does every instance require its own particularistic explanation?

Before I turn to these questions I will outline the main recurrent kinds of trouble as they appear to me. Many of my ideas on this subject are similar to Kaufman's, although I put them in different words and with somewhat different emphases.

All institutions, and especially states, must have resources at their disposal in order to persist: goods, services, and (where it exists) money. Most resources are perishable or expended in the process of being used, so they must constantly be supplied afresh. More durable resources and facilities (such as buildings, fortifications, roads, and hydraulic works) require expenditures for their maintenance. In other words, states need enough income to do what they have to do. It is hardly surprising that this is one of the problems they often face, but I do not think we pay enough attention to how many states, how large a part of the time, find this a major problem. Occasionally, as by rapid expansion through easy conquest of rich neighbors, a state acquires income that vastly exceeds its immediate needs. But such periods are invariably brief. In Chapter 4 Culbert asks what happens when the sources of easy income dry up. Sometimes the state itself disappears, or at least fragments. But often political integration of a large region persists long after there is no more easy income from expansion, as in both the western and eastern Roman empires, many Chinese dynasties, and the Teotihuacan state. In other cases, such as the Old and Middle Kingdoms of Egypt, income from conquests was perhaps never significant. How did large states balance their costs and expenses when they could not simply capture resources from others?

In cases in which states did succeed in establishing a long-term (or potentially long-term) balance between costs and expenses, the inverse question arises. Why were they not able to do so indefinitely? The histories of empires that persisted much longer than their times of rapid growth can be read as struggles over the generation, control, and use of scarce resources, and of the consequences of these struggles. The systematic comparative study of such struggles is largely a task for the future. Here I will attempt only an outline of such an analysis.

The fundamental problem faced by states is put by Micawber's Principle: income must be greater than or equal to expenditures. There can be accounting deficits, but the state must, somehow, maintain long-term access to sufficient quantities of goods and services. It is not the absolute amount of income or expenditures that matters, nor is it necessary that income exceed expenditures by very much. What is critical is that (since reserves were always finite and mostly perishable) expenditures cannot exceed income for very long without disastrous consequences. Because the processes that reduce income are different from those that increase costs, it is useful to discuss them separately.

Troubles in Getting Income

If a rapidly expanding state depends heavily on captured income it may be that, all along, it is "living on capital," that is, making expenditures at a rate that could not possibly be sustained for long by the conquered territories. I am not certain that there are any really clear examples of this. If there are, it seems such a state would have to find ways of quickly reducing its expenditures or else collapse.

Often, however, a large state controls territory that, in terms of environment and available technology, can produce a large income over a long time. At least five kinds of things can reduce the income available to the central authority. Kaufman has a similar list but we differ in the relative importance we assign to different factors.

The first on my list is increasing avoidance of taxes. Tax obligations imposed by a state are probably rarely equal even in theory or equally effectively enforced for everyone. However, inequalities may increase over time. This can occur through reduction of taxes or total exemption for certain institutions, individuals, or social categories—for example, religious foundations in ancient Egypt and many other places, gentry in Han China, nobility in prerevolutionary France. It can also occur through widespread fraud or simply defaulting on taxes, as may have happened increasingly in the later western Roman empire. In either case, three consequences are likely. First, the central authority has less revenue at its disposal. Second, those whose tax burden is lightened can use a higher proportion of their income for their own purposes (including transmission to heirs or successors). This strengthens them and makes them more independent of the central authority at the same time that the latter's resources are declining. Those who are already relatively wealthy tend to be the most successful in reducing the taxes they pay, and this further increases socioeconomic differences within the state. Third, since it is extremely unlikely that the central authority will cut its costs in proportion to the reduction in the revenue obtained from some elements of the society, it is highly likely that tax burdens will be increased for the remainder, who tend to be the less wealthy. This causes further hardships for them.

One important consequence of overtaxing the less powerful is that (whether or not land or anything else is "private property" in our sense) unless the units collectively responsible for taxes are quite large (certainly larger than extended families) their capacity to weather short-term crises such as crop failures or inopportune deaths of key members will be significantly reduced. Few nonindustrialized states seem to have been effective sources of credit to the majority of the people they ruled. This means that households without reserves to tide themselves over brief but severe crises must often seek loans from local individuals or institutions with more resources, who can exploit the situation to extend their own control over resources at the expense of those who controlled fewer resources to begin with. The details of how this happens will vary according to differences in rules about the transmission and alienation of rights over resources, but I strongly suspect that the general process is nearly universal. For example, some scholars are puzzled by evidence for a significant number of households without rights to land in late pre-conquest Aztec society, in view of rules that made communal (*calpulli*) rights to land theoretically inalienable. I would have been puzzled by the opposite—by evidence that, in a society as stratified as that of the later Aztecs, aristocrats had failed to find a way to dispossess some of the weaker commoner households.

I realize that, in spite of references to some examples, I, like Kaufman, am sketching a generic trajectory, rather than an account of what actually happened in any specific case. Future studies should test the applicability of my model to specific instances and reject, modify, or elaborate it as seems best. For example, many states have gone through periods of reorganization, often provoked by crises, in which the procedures for obtaining revenue were reformed. These efforts were usually only partially successful. Nevertheless, they may have substantially prolonged the lives of many states. Systematic study and comparison of various reform efforts, of different methods used and different degrees of success, should be very worthwhile.

A second kind of trouble is a tendency for a higher proportion of government revenues to accrue to holders of intermediate-level offices, especially those in the provinces, and never become available to the central authority. The effect is much the same as for the problem previously discussed: the central authority is weakened while other relatively powerful elements in the state are strengthened. Furthermore, both central and regional authorities are trying to get revenue from the same population, and it is likely that there will be an increase in the overall tax burden.

The third way a state can lose income is by declining productivity of the sources of income. In principle, this could occur as a result of long-term environmental changes, but in most instances of political fragmentation there is little or no evidence that such changes were important. (They should be distinguished from brief environmental crises, in which the key point is not the existence of the crisis, but the ability of the state and society to react effectively to it.) In some instances politically motivated overexploitation seems to have led to environmental damage that seriously impaired the government's sources of income. In Chapter 3, Yoffee describes how in Mesopotamia the necessities of empire, or what were perceived as necessities, seem to have been exceptionally destructive to regions outside the core area. Centralized governments repeatedly made demands that could be met only by damaging capacity for future production. An implication is that Mesopotamia was never amenable to Geertzian agricultural involution. Did heads of empires never understand this, did they understand it but succumb to temptations to maximize present profits at the expense of the future, or did they feel subject to necessities that left them no choice?

Politically motivated environmental damage may also have been important in the Southern Maya Lowlands, although the evidence from that region is not yet clear. Kaufman gives a good deal of emphasis to this factor. It was important in some cases, but so far I see no good evidence for it in many other instances.

A variant of this kind of trouble occurs when the damage is not to the physical environment, but to households or other productive institutions. Extraction of taxes (in the form of goods, services, or both) by the government may take so much from these institutions that they are left without the resources or the will to be as productive as before. Stated as an abstract principle, without quantification, this point seems undeniable. What is unclear—seemingly as unclear in the United States in the 1980s as in any ancient empire—is how much impact a given degree and kind of taxation on which persons and institutions, in which circumstances, will have on their productivity.

The fourth way in which income can be lost is through loss of political control over territories, either because they have been captured by outsiders or because political fragmentation is already underway. Kaufman mentions a fifth way. Lucrative foreign trade may decline, often for reasons beyond the state's control. The collapse of the Old Assyrian state described by Yoffee in Chapter 3 is an excellent example.

Higher Costs in Doing What Is Required of the State

By an increase in costs I mean an increase in real costs, aside from apparent increases due to inflation. One reason for such an increase is that the state may actually be required to do more. Sometimes other states or barbarians pose increasingly serious military threats, although, as Hsu points out in Chapter 7, we should never take this for granted. It needs to be demonstrated independently in each case. A second possibility is that the state needs to do more, or at least is called upon to try to do more, to offset environmental problems. These problems may themselves be of the state's making, as I pointed out above. Third, if population increases, the state may be called upon to provide services for more people. (My view about population increase [Cowgill 1975] is not that it rarely happens, but that we should not assume that there is always a natural tendency toward increase.) Finally, modern states are sometimes required to do more because their inhabitants develop new expectations about state services. I do not know if this was a significant factor for any nonindustrialized state, but it is a possibility that should be borne in mind.

The other major kind of reason for rising real costs is less effective use of revenue due to bureaucratic proliferation and/or increasing corruption, rigidity, incompetence, extravagance, and (perhaps) inefficiency. These are often lumped, but we should think about each separately. By bureaucratic proliferation I mean an increase in the number of offices (and officeholders) required to do much the same tasks as before. The tendency of bureaucracies to proliferate is perhaps the best example of a unidirectional trend furnished by any class of social phenomena. As Parkinson (1957) points out, one of the major effects is for the officeholders to make more work for one another. Thus, they may be incorruptible, highly competent, adaptable within limits, and keenly interested in managing the state's affairs thriftily and efficiently. That is, there may be no increase in corruption, rigidity, incompetence, extravagance, or willful inefficiency, yet less gets accomplished with a given amount of revenue. Similarly, grafters may be highly competent, resources may be used efficiently but toward extravagant ends, and so forth. Rigidity, proliferation, corruption, incompetence, and extravagance are distinct concepts. I am not sure if inefficiency should be defined as something distinct from all these or used as just a general term for their combined effects.

Bronson and Bowersock both point out that we should not assume that the prevalence of corrupt or incompetent officeholders always increases over time. This is true, but we should also not think that the existence of a few flagrant examples in the early stages of empires settles the matter. There may be increases in one or more of the factors I listed above. It is hard to get good quantitative data on amounts of corruption, inefficiency, incompetence, and extravagance. Bureaucratic proliferation should be relatively easy to quantify, because it is reflected in official tables of organization and other documents. We also need to study how all these factors work together systematically to affect adversely the ratio of income to accomplishments in specific instances.

Accountability of Officeholders

Eisenstadt (1969) uses *accountability* to refer to the idea that a ruler, even if he is politically supreme, must nevertheless conform to some set of moral principles in order to maintain his legitimacy. I use the term with reference to holders of subordinate offices. Subordinates are *accountable* to the extent that those above them can effectively detect and penalize poor performance or nonperformance of whatever superordinates want subordinates to do. Rulers, especially "strong" rulers, usually try to make their subordinates highly accountable. Subordinates often try to reduce their accountability. Struggles between these two opposing motives loom large in the histories of nearly all states. They have much to do with the collapse of states, partly because the struggles interfere with achieving other political objectives and partly because the logical extreme of reduced accountability for provincial officials is total autonomy—that is, political fragmentation.

No study of political collapse can ignore the tension between accountability and autonomy. However, to suggest that this opposition "explains" what happens to states is roughly like "explaining" what happens in a chess game by saying that white wants to checkmate black's king and black wants to checkmate white's king. We have to try to understand how the struggle between accountability and autonomy gets carried out in specific circumstances. What resources and maneuvers are available to rulers, and what are available to their subordinates? The struggle over control of government income (or potential government income), discussed above, is vital, but it is not the whole story. Rules of the political system are also important—for example, whether the state is in theory absolutist, whether the rulers are accountable (in Eisenstadt's sense) to other aristocrats, or whether (as in the United States) authority is parceled out through deliberate "checks and balances." It is important to know whether there are other elements of society, such as wealthy merchants or numerous (but rarely wealthy) peasants, that different players can try to use as allies or can try to pit against one another. Ideology can also be important, especially if ideological differences tend to separate rulers and their supporters from holders of subordinate offices.

As I said, I cannot offer anything like a systematic analysis along the lines I have outlined. I have tried, however, to establish a basis for further discussion. I will also offer some suggestions about possible differences in the kinds of troubles most characteristic of different kinds of states.

Different Kinds of Problems for Different Kinds of States

States vary greatly in their territorial extent. The relevance of this obvious point, especially for large, nonindustrialized states, is that sheer difficulty in communication can make it much harder for a ruler to keep physically distant subordinates accountable. It is not because of the amount of information that needs to be processed, but the time it takes for messages and responses to messages to get from one place to another. It is harder to check up on distant subordinates, and it is also necessary to give them greater legitimate powers of discretion, because they must frequently react to local events without taking time to get instructions from the political center.

The difficulties imposed by geographic distance are part of the problems that Hsu refers to in his discussion of "regionalism." Kaufman mentions techniques to keep subordinates more accountable. These include frequent rotation from one region to another, not sending an official to a region where he has family or property, keeping close relatives of regional officeholders in the capital (where they are, in effect, hostages), and using special agents of the ruler to check on what is going on in the provinces. Different rulers have employed some or all of these techniques to varying degrees. Nevertheless, officials have often succeeded in reducing their accountability, above all by gaining lifetime tenure in a specific region, acquiring increased control over land and other regional resources, and getting control over selection of their successors (which means that they can keep their offices as a sort of family property).

Besides differences in communication difficulties, states vary in how they administer territories, as many other writers have recognized. Some territories are simply *subjugated*. Local rulers may be left in place if they are obedient, or they may be replaced by governors. In either case, the central authority does little on the local level except claim a proportion of taxes, impose penalties if demands (taxes, and perhaps people for military or other service) are not adequately met, suppress fighting with other regions within the state, and offer protection against foreign invaders. In other cases territories are *incorporated*, by which I mean that the central authority takes part in local administration and provides substantial goods and services, especially management of public works and reserves of food and other resources.

I am not entirely happy with the terms *subjugation* and *incorporation*, but other terms that have been proposed, such as *indirect* versus *direct* rule or *hegemonic* versus *territorial* empires, seem to me to have at least as many problems or not to refer to quite the same distinction.

A large state may handle some regions by subjugation and others by incorporation, or use one or the other of these forms exclusively. Subjugation and incorporation are ideal types. It is not clear to me whether most real-world instances are plainly one or the other, or whether many instances fall somewhere between these types. I also am not sure if subjugation and incorporation, as I have defined them, are most usefully seen as values of a single variable. It may well be better to disaggregate them into several variables.

At any rate, it seems that a subjugated region might easily gain its autonomy simply because local dignitaries assert (or reassert) their lack of accountability to the central authority. This might happen with little impact on the general population. In contrast, incorporated regions are more dependent on the effective functioning of the central authority. If the central authority has trouble doing what is locally expected of it (for any of the reasons outlined above), the effect is likely to be felt by the general population, as well as by regional officeholders. In systems talk, a state that operates by subjugation is more nearly decomposable, whereas the systemic linkages are much stronger when rule is by incorporation. A simple-minded prediction is that subjugation states should tend to be fragile, short-lived, and suffer relatively moderate social and economic consequences when they break up, whereas incorporation states will tend to last longer but suffer relatively severe social and economic troubles when they do break down. However, it is doubtful that these simple predictions fit all the evidence. Can all the short-lived empires of Mesopotamia be considered subjugation states? The Teotihuacan state was long-lived but it is unlikely that it ruled more than its core area by incorporation. Nevertheless, the contrast between subjugation and incorporation may prove useful. At any rate, it suggests one axis of differentiation within the broad and quite heterogeneous category of nonindustrialized state.

A distinction roughly similar to what I have called incorporation and subjugation has been made by many scholars. Nevertheless, this and many of the other matters I have discussed above were not emphasized during the seminar, and the preceding chapters do not systematically present data that bears on all the questions I have raised. They do, however, provide much that is highly relevant to these questions, as well as to a diversity of other important topics.

SOME ISSUES RAISED IN THIS VOLUME

The Maya

Political troubles almost surely contributed to the Maya collapse, but it was probably not an instance of political fragmentation, since Late Classic southern lowland Maya society was probably never unified politically. However, the Maya collapse may be one of the few instances of the end of a great tradition, if one regards the southern lowlands tradition as a distinct civilization rather than a variant of a more generalized Maya civilization. It was certainly the end of one major line in a family of closely related Maya traditions. Other lines survived, with more or less drastic changes, in the highlands and in the northern lowlands, but the demographic collapse in the southern lowlands seems severe enough to have, just by itself, terminated the southern lowlands variant of the Maya great tradition. Whatever other factors may have also worked for or against its continuance, there probably simply weren't enough people left to sustain it any longer.

Culbert (Chapter 4) also stresses ecological instability. This deserves some elaboration. As I understand Geertz's (1963) argument in *Agricultural Involution*, some environments can sustain certain techniques of agricultural intensification almost indefinitely. There is a limit to output because (without some drastic innovation in technology) a point is reached at which an excessively large increase in labor per hectare is needed to achieve a very slight increase in output per hectare. However, the situation is "stable" in the sense that there is no limit to the intensity of land use that the environment can indefinitely sustain. The point along the curve of agricultural output per hectare as a function of labor input per hectare that a given farming household will actually occupy is determined by all the complex factors (costs of labor, household labor supply, land rents, taxes, prices of crops, household demand for income, political and social pressures, etc.) that determine an acceptable, desired, or needed ratio of labor input to crop output. The only limit to intensification, however, is that, although in principle a household can intensify its labor input per hectare indefinitely by concentrating all its labor on smaller and smaller patches of ground, there is an ill-defined limit beyond which the household (not the environment) cannot possibly sustain a further worsening of the ratio of labor input to produce output.

Some environments offer a contrasting situation. Up to a point, higher labor inputs per hectare result in higher outputs per hectare, as in the previous case. Beyond that point, however, the environment is damaged in ways that sharply reduce the amount that can be produced per hectare. When Culbert and others speak of the instability of agricultural intensification in the Maya lowlands, or fragility of the environment, I believe they refer to this kind of relation to the environment.

Culbert argues convincingly that a subsistence crisis may have contributed to the Maya collapse. However, although I strongly agree that the ultimate population reduction was very great, according to Culbert's evidence it took a century or so for the depopulation to run its course. This implies that something other than a single nearly instantaneous demographic disaster was involved. If survivors of whatever caused cessation of the erection of monumental structures and hieroglyphic inscriptions at Tikal and other sites could hang on for a few generations, why did they not hang on indefinitely? Were they forced out by continuing problems of the environment or by political or other troubles, or did they choose to leave because the central southern lowlands had finally become less attractive than other regions available to them?

This leads to a related problem: the duration of depopulation in the southern lowlands. In the twentieth century, for a variety of social and political reasons, population growth in the southern Maya lowlands has been very rapid, partly through migration and partly through natural increase. Persistently sparse population from the sixteenth through the nineteenth centuries can be understood as one aspect of the general Meso-american demographic disaster in the wake of the Spanish conquest. But why did the southern lowlands, especially the Petén, fill up so slowly between the tenth and the sixteenth centuries? Even a moderate amount of in-migration, plus a very moderate local rate of natural increase, would have led to more people than were there at the time of Spanish contact. It is hard to believe that, whatever environmental disaster may have occurred in the ninth and tenth centuries, it took many centuries for the land to recover to the point at which long-fallow swidden, at least, would have been again feasible over large areas. Perhaps environmental recovery was much slower than I suppose. Pertinent evidence on this point is badly needed. I suspect that a more important cause of the slowness of repop-ulation may have been economic and political factors that limited the appeal of the southern lowlands for Postclassic Mesoamericans. As Cul-bert and others have suggested, new patterns and routes of trade may have impeded recovery of the southern lowlands.

Teotihuacan

Millon (Chapter 5) distinguishes the final dramatic and violent de-struction of the city from the events that made its destruction possible. Hsu makes a similar distinction between the Yellow Turban rebellion and other immediate agents or symptoms of Han political fragmentation, and the phenomena that made these troubles possible. In both cases to look behind the immediate causes does not mean that we must follow an endless chain of causality into the remote past. It is rather a matter of looking for deeper or more general processes, and if there is no ab-solutely given end to this effort, there are are least strategic points at which to pause.

Yoffee points out that the very practices that made it possible for rulers of some Mesopotamian city-states to build empires contributed to the collapse of those empires. Millon also suggests that certain practices that were highly useful early in the development of the Teotihuacan state later contributed to its downfall. In both cases the arguments are plausible, but the Mesopotamian empires usually fell within a few generations, whereas Teotihuacan held on nearly ten times as long, for some seven centuries. Do we have any idea what explains the difference?

Rome

Bowersock (Chapter 6) shows how skeptical we must be about popular suppositions. The eastern (Byzantine) part of the Roman empire lasted into the fifteenth century, and Bowersock argues that, at least until the Arab invasions of the seventh century, the western empire itself did not collapse or even, in any clear sense, decline. He argues further that a clearcut Roman climax, a high point that could mark the onset of decline, is itself hard to define.

Bowersock points out that different parts of a state can undergo quite different experiences. There can be clear evidence for decline or destruction of specific cities or districts at the same time that other areas are flourishing as never before. I add that this can also be true for different social sectors. The worst of times for some may be the best of times for others.

If local decline is detectable, then, by the same token, local prosperity is identifiable. The implication is not that overall tendencies in large states are unknowable, but that evidence about a particular region cannot be considered generally applicable to an entire empire.

Bowersock's challenges to comfortable common knowledge are salutary. An "instance of collapse" about which so much is known proves to be much more complex, puzzling, and even paradoxical than the models we put forward, often with considerable confidence and satisfaction, to explain instances for which the data are far more sparse.

Nevertheless, I am reluctant to think that the western Roman empire had little in common with other instances discussed in this volume. Clearly the transition to the so-called Dark Ages was a transformation far more than a collapse of the Greco-Roman great tradition. However, political fragmentation is another matter. By the fifth century the western empire had broken up into a number of independent states. Peter Brown (1971:118–19) writes that

> Two generations . . . [after about A.D. 400], the western empire had disappeared. . . . The failure of the western emperors to defend themselves against the pressure of barbarian attacks after 400, and, when attacked, to win back lost territories, can be largely explained in terms of the basic economic and social weaknesses of western society. . . .
>
> The reasons for the collapse of the imperial government, in the west, are far from simple. Questions of morale came into play, as well as economic and social factors. Perhaps the most basic reason for the failure of the imperial government, in the years between 380 and 410, was that the two main groups in the Latin world—the senatorial aristocracy and the Catholic Church—dissociated themselves from the fate of the Roman army that defended them. Both groups unwittingly sapped the strength of the army and of the imperial administration; and, having hamstrung their protectors, they found, somewhat to their surprise, that they could do without them. . . . The disappearance of the western empire, therefore, was the price for the survival of the Senate and the Catholic Church.

And, a few pages later,

> The barbarian invasions did not destroy west Roman society, but they drastically altered the scale of life in the western provinces. The imperial government . . . lost so much land and taxes that it remained bankrupt to the time of its extinction in 476. The senators lost the income of their scattered estates. They were able to make good some of their losses by rack-renting and chicanery in the areas where their power was strongest. . . . Communications suffered. . . . In western Europe, the fifth century was a time of narrowing horizons, of the strengthening of local roots, and the consolidating of old loyalties. (Brown 1971:126)

Again, "the politics of Roman courtiers at the new barbarian courts were local politics. The idea of a united western empire was increasingly ignored" (Brown 1971:129).

To be sure, in the sixth century much of the west was reconquered by the eastern empire, and it remained under Byzantine control for centuries (Brown 1971:132–34). But by the seventh century, the classical tradition rapidly disappeared in the west, according to Brown (1971:176), who characterizes the change as a "simplification of culture" (Brown 1971:174).

Brown, like Bowersock, stresses the survival, or transformation rather than collapse, of many aspects of Antique culture. Moreover, there was no single, brief, decisive crisis, but a complex series of political, social, economic, ideological, religious, and ethnic changes, lasting over centuries. Nevertheless, the political system of the Roman west did come apart. Recapture of parts of it by the eastern empire was not the same as reconstitution of a political system from within.

Questions of socioeconomic decline do not seem settled. There was certainly no simple monotonous downward trend in all aspects in all parts of the later western empire. Gunderson's (1976) evidence that in many places land prices did not fall cannot be lightly dismissed. Neither should it be taken as the last word on the subject. For example, the failure of nominally higher rates of taxation to depress land prices cannot be interpreted unless the extent of tax evasion is also considered. The government's willingness to negotiate tax exemptions in return for lump-sum payments suggests that it had become difficult to collect all the taxes owed by large landholders. A full assessment of economic well-being must also consider commodity prices and the state of industry as well as land prices. Gunderson suggests that a surge of urbanization will accompany the diffusion of new manufacturing techniques, followed naturally by a subsequent decline in urban populations as new techniques are assimilated and industry spreads to the countryside. I do not think evidence from other societies supports this idea.

My own guess is that land prices may have stayed high because, for those who could afford the prices at all, large landholdings were becoming more and more necessary for maintaining reasonably secure high status, while theoretical tax rates were becoming less related to the amounts the imperial government could actually extract from wealthy individuals.

Gunderson also argues that the labor shortage of Late Antiquity need not imply a decline in population. Evidence for a population decline is ambiguous. Much of the earlier literature on Roman population is demographically naive and unsatisfactory (e.g., Boak 1955). Other population studies (e.g., Finley 1969:153–61) are much better. I think no one could seriously argue that population in the west increased more than slightly between the second and the fifth centuries. I suspect that there was actually a general decline in numbers, at least in central Italy, though there may have been increases in some more distant parts of the empire.

It is incongruous that questions of population remain so controversial for such a "historic" society as the Roman empire, while archaeologists often discuss prehistoric population levels and trends with great confidence. There are probably faults on both sides. Anyone who thinks seriously about problems in deriving good population estimates from archaeological data has to recognize the wide range of uncertainty in such estimates. The archaeologists who actually do the work often acknowledge these uncertainties (as Culbert does in this volume), but readers tend to lose sight of them. Even so, we may have a better idea of population trends in the southern Maya lowlands than in the Roman empire. This may be more a result of different kinds of archaeological fieldwork than of greater caution on the part of students of Classical Antiquity. Serious application of modern techniques of settlement archaeology to substantial parts of the Roman world (now underway in some places) should make important contributions to our knowledge of ancient population trends.

This leads to a final point. The abundance of historical materials for Rome is undeniably an immense advantage, yet I think that only a few Classical archaeologists are beginning to make good use of recent developments in anthropological archaeology. An example is the 1983 book by Hodges and Whitehouse, which challenges some views about Late Antiquity and exemplifies approaches that may shed a great deal of light on large questions that have not been resolved by the methods hitherto employed.

China

In emphasizing ideological differences between the Confucian bureaucracy and the inner court of the Han emperors, Hsu (Chapter 7) takes a strongly idealist position. During the earlier Han, the bureaucrats elaborated the doctrine that, according to Confucian principles, they were persons of a special kind, with both the right and the duty, by virtue of their training, to criticize the conduct of the government in general and of the emperor in particular. In the terms of Eisenstadt and Jaspers, their efforts made China into an "Axial Age" society.

I agree that ideology made a difference, but I find it hard to say how much difference. How much longer would the Han dynasty have lasted if the bureaucracy had had no coherent ideological basis for their conflicts with the inner court? Many of the Confucian bureaucrats used their high offices in order to acquire wealth in land, and as Hsu says (p. 185), at least the most influential "were able to weld successions of leadership lasting several generations and actually constituting a form of hereditary nobility." Thus, although the high level of ideological consciousness among the literati undoubtedly exacerbated the conflict and perhaps hastened the end, could it have been more important that bureaucrats were increasingly independent of the emperors for their wealth and positions?

Hsu says little about taxation, revenues, and the funding of the Han government. In his position paper prepared before the seminar met he indicated that, during the earlier part of the Western Han, suppression of the descendants of "meritorious generals" and other quasi-feudal aristocrats left over from before the Han resulted, by the reign of Emperor Wu (141–87 B.C.), in a very high degree of centralization, with all officers of government highly accountable to the emperor and with an effective and relatively equitable tax system. Fairbank, Reischauer, and Craig (1973:70–81) say that thereafter the general trend (with some partial reversals) was toward greater avoidance of taxes by the wealthy (including Confucian bureaucrats), heavier tax burdens on those who could not avoid taxation, and increasingly severe problems in financing government operations. However, during our seminar Hsu questioned whether financial problems were especially severe for the Han government. He has subsequently emphasized (personal communication) that fiscal conditions in the reign of Emperor Wu were even worse than during the last part of the Han dynasty. Nevertheless, there was no sign of collapse at the time of Emperor Wu. This underlines the hazards of relying too much on a single source such as Fairbank, Reischauer, and Craig (1973). It also shows we should not take it for granted that (as I suggested earlier in this chapter) fiscal conditions always tend to get worse as empires get older. It seems there is no simple correlation between solvency and effectiveness of centralized political control.

South Asia

Bronson (Chapter 8) argues that we underestimate the role of "barbarians" in the fragmentation of states and overestimate the tendency for corruption and incompetence to get worse as empires get older. These are provocative ideas that deserve consideration, but more data are needed before either can be accepted as fully established.

Periods of political unification have been atypical and relatively brief in South Asia. Bronson suggests this may be due to vulnerability to incursions by barbarians from the north. This is a debatable conclusion. For example, the Mughals, themselves invaders from the north, imposed an unusually high degree of political unification. Their empire was short-lived, but I do not think troubles on its northern frontier had much to do with its demise. European traders and their armies played a role, but I doubt if they were decisive either. I suspect the relative infrequency and short duration of large states in South Asia is better explained by features of the South Asian environment, by a political "style" that was part of the South Asian great tradition, or by some combination of both. Bronson considers these possibilities but rejects them. I do not think they should be ruled out.

The contrast between South Asia and modern China is interesting. After the fall of the Ch'ing dynasty in the early 1900s, China experienced several decades during which effective rule was largely by regional "warlords." Reestablishment of a strong, centralized government was a wholly internal achievement, carried out *in spite of* foreign interventions and invasions. In some ways it matters profoundly that the ideology of the new government is Marxist-Leninist rather than Confucian. However, I strongly suspect that even if Marxist-Leninist ideology did not exist China would be reunified by now. In South Asia, on the other hand, a major effect of nineteenth-century British imperialism was to impose much more political unification than had existed before. Immediate fragmentation into Pakistan, India, and Sri Lanka was concomitant with British withdrawal, and a few years later east Pakistan split off as Bangladesh. Even within some of these four states, separatist tendencies (regional, ethnic, and religious) are very strong and troublesome.

In spite of whatever differences modern technology makes, I suspect these twentieth-century contrasts reflect some very enduring differences between China and South Asia. The natural environments of central and southern India are perhaps not hospitable to nonindustrialized empires. The troubles of empires (or would-be empires) in the plains of the Indus and Ganges probably had more to do with their neighbors to the south than with those in the north. Marvin Harris (1979:107–8) argues that political and social differences between China and South Asia can largely be explained by environmental differences. Harris probably has part of the answer. However, I suspect that there is much that is not explained by either external barbarians or internal environments, that Chinese ideologies and techniques of statecraft have facilitated political centralization, whereas those of South Asia have favored smaller states and have not been so useful to persons who have tried to build or maintain empires. This is scarcely an original idea. I regret that I cannot discuss it further here.

Both Bronson and Bowersock point out that corruption and scandalous behavior can easily be found in the early days of empires. Some of the most flagrant rogues and self-seekers were in at the beginnings of empires, and blithering incompetents can be found there also. Possibly their proportions tend to increase as empires get older, but quantitative data on this point will be difficult to obtain. More significant is that a flourishing empire, especially one making huge profits through successful wars (a theme Bronson stresses), can tolerate relatively high costs due to corruption and incompetence. Still more important, and not emphasized by Bronson, is the ability of strong central authorities to intimidate, coopt, manipulate, or liquidate scoundrels, and to get rid of at least some of the worst incompetents. As middle and lower levels of bureaucracies entrench themselves, it becomes virtually impossible to weed out the lazy and incompetent. Also, as holders of higher offices acquire independent power bases and a large say in who succeeds them in office (so that recruitment is more nearly by ascription than achievement), the central authorities must find it harder to place competent and loyal persons in key positions, and harder to control action at cross-purposes to their own. It is not the *existence* of scandalous behavior, rule-breaking, and bungling that is crucial: it is the impact that all of these actions have.

Boundaries

Boundaries received much attention during the seminar, and Eisenstadt, especially, discusses them in this volume (Chapter 10). They are important, especially because boundary-maintaining mechanisms are part of what systems need to ensure their continued reproduction. However, what goes on inside and outside the boundaries is also important. When boundaries disappear or lose their significance, it is probably because differences between what is happening inside and what is happening outside have become unimportant, rather than because boundary-maintaining mechanisms per se have failed. More specifically, as an empire moves toward political fragmentation, regions become more autonomous, and it makes less difference whether a region is nominally part of the empire or not. This seems, for example, a useful way of looking at events around the western Mediterranean in Late Antiquity.

Costs of Stability

A theme throughout this chapter is that states do not simply persist of their own accord. Political systems must constantly confront problems, and resources and human skills must be employed unceasingly in maintaining the state. However, concentration on this fact makes it easy to assume that political fragmentation is always a bad thing, to be avoided if possible. There are costs as well as benefits in maintaining a political system indefinitely. Fragmentation may offer new opportunities and facilitate change. Can a large state be stabilized without inhibiting innovation and stifling cultural creativity? Excessive instability is bad, but too much stability may not be good either. We should try to provide a balanced assessment of the costs as well as the benefits of the techniques by which states, modern as well as ancient, have coped with challenges to their continued existence.

SOME DIRECTIONS FOR THE FUTURE

I shall mention only a few of the topics for further research suggested by the chapters in this volume. Why did some empires last so much longer than others? How closely is their duration connected to degrees and kinds of integration, economic and social as well as political? How do empires solve (or not solve) the problem of adequate income when fast wealth through easy conquest of rich neighbors is no longer possible? How do empires respond to crises? Why are some times of trouble fatal, whereas others are not? What orderly relations, if any, hold between fiscal troubles and developmental cycles of empires? Are there trends over time in the incidence of scoundrels or incompetents in governments? Is the incidence of either fiscal troubles or misbehavior really just as high early as late? If so, are there structural reasons why the effects of such sources of trouble are sometimes less serious, or is it simply that part of the time an empire is so successful that it can tolerate a startling amount of systemic malfunctioning?

Struggles between heads and important subordinates over accountability and autonomy seem universal, but can we identify important variants? Were certain strategies in these struggles given much greater emphasis in some instances than in others? If so, are the differences explainable by differences in environments, technologies, and relations of production, or were differences in ideas about rules, techniques, and purposes of political activity also important?

Finally, what of the role of ideology in imperial expansion? Conrad and Demarest (1984) argue that ideologies gave the Incas and Aztecs decisive edges over their competitors. Ideology was also important in the explosive Islamic conquests of the seventh century. Other peoples, however, such as the Romans, were very successful empire builders on a much lower ideological plane, motivated less by a sense of mission than by quite pragmatic appetites for power and wealth. Was strong dependence on ideology one reason some empires were short-lived, since there may be little else to hold things together if ideological fervor wanes?

Underlying all these questions is the insistence that, if ideas are not merely epiphenomenal, we need greatly improved concepts, especially hypotheses that have withstood testing against substantial bodies of evidence, about causal connections between ideas and material phenomena.

NOTE

Parts of this chapter somewhat resemble the position paper I wrote in advance of the seminar, but I have made many changes in response to comments by the other seminar participants, and by Jane Kepp and an anonymous reader. Norm Yoffee tried to get me to prune back a number of my more florid digressions. I resisted many of these suggestions, but the chapter is better than it would have been without all the comments on earlier versions.

Bibliography

Acosta, Jorge R.

1964   *El palacio del Quetzalpapalotl.* Mexico City: Instituto Nacional de Antropología e Historia, Memoir No. 10.

1970   Sección 1: La Gran Cala. In *Proyecto Cholula,* coord. Ignacio Marquina, pp. 119–28. Mexico City: Instituto de Antropología e Historia, Investigaciones No. 19.

Adams, Richard E. W.

1971   *The Ceramics of Altar de Sacrificios, Guatemala.* Papers of the Peabody Museum of Archaeology and Ethnology, vol. 63. Cambridge, Mass.: Harvard University Press.

1973   Maya Collapse: Transformation and Termination in the Ceramic Sequence at Altar de Sacrificios. In *The Classic Maya Collapse,* ed. T. P. Culbert, pp. 133–63. Albuquerque: University of New Mexico Press.

1977   *Prehistoric Mesoamerica.* Boston: Little, Brown.

1980   Swamps, Canals, and the Location of Ancient Maya Cities. *Antiquity* 80:206–14.

1981   Settlement Patterns of the Central Yucatán and Southern Campeche Regions. In *Lowland Maya Settlement Patterns,* ed. W. Ashmore, pp. 211–57. Albuquerque: University of New Mexico Press.

1984   The Río Azul Archaeological Project: 1984 Preliminary Report. Manuscript.

Adams, Richard E. W., W. E. Brown, Jr., and T. Patrick Culbert

1981   Radar Mapping, Archaeology and Ancient Maya Land Use. *Science* 213:1457–63.

Adams, Richard E. W., and Richard C. Jones
1981   Spatial Patterns and Regional Growth Among Classic Maya Cities. *American Antiquity* 46:301–22.
Adams, Richard E. W., and Woodruff D. Smith
1981   Feudal Models for Classic Maya Civilization. In *Lowland Maya Settlement Patterns*, ed. W. Ashmore, pp. 335–49. Albuquerque: University of New Mexico Press.
Adams, Robert McC.
1966   *The Evolution of Urban Society: Early Mesopotamia and Prehispanic Mexico*. Chicago: Aldine.
1978   Strategies of Maximization, Stability, and Resilience in Mesopotamian Society, Settlement, and Agriculture. *Proceedings of the American Philosophical Society* 122(5):329–35.
1981   *Heartland of Cities: Surveys of Ancient Settlement and Land Use on the Central Floodplain of the Euphrates*. Chicago: University of Chicago Press.
1984   Mesopotamian Social Evolution: Old Outlooks, New Goals. In *On the Evolution of Complex Societies: Essays in Honor of Harry Hoijer, 1982*, ed. T. Earle, pp. 79–129. Malibu: Undena.
Adams, Robert McC., and Hans J. Nissen
1972   *The Uruk Countryside: The Natural Setting of Urban Societies*. Chicago: University of Chicago Press.
Aldenderfer, Mark S.
1981   Computer Simulation for Archaeology: An Introductory Essay. In *Simulations in Archaeology*, ed. Jeremy A. Sabloff pp. 11–49. School of American Research Advanced Seminar Series. Albuquerque: University of New Mexico Press.
Almaraz, Ramón
1865   *Memoria de los trabajos ejecutados por la Comisión de Pachuca . . . 1864. Mexico City*.
Anderson, Perry
1979   Note B. The Asiatic Mode of Production. In *Lineages of the Absolutist State*, pp. 462–549. London: Verso.
1980   *Arguments within English Marxism*. London: Verso.
Andrews, E. Wyllys, IV
1942   Yucatán: Architecture. *Carnegie Institution of Washington Yearbook* 41:257–63.
1965   Archaeology and Prehistory in the Northern Maya Lowlands: An Introduction. In *Archaeology of Southern Mesoamerica*, Part 1, *Handbook of Middle American Indians*, ed. Robert Wauchope and Gordon R. Willey, pp. 288–330. Austin: University of Texas Press.
Andrews, E. Wyllys, IV, and E. Wyllys Andrews V
1980   *Excavations at Dzibilchaltún, Yucatán, Mexico*. Middle American Research Institute Publication 48. New Orleans: Tulane University Press.
Andrews, E. Wyllys, V
1979   Early Central Mexican Architectural Traits at Dzibilchaltún, Yu-

catán. In *Actes du 42e Congrès International des Américanistes* 8:237–49 (Paris).

1981   Dzibilchaltún. In *Supplement to the Handbook of Middle American Indians*, vol. 1, *Archaeology*, ed. Victoria R. Bricker and Jeremy A. Sabloff, pp. 313–41. Austin: University of Texas Press.

Angulo, Jorge V., and Kenneth G. Hirth

1981   Presencia teotihuacana en Morelos. In *Interacción cultural en México central*, comp. Evelyn C. Rattray, Jaime Litvak King, and Clara Díaz O., pp. 81–99. Mexico City: Universidad Nacional Autónoma de México.

Appleby, J. O.

1978   *Economic Thought and Ideology in Seventeenth-Century England.* Princeton: Princeton University Press.

Arce, Javier, with M. Fernández-Galiano, Juan José Sayas, José M. Blázquez, and Luis A. García Moreno

1980   *La caida del imperio romano de occidente en el año 476.* Madrid: Cuadernos de la Fundación Pastor 24.

Armillas, Pedro

1944   Exploraciones recientes en Teotihuacán, México. *Cuadernos Americanos* 16(4):121–36.

1950   Teotihuacán, Tula y los toltecas: Las culturas post-arcáicas y preaztecas del centro de México: Excavaciones y estudios, 1922–1950. *Runa* 3:37–70 (Buenos Aires).

1969   The Arid Frontier of Mexican Civilization. *Transactions, New York Academy of Sciences* 31:697–704.

Athens, Stephen

1977   Theory Building and the Study of Evolutionary Processes in Complex Societies. *For Theory Building in Archaeology*, ed. Lewis R. Binford, pp. 353–84. New York: Academic Press.

Aveni, Anthony F., Horst Hartung, and J. Charles Kelley

1982   Alta Vista (Chalchihuites), Astronomical Implications of a Mesoamerican Ceremonial Outpost at the Tropic of Cancer. *American Antiquity* 47(2):316–35.

Balazs, Etienne

1964   *Chinese Civilization and Bureaucracy*, trans. M. Wright. New Haven: Yale University Press.

Balkan, Kemal

1954   *Kassitenstudien.* New Haven: American Oriental Society.

Ball, Joseph W.

1974a   A Teotihuacán-style Cache from Becán, Campeche. *Archaeology* 27(1):2–9.

1974b   A Regional Ceramic Sequence for the Río Bec Area. In *Preliminary Reports on Archaeological Investigations in the Río Bec Area, Campeche, Mexico*, comp. Richard E. W. Adams, pp. 113–17. Middle American Research Institute Publication No. 31. New Orleans: Tulane University Press.

1979   Southeastern Campeche and the Mexican Plateau: Early Classic Contact Situations. In *Actes du 42e Congrès International des Américanistes* 8:271–80 (Paris).

1983   Teotihuacán, the Maya, and Ceramic Interchange: A Contextual Perspective. In *Highland-Lowland Interaction in Mesoamerica: Interdisciplinary Approaches*, ed. Arthur G. Miller, pp. 125–45. Washington, D.C.: Dumbarton Oaks.

Barbour, Warren T. D.
1976   The Figurines and Figurine Chronology of Ancient Teotihuacán, Mexico. Ph.D. dissertation, University of Rochester.

Barth, Fredrik
1965   *Political Leadership among the Swat Pathans*. London: London School of Economics Monographs on Social Anthropology 19.

Barthel, Thomas S.
1982   Veritable "Texts" in Teotihuacán Art? *The Masterkey* 56(1):4–12.

Bates, D. G.
1980   The Middle Eastern Village in Regional Perspective. In *Village Viability in Contemporary Society*, ed. P. C. Reining and B. Lenkerd, pp. 161–83. American Association for the Advancement of Science Selected Symposium 34. Boulder: Westview.

Batres, Leopoldo
1906   *Teotihuacán*. Mexico City: Fidencio S. Soria.

Beckerman, Wilfred
1979   Small Is Stupid. *The Times Higher Education Supplement*, 23 November, pp. 14–15 (London).

Bejarano, Emilio J.
1979   Presencia teotihuacana en Guanajuato. *Los procesos de cambio, XV Mesa Redonda* 2:335–42 (Mexico City: Sociedad Mexicana de Antropología).

Bender, Barbara
1978   Gatherer-Hunter to Farmer: A Social Perspective. *World Archaeology* 10:204–22.

Berlo, Janet Catherine
1983a   The Warrior and the Butterfly: Central Mexican Ideologies of Sacred Warfare and Teotihuacán Iconography. In *Text and Image in Pre-Columbian Art*, ed. J. C. Berlo, pp. 79–117, BAR International Series No. 180. Oxford: British Archaeological Reports.

1983b   Teotihuacán-Maya Syncretism at Lake Amatitlan, Guatemala. Paper presented at Symposium on Art and the Rise of the Teotihuacán State, Department of Art, University of California at Los Angeles.

1984   *Teotihuacán Art Abroad: A Study of Metropolitan Style and Provincial Transformation in Incensario Workshops*. BAR International Series 199, parts i and ii. Oxford: British Archaeological Reports.

Bernal, Ignacio
1965   Archaeological Synthesis of Oaxaca. In *Handbook of Middle American Indians*, vol. 3, ed. Robert Wauchope and Gordon R. Willey, pp. 788–813. Austin: University of Texas Press.

Biddiss, Michael
    1980   Purveyor of Harsh Prophecies and Poetic Truths. *The Times Higher Education Supplement*, 1 August, p. 9 (London).
Bielenstein, Hans
    1954;   The Restoration of the Han Dynasty. *Bulletin of the Museum of Far*
    1959   *Eastern Antiquities* 26:1–209; 31:1–287 (Stockholm).
Biggs, Robert
    1967   Semitic Names in the Fara period. *Orientalia N. S.* 36:55–66.
Blalock, Hubert M., Jr.
    1984   *Basic Dilemmas in the Social Sciences.* Beverly Hills: Sage Publications.
Blanton, Richard E.
    1976   Anthropological Studies of Cities. *Annual Review of Anthropology* 5:249–64.
    1978   *Monte Albán: Settlement Patterns at the Ancient Zapotec Capital.* New York: Academic Press.
Blanton, Richard E., and Stephen A. Kowalewski
    1981   Monte Albán and After in the Valley of Oaxaca. In *Supplement to the Handbook of Middle American Indians*, vol. 1, *Archaeology*, ed. Victoria R. Bricker and Jeremy A. Sabloff, pp. 94–116. Austin: University of Texas Press.
Boak, A. E. R.
    1955   *Manpower Shortage and the Fall of the Roman Empire in the West.* Ann Arbor: University of Michigan Press.
Bodde, Derk
    1938   *China's First Unifier.* Leiden: Brill.
Bottéro, Jean
    1967   The First Semitic Empire. In *The Near East: The Early Civilizations*, ed. J. Bottéro, E. Cassin, and J. Vercoutter, pp. 91–132. London: Weidenfeld and Nicolson.
Boudon, R.
    1982   *The Unintended Consequences of Social Action.* New York: St. Martin's Press.
Bove, Frederick J.
    1987   Teotihuacan Impact on the Pacific Coast of Guatemala: Myth or Reality? Paper presented at the Society for American Archaeology, Toronto, May 1987.
Brainerd, George W.
    1942   Yucatán: Ceramics. *Carnegie Institution of Washington Yearbook* 41:253–57 (Washington, D.C.).
Brewbaker, James L.
    1979   Diseases of Maize in the Wet Lowland Tropics and the Collapse of the Classic Maya Civilization. *Economic Botany* 33:101–18.
Brinkman, John A.
    1968   *A Political History of Post-Kassite Babylonia, 1158–722 B.C.* Rome: Pontifical Biblical Institute.

1973   Sennacherib's Babylonian Problem: An Interpretation. *Journal of Cuneiform Studies* 25:89–95.

1980   Kassiten. *Reallexikon der Assyriologie* 5:464–73.

1981   Hurrians in Babylonia in the Late Second Millennium B.C.: An Unexploited Minority Resource for Socioeconomic and Philological Analysis. In *Studies on the Civilization and Culture of Nuzi and the Hurrians*, ed. M. A. Morrison and D. I. Owen, pp. 27–35. Winona Lake, Indiana: Eisenbrauns.

1984   *Prelude to Empire: Babylonian Society and Politics, 747–626 B.C.* Philadelphia: Occasional Publications of the Babylonian Fund, No. 7.

Bronson, Bennet

1966   Roots and the Subsistence of the Ancient Maya. *Southwestern Journal of Anthropology* 22:251–79.

1977   Notes Toward a Functional Model of the Coastal State in Southeast Asia. In *Economic Exchange and Social Interaction in Southeast Asia* 13:39–52, ed. Karl L. Hutterer. Ann Arbor: Michigan Papers on South and Southeast Asia.

Brown, Kenneth L.

1977a   The Valley of Guatemala: A Highland Port of Trade. In *Teotihuacán and Kaminaljuyu*, ed. William T. Sanders and Joseph W. Michels, pp. 205–395. University Park: Pennsylvania State University Press.

1977b   Toward a Systematic Explanation of Culture Change within the Middle Classic Period of the Valley of Guatemala. In *Teotihuacán and Kaminaljuyu*, ed. William T. Sanders and Joseph W. Michels, pp. 411–40. University Park: Pennsylvania State University Press.

Brown, Peter R. L.

1971   *The World of Late Antiquity: A.D. 150–750.* London: Thames and Hudson.

1972   *Religion and Society in the Age of Saint Augustine.* London: Faber and Faber.

1978   *The Making of Late Antiquity.* Cambridge, Mass.: Harvard University Press.

1981   *The Cult of the Saints.* Chicago: University of Chicago Press.

1982   *Society and the Holy in Late Antiquity.* Berkeley and Los Angeles: University of California Press.

Buccellati, Giorgio

1966   *The Amorites of the Ur III Period.* Naples: Instituto Orientale de Napoli.

Bury, J. B.

1927   *The Invasion in Europe by the Barbarians.* Reprint of 1902 edition. London: Macmillan.

Butzer, Karl

1980   Civilizations: Organisms or Systems? *American Scientist* 68:517–23.

Cabrera Castro, Rubén, Ignacio Rodríguez García, and Noel Morelos García (coord.)

1982a   *Teotihuacán 80–82: Primeros resultados.* Mexico City: Instituto Nacional de Antropología e Historia.

1982b   *Memoria del proyecto arqueológico Teotihuacán 80–82*, vol. 1. Mexico City: Instituto Nacional de Antropología e Historia.

Cabrera Castro, Rubén, and Saburo Sugiyama
1982   La reexploración y restauración del Templo Viejo de Quetzalcoatl. In *Memoria del proyecto arqueológico Teotihuacán 80–82*, vol. 1, coord. Rubén Cabrera C., Ignacio Rodríguez G., and Noel Morelos G., pp. 163–83. Mexico City: Instituto Nacional de Antropología e Historia.

Cagni, L.
1977   The Poem of Erra. *Sources and Monographs on the Ancient Near East*, 1:3 (Malibu: Undena).

Cameron, Alan
1977   Paganism and Literature in Late Fourth Century Rome. In *Christianisme et formes littéraires de l'antiquité tardive en occident*, ed. Manfred Fuhrmann. Geneva: Fondation Hardt, Entretiens sur l'antiquité classique, tome 23.

Cameron, Averil
1982   From Freedom to Serfdom. *The Times Higher Education Supplement*, 2 February, p. 12 (London).

Cardascia, Guillaume
1951   *Les archives des Murašû*. Paris: Imprimerie Nationale.

Carneiro, R. L.
1970   A Theory of the Origin of the State. *Science* 169:733–38.

Caroe, Olaf
1976   *The Pathans, 550 B.C.–A.D. 1957*. Karachi: Oxford University Press.

Carr, Robert F., and James E. Hazard
1961   *Map of the Ruins of Tikal, El Petén, Guatemala*. Tikal Report 11, University Museum Monographs. Philadelphia: University of Pennsylvania.

Carrasco, Pedro
1982   The Political Economy of the Aztec and Inca States. In *The Inca and Aztec States 1400–1800: Anthropology and History*, ed. George A. Collier, R. I. Rosaldo, and J. D. Wirth, pp. 23–40. New York: Academic Press.

Caso, Alfonso
1936–   ¿Tenían los teotihuacanos conocimiento del tonalpohualli? *El México*
1939   *Antiguo* 4:131–44.
1958–   Glifos teotihuacanos. *Revista Mexicana de Estudios Antropológicos*
1959   15:51–71.
1967   Dioses y signos teotihuacanos. In *Teotihuacán: XI Mesa Redonda* 1:249–75. Mexico City: Sociedad Mexicana de Antropología.

Chadwick, Robert
1971   Archaeological Synthesis of Michoacán and Adjacent Regions. In *Handbook of Middle American Indians*, vol. 11, ed. Robert Wauchope, Gordon F. Ekholm, and Ignacio Bernal, pp. 657–93. Austin: University of Texas Press.

Chandler, Tertius, and Gerald Fox
   1974   *3000 Years of Urban Growth*. New York: Academic Press.
Chang, Kwang-chih
   1980   *Shang Civilization*. New Haven: Yale University Press.
Charlton, Thomas H.
   1978   Teotihuacán, Tepeapulco, and Obsidian Exploitation. *Science* 200:1227–36.
Charnay, Désiré
   1888   *The Ancient Cities of the New World*. New York: Harper and Brothers.
Charpin, Dominique
   1977   L'onomastique hurrite à Dilbat et ses implications historiques. In *Problèmes concernant les Hurrites*, ed. M. T. Barrelet, pp. 51–70. Paris: Centre Nationale de la Recherche Scientifique.
   1978   Recherches sur la "dynastie de Manana." *Revue d'assyriologie* 72:13–40.
Chase, Arlen F., and Prudence M. Rice (eds.)
   1985   *The Lowland Maya Postclassic*. Austin: University of Texas Press.
Chase, Diane Z., and Arlen F. Chase
   1982   Yucatec Influence in Terminal Classic Northern Belize. *American Antiquity* 47:596–614.
Cheek, Charles D.
   1976   Teotihuacán Influence at Kaminaljuyu. In *Las fronteras de Mesoamérica: XIV Mesa Redonda* 2:55–71. Mexico City: Sociedad Mexicana de Antropología.
   1977a   Teotihuacán Influence at Kaminaljuyu. In *Teotihuacán and Kaminaljuyu*, ed. William T. Sanders and Joseph W. Michels. pp. 441–52. University Park: Pennsylvania State University Press.
   1977b   Excavations at the Palangana and the Acropolis, Kaminaljuyu. In *Teotihuacán and Kaminaljuyu*, ed. William T. Sanders and Joseph W. Michels, pp. 1–204. University Park: Pennsylvania State University Press.
Childe, V. G.
   1941   *Man Makes Himself*. London: Watts.
   1950   The Urban Revolution. *Town Planning Review* 21:3–17.
Chin, Fa-ken
   1963   Tung-Han Tang-ku jen-wu ti fen-hsi. *Bulletin of the Institute of History and Philosophy* 34(B):505–58.
Chu, T. C.
   1972   *Han Social Structure*. Seattle: University of Washington Press.
Cipolla, Carlo
   1970   *The Economic Decline of Empires*. London: Methuen.
Civil, Miguel
   1980   Les limites de l'information textuelle. In *L'archéologie de l'Iraq*, ed. M. T. Barrelet, pp. 225–323. Paris: Centre Nationale de la Recherche Scientifique.

Clark, Colin, and Margaret Haswell
1964   *The Economics of Subsistence.* London: Macmillan.
Clark, John E.
1986   From Mountains to Molehills: A Critical Review of Teotihuacan's Obsidian Industry. In *Economic Aspects of Prehispanic Highland Mexico*, ed. Barry L. Isaac, pp. 23–74. Research in Economic Anthropology, Supplement 2, 1986. JAI Press, Greenwich, Conn.
Cobean, Robert H.
1978   The Pre-Aztec Ceramics of Tula, Hidalgo, Mexico. Ph.D. dissertation, Harvard University.
Cobean, Robert H., Alba Guadalupe Mastache, Ana María Crespo, and Clara L. Díaz
1981   La cronología de la región de Tula. In *Interacción cultural en México central*, comp. Evelyn C. Rattray, Jaime Litvak King, and Clara Díaz, O., pp. 187–214. Mexico City: Universidad Nacional Autónoma de México.
Coe, Michael D.
1965   Archaeological Synthesis of Southern Veracruz and Tabasco. In *Handbook of Middle American Indians*, vol. 3, ed. Robert Wauchope and Gordon R. Willey, pp. 679–715. Austin: University of Texas Press.
1968   San Lorenzo and the Olmec Civilization. In *Dumbarton Oaks Conference on the Olmec*, ed. Elizabeth P. Benson, pp. 41–77. Washington, D.C.: Dumbarton Oaks.
1980   *The Maya*, rev. ed. London: Thames and Hudson.
1981   Religion and the Rise of Mesoamerican States. In *The Transition to Statehood in the New World*, ed. Grant D. Jones and Robert R. Kautz, pp. 157–71. Cambridge: Cambridge University Press.
Coe, Michael D., and Richard A. Diehl
1980   *In the Land of the Olmec*, 2 vols. Austin: University of Texas Press.
Coe, William R.
1965   Tikal: Ten Years of Study of a Maya Ruin in the Lowlands of Guatemala. *Expedition* 8(1):5–56.
Coedes, G.
1968   *The Indianized States of Southeast Asia.* Honolulu: University Press of Hawaii.
Coggins, Clemency
1975   Painting and Drawing Styles at Tikal: An Historical and Iconographic Reconstruction. Ph.D. dissertation, Harvard University.
1979   Teotihuacán at Tikal in the Early Classic Period. In *Actes du 42e Congrès International des Américanistes* 8:251–69. Paris.
Conrad, Geoffrey W., and Arthur A. Demarest
1984   *Religion and Empire: The Dynamics of Aztec and Inca Expansionism.* Cambridge: Cambridge University Press.
Cook de Leonard, Carmen
1956   Dos atlatl de la época teotihuacana. In *Estudios antropológicos publicados en homenaje al Doctor Manuel Gamio*, pp. 183–200.

Mexico City: Universidad Nacional Autónoma de México and Sociedad Mexicana de Antropología.

Cooper, Jerrold
1983   *The Curse of Agade*. Baltimore: Johns Hopkins University Press.

Corona Nuñez, José
1972   Los teotihuacanos en el occidente de México. In *Teotihuacán: XI Mesa Redonda* 2:253–56. Mexico City: Sociedad Mexicana de Antropología.

Cowgill, George L.
1964   The End of Classic Maya Culture: A Review of Recent Evidence. *Southwestern Journal of Anthropology* 20:145–59.
1975   On Causes and Consequences of Ancient and Modern Population Changes. *American Anthropologist* 77:505–25.
1979a   Processes of Growth and Decline at Teotihuacán: The City and the State. In *Los procesos de cambio, XV Mesa Redonda* 1:183–93. Mexico City: Sociedad Mexicana de Antropología.
1979b   Teotihuacán, Internal Militaristic Competition, and the Fall of the Classic Maya. In *Maya Archaeology and Ethnohistory*, ed. Norman Hammond and Gordon R. Willey, pp. 51–62. Austin: University of Texas Press.
1979c   Politico-Economic Factors in the Disintegration of Early States. Paper prepared for the 44th Annual Meeting of the Society for American Archaeology, Vancouver, British Columbia.
1983a   Guide to Random Access Version of DF8. Manuscript, Brandeis University.
1983b   Rulership and the Ciudadela: Political Inferences from Teotihuacán Architecture. In *Civilization in the Ancient Americas: Essays in Honor of Gordon R. Willey*, ed. Richard M. Leventhal and Alan L. Kolata, pp. 313–43. Albuquerque: University of New Mexico Press, and Peabody Museum of Archaeology and Ethnology, Harvard University.

Cowgill, Ursula M.
1962   An Agricultural Study of the Southern Maya Lowlands. *American Anthropologist* 64:273–86.

Craddock, Patricia B.
1972   *The English Essays of Edward Gibbon*. Oxford: Clarendon Press.

Crespo, Ana María, and Alba Guadalupe Mastache de Escobar
1981   La presencia en el área de Tula, Hidalgo, de grupos relacionados con el barrio de Oaxaca en Teotihuacán. In *Interacción cultural en México central*, comp. Evelyn C. Rattray, Jaime Litvak King, and Clara Díaz O., pp. 99–106. Mexico City: Universidad Nacional Autónoma de México.

Culbert, T. Patrick
1973   The Downfall at Tikal. In *The Classic Maya Collapse*, ed. T. P. Culbert, pp. 63–92. Albuquerque: University of New Mexico Press.
1974   *The Lost Civilization: The Story of the Classic Maya*. New York: Harper and Row.
1977   Maya Development and Collapse: An Economic Perspective. In *So-*

cial Process in Maya Prehistory, ed. N. Hammond, pp. 510–30. New York: Academic Press.

Culbert, T. Patrick (ed.)
1973   *The Classic Maya Collapse*. Albuquerque: University of New Mexico Press.

Culbert, T. Patrick, Laura J. Kosakowsky, Robert E. Fry, and William A. Haviland
n.d.   The Demography of Tikal, Guatemala. In preparation for *Lowland Maya Demography*, ed. T. Patrick Culbert and Don S. Rice.

Culbert, T. Patrick, Mara L. Spencer, and Pamela C. Magers
1976   Slash-and-Burn Agriculture in the Maya Lowlands. *Actes du 42e Congrès des Américanistes* 8:335–44 (Paris).

Davies, Nigel
1983   *The Ancient Kingdoms of Mexico*. New York: Penguin Books.

de Crespigny, Rafe
1970   *The Last of the Han*. Canberra: Australian National University Press.

Deevey, Edward S., D. S. Rice, P. M. Rice, H. H. Vaughan, M. Brenner, and M. S. Flannery
1979   Maya Urbanism: Impact on a Tropical Karst Environment. *Science* 206:298–306.

Denevan, William M.
1982   Hydraulic Agriculture in the American Tropics: Forms, Measures, and Recent Research. In *Maya Subsistence: Studies in Memory of Dennis E. Puleston*, ed. K. V. Flannery, pp. 181–203. New York: Academic Press.

de Ste Croix, G. E. M.
1981   *The Class Struggle in the Ancient Greek World*. London: Duckworth.

Diakonoff, Igor M.
1969   The Rise of the Despotic State in Ancient Mesopotamia. In *Ancient Mesopotamia*, ed. I. M. Diakonoff, pp. 173–203. Moscow: Nauka Publishing House.

Díaz Oyarzábal, Clara Luz
1980   *Chingú: Un sitio clásico del área de Tula, Hidalgo*. Mexico City: Instituto Nacional de Antropología e Historia.

1981   Chingú y la expansión teotihuacana. In *Interacción cultural en México central*, comp. Evelyn C. Rattray, Jaime Litvak King, and Clara Díaz O., pp. 107–12. Mexico City: Universidad Nacional Autónoma de México.

Diehl, Richard A.
1981   Tula. In *Supplement to the Handbook of Middle American Indians*, vol. 1, *Archaeology*, ed. Victoria R. Bricker and Jeremy A. Sabloff, pp. 277–95. Austin: University of Texas Press.

Doeppers, Daniel Frederick
1968   Hispanic Influences on Demographic Patterns in the Central Plains of Luzon, 1565–1780. *Journal of East Asiatic Studies* 12 (September): 13–96 (University of Manila).

Donbaz, Veysel, and Norman Yoffee
1986   *Old Babylonian Texts from Kish Conserved in the Istanbul Ar-chaeological Museums*. Malibu: Undena.
Doran, James
1970   Systems Theory, Computer Simulations and Archaeology. *World Archaeology* 1:289–98.
Dosch, Gudrun, and Karlheinz Deller
1981   Die Familie Kizzuk—Sieben Kassitengenerationen im Temtena und Šuriniwe. In *Studies in the Civilization and Culture of Nuzi and the Hurrians*, ed. Martha Morrison and David Owen, pp. 91–113. Winona Lake, Indiana: Eisenbrauns.
Doty, Lawrence T.
1977   *Cuneiform Archives from Hellenistic Uruk*. Ph.D. dissertation, Yale University.
Drennan, Robert D.
1984   Long-Distance Movement of Goods in the Mesoamerican Formative and Classic. *American Antiquity* 49(1):27–43.
Drennan, Robert D., and Judith A. Nowak
1979   El posible papel de Teotihuacán en el desarrollo clásico del Valle de Tehuacán. In *Los procesos de cambio, XV Mesa Redonda* 2:351–58. Mexico City: Sociedad Mexicana de Antropología.
Dumond, Don E., and Florencia Müller
1972   Classic to Postclassic in Highland Central Mexico. *Science* 175:1208–15.
Dunnell, Robert
1980   Evolutionary Theory and Archaeology. *Advances in Archaeological Method and Theory* 3:35–99.
Eisenstadt, Shmuel N.
1967   *The Decline of Empires*. Englewood Cliffs, N.J.: Prentice-Hall.
1969   *The Political Systems of Empires: The Rise and Fall of the Historical Bureaucratic Societies*. Reprint, with a new introduction, of 1963 edition. New York: Free Press.
Eisenstadt, Shmuel N. (ed.)
1986   *The Origins and Diversity of Axial Age Civilizations*. Albany: State University of New York Press.
Eph'al, Israel
1982   *The Ancient Arabs*. Jerusalem: Magnes Press.
Fairbank, John K., Edwin O. Reischauer, and Albert M. Craig
1973   *East Asia: Tradition and Transformation*. Boston: Houghton Mifflin.
Fales, Mario
1973   *Censimenti e catasti epoca neo-assira*. Rome: Studi economici e technologici, vol. 2.
Falkenstein, Adam
1957   *Die neusumerischen Gerichtsurkunden*. Munich: Bavarian Academy of Sciences.

1963   Zu den Inschriftfunden der Grabung in Uruk-Warka. *Baghdader Mitteilungen* 2:1–82.

1966   *Die Inschriften Gudeas von Lagaš. Einleitung.* Rome: Pontifical Biblical Institute.

Farber, Howard
1978   A Price and Wage Study for Northern Babylonia During the Old Babylonian Period. *Journal of the Economic and Social History of the Orient* 21:1–51.

Farber, Walter
1983   Die Vergöttlichung Narām-Sîns. *Orientalia N. S.* 52:67–72.

Finkelstein, Jacob J.
1961   Ammiṣaduqa's Edict and the Babylonian "Law Codes." *Journal of Cuneiform Studies* 15:91–104.

1966   Sex Offenses in Sumerian Laws. *Journal of the American Oriental Society* 86:355–72.

Finley, Moses I.
1969   *Aspects of Antiquity: Discoveries and Controversies.* New York: Viking Press.

Flannery, Kent V.
1972   The Cultural Evolution of Civilizations. *Annual Review of Ecology and Systematics* 3:399–426.

Flannery, Kent V., and Joyce Marcus (eds.)
1983   *The Cloud People: Divergent Evolution of the Zapotec and Mixtec Civilizations.* New York: Academic Press.

Foncerrada de Molina, Marta
1978   Reflexiones en torno a la pintura mural de Cacaxtla. *Comunicaciones* 15:103–30 (Puebla: Fundación Alemana para la Investigación Científica).

1980   Mural Painting in Cacaxtla and Teotihuacán Cosmopolitanism. *Third Palenque Round Table, 1978,* Part 2, ed. Merle Greene Robertson, pp. 183–98. Austin: University of Texas Press.

Ford, Anabel
1981   Conditions for the Evolution of Complex Societies: The Development of the Central Lowland Maya. Ph.D. dissertation, University of California, Santa Barbara.

Forrester, Jay Wright
1961   *Industrial Dynamics.* Cambridge, Mass.: MIT Press.

1969   *Urban Dynamics.* Cambridge, Mass.: MIT Press.

Foster, Benjamin
1982   *Umma in the Sargonic Period.* Hamden, Conn.: Memoirs of the Connecticut Academy of Sciences.

Franco, José Luis
1970a   Trabajos y excavaciones arqueológicos. In *Minería prehispánica en la Sierra de Querétaro,* pp. 23–26. Mexico City: Secretaría del Patrimonio Nacional.

1970b   Material recuperado. In *Minería prehispánica en la Sierra de*

Querétaro, pp. 27–44. Mexico City: Secretaría del Patrimonio Nacional.

Frankfort, Henri

1956   *The Birth of Civilization in the Near East.* New York: Doubleday.

Frankfort, Henri, Lloyd Seton, and Thorkild Jacobsen

1940   *The Gimil-Sin Temple and the Palace of the Rulers at Tell Asmar.* Chicago: Oriental Institute.

Frayne, Douglas

1981   The Historical Correlations of the Sumerian Royal Hymns (2400–1900). Ph.D. dissertation, Yale University.

Freidel, David A.

1985   Terminal Classic Lowland Maya: Successes, Failures, and Aftermaths. In *Late Lowland Maya Civilization: Classic to Postclassic,* ed. J. A. Sabloff and E. W. Andrews V, pp. 409–30. Albuquerque: University of New Mexico Press.

Freidel, David A., and Vernon Scarborough

1982   Subsistence, Trade, and Development of the Coastal Maya. In *Maya Subsistence: Studies in Memory of Dennis E. Puleston,* ed. K. V. Flannery, pp. 131–55. New York: Academic Press.

Friberg, Jöran

1978–   The Third Millennium Roots of Babylonian Mathematics. *Research*
1979   *Report,* Department of Mathematics, Chalmers University of Technology, University of Göteborg. Göteborg.

Fried, Morton H.

1960   On the Evolution of Social Stratification and the State. In *Culture in History: Essays in Honor of Paul Radin,* ed. S. Diamond, pp. 713–31. New York: Columbia University Press.

1967   *The Evolution of Political Society.* New York: Random House.

1975   *The Notion of Tribe.* Menlo Park: Cummings.

1978   The State, the Chicken, and the Egg: or, What Came First? In *Origins of the State: The Anthropology of Political Evolution,* ed. Ronald Cohen and Elman R. Service. Philadelphia: Institute for the Study of Human Issues.

Friedman, Jonathan, and Michael Rowlands

1977   Notes Toward an Epigenetic Model of the Evolution of Civilisation. In *The Evolution of Social Systems,* ed. Jonathan Friedman and Michael Rowlands, pp. 201–76. London: Duckworth.

Fry, Robert E.

1969   Ceramics and Settlement in the Periphery of Tikal, Guatemala. Ph.D. dissertation, University of Arizona.

Gadd, Cyril J.

1965   Assyria and Babylonia, c. 1370–1300 B.C. *Cambridge Ancient History,* vol. 2, pt. 2, ch. 18. Cambridge: Cambridge University Press.

Gale, E. M.

1931   *Discourses on Salt and Iron.* Leiden: Brill.

Gamio, Manuel
   1922   *La población del Valle de Teotihuacán,* 3 vols. Mexico City: Secretaría de Agricultura y Fomento.
García Cook, Angel
   1981   The Historical Importance of Tlaxcala in the Cultural Development of the Central Highlands. In *Supplement to the Handbook of Middle American Indians,* vol. 1, *Archaeology,* ed. Victoria R. Bricker and Jeremy A. Sabloff, pp. 244–76. Austin: University of Texas Press.
García Cook, Angel, and Elia del Carmen Trejo
   1977   Lo teotihuacano en Tlaxcala. *Comunicaciones* 14:57–70 (Puebla: Fundación Alemana para la Investigación Científica).
García Payón, José
   1971   Archaeology of Central Veracruz. In *Handbook of Middle American Indians,* vol. 11, ed. Robert Wauchope, Gordon F. Ekholm, and Ignacio Bernal, pp. 505–42. Austin: University of Texas Press.
Garelli, Paul
   1958   Nabonide. *Supplément au dictionaire de la Bible,* vol. 6, columns 269–86.
   1963   *Les assyriens en cappadoce.* Paris: Librairie Adrien Maisonneuve.
   1969   *Le proche-orient asiatique.* Paris: Presses Universitaires de France.
   1974   Remarques sur l'administration de l'empire assyrienne. *Revue d'assyriologie* 68:129–48.
Garelli, Paul, and Valentin Nikiprowetzky
   1974   *Le proche-orient asiatique,* vol. 2. Paris: Presses Universitaires de France.
Geertz, Clifford
   1963   *Agricultural Involution: The Process of Ecological Change in Indonesia.* Berkeley: University of California Press.
Gelb, Ignace J.
   1969   On the Alleged Temple and State Economies in Ancient Mesopotamia. *Studi in onore di Edouardo Volterra* 6:132–56 (Milan).
   1977   Thoughts about Ibla: A Preliminary Evaluation, March 1977. *Syro-Mesopotamian Studies* 1(1):3–30.
   1980   *Computer-aided Analysis of Amorite.* Chicago: Oriental Institute.
   1981   Ebla and the Kish Civilization. In *La Lingua de Ebla,* ed. Luigi Cagni, pp. 10–65. Naples: Istituto Universitario Orientale.
Geyl, Pieter
   1958   *Debates with Historians.* Cleveland: World Publishing.
Glassner, Jean-Jacques
   1979   *La chute de l'empire d'Akkade.* Thesis, Ecole Pratique des Hautes Etudes, Paris.
Gliessman, Stephen R., B. L. Turner II, F. J. Rosado May, and M. F. Amador
   1983   Ancient Raised Field Agriculture in the Maya Lowlands of Southeastern Mexico. In *Drained Field Agriculture in Central and South America,* ed. J. P. Darch, pp. 91–110. BAR International Series No. 189. Oxford: British Archaeological Reports.

Godelier, M.
1978   The Concept of the Asiatic Mode of Production and Marxist Models of Social Evolution. In *Relations of Production: Marxist Approaches to Economic Anthropology*, ed. D. Seddon, pp. 209–57. London: Frank Cass.

Gómez-Pompa, Arturo, Epifanio Jiménez, A. Orozco, and Julio Jiménez
1976   *La chinampa tropical, estudio ecologico de la región de Balancan-Tenosique*. Xalapa, Veracruz: Informes del Instituto de Investigaciones sobre Recursos Bióticos.

Gómez-Pompa, Arturo, Hector Luis Morales, Epifanio Jiménez Avila, and Julio Jiménez Avila
1982   Experiences in Traditional Hydraulic Agriculture. In *Maya Subsistence: Studies in Memory of Dennis E. Puleston*, ed. K. V. Flannery, pp. 327–42. New York: Academic Press.

González Miranda, Luis Alfonso, and David Fuentes González
1982   Informe de labores realizados por la sección de antropología física en el proyecto arqueológico Teotihuacán. In *Memoria del proyecto arqueológico Teotihuacán 80–82*, vol. 1, ed. Rubén Cabrera C., Ignacio Rodríguez G., and Noel Morelos G., pp. 421–49. Mexico City: Instituto Nacional de Antropología e Historia.

Goodchild, R. G.
1976   *Libyan Studies*, ed. Joyce Reynolds. London: Paul Elek.

Goodland, R. J. A., and H. S. Irwin
1975   *Amazon Jungle: Green Hell to Red Desert? Developments in Landscape Management and Urban Planning*, vol. 1. New York: Elsevier Scientific Publishing.

Gordon, E. I.
1959   *Sumerian Proverbs: Glimpses of Everyday Life in Ancient Mesopotamia*. Philadelphia: Museum Monographs.

Goubert, Pierre
1966   *Louis XIV and Twenty Million Frenchmen*. New York: Vintage Books.

Graham, John A.
1973   Aspects of Non-Classic Presences in the Inscriptions and Sculptural Art of Seibal. In *The Classic Maya Collapse*, ed. T. P. Culbert, pp. 207–19. Albuquerque: University of New Mexico Press.

Grayson, A. Kirk
1971   The Early Development of the Assyrian Monarchy. *Ugarit Forschungen* 3:311–19.

1975   *Assyrian and Babylonian Chronicles*. Locust Valley, N.Y.: J. J. Austin.

Grayson, A. Kirk, and Edmond Sollberger
1976   L'insurrection générale contre Naramsuen. *Revue d'assyriologie* 70:103–28.

Green, Margaret W.
1981   The Construction and Implementation of the Cuneiform Writing System. *Visible Language* 15:345–72.

Greene, Merle, Robert L. Rands, and John A. Graham
1972   *Maya Sculpture from the Southern Lowlands, the Highlands, and Pacific Piedmont, Guatemala, Mexico, Honduras.* Berkeley: Lederer, Street and Zeus.
Greene, Virginia, and Hattula Moholy-Nagy
1966   A Teotihuacán-Style Vessel from Tikal: A Correction. *American Antiquity* 31:432–34.
Greengus, Samuel
1979   *Old Babylonian Tablets from Ishchali and Vicinity.* Istanbul: Nederlands Historisch-Archaeologisch Instituut.
Grégoire, Jean-Pierre
1980   L'origine et le développement de la civilisation mésopotamienne du troisième millénaire avant notre ère. In *Production, pouvoir et parenté dans le monde mediterranéen,* pp. 27–101. Paris: Centre Nationale de la Recherche Scientifique.
Grove, David C.
1981   Olmec Monuments: Mutilation as a Clue to Meaning. In *The Olmec and Their Neighbors: Essays in Honor of Matthew W. Stirling,* ed. Elizabeth Benson, pp. 49–68. Washington, D.C.: Dumbarton Oaks.
Gunderson, Gerald
1976   Economic Change and the Demise of the Roman Empire. *Explorations in Economic History* 13:43–68.
Güterbock, Hans
1934   Die historische Tradition und ihre literarische Gestaltung bei Babyloniern und Hethitern bis 1200. *Zeitschrift für Assyriologie* 42:1–91.
Haas, Jonathan
1982   *The Evolution of the Prehistoric State.* New York: Columbia University Press.
Hall, D. G. E.
1968   *A History of Southeast Asia.* London: Macmillan.
Hall [Millon], Clara
1962   A Chronological Study of the Mural Art of Teotihuacán. Ph.D. dissertation, University of California, Berkeley.
Hallo, William W.
1957   *Early Mesopotamian Royal Titles.* New Haven: American Oriental Society.
1960   A Sumerian Amphictyony. *Journal of Cuneiform Studies* 14:88–114.
1962   The Royal Inscriptions of Ur: A Typology. *Hebrew Union College Annual* 33:1–43.
1963a   Beginning and Ending of the Sumerian King List in the Nippur Recension. *Journal of Cuneiform Studies* 17:52–57.
1963b   Royal Hymns and Mesopotamian Unity. *Journal of Cuneiform Studies* 17:113–18.
1971a   *The Ancient Near East: A History.* New York: Harcourt Brace Jovanovich.

1971b   Gutium. *Reallexikon der Assyriologie* 3:707–20.
Hallo, William W., and J. J. van Dijk
1968   *The Exaltation of Inanna.* New Haven: Yale University Press.
Hamblin, Robert L., and Brian L. Pitcher
1980   The Classic Maya Collapse: Testing the Class Conflict Hypothesis. *American Antiquity* 45:246–67.
Hammond, Norman
1977   The Earliest Maya. *Scientific American* 236:116–33.
1982   The Exploration of the Maya World. *American Scientist* 70:482–95.
Harbottle, G., and E. V. Sayre
1979   Neutron Activation Analyses: Teotihuacán Trade Ceramics. In *Los procesos de cambio, XV Mesa Redonda* 2:313–16. Mexico City: Sociedad Mexicana de Antropología.
Harner, M.
1970   Population pressure and the Social Evolution of Agriculturalists. *Southwestern Journal of Anthropology* 26:67–86.
Harris, Marvin
1979   *Cultural Materialism: The Struggle for a Science of Culture.* New York: Random House.
Harris, Rivkah
1960   Old Babylonian Temple Loans. *Journal of Cuneiform Studies* 14:126–32.
1961   On the Process of Secularization under Hammurabi. *Journal of Cuneiform Studies* 15:117–20.
Harrison, Peter D.
1978   Bajos Revisited: Visual Evidence for One System of Agriculture. In *Pre-Hispanic Maya Agriculture*, ed. P. D. Harrison and B. L. Turner II, pp. 247–53. Albuquerque: University of New Mexico Press.
Harrison, Peter D., and B. L. Turner II (eds.)
1978   *Pre-Hispanic Maya Agriculture.* Albuquerque: University of New Mexico Press.
Haviland, William A.
1970   Tikal, Guatemala, and Mesoamerican Urbanism. *World Archaeology* 2:186–97.
Hellmuth, Nicholas
1975   *The Escuintla Hoards: Teotihuacán Art in Guatemala.* Guatemala: Foundation for Latin American Anthropological Research, Progress Reports 1(2).
1978   Teotihuacán Art in the Escuintla, Guatemala, Region. In *Middle Classic Mesoamerica: A.D. 400–700*, ed. Esther Pasztory, pp. 71–85. New York: Columbia University Press.
Hester, Thomas R., Harry J. Shafer, and Jack D. Eaton
1982   *Archaeology at Colha, Belize: The 1981 Interim Report.* San Antonio: Center for Archaeological Research, University of Texas at San Antonio, and Venice: Centro Studi e Richerche Ligabue.

Heyden, Doris
  1975   An Interpretation of the Cave Underneath the Pyramid of the Sun
          in Teotihuacán, Mexico. *American Antiquity* 40:131–47.
Hindness, B., and P. Q. Hirst
  1975   *Pre-capitalist Modes of Production*. London: Routledge and Kegan
          Paul.
Hirth, Kenneth G.
  1974   Precolumbian Population Development along the Río Amatzinac:
          The Formative through Classic Periods in Eastern Morelos, Mexico.
          Ph.D. dissertation, University of Wisconsin, Milwaukee.
  1976   Teotihuacán Influence in the Eastern Valley of Morelos, Mexico.
          Las fronteras de Mesoamérica, XIV Mesa Redonda 2:33–43. Mex-
          ico City: Sociedad Mexicana de Antropología.
  1978   Teotihuacán Regional Population Administration in Eastern Mo-
          relos. *World Archaeology* 9:320–33.
Hirth, Kenneth G., and William Swezey
  1976   The Changing Nature of the Teotihuacán Classic: A Regional Per-
          spective from Manzanilla, Puebla. *Las fronteras de Mesoamérica,
          XIV Mesa Redonda* 2:11–23. Mexico City: Sociedad Mexicana de
          Antropología.
Ho, Ch'ang-chun
  1956   *Liang-Han tu-ti chan-yu hsin-pt'ai-ti fa-chan*. Shanghai: Jen-min.
Hodder, Ian (ed.)
  1982   *Symbolic and Structural Archaeology*. Cambridge: Cambridge Uni-
          versity Press.
Hodges, Richard, and David Whitehouse
  1983   *Mohammed, Charlemagne and the Origins of Europe: Archaeology
          and the Pirenne Thesis*. Ithaca: Cornell University Press.
Hoffman, Michael A.
  1976   The City of the Hawk: Seat of Egypt's Ancient Civilization. *Expe-
          dition* 18(3):32–41.
  1983   Where Nations Began. *Science 83* 4(8):42–51.
Hosler, Dorothy, Jeremy A. Sabloff, and Dale Runge
  1977   Simulation Model Development: A Case Study of the Classic Maya
          Collapse. In *Social Process in Maya Prehistory*, ed. N. Hammond,
          pp. 553–90. London: Academic Press.
Hsu, Cho-yun
  1965a   *Ancient China in Transition*. Stanford: Stanford University Press.
  1965b   The Changing Relationship Between Local Society and the Central
          Political Power in Former Han. *Comparative Studies in Society and
          History* 7:358–70.
  1980   *Han Agriculture*. Seattle: University of Washington Press.
Hsu, Fu-Kuan
  1972   *Chou-Ch'in-Han cheng-chih she-hui chieh-kou-chih-yen-chiu*. Hong
          Kong: New Asia Institute.
  1975   *Li'ang-Han Shih-hsiang-shih*. Hong Kong: New Asia Institute.

Ikeda, Yuichi
  1976   Chogoku Kodaini Okeru. *Chugoku Kodaishi Kenkyu* 4. Tokyo: Yuzan Kaku.

Jacobsen, Thorkild
  1939a   *The Sumerian King List.* Chicago: University of Chicago Press.
  1939b   The Assumed Conflict Between the Sumerians and the Semites in Early Mesopotamian History. *Journal of the American Oriental Society* 59:485–95.
  1953   The Reign of Ibbi-Sin. *Journal of Cuneiform Studies* 7:36–47.
  1957   Early Political Development in Mesopotamia. *Zeitschrift für Assyriologie* 52:91–140.
  1978–   Iphur-kishi and His Times. *Archiv für Orientforschung* 26:1–14.
  1979

Jacobsen, Thorkild, and Robert McC. Adams
  1958   Salt and Silt in Ancient Mesopotamian Agriculture. *Science* 128:1251–58.

Janzen, Daniel H.
  1970   The Unexploited Tropics. *Bulletin of the Ecological Society of America* 51:4–7.

Jarquín P., Ana María, and Enrique Martínez V.
  1982a   Las excavaciones en el Conjunto 1D. In *Memoria del proyecto arqueológico Teotihuacán 80–82*, vol. 1, coord. Rubén Cabrera C., Ignacio Rodríguez G., and Noel Morelos G., pp. 89–126. Mexico City: Instituto Nacional de Antropología e Historia.
  1982b   Una escultura tardía teotihuacana. In *Teotihuacán 80–82: Primeros resultados*, ed. Rubén Cabrera C., Ignacio Rodríguez G., and Noel Morelos G., pp. 121–27. Mexico City: Instituto Nacional de Antropología e Historia.
  1982c   Exploración en el lado este de la Ciudadela (Estructuras: 1G, 1R, 1Q, y 1P). In *Memoria del proyecto arqueológico Teotihuacán 80–82*, vol. 1, coord. Rubén Cabrera C., Ignacio Rodríguez G., and Noel Morelos G., pp. 19–47. Mexico City: Instituto Nacional de Antropología e Historia.

Jefferson, Mark
  1939   The Law of the Primate City. *Geographical Review* 29(2):226–32.

Johnson, Gregory A.
  1975   Locational Analysis and the Investigation of Uruk Local Exchange Systems. In *Ancient Civilization and Trade*, ed. J. A. Sabloff and C. C. Lamberg-Karlovsky, pp. 285–339. Albuquerque: University of New Mexico Press.
  1980   Rank-Size Convexity and System Integration: A View from Archaeology. *Economic Geography* 36:234–47.

Jones, A. H. M.
  1964   *The Later Roman Empire, 284–602*, 3 vols. with a volume of maps. Oxford: Basil Blackwell.
  1967   Comparison of the Processes of Decline in the Eastern and Western

Parts of the Roman Empire. (Originally published in 1955.) In *The Decline of Empires*, ed. S. N. Eisenstadt, pp. 159–64. Englewood Cliffs: Prentice-Hall.

Jones, Christopher
1979   Tikal as a Trading Center: Why it Rose and Fell. Paper presented at the XLIII International Congress of Americanists, Vancouver, B.C., Canada.

Jones, Christopher, and Linton Satterthwaite
1982   *The Monuments and Inscriptions of Tikal: The Carved Monuments.* Tikal Report 33, Part A. University Museum Monograph 44. Philadelphia: University of Pennsylvania.

Jones, Tom B.
1976   Sumerian Administrative Documents. In *Sumerological Studies in Honor of Thorkild Jacobsen on his Seventieth Birthday*, ed. Stephen Lieberman, pp. 41–62. Chicago: University of Chicago Press.

Kamada, Shigeo
1962   *Sinkan seiji seido no Kenkyu.* Toyko: Nihongakujutsu shinko-kai.

Kamp, Kathryn, and Norman Yoffee
1980   Ethnicity in Ancient Western Asia During the Early Second Millennium B.C. *Bulletin of the American Schools of Oriental Research* 237:85–103.

Kelley, J. Charles
1976   Alta Vista: Outpost of Mesoamerican Empire on the Tropic of Cancer. *Las fronteras de Mesoamérica, XIV Mesa Redonda* 2:21–40. Mexico City: Sociedad Mexicana de Antropología.
1980   Alta Vista, Chalchihuites: "Port of Entry" on the Northwestern Frontier of Mesoamerica. In *Rutas de intercambio en Mesoamérica y el norte de México, XVI Mesa Redonda* 1:53–64. Saltillo: Sociedad Mexicana de Antropología.
1985   The Chronology of the Chalchihuites Culture. In *The Archaeology of West and Northwest Mesoamerica*, ed. Michael S. Foster and Phil C. Weigand, pp. 269–87. Westview Press, Boulder, Colo.

Kidder, Alfred V., Jesse Jennings, and Edwin M. Shook
1946   *Excavations at Kaminaljuyu, Guatemala.* Washington, D.C.: Carnegie Institution of Washington, Publ. 561.

Kiefer, Thomas M.
1972   The Tausug Polity and the Sultanate of Sulu: A Segmentary State in the Philippines. *Sulu Studies* 1:19–64 (Jolo, Philippines).

Klengel, Horst
1982   "Fremde" im Herrschaftsbereich des Samsuditana von Babylon. In *Schriften zur Geschichte und Kultur des Alten Orients*, vol. 15, ed. Horst Klengel, pp. 143–48. Berlin: Akademie-Verlag.

Klotchkoff, Igor S.
1982   The Late Babylonian List of Scholars. In *Schriften zur Geschichte und Kultur des Alten Orients*, vol. 15, ed. Horst Klengel, pp. 149–54. Berlin: Akademie-Verlag.

Kohl, Philip
  1979   The "World Economy" of West Asia in the Third Millennium B.C. *South Asian Archaeology 1977*:55–85.

Kohl, Philip L., and Rita P. Wright
  1977   Stateless Cities: The Differentiation of Societies in the Near Eastern Neolithic. *Dialectical Anthropology* 2:271–83.

Kramer, Samuel N.
  1940   *Lamentation Over the Destruction of Ur*. Assyriological Studies 12. Chicago: University of Chicago Press.
  1964   *The Sumerians*. Chicago: University of Chicago Press.
  1969   *The Sacred Marriage Rite*. Bloomington: University of Indiana Press.

Kraus, Fritz R.
  1970   *Sumerer und Akkader*. Amsterdam: North Holland.

Krecher, Joachim
  1980   Klagelied. *Reallexikon der Assyriologie* 6:1–6.

Krotser, Paula H.
  1981   Veracruz: Corredor hacia el sureste. In *Interacción cultural en México central*, comp. Evelyn C. Rattray, Jaime Litvak King, and Clara Díaz O., pp. 175–85. Mexico City: Universidad Nacional Autónoma de México.

Kubler, George
  1967   *The Iconography of the Art of Teotihuacán*. Studies in Pre-Columbian Art and Archaeology No. 4. Washington, D.C.: Dumbarton Oaks.
  1980   Eclecticism at Cacaxtla. *Third Palenque Round Table 1978*, Part 2, ed. Merle Greene Robertson, pp. 163–72. Austin: University of Texas Press.

Kuhn, Thomas S.
  1970   *The Structure of Scientific Revolutions*, 2nd ed. Chicago: University of Chicago Press.

Kurjack, Edward B.
  1974   *Prehistoric Lowland Maya Community and Social Organization*. Middle American Research Institute, Publication 38. New Orleans: Tulane University Press.

Lambert, J. D. H., and J. T. Arnason
  1982   Ramón and Maya Ruins: An Ecological, Not an Economic, Reality. *Science* 216:298–99.

Lambert, Wilfred G.
  1967   *Babylonian Wisdom Literature*. Oxford: Clarendon Press.

Langley, James C.
  1983   Teotihuacán: Illiterate Metropolis? *Country Life*, July 28, pp. 238–39.
  1986   *Symbolic Notation of Teotihuacán*. BAR International Series 313. Oxford: British Archaeological Reports.

Lao, Kan
  1935   Liang Han chung-kuo mien-chi chih ku-chi ch'i kou-shu tseng-chien

chih-tui-tse. *Bulletin of the Institute of History and Philology* 5:215–40.

1948   Lun Han-tai-ti nei-chao yu wai-ch'ao. *Bulletin of the Institute of History and Philology* 13:227–67.

LaPorte, Juan Pedro

1985   El "Talud-Tablero" en Tikal, Petén: Nuevos Datos. Paper presented at symposium on the life and work of Román Piña Chan, Instituto de Investigaciones Antropológicas y Centro de Estudios Mayas, Universidad Nacional Autónoma de México (UNAM), Mexico City, July 1985.

Larsen, Mogens T.

1974   The Old Assyrian Colonies in Anatolia. *Journal of the American Oriental Society* 94:468–75.

1976   *The Old Assyrian City-State and Its Colonies.* Copenhagen: Akademisk Forlag.

1977   Partnerships in the Old Assyrian Trade. In *Trade in the Ancient Near East,* ed. J. D. Hawkins, pp. 119–45. London: British School of Archaeology in Iraq.

Larsen, Mogens T. (ed.)

1978   *Power and Propaganda: A Symposium on Ancient Empires. Mesopotamia,* vol. 7. Copenhagen: Akademisk Forlag.

Levy, Howard

1956   Yellow Turban Religion and Rebellion at the End of Han. *Journal of the American Oriental Society* 76:214–17.

Lewis, Brian

1980   *The Sargon Legend.* Cambridge, Mass.: American Schools of Oriental Research.

Lewontin, Richard

1983   Darwin's Revolution. *New York Review of Books* 30(10), 16 June, pp. 21–27.

Lilley, S.

1973   Technological Progress and the Industrial Revolution, 1700–1914. In *The Fontana Economic History of Europe, 3. The Industrial Revolution,* ed. C. M. Cipolla, pp. 187–254. London: Collins/Fontana.

Linné, Sigvald

1942   *Mexican Highland Cultures: Archaeological Researches at Teotihuacán, Calpulalpan, and Chalchicomula in 1934–35.* Stockholm: Ethnographic Museum of Sweden, N.S., Pub. 7.

Lister, Robert H.

1971   Archaeological Synthesis of Guerrero. In *Handbook of Middle American Indians,* vol. 11, ed. Robert Wauchope, Gordon F. Ekholm, and Ignacio Bernal, pp. 619–31. Austin: University of Texas Press.

Litvak King, Jaime

1970   Xochicalco en la caída del clásico: Una hipótesis. *Anales de Antropología* 7:131–44 (Mexico City: Universidad Nacional Autónoma de México).

1978   Central Mexico as a Part of the General Mesoamerican Commu-
          nications System. In *Mesoamerican Communication Routes and Cul-
          tural Contacts*, ed. Thomas A. Lee, Jr., and Carlos Navarrete, pp.
          115–22. Provo, Utah: Papers of the New World Archaeological
          Foundation No. 40.

Lloyd, Seton
1978   *The Archaeology of Mesopotamia*. London: Thames and Hudson.

Lorenzo, José Luis
1968   Clima y agricultura en Teotihuacán. In *Materiales para la arqueo-
          logía de Teotihuacán*, ed. José Luis Lorenzo, Serie Investigaciones
          17:51–72 (Mexico City: Instituto Nacional de Antropología e His-
          toria).

Lounsbury, Floyd G.
1978   Maya Numeration, Computation, and Calendrical Astronomy. In
          Dictionary of Scientific Biography, vol. 15, supp. 1, Topical Essays,
          pp. 759–818. New York: Charles Scribner's Sons.

Lovejoy, Thomas E., and Eneas Salati
1983   Precipitating Change in Amazonia. In *The Dilemma of Amazonian
          Development*, ed. E. F. Moran, pp. 211–20. Boulder: Westview
          Press.

Lowe, John G. W.
1982   On Mathematical Models of the Classic Maya Collapse: The Class
          Conflict Hypothesis Re-examined. *American Antiquity* 47:643–52.

McClung de Tapia, Emily
1978   Aspectos ecológicos del desarrollo y la decadencia de Teotihuacán.
          Anales de Antropología 15:53–65 (Mexico City: Universidad Na-
          cional Autónoma de México).

McGuire, Randall
1983   Breaking Down Cultural Complexity: Inequality and Heterogeneity.
          Advances in Archaeological Method and Theory 6:91–117.

Machinist, Peter
1976   Literature as Politics: The Tukulti-Ninurta Epic and the Bible. *Cath-
          olic Biblical Quarterly* 38:455–82.

1982   Provincial Governance in Middle Assyria and Some New Texts from
          Yale. *Assur* 3:65–105.

1985   On Self-consciousness in Mesopotamia. In *The Origins and Diversity
          of Axial Age Civilizations*, ed. S. N. Eisenstadt, pp. 183–202. Al-
          bany: State University of New York Press.

MacKendrick, Paul
1971   *Roman France*. London: G. Bell.

Maekawa, Kazuya
1984   Cereal Cultivation in the Ur III Period. *Bulletin of Sumerian Agri-
          culture* 1:73–96.

Maidman, Maynard
1984   Kassites Among the Hurrians: A Case Study from Nuzi. *Bulletin of
          the Society for Mesopotamian Studies* 8:15–21.

Mallowan, Max
  1972   Cyrus the Great (558–529 B.C.). *Iran* 10:1–17.
Malmstrom, Vincent
  1978   A Reconstruction of the Chronology of Mesoamerican Calendrical
          Systems. *Journal of the History of Astronomy* 9(2)(25):105–16.
Mannheim, Karl
  1936   *Ideology and Utopia: An Introduction to the Sociology of Knowl-
          edge*, trans. Louis Wirth and Edward Shils. New York: Harcourt,
          Brace and World.
Marcus, Joyce
  1976   *Emblem and State in the Classic Maya Lowlands*. Washington, D.C.:
          Dumbarton Oaks.
  1980   Zapotec Writing. *Scientific American* 242:50–64.
  1983   Teotihuacán Visitors on Monte Albán Monuments and Murals. In
          The Cloud People, ed. Kent V. Flannery and Joyce Marcus, pp. 175–
          81. New York: Academic Press.
Marquina, Ignacio
  1964   *Arquitectura prehispánica*, 2nd ed. Memorias del Instituto Nacional
          de Antropología e Historia, No. 1. Mexico City: Instituto Nacional
          de Antropología e Historia.
  1970a   Pirámide de Cholula. In *Proyecto Cholula*, coord. Ignacio Marquina,
          pp. 31–45. Mexico City: Instituto Nacional de Antropología e His-
          toria, Investigaciones No. 19.
  1970b   *Proyecto Cholula*. Mexico City: Instituto Nacional de Antropología
          e Historia, Investigaciones No. 19.
Mastache de Escobar, Alba Guadalupe, and Ana María Crespo
  1974   La ocupación prehispánica en el área de Tula, Hgo. In *Proyecto
          Tula, 1a parte*, coord. Eduardo Matos Moctezuma, pp. 71–103.
          Mexico City: Instituto Nacional de Antropología e Historia.
Mathews, Peter
  1985   Maya Early Classic Monuments and Inscriptions. In *A Consideration
          of the Early Classic Period in the Maya Lowlands*, ed. Gordon R.
          Willey and Peter Mathews, pp. 5–54. Institute for Mesoamerican
          Studies, Publication No. 10, State University of New York at Albany.
Matos Moctezuma, Eduardo
  1980   Teotihuacán: Excavaciones en la calle de los muertos (1964). *Anales
          de Antropología* 17(1):69–90 (Mexico City: Universidad Nacional
          Autónoma de México).
Matos Moctezuma, Eduardo, María Teresa García G., Fernando López A., and
Ignacio Rodríguez G.
  1981   Proyecto Tepeapulco: Resumen preliminar de los actividades reali-
          zados en la primera temporada de trabajo. In *Interacción cultural
          en México central*, comp. Evelyn C. Rattray, Jaime Litvak King, and
          Clara Díaz O., pp. 113–48. Mexico City: Universidad Nacional
          Autónoma de México.

Mayr, Ernst
1974   Teleological and Teleonomic, a New Analysis. *Boston Studies in the Philosophy of Science* 14:91–117.
Meadows, Donella, Dennis L. Meadows, Jørgen Randers, and William W. Behrens III
1972   *Limits to Growth.* New York: Universe Books.
Medawar, Peter
1961   *The Art of the Soluble.* London: Pelican.
Mercado Rojano, Antonio
1987   ¿Una sacerdotisa en Teotihuacan? *México Desconocido,* no. 121, March 1987, pp. 6–9. Mexico City.
Mesarović, Mihajlo, and Eduard Pestel
1974   *Mankind at the Turning Point.* New York: Dutton.
Meyer, Karl E.
1973   *Teotihuacán.* New York: Newsweek.
Michałowski, Piotr
1976   *The Royal Correspondence of Ur.* Ph.D. dissertation, Yale University.
1980   New Sources Concerning the Reign of Naram-Sin. *Journal of Cuneiform Studies* 32:233–46.
1983   History as Charter: Some Observations on the Sumerian King List. *Journal of the American Oriental Society* 103:237–48.
n.d.   The Strange Career of King Nabonidus. Manuscript on file in Jerusalem, Assyriological Seminar.
Michelet, Dominique
1984   *Río Verde, San Luis Potosí (Mexique).* Mexico City: Centre d'Etudes Mexicaines et Centramericaines, Collection Etudes Mesoamericaines, vol. 9.
Michels, Joseph W.
1979   A History of Settlement at Kaminaljuyu. In *Settlement Pattern Excavations at Kaminaljuyu, Guatemala,* ed. Joseph W. Michels, pp. 277–306. University Park: Pennsylvania State University Press.
Miksicek, Charles S., K. J. Elsesser, I. A. Wuebber, K. O. Bruhns, and N. Hammond
1981   Rethinking Ramón: A Comment on Reina and Hill's Lowland Maya Subsistence. *American Antiquity* 49:916–19.
Millar, Fergus
1982   Rich and Poor in the Ancient World. *London Review of Books,* 17–30 June, pp. 17–18.
Miller, Arthur G.
1973   *The Mural Painting of Teotihuacán.* Washington, D.C.: Dumbarton Oaks.
Millon, Clara
1972   The History of Mural Art at Teotihuacán. In *Teotihuacán, XI Mesa Redonda* 2:1–16 (Mexico City: Sociedad Mexicana de Antropología).

1973   Painting, Writing, and Polity in Teotihuacán, Mexico. *American Antiquity* 38:294–314.

Millon, René
1967   Urna de Monte Albán 111A encontrada en Teotihuacán. *Boletín del Instituto Nacional de Antropología e Historia* 29:42–44 (Mexico City).
1970   Teotihuacán: Completion of Map of Giant Ancient City in the Valley of Mexico. *Science* 170:1077–82.
1973   *Urbanization at Teotihuacán, Mexico*, vol. 1, *The Teotihuacán Map*, part 1, *Text*. Austin: University of Texas Press.
1976   Social Relations in Ancient Teotihuacán. In *The Valley of Mexico: Studies in Pre-Hispanic Ecology and Society*, ed. Eric R. Wolf, pp. 205–48. Albuquerque: University of New Mexico Press.
1981   Teotihuacán: City, State, and Civilization. In *Supplement to the Handbook of Middle American Indians*, vol. 1, *Archaeology*, ed. Victoria R. Bricker and Jeremy A. Sabloff, pp. 198–243. Austin: University of Texas Press.
1983   Informe . . . de descubrimientos demostrando la procedencia en Teotihuacán de pinturas murales saqueadas. . . . Report to Instituto Nacional de Antropología e Historia (Mexico City).

Millon, René, R. Bruce Drewitt, and George L. Cowgill
1973   *Urbanization at Teotihuacán, Mexico*, vol. 1, *The Teotihuacán Map*, part 2, *Maps*. Austin: University of Texas Press.

Milner, A. C., E. E. McKinnon, and T. Luckman Sinar
1978   A Note on Aru and Kota Cina. *Indonesia* 26:1–42 (Ithaca, New York).

Moholy-Nagy, Hattula
1975   Obsidian at Tikal, Guatemala. In *Actas del XLI Congreso Internacional de Americanistas* 1:511–18 (Mexico City).
1987   Late Early Classic Problematical Deposits: A Preliminary Report on Teotihuacán-Style Burials at Tikal, Guatemala. Paper presented at 52d annual meeting of the Society for American Archaeology, Toronto, May 1987.

Moholy-Nagy, Hattula, Frank Asaro, and Fred H. Stross
1984   Tikal Obsidian: Sources and Typology. *American Antiquity* 49(1):104–17.

Molloy, B. J., and J. P. Molloy
n.d.   The Xolalpan-Monte Albán IIIA and Metepec-Monte Albán IIIB Periods in Mesoamerican History. Manuscript.

Momigliano, Arnaldo
1973   La caduta senza rumore di un impero nel 476 d.C. *Annali della Scuola Normale Superiore di Pisa* 3.3:397–418, reprinted in A. Momigliano, *Sesto contributo alla storia degli studi classici e del mondo antico* 1, 1980, pp. 159–79. Rome: Edizioni di Storia e Letteratura.
1976   Gibbon from an Italian Point of View. *Daedalus* 105:125–35.

Morley, Sylvanus G.
   1946   *The Ancient Maya*. Stanford: Stanford University Press.
Mountjoy, Joseph, and David Peterson
   1973   *Man and Land at Prehispanic Cholula*. Nashville: Vanderbilt University Publications in Anthropology 4.
Müller, Florencia
   1970   La Cerámica de Cholula. In *Proyecto Cholula*, coord. Ignacio Marquina, pp. 129–42. Mexico City: Instituto Nacional de Antropología e Historia, Investigaciones No. 19.
   1978   *La alfarería de Cholula*. Instituto Nacional de Antropología e Historia, serie Arqueología, SEP INAH, Mexico City.
   1979   ¿Que significado tiene la distribución de los elementos teotihuacanos en Guerrero? In *Los procesos de cambio, XV Mesa Redonda* 2:343–50. Mexico City: Sociedad Mexicana de Antropología.
Netting, Robert M.
   1972   Sacred Power and Centralization: Aspects of Political Adaptation in Africa. In *Population Growth: Anthropological Implications*, ed. B. Spooner, pp. 219–44. Cambridge, Mass.: MIT Press.
   1977   Maya Subsistence: Mythologies, Analogies, Possibilities. In *The Origins of Maya Civilization*, ed. R. E. W. Adams, pp. 299–333. Albuquerque: University of New Mexico Press.
Noguera, Eduardo
   1940   Excavations at Tehuacan. In *The Maya and Their Neighbors*, ed. Clarence L. Hay, Ralph L. Linton, Samuel K. Lothrop, Harry L. Shapiro, and George C. Vaillant, pp. 306–19. New York: D. Appleton Century.
   1956   Un edificio preclásico en Cholula. In *Estudios antropológicos publicados en homenaje al Doctor Manuel Gamio*, pp. 213–24. Mexico City: Universidad Nacional Autónoma de México and Sociedad Mexicana de Antropología.
Oates, Joan
   1979   *Babylon*. London: Thames and Hudson.
Oded, Bustenay
   1979   *Mass Deportations and Deportees in the Neo-Assyrian Empire*. Wiesbaden: Dr. Ludwig Reichert Verlag.
Odell, Rice
   1977   History Offers Warnings on the Environment. *Letter of the Conservation Foundation*, October (Washington, D.C.).
   1979   Can Technology Avert the Errors of the Past? *Letter of the Conservation Foundation*, November (Washington, D.C.).
   1980   *Environment Awaking*. Cambridge, Mass.: Balinger.
O'Donnell, James J.
   1979   *Cassiodorus*. Berkeley and Los Angeles: University of California Press.
Paradis, Louise
   1987   Teotihuacan and Precolumbian Guerrero. Paper presented at the

52nd annual meeting of the Society for American Archaeology in Toronto, May 1987.

Parkinson, C. Northcote
1957   *Parkinson's Law and Other Studies in Administration*. Boston: Houghton Mifflin.

Parsons, Lee A.
1978   The Peripheral Coastal Lowlands and the Middle Classic Period. In *Middle Classic Mesoamerica: A.D. 400–700*, ed. Esther Pasztory, pp. 25–34. New York: Columbia University Press.

Pasztory, Esther
1972   The Murals of Tepantitla, Teotihuacán. Ph.D. dissertation, Columbia University.
1973   The Gods of Teotihuacán: A Synthetic Approach in Teotihuacán Iconography. In *40th International Congress of Americanists, Rome-Genoa 1972*, vol. 1, pp. 147–59. Genoa.
1974   The Iconography of the Teotihuacán Tlaloc. *Studies in Pre-Columbian Art and Archaeology 15*. Washington, D.C.: Dumbarton Oaks.
1976a   *The Murals of Tepantitla, Teotihuacán*. New York: Garland.
1976b   The Xochicalco Stelae and a Middle Classic Deity Triad in Mesoamerica. *XXIII International Congress of the History of Art, Granada 1973* 1:185–215. Granada: Universidad de Granada.
1978   Artistic Traditions of the Middle Classic Period. In *Middle Classic Mesoamerica: A.D. 400–700*, ed. Esther Pasztory, pp. 108–42. New York: Columbia University Press.

Pelikan, Jaroslav
1982   The Two Cities: The Decline and Fall of Rome as Historical Paradigm. *Daedalus* 111:85–91.

Pendergast, David M.
1971   Evidence of Early Teotihuacán-Lowland Maya Contact at Altún Ha. *American Antiquity* 36:455–60.

Piña Chan, Román
1972   Teotenango prehispánico. *Boletín del Instituto Nacional de Antropología e Historia*, época 2, 2:17–20 (Mexico City).

Postgate, J. Nicholas
1974   Some Remarks on Conditions in the Assyrian Countryside. *Journal of the Economic and Social History of the Orient* 17:225–40.
1977   *The First Empires*. Oxford: Elsevier.

Powell, Marvin
1973   Review of E. Sollberger, *Pre-Sargonic and Sargonic Economic Texts (CT 50)*. *Zeitschrift für Assyriologie* 63:99–106.
1975   Review of H. Limet, *Etude de documents de la periode d'Agadé appartenant à l'université de Liège*. *Journal of Cuneiform Studies* 27:180–88.
1981   Three Problems in the History of Cuneiform Writing: Origins, Direction of Script, Literacy. *Visible Language* 15:419–40.

Price, Thomas, and James Brown (eds.)
1985   *Prehistoric Hunter-Gatherers: The Emergence of Cultural Complexity*. New York: Academic Press.

Pring, D. C.
  1977   Influence or Intrusion? The "Protoclassic" in the Maya Lowlands.
          In *Social Process in Maya Prehistory: Studies in Honour of Sir Eric
          Thompson*, ed. Norman Hammond, pp. 135–65. New York: Ac-
          ademic Press.
Pritchard, J. B.
  1969   *Ancient Near Eastern Texts Relating to the Old Testament*, 3rd ed.
          Princeton: Princeton University Press.
Proskouriakoff, Tatiana
  1960   Historical Implications of a Pattern of Dates at Piedras Negras,
          Guatemala. *American Antiquity* 25:454–75.
  1963   Historical Data in the Inscriptions of Yaxchilán, Part 1. *Estudios de
          Cultura Maya* 3:149–67.
  1964   Historical Data in the Inscriptions of Yaxchilán, Part 2. *Estudios de
          Cultura Maya* 4:177–201.
Puleston, Dennis E.
  1971   An Experimental Approach to the Function of Classic Maya Chul-
          tuns. *American Antiquity* 36:322–35.
  1974   Intersite Areas in the Vicinity of Tikal and Uaxactún. In *Mesoamer-
          ican Archaeology: New Approaches*, ed. N. Hammond, pp. 301–
          12. Austin: University of Texas Press.
  1978   Terracing, Raised Fields and Tree Cropping in the Maya Lowlands:
          A New Perspective on the Geography of Power. In *Pre-Hispanic
          Maya Agriculture*, ed. P. D. Harrison and B. L. Turner II, pp. 225–
          45. Albuquerque: University of New Mexico Press.
Quirarte, Jacinto
  1983   Outside Influence at Cacaxtla. In *Highland-Lowland Interaction in
          Mesoamerica: Interdisciplinary Approaches*, ed. Arthur G. Miller,
          pp. 201–21. Washington, D.C.: Dumbarton Oaks.
Rapp, Rayna
  1977   Gender and Class: An Archaeology of Knowledge Concerning the
          Origin of the State. *Dialectical Anthropology* 2:309–16.
Rappaport, Roy
  1977   Maladaptation in Social Systems. In *The Evolution of Social Systems*,
          ed. Jonathan Friedman and Michael Rowlands, pp. 49–73. London:
          Duckworth.
Rathje, William L.
  1971   The Origin and Development of Lowland Classic Maya Civilization.
          American Antiquity 36:275–85.
  1972   Praise the Gods and Pass the Metates: An Hypothesis of the De-
          velopment of Lowland Rainforest Civilizations in Mesoamerica. In
          Contemporary Archaeology, ed. M. P. Leone, pp. 365–92. Car-
          bondale: Southern Illinois University Press.
  1973   Classic Maya Development and Denouement: A Research Design.
          In *The Classic Maya Collapse*, ed. T. P. Culbert, pp. 405–54. Al-
          buquerque: University of New Mexico Press.

Rattray, Evelyn C.
1978   Los contactos Teotihuacán-Maya vistos desde el centro de México. *Anales de Antropología* 15:34–52. Mexico City: Universidad Nacional Autónoma de México.
1979a   Los contactos entre Teotihuacán y Veracruz. In *Los procesos de cambio, XV Mesa Redonda* 2:301–11. (Mexico City: Sociedad Mexicana de Antropología).
1979b   La cerámica de Teotihuacán: Relaciones externas y cronología. *Anales de Antropología* 16:51–70. (Mexico City: Universidad Nacional Autónoma de México).
1981a   Los barrios foráneos de Teotihuacán. Paper presented at symposium on Teotihuacán by Instituto de Investigaciones Antropológicas, Universidad Nacional Autónoma de Mexico (Mexico City).
1981b   La industria de obsidiana durante el período Coyotlatelco. *Revista Mexicana de Estudios Antropológicos* 27(2):213–23.
n.d.a   El barrio de los comerciantes en Teotihuacán. Manuscript.
n.d.b   The Teotihuacán Ceramic Chronology. Manuscript.
Redfield, Robert
1956   *Peasant Society and Culture.* Chicago: University of Chicago Press.
Redfield, Robert, and Milton Singer
1954   The Cultural Role of Cities. *Economic Development and Cultural Change* 3:53–73.
Reina, Rubén E.
1967   Milpas and Milperos: Implications for Prehistoric Times. *American Anthropologist* 69:1–20.
Renfrew, Colin
1978   Trajectory Discontinuity and Morphogenesis: The Implications of Catastrophe Theory for Archaeology. *American Antiquity* 43:203–22.
Renger, Johannes
1970   Zur Lokalisierung von Karkar. *Archiv für Orientforschung* 23:73–78.
Rice, Don S.
1978   Population Growth and Subsistence Alternatives in a Tropical Lacustrine Environment. In *Pre-Hispanic Maya Agriculture,* ed. P. D. Harrison and B. L. Turner II, pp. 35–61. Albuquerque: University of New Mexico Press.
1985   The Petén Postclassic: Perspectives from the Central Petén Lakes. In *Late Lowland Maya Civilization: Classic to Postclassic,* ed. J. A. Sabloff and E. W. Andrews V, pp. 301–44. Albuquerque: University of New Mexico Press.
Rice, Don S., and Prudence M. Rice
n.d.   Proyecto Lacustre Project Summary Report: 1979, 1980, and 1981 Seasons. Manuscript.
Rice, Don S., Prudence M. Rice, and Edward S. Deevey
1985   Paradise Lost: Classic Maya Impact on a Lacustrine Environment. In *Prehistoric Lowland Maya Environment and Subsistence Econ-*

omy, ed. M. Pohl, pp. 91–105. Cambridge, Mass.: Harvard University Press.

Rindos, David
1985   Darwinian Selection and Cultural Evolution. *Current Anthropology* 26:65–88.

Romero R., Erica Ma. Eugenia
1982   Evidencias post-teotihuacanas en el lado este de la Ciudadela. In *Teotihuacán 80–82: Primeros resultados*, ed. Rubén Cabrera C., Ignacio Rodríguez G., and Noel Morelos G., pp. 149–54. Mexico City: Instituto Nacional de Antropología e Historia.

Rostovtzeff, Michael
1957   *The Social and Economic History of the Roman Empire*, 2 vols., revised by P. M. Fraser. Oxford: Clarendon Press.

Rovner, Irwin
1974   Implications of the Lithic Analysis at Becán. In *Preliminary Reports on Archaeological Investigations in the Río Bec Area, Campeche, Mexico*, comp. Richard E. W. Adams, pp. 128–32. Middle American Research Institute Publ. 31. New Orleans: Tulane University Press.

Sabloff, Jeremy A.
1971   The Collapse of Classic Maya Civilization. In *The Patient Earth*, ed. J. Harte and R. Socolow, pp. 16–27. New York: Holt, Rinehart and Winston.
1973   Continuity and Disruption during Terminal Late Classic Times at Seibal: Ceramic and Other Evidence. In *The Classic Maya Collapse*, ed. T. P. Culbert, pp. 107–31. Albuquerque: University of New Mexico Press.

Sabloff, Jeremy A., and E. Wyllys Andrews V (eds.)
1985   *Late Lowland Maya Civilization: Classic to Postclassic*. Albuquerque: University of New Mexico Press.

Sabloff, Jeremy A., and Gordon R. Willey
1967   The Collapse of Maya Civilization in the Southern Lowlands: A Consideration of History and Process. *Southwestern Journal of Anthropology* 23:311–16.

Sachs, Abraham
1976   The Latest Datable Cuneiform Tablets. In *Kramer Anniversary Volume*, ed. Barry L. Eichler, pp. 379–98. Neukirchen-Vluyn: Neukirchner Verlag.

Sahlins, Marshall
1960   Evolution: Specific and General. In *Evolution and Culture*, ed. Marshall Sahlins and Elman Service, pp. 12–44. Ann Arbor: University of Michigan Press.
1961   The Segmentary Lineage: An Organization of Predatory Expansion. *American Anthropologist* 63:322–45.
1968   *Tribesmen*. Englewood Cliffs: Prentice-Hall.

Salmon, Merrilee H.
1978   What Can Systems Theory Do for Archaeology? *American Antiquity* 43:174–83.

1982   *Philosophy and Archaeology.* New York: Academic Press.
Sanders, William T.
1973   The Cultural Ecology of the Lowland Maya: A Reevaluation. In *The Classic Maya Collapse,* ed. T. P. Culbert, pp. 325–65. Albuquerque: University of New Mexico Press.
1977   Ethnographic Analogy and the Teotihuacán Horizon Style. In *Teotihuacán and Kaminaljuyu,* ed. W. T. Sanders and Joseph W. Michels, pp. 397–410. University Park: Pennsylvania State University Press.
1978   Ethnographic Analogy and the Teotihuacán Horizon Style. In *Middle Classic Mesoamerica: A.D. 400–700,* ed. Esther Pasztory, pp. 35–44. New York: Columbia University Press.
1981a   Ecological Adaptation in the Basin of Mexico: 23,000 B.C. to the Present. In *Supplement to the Handbook of Middle American Indians,* vol. 1, *Archaeology,* ed. Victoria R. Bricker and Jeremy A. Sabloff, pp. 147–97. Austin: University of Texas Press.
1981b   Classic Maya Settlement Patterns and Ethnographic Analogy. In *Lowland Maya Settlement Patterns,* ed. W. Ashmore, pp. 351–69. Albuquerque: University of New Mexico Press.
Sanders, William T., and Joseph W. Michels (eds.)
1977   *Teotihuacán and Kaminaljuyu.* University Park: Pennsylvania State University Press.
Sanders, William T., and Carson N. Murdy
1982   Cultural Evolution and Ecological Succession in the Valley of Guatemala: 1500 B.C.–A.D. 1524. In *Maya Subsistence: Studies in Memory of Dennis E. Puleston,* ed. K. V. Flannery, pp. 19–63. New York: Academic Press.
Sanders, William T., Deborah Nichols, Rebecca Storey, and Randolph Widmer
1982   A Reconstruction of a Classic Period Landscape in the Teotihuacán Valley. Final Report to the National Science Foundation (Grant BNS 8005754).
Sanders, William T., Jeffrey R. Parsons, and Robert S. Santley
1979   *The Basin of Mexico: Ecological Processes in the Evolution of a Civilization* (text and maps). New York: Academic Press.
Sanders, William T., and Robert S. Santley
1983   A Tale of Three Cities: Energetics and Urbanization in Pre-Hispanic Central Mexico. In *Prehistoric Settlement Patterns: Essays in Honor of Gordon R. Willey,* ed. E. Z. Vogt and R. M. Leventhal, pp. 243–91. Albuquerque: University of New Mexico Press.
Santley, Robert S.
1983   Obsidian Trade and Teotihuacán Influence in Mesoamerica. In *Highland-Lowland Interaction in Mesoamerica: Interdisciplinary Approaches,* ed. Arthur G. Miller, pp. 69–124. Washington, D.C.: Dumbarton Oaks.
1987   Teotihuacan Influence at Matacapan: Alternative Models and Explanatory Frameworks. Paper presented at the 52d annual meeting of the Society for American Archaeology, Toronto, May 1987.

Schele, Linda
 1986   The Tlaloc Complex in the Classic Period: War and the Interaction
         between the Lowland Maya and Teotihuacan. Paper presented at
         the symposium on *The New Dynamics*, Kimbell Art Museum, Fort
         Worth, Texas, May 1986.
Scott, Sue
 1982   Figurines from Hacienda Metepec, Teotihuacán, Mexico: A Stylistic
         Analysis. M.A. thesis, Universidad de las Americas.
Secretaría del Patrimonio Nacional
 1970   *Minería prehispánica en la Sierra de Querétaro.* Mexico City.
Séjourné, Laurette
 1966   *El lenguaje de las formas en Teotihuacán.* Mexico City.
Seler, Eduard
 1915   Die Stuckfassade von Acanceh in Yucatán. *Gesammelte Abhand-
         lungen zur Amerikanischen Sprach- und Altertumskunde* 5:389–
         404. Berlin: Verlag Behrend.
Sempowski, Martha
 1979   TE27: Test Excavation in the Puma Mural group—Plaza and Main
         Temple-Pyramid (73A:N4E1), Teotihuacán. Manuscript, Depart-
         ment of Anthropology, University of Rochester.
 1981   Differential Mortuary Treatment: Its Implications for Social Status
         at Three Residential Compounds in Teotihuacán, Mexico. Paper
         presented at symposium on Teotihuacán sponsored by Instituto de
         Investigaciones Antropológicas, Universidad Nacional Autónoma de
         México, Mexico City.
 1982   Mortuary Practices at Teotihuacán, Mexico: Their Implications for
         Social Status. Ph.D. dissertation, University of Rochester.
Service, Elman R.
 1960   The Law of Evolutionary Potential. In *Evolution and Culture*, ed.
         Marshall Sahlins and Elman Service, pp. 93–122. Ann Arbor: Uni-
         versity of Michigan Press.
 1975   *Origins of the State and Civilization: The Process of Cultural Ev-
         olution.* New York: W. W. Norton.
 1978   Classical and Modern Theories of the Origins of Government. In
         Origins of the State: The Anthropology of Political Evolution, ed.
         Ronald Cohen and Elman R. Service, pp. 21–34. Philadelphia: In-
         stitute for the Study of Human Issues.
Shankman, Paul
 1984   The Thick and the Thin: On the Interpretive Theoretical Program
         of Clifford Geertz. *Current Anthropology* 25:261–79.
Sharer, Robert J.
 1977   The Maya Collapse Revisited: Internal and External Perspectives.
         In *Social Process in Maya Prehistory*, ed. N. Hammond, pp. 531–
         52. New York: Academic Press.
 1980   The Quiriguá Project, 1974–1979. *Expedition* 23:5–10.
Sharpless, J. B., and S. B. Warner
 1977   Urban History. *American Behavioral Scientist* 21:221–44.

Shook, Edwin M.
1965   Archaeological Survey of the Pacific Coast of Guatemala. In *Handbook of Middle American Indians*, vol. 2, ed. Robert Wauchope and Gordon R. Willey, pp. 180–94. Austin: University of Texas Press.

Sidrys, Raymond, and Rainer Berger
1979   Lowland Maya Radiocarbon Dates and the Classic Maya Collapse. *Nature* 277:269–74.

Siemens, Alfred H.
1978   Karst and the Pre-Hispanic Maya in the Southern Lowlands. In *Pre-Hispanic Maya Agriculture*, ed. P. D. Harrison and B. L. Turner II, pp. 117–43. Albuquerque: University of New Mexico Press.

Siemens, Alfred H., and Dennis E. Puleston
1972   Ridged Fields and Associated Features in Southern Campeche: New Perspectives on the Lowland Maya. *American Antiquity* 37:228–39.

Sigrist, R. Marcel
1977   Nippur entre Isin et Larsa de Sin-iddinam à Rim-Sin. *Orientalia NS* 46:363–74.
1984   *Le satukku dans l'Ešumeša*. Malibu: Undena.

Simmons, Steven
1959–   Early Old Babylonian Tablets from Harmal and Elsewhere. *Journal*
1961   *of Cuneiform Studies* 13:71–93, 105–19; 14:23–32, 49–55, 75–87, 117–25; 15:49–58, 81–83.
1978   *Early Old Babylonian Documents*. New Haven: Yale University Press.

Simon, Herbert
1965   The Architecture of Complexity. *Yearbook of the Society for General Systems Research* 10:63–76.
1977   The Complexity, Section 4. In H. Simon, *Models of Discovery and Other Topics in the Methods of Science*, pp. 175–265. Boston: D. Reidel.

Skinner, G. William
1964   Marketing and Social Structure in Rural China, Part 1. *Journal of Asian Studies* 24:3–43.
1971   Chinese Peasants and the Closed Community: An Open and Shut Case. *Comparative Studies in Society and History* 13:270–81.

Smith, Carol A.
1976a   Regional Economic Systems: Linking Geographical Models and Socioeconomic Problems. In *Regional Analysis*, ed. Carol A. Smith, vol. 1, pp. 3–63. New York: Academic Press.
1976b   Exchange Systems and the Spatial Distribution of Elites: The Organization of Stratification in Agrarian Societies. In *Regional Analysis*, ed. Carol A. Smith, vol. 2, pp. 309–74. New York: Academic Press.
1985a   Theories and Measures of Urban Primacy. In *Urbanization and the World Economy*, ed. Michael Timberlake, pp. 87–117. New York: Academic Press.
1985b   Class Relations and Urbanization in Guatemala: Toward an Alternative Theory of Urban Primacy. In *Urbanization and the World*

Economy, ed. Michael Timberlake, pp. 121–67. New York: Academic Press.

Smith, W. Stevenson
1981   The Art and Architecture of Ancient Egypt, revised with additions by William Kelly Simpson. New York: Penguin Books.

Sollberger, Edmond
1954–   Sur la chronologie des rois d'Ur et quelques problèmes connexes.
1956   Archiv für Orientforschung 17:10–48.
1967   The Rulers of Lagash. Journal of Cuneiform Studies 21:279–91.

Sotomayor C., Alfredo, and Noemí Castillo T.
1965   Estudio petrográfico de las cerámicas "Anaranjado Delgado." Mexico City: Instituto Nacional de Antropología e Historia.

Spaulding, Albert C.
1973   Archaeology in the Active Voice: The New Anthropology. In Research and Theory in Current Archaeology, ed. C. L. Redman, pp. 337–54. New York: Wiley.

Speiser, Ephraim A.
1952   Some Factors in the Collapse of Akkad. Journal of the American Oriental Society 72:97–101.

Spence, Michael W.
1967   The Obsidian Industry of Teotihuacán. American Antiquity 32:507–14.
1974   Residential Practices and the Distribution of Skeletal Traits in Teotihuacán, Mexico. Man n.s. 9:262–73.
1981   Obsidian Production and the State in Teotihuacán, Mexico. American Antiquity 46(4):769–88.
n.d.   Commodity or Symbol: The Role of Teotihuacán Obsidian in the Maya Region. Manuscript, University of Western Ontario, London.

Spengler, Oswald
1918–   The Decline of the West. Trans. C. F. Atkinson. New York: Alfred
1922   Knopf. See also abridged edition prepared by A. Helps; London: George Allen and Unwin, 1961.

Starbuck, David R.
1975   Man-Animal Relationships in Pre-Columbian Central Mexico. Ph.D. dissertation, Yale University.

Steinkeller, Piotr
1976   Sale Documents of the Ur III Period. Ph.D. dissertation, University of Chicago.

Stol, Marten
1976   Studies in Old Babylonian History. Istanbul: Nederlands Historisch-Archaeologisch Instituut.

Stolper, Matthew W.
1974   Management and Politics in Later Achaemenid Babylonia: New Texts from the Murašû Archive. Ph.D. thesis, University of Michigan.

Stone, Elizabeth C.
1977   Economic Crisis and Social Upheaval in Old Babylonian Nippur. In

Mountains and Lowlands: Essays in the Archaeology of Greater Mesopotamia, ed. L. D. Levine and T. C. Young, Jr., pp. 267–89. Malibu: Undena.

Storey, Rebecca
    1983   Mortality and Health at Tlajinga 33, Teotihuacán. Paper presented at 48th Annual Meeting of Society for American Archaeology, Pittsburgh.
    1985   An Estimate of Mortality in a Pre-Columbian Population. *American Anthropologist*, 87:519–35.

Storey, Rebecca, and Randolph J. Widmer
    1982   Excavations at Tlajinga 33. In *A Reconstruction of a Classic Period Landscape in the Teotihuacán Valley*, by William T. Sanders, Deborah Nichols, Rebecca Storey, and Randolph Widmer. Final report to the National Science Foundation (Grant BNS 8005754).

Stross, Fred H., Payson Sheets, Frank Asaro, and Helen V. Michel
    1983   Precise Characterization of Guatemalan Obsidian Sources, and Source Determination of Artifacts from Quirigua. *American Antiquity* 48(2):323–48.

Sugiura Yamamoto, Yoko
    1981   Cerámica de Ojo de Agua, Estado de México, y sus posibles relaciones con Teotihuacán. In *Interacción cultural en México central*, comp. Evelyn C. Rattray, Jaime Litvak King, and Clara Díaz O., pp. 159–68. Mexico City: Universidad Nacional Autónoma de México.

Sugiyama, Saburo
    n.d.   Burials Dedicated to the Old Temple of Quetzalcoatl at Teotihuacan, Mexico. *American Antiquity*, in press.

Swinson, Arthur
    1967   *North-West Frontier*. New York: Praeger.

Taube, Karl A.
    1986   The Teotihuacan Cave of Origin. *Res*, v. 12, pp. 51–82.

Thomas, Prentice
    1981   *Prehistoric Maya Settlement Patterns at Becán, Campeche, Mexico*. Middle American Research Institute, Publication 45. New Orleans: Tulane University Press.

Thompson, J. Eric S.
    1954   *The Rise and Fall of Maya Civilization*. Norman: University of Oklahoma Press.
    1967   The Maya Central Area at the Spanish Conquest and Later: A Problem in Demography. *Proceedings of the Royal Anthropological Institute of Great Britain and Ireland for 1966*:23–37.

Torres Montes, Luis
    1972   Materiales y técnicas de la pintura mural de Teotihuacán. In *Teotihuacán, XI Mesa Redonda* 2:17–42. (Mexico City: Sociedad Mexicana de Antropología).

Tourtellot, Gair
    1970   The Peripheries of Seibal: An Interim Report. In *Monographs and Papers in Maya Archaeology*. Papers of the Peabody Museum of

American Archaeology and Ethnology, ed. W. R. Bullard, 61:405–
15. (Cambridge, Mass.: Harvard University).

Toynbee, Arnold
1933–   A Study of History, vol. 1 (1946): abridgment of vols. 1–6; vol. 2
1954   (1957): abridgment of vols. 7–10, by D. C. Somervell. Oxford:
Oxford University Press.

Tuchman, Barbara W.
1984   The March of Folly from Troy to Vietnam. New York: Knopf.

Turner, B. L., II
1974   Prehistoric Intensive Agriculture in the Maya Lowlands: New Evidence from the Río Bec Region. Ph.D. dissertation, University of
Wisconsin, Madison.
1978   Ancient Agricultural Land Use in the Central Maya Lowlands. In
Pre-Hispanic Maya Agriculture, ed. P. D. Harrison and B. L. Turner
II, pp. 163–83. Albuquerque: University of New Mexico Press.

Turner, B. L., II, and Peter D. Harrison
1978   Implications from Agriculture for Maya Prehistory. In Pre-Hispanic
Maya Agriculture, ed. P. D. Harrison and B. L. Turner II, pp. 337–
73. Albuquerque: University of New Mexico Press.
1981   Prehistoric Raised-field Agriculture in the Maya Lowlands. Science
213:399–405.

Turner, Margaret Hempenius
1981   The Lapidaries of Teotihuacán, Mexico: A Preliminary Study of Fine
Stone Working in the Ancient Mesoamerican City. Paper presented
at symposium on Teotihuacán sponsored by Instituto de Investigaciones Antropológicas, Universidad Nacional Autónoma de México, Mexico City.
1983   The Lapidary Industry of Teotihuacán, Mexico. Paper presented at
48th Annual Meeting of Society for American Archaeology, Pittsburgh.

Utsunomiya, Kiyoyoshi
1954   Kandai Shaki Keizaishi Kenkyu. Tokyo: Kobun-do.

Valenzuela, Juan
1945   Las exploraciones efectuadas en Los Tuxtlas, Veracruz. Anales del
Museo Nacional de Arqueología, Historia y Etnología 3:83–107
(Mexico City).

Vargas Pacheco, Ernesto
1980   Consideraciones sobre Teotenango y Ojo de Agua, Edo. de México.
Anales de Antropología 17(1):53–67. (Mexico City: Universidad
Nacional Autónoma de México).

Veenhof, Klaus
1972   Aspects of Old Assyrian Trade and Its Terminology. Leiden: Brill.

Vidal, Gore
1981   Creation. New York: Random House.

Villa Rojas, Alfonso
1945   The Maya of East Central Quintana Roo. Washington, D.C.: Carnegie Institution of Washington, Publication 559.

Vlacek, David T., Sylvia Garza de González, and Edward B. Kurjack
  1978   Contemporary Farming and Ancient Maya Settlements: Some Dis-
            concerting Evidence. In *Pre-Hispanic Maya Agriculture*, ed. P. D.
            Harrison and B. L. Turner II, pp. 211–23. Albuquerque: University
            of New Mexico Press.
von Winning, Hasso
  1948   The Teotihuacán Owl-and-Weapon Symbol and Its Association with
            "Serpent Head X" at Kaminaljuyu. *American Antiquity* 14(2):129–
            32.
  1961   Teotihuacán Symbols: The Reptile's Eye Glyph. *Ethnos* 26:121–66.
  1968   Der Netzjaguar in Teotihuacán, Mexico: Eine ikonographische Un-
            tersuchung. *Baessler-Archiv* n.f., Band 16, pp. 31–46. (Berlin: Verlag
            von Dietrich Reimer).
  1977   The Old Fire God and His Symbolism at Teotihuacán. *Indiana* 4:7–
            61 (Berlin).
  1979a   The Binding of the Years and the New Fire at Teotihuacán. *Indiana*
            5:15–32 (Berlin).
  1979b   Teotihuacán Symbols: The Fire God Complex. In *Actes du 42e
            Congrès International des Américanistes* 7:425–37 (Paris).
  1979c   Los incensarios teotihuacanos y los del litoral pacífico de Guatemala:
            Su iconografía y función ritual. In *Los procesos de cambio, XV Mesa
            Redonda* 2:327–34. (Mexico City: Sociedad Mexicana de Antro-
            pología).
  1984   Insignias de oficio en la iconografía de Teotihuacán. *Pantoc*, no. 8,
            Publicaciones Antropológicas de Occidente, Universidad Autónoma
            de Guadalajara, June–December 1984, pp. 5–54. Guadalajara,
            Mexico.
Wallaker, B. E.
  1978   Han Confucianism and Confucians in Han. In *Ancient China: Studies
            in Early Civilization*, ed. David Roy and T. H. Tsien, pp. 215–28.
            Hong Kong: Hong Kong Press.
Webb, Malcolm C.
  1973   The Petén Maya Decline Viewed in the Perspective of State For-
            mation. In *The Classic Maya Collapse*, ed. T. P. Culbert, pp. 367–
            404. Albuquerque: University of New Mexico Press.
Weber, Max
  1978   *Economy and Society: An Outline of Interpretive Sociology.* Berke-
            ley: University of California Press.
Weigand, Phil C.
  1968   The Mines and Mining Techniques of the Chalchihuites Culture.
            American Antiquity 33:45–61.
  1978   The Prehistory of the State of Zacatecas: An Interpretation, Parts I
            and II. *Anthropology* 2(1,2):67–87, 103–17. Stony Brook: State
            University of New York Press.
  1982   Mining and Mineral Trade in Prehispanic Zacatecas. In *Mining and
            Mining Techniques in Ancient Mesoamerica*, ed. P. C. Weigand and
            G. Gwynne. *Anthropology* 6(1–2):175–88 (special issue).

Weigand, Phil C., Garman Harbottle, and Edward V. Sayre
1977   Turquoise Sources and Source Analysis: Mesoamerica and the Southwestern U.S.A. In *Exchange Systems in Prehistory*, ed. Timothy K. Earle and Jonathan E. Ericson, pp. 15–34. New York: Academic Press.

Weiss, Harvey
1975   Kish, Akkad, and Agade. *Journal of the American Oriental Society* 95:434–53.

Wilcke, Claus
1969   Zur Geschichte der Amurriter der Ur III-Zeit. *Die Welt des Orients* 5:1–31.
1970   Drei Phasen des Niedergangs des Reiches von Ur III. *Zeitschrift für Assyriologie* 60:54–69.
1971   Zum Königtum in der Ur III-Zeit. In *Le palais et la royauté*, ed. P. Garelli, pp. 177–223. Paris: Paul Geuthner.
1975   Politische Opposition nach Sumerischen Quellen. In *La voix de l'opposition en Mésopotamie*, ed. A. Finet, pp. 37–65. Brussels: Institut des Hautes Etudes.

Wilhelm, Helmut
1957   The Scholar's Frustration: Notes on a Type of *fu*. In *Chinese Thought and Institutions*, ed. J. K. Fairbank, pp. 310–19. Chicago: University of Chicago Press.

Willey, Gordon R.
1973a   *The Altar de Sacrificios Excavations: General Summary and Conclusions*. Papers of the Peabody Museum of American Archaeology and Ethnology 64, no. 3. Cambridge, Mass.: Harvard University Press.
1973b   Certain Aspects of the Classic to Postclassic Periods in the Belize Valley. In *The Classic Maya Collapse*, ed. T. P. Culbert, pp. 93–106. Albuquerque: University of New Mexico Press.
1977   External Influences on the Lowland Maya: 1940 and 1975 Perspectives. In *Social Process in Maya Prehistory: Studies in Honour of Sir Eric Thompson*, ed. Norman Hammond, pp. 58–75. New York: Academic Press.
1979   Highland Culture Contacts in the Lowland Maya Area: An Introductory Commentary. In *Actes du 42e Congrès International des Américanistes* 8:214–20 (Paris).
1986   The Postclassic of the Maya Lowlands: A Preliminary Overview. In *Late Lowland Maya Civilization: Classic to Postclassic*, ed. J. A. Sabloff and E. W. Andrews V, pp. 17–51. Albuquerque: University of New Mexico Press.

Willey, Gordon R., William R. Bullard, Jr., John B. Glass, and James C. Gifford
1965   *Prehistoric Settlements in the Belize Valley*. Papers of the Peabody Museum of American Archaeology and Ethnology 54. Cambridge, Mass.: Harvard University Press.

Willey, Gordon R., and Richard M. Leventhal
1979   Prehistoric Settlement at Copán. In *Maya Archaeology and Eth-*

nohistory, ed. N. Hammond and G. R. Willey, pp. 75–102. Austin: University of Texas Press.

Willey, Gordon R., and Demitri B. Shimkin

1973   The Maya Collapse: A Summary View. In *The Classic Maya Collapse*, ed. T. P. Culbert, pp. 457–501. Albuquerque: University of New Mexico Press.

Winter, Marcus C.

1979   El impacto teotihuacano y procesos de cambio en Oaxaca. In *Los procesos de cambio, XV Mesa Redonda* 2:359–67. (Mexico City: Sociedad Mexicana de Antropología).

Wiseman, Frederick M.

1978   Agricultural and Historical Ecology in the Southern Lowlands. In *Pre-Hispanic Maya Agriculture*, ed. P. D. Harrison and B. L. Turner II, pp. 63–115. Albuquerque: University of New Mexico Press.

Wittfogel, Karl A.

1957   *Oriental Despotism: A Comparative Study of Total Power.* New Haven: Yale University Press.

Wolf, Eric R.

1955   The Mexican Bajio in the Eighteenth Century: An Analysis of Cultural Integration. *Middle American Research Institute*, Publication 17:177–200.

Wolters, O. W.

1967   *Early Indonesian Commerce.* Ithaca: Cornell University Press.

Wright, Henry

1977   Recent Research on the Origin of the State. *Annual Review of Anthropology* 6:379–97.

Yang, Lien-sheng

1936   Tung-Han-ti hao-tsu. *Ts'ing hua Hs'ueh pao* 11(4):1007–63.

Yoffee, Norman

1977   *The Economic Role of the Crown in the Old Babylonian Period.* Malibu: Undena.

1979   The Decline and Rise of Mesopotamian Civilization: An Ethnoarchaeological Perspective on the Evolution of Social Complexity. *American Antiquity* 44:5–35.

1981   *Explaining Trade in Ancient Western Asia.* Malibu: Undena.

n.d.   Mesopotamian Interaction Spheres. Manuscript.

Yu, Ying-shih

1956   Tung-Han cheng-chuan chih chien-li yu shih-chu-ta-hsin-chih kuan-hsi. *Hsin-yao hsueh-pal* 1(2):209–80.

1976   *Li-shih yu shih-hsiang.* Taipei: Lien-ching.

Zadok, Ran

1977   *On West Semites in Babylonia During the Chaldean and Achaemenian Periods: An Onomastic Study.* Jerusalem: H. J. and Z. Wanaarta.

1979   On Some Foreign Population Groups in First-Millennium Babylonia. *Tel-Aviv* 6:164–81.

1981   Arabians in Mesopotamia During the Late Assyrian, Chaldean,

Achaemenian and Hellenistic Periods, Chiefly According to Cuneiform Sources. *Zeitschrift des Deutschen Morgenländischen Gesells-
chaft* 31:42–84.

1984   Assyrians in Chaldean and Achaemenian Babylonia. *Assur* 4:71–
98.

Index

Abandonment of land, 172
Acancéh, 128
Acapulco, 132
Accountability, 64, 226–27, 263–64
Acephalous organization, 205, 206
Achievement, selection by, 206
Adams, Richard E. W., 73, 96
Adams, Robert McC., 15, 53, 100,
 137, 149
Adaptation, 5, 7, 175
"Additive" improvements of theory,
 249, 251
Administration: benefits of, 221;
 fragmentation of, 228; intervention
 by, 138; provincial, 52, 56; struggles between central authority and
 subordinates, 189–92, 239, 261,
 263–64, 272, 274, 275
Afghans, 203, 209
Afridi, 207
Agade, 46, 62
Agriculture, 57; centralized management of, 91, 92; destructive use of
 land in, 230; double cropping, 89,
 93, 95; intensification of, 16–17,
 36, 73, 91, 99–100, 140, 188–89,
 267; involution of, 261–62, 267;
 kitchen gardens, 89, 95; management of, 99; market oriented, 216;

raised field, 73, 90, 91, 92, 93, 95–
 96, 97, 98, 99; risks, 97–99, 100;
 root crops, 89, 95; swidden, 89,
 95, 97, 98, 268; terracing, 90, 91,
 93, 95, 98, 99
Aké, 128
Albanians, 203
Alienation, 223
Almoravids, 217
Alta Vista (Chalchihuites culture),
 133
Altar de Sacrificios, 75, 79, 82, 83,
 89
Altún Há, 120
Ambiguity, 247
Ambrose (bishop of Milan), 170
Amorites, 50–51, 55, 64, 65
Anatolia, 54, 55
Anderson, Perry, 27
Angkor state, 212
Anthropological archaeology, 271
Antisystems, 241
Aquileia, 170–71, 173
Arabs, 171, 173, 208, 214, 269, 276
Arameans, 56, 58
Archaeology, anthropological, 271
Architecture: domestic, 127; residen-
 tial, 107–8
Aristocrats, 170

319

About the Contributors

ROBERT McC. ADAMS, Secretary of the Smithsonian Institution, was from 1975 to 1984 the Harold H. Swift Distinguished Service Professor of Anthropology at the University of Chicago, and from 1962 to 1968 and 1981 to 1983 director of the university's Oriental Institute. Among his many publications are *Heartland of Cities: Surveys of Ancient Settlement and Land Use on the Central Floodplain of the Euphrates* and *The Evolution of Urban Society: Early Mesopotamia and Prehispanic Mexico*.

G. W. BOWERSOCK'S books include *Augustus and the Greek World*, *Roman Arabia*, and the coedited volume *Edward Gibbon and the Decline and Fall of the Roman Empire*. He was professor of Greek and Latin at Harvard University from 1969 to 1980 and became professor at the School of Historical Studies at the Institute for Advanced Study, Princeton, in 1980.

BENNET BRONSON, Associate Curator of Asian Anthropology at the Field Museum of Natural History in Chicago since 1968, has published many articles about South and East Asian archaeology and anthropology, cultural process and change, ethnoarchaeology, archaeometallurgy, and related subjects.

GEORGE L. COWGILL has been a professor of anthropology at Brandeis University since 1976. He has served as visiting professor at Harvard

University and the Universidad Nacional Autónoma de México in Mexico City. His research interests include the use of quantitative methods in archaeology, complex societies in Mesoamerica, and fertility in Third World countries. His volume *Mathematical and Computer Methods in Archaeology* is forthcoming.

T. PATRICK CULBERT, professor in the Department of Anthropology, University of Arizona, has written extensively about the Classic Maya. His publications include *The Lost Civilization: The Story of the Classic Maya* and the edited volume *The Classic Maya Collapse*.

SHMUEL N. EISENSTADT, professor of sociology at the Hebrew University of Jerusalem, is a member of the Israeli Academy of Sciences and Humanities, a Foreign Honorary Fellow of the American Academy of Arts and Sciences, and an Honorary Fellow of the London School of Economics. He has served as visiting professor at numerous universities, including Harvard, Stanford, and Chicago. His research specialties are historical sociology and culture change, and his many books include *The Political Systems of Empires* and the edited volume *The Origins and Diversity of Axial Age Civilizations*.

CHO-YUN HSU, professor of history at the University of Pittsburgh, has specialized in the history of Han and pre-Han China. His publications include *Ancient China in Transition* and *Han Agriculture*.

HERBERT KAUFMAN, who studies organizational theory and bureaucracies, was professor of political science at Yale University from 1953 to 1969, Senior Fellow at the Brookings Institution from 1969 to 1983, Visiting Scholar at the Russell Sage Foundation from 1981 to 1982, and the Thomas P. O'Neill, Jr., Professor of American Politics at Boston College from 1986 to 1987. Among his numerous publications are *The Limits of Organizational Change, Are Governments Immortal?* and *Time, Chance, and Organizations: Natural Selection in a Perilous Environment.*

RENÉ MILLON, professor emeritus in the Department of Anthropology, University of Rochester, is director of the Teotihuacan Mapping Project, which began in 1962. Among his publications are *Urbanization at Teotihuacan: The Teotihuacan Map, Parts I and II (Part II* coauthored with R. Bruce Drewitt and George L. Cowgill). *Teotihuacan: Ancient Metropolis in the Valley of Mexico* is forthcoming.

NORMAN YOFFEE, professor of anthropology at the University of Arizona was in 1979–80 and 1987–88 a Visiting Fellow at Wolfson College,

Oxford, and in 1984–85 a Fulbright Senior Fellow at the University of Sydney. His publications include *The Economic Role of the Crown in the Old Babylonian Period* and (with V. Donbaz) *Old Babylonian Texts from Kish Conserved in the Istanbul Archaeological Museums.*